People and Buildings

PEOPLE AND BUILDINGS

EDITED BY ROBERT GUTMAN

Basic Books, Inc., Publishers

NEW YORK   LONDON

To the Memory

of

JOHN MADGE (1914–1968)

Contributors

CHRISTOPHER ALEXANDER is Professor of Architecture at the College of Environmental Studies at the University of California, Berkeley. He is the author of *Notes on the Synthesis of Form* (1964) and one of the co-authors of *A Pattern Language Which Generates Multi-Service Centers* (1968).

BERNARD BARBER is Professor and Chairman of the Department of Sociology at Barnard College. His works include *Science and Social Order* (1952), *Social Stratification* (1957), and *Drugs and Society* (1967).

MAURICE BROADY is Professor of Social Administration at the University College of Swansea, England. Several of his articles have been collected in *Planning for People: Essays on the Social Context of Planning* (1968).

JOHN CASSEL is Professor and Chairman of the Department of Epidemiology in the School of Public Health at the University of North Carolina. He is a specialist in the epidemiology of chronic and non-infectious diseases and has written many articles on that subject.

ALAN COLQUHOUN is an architect in private practice in London. He has taught at the Architectural Association School, at Cambridge University, and at Princeton University.

DERK DE JONGE, a research sociologist, is with the Housing and Planning Research Section at the Technical University in Delft, the Netherlands.

LEE E. FARR, currently Chief of the Bureau of Emergency Health Services for the city of Berkeley, has published articles on nuclear medicine, nuclear reactors, and protein metabolism.

NANCY JO FELIPE is Assistant Professor of Psychology at the American University in Washington, D.C. She has written articles on personal space and the significance of seating patterns.

LEON FESTINGER is Else and Hans Staudinger Professor of Psychology at the New School for Social Research. He is the author of *Conflict, Decision and Dissonance* (1964) and senior author of the classic *Social Pressures in Informal Groups* (1950).

JAMES MARSTON FITCH is Professor of Architecture at Columbia University and the author of several books, including *Architecture and the Esthetics of Plenty* (1961) and *American Building* (1966).

MARC FRIED is Research Professor at the Institute of Human Sciences at Boston College, a lecturer in psychology at the Harvard Medical School, and a psychologist at the Massachusetts General Hospital. His special fields of interest are the epidemiology of mental health and illness and the relationship between personality and sociocultural patterns.

ROBERT GUTMAN is Professor of Sociology at Rutgers University and currently Class of 1913 Lecturer in Architecture at Princeton University. He recently coedited *Neighborhood, City, and Metropolis* (1970).

EDWARD T. HALL is Professor of Anthropology at Northwestern University and the author of *The Silent Language* (1959) and *The Hidden Dimension* (1966).

JOHN N. HAZARD is Professor of Public Law at Columbia University and is well known as a specialist in Soviet law.

ALEXANDER KIRA is Professor of Architecture at Cornell University. He is preparing a revised edition of *The Bathroom* (1967) and is planning a similar volume on the bedroom.

STANFORD M. LYMAN is Associate Professor of Sociology at the University of Nevada and the author of articles on deviant behavior.

ABRAHAM H. MASLOW (1908–1970) was for many years Professor of Psychology at Brandeis University. Among his books are *Toward a Psychology of Being* (1962) and *Religion, Values, and Peak Experiences* (1964).

THE MINISTRY OF HOUSING AND LOCAL GOVERNMENT in Great Britain maintains The Architects Research and Development Group, which has designed a number of demonstration housing projects for selected local authorities. It also conducts programming and evaluation studies in connection with these projects.

NORBETT L. MINTZ is currently a psychologist at McLean Hospital. His fields of interest include personality, abnormal psychology, and esthetics.

THOMAS C. PINKERTON is a psychologist and biophysicist who presently holds a research appointment at the University of California, San Diego.

LEE RAINWATER is Professor of Sociology at Harvard University and a faculty associate of the Joint Committee for Urban Studies of Massachusetts Institute of Technology and Harvard University. His recent book, *Behind Ghetto Walls: Black Family Life in a Federal Slum* (1970), also deals with the housing project described in his article.

AMOS RAPOPORT is a member of the Department of Architecture at the University of Sydney and the author of *House Form and Culture* (1969), as well as many articles dealing with the relation of the behavioral sciences to architecture.

BARRY SCHWARTZ is a doctoral candidate in sociology at the University of Pennsylvania, whose special fields of interest are crime and delinquency and social psychology.

MARVIN B. SCOTT is Associate Professor and Chairman of the Department of Sociology at Sonoma State College in California. He is a specialist in theory and social psychology.

MURRAY SILVERSTEIN teaches in the School of Architecture at the University of Washington and is currently engaged in an examination of the teenager's place in urban culture.

ROBERT SOMMER is Professor and Chairman of the Department of Psychology at the University of California, Davis, and is the author of *Personal Space* (1969) and of numerous articles on the effects of the physical setting on attitudes and behavior.

MATTHEW TAYBACK is presently Assistant Secretary of the Department of Health and Mental Hygiene of the state of Maryland.

SIM VAN DER RYN is Associate Professor of Architecture at the College of Environmental Design at the University of California, Berkeley.

THORSTEIN VEBLEN (1857–1929), American sociologist, economist, and social critic, was the author of many well known and influential books, including *The Theory of the Leisure Class* (1899), *The Theory of Business Enterprise* (1904), *The Higher Learning in America* (1918), and *The Vested Interests and the State of the Industrial Arts* (1919).

ROSABELLE PRICE WALKLEY is Lecturer in Behavioral Sciences and Associate Research Behavioral Scientist at the University of California, Los Angeles.

NEWTON WATSON is Professor of Architecture in the School of Environmental Studies at University College in London.

B. W. P. WELLS is a member of the Department of Psychology at the University of Strathclyde, Scotland, and a member of the research staff of the Building Performance Research Unit at that university.

BARBARA WESTERGAARD is a Research Associate of the Built Environment Research Project in the Department of Sociology at Rutgers University.

DANIEL M. WILNER is Professor of Public Health and Professor of Preventive and Social Medicine and Chairman of the Department of Public Health at the University of California, Los Angeles. He is the co-author of the influential *Human Relations in Interracial Housing* (1955) and author of *Narcotics* (1965).

JOACHIM F. WOHLWILL is Professor of Psychology at Pennsylvania State University. He is the author of many articles on environmental and developmental psychology.

Preface

There is at the present time an enormous interest in relating the behavioral sciences to the design disciplines. Most schools of architecture now require their students to take courses in the behavioral sciences, with particular attention being paid to urban sociology. Sociologists and social psychologists are being added to the faculties of architecture schools, where they offer lectures and seminars and participate as programming specialists and design critics in studio courses. For a number of years sociologists and other behavioral scientists in many European countries have collaborated with architects and planners in the design work undertaken by governmental ministries, and more recently have been participating in the work of private design firms. Similar developments are now occurring in the United States. Within the last few years, in both this country and abroad, several new magazines and journals have been published that are specifically devoted to reporting on the interaction between the behavioral sciences and the design professions.

The demand for collaboration was initiated by the design professions. The behavioral science disciplines have not always responded helpfully, but reciprocity is now beginning to occur. A few graduate departments in the behavioral sciences have begun to offer specialized doctoral training programs in what is coming to be called "environmental psychology" or "environmental sociology," and papers and monographs dealing with this subject have begun to appear in increasing numbers. The meetings of the American Sociological Association, the American Psychological Association, and the Society of Applied Anthropology now regularly include sessions in which the problems of environmental studies are discussed. Each of these organizations has developed liaison activities with the Interprofessional Council on Environmental Design, an organization representing six design groups, including the American Institute of Architects, the American Institute of Planners, and the American Society of Landscape Architects.

The interest in joining the resources of the social and design disciplines arises from several sources. Probably the major factor in this process is the realization by the design professions that the intellectual traditions of architecture and planning are simply not adequate for grasping the complexity of the building needs of urbanized and industrialized societies. Architects find themselves facing tasks and clients for which their training did not prepare them. Instead, for example, of designing villas and palaces for the wealthy, architects must now design projects to house the black and disadvantaged populations. Where once they were hired by a college to propose a scheme for one or two dormitories, a library, or an administration building, very often now designers are expected to take charge of the design of a complete campus. In these settings architects encounter questions that they are unable to answer through informal programming techniques—questions about the life styles of the poor, about the housing needs of different racial groups, about the ultimate purposes of a college or university—and they turn to the behavioral scientist in the hope that he can provide the answers.

The design professions are also setting higher standards of social responsibility for themselves. The modern movement in architecture has been characterized by a utopian thrust, but the aspiration to increase welfare and improve justice demands more than good intentions. Architects evidence an increasing desire to be sure ahead of time that the buildings they design will have a beneficial effect upon the ultimate users. Of course, the architect's greater interest in the users' requirements is also a response to the increasing articulateness of clients and users. With building resources becoming scarcer at the same time that unmet needs for shelters are apparently increasing, those who pay for and use buildings want clear evidence that the final product will satisfy their needs.

At the same time that designers have become more self-conscious, behavioral scientists have developed a new concern for the practical applications of their research. During the years immediately following World War II, sociologists and psychologists often argued that their main task was to describe and explain the principles that govern human behavior, whereas the application of that knowledge was the responsibility of the policy makers, administrators, and the public. It became evident, however, to many behavioral scientists that their reports were being used in pursuit of goals they did not support. Furthermore, they came to realize that much of their research, for all of its contribution to knowledge, was not really apposite to the problems of industrialized society. As a result, many more behavioral scientists now wish to focus their research efforts on contemporary social problems and to try to maintain control over the development and use of their investigations.

The social disciplines also exhibit a renewed awareness of the relevance of environmental factors to human behavior. A body of coherent theory and research is now emerging that examines those needs of the human organism and of group functioning that are best satisfied through the provision of specific conditions in the physical, as distinguished from the social, environment. Examples of such studies are those based on the need for personal space and for territory. Both of these needs, it is coming to be thought, must be met if organisms and groups are to function effectively, and both needs imply certain constraints on the form of buildings and urban settlements. Investigations are also being carried out, particularly within the field of anthropology, on the communication function of symbol systems. Some of these investigations take into account the role of architecture and urban form as "languages," through which men and groups define the boundaries of relevant social interaction and through which the social values and norms that produce social order and integration are reinforced. One can also point to the expansion of research in social biology, epidemiology, and social control. Studies in these fields consider the influence of the physical environment on physiological stress, mental illness, and symptoms of social pathology, such as family disorganization, urban violence, and delinquency.

It is important to emphasize that these developments are not taking place primarily because of demands from the design professions for useful behavioral knowledge. In large part they reflect the sense within the behavioral sciences that the tradition that assumed that human personality was formed by culture and that the causes of social distress could therefore be found in social and cultural conditions was an extreme overreaction against an earlier period of evolutionary and biological determinism in American social theory. As in many other fields concerned with human behavior, the idea has suddenly taken hold that many of our social problems may stem from a failure to be sensitive to the limits on human progress and perfectability. To put the same thought in a less negative light, civilization can advance further only by respecting the constraints that the nature of the organism and the nature of the environment impose on human adaptability.

Those of us who have tried to work in the middle ground between environmental design and sociology are aware of the many issues about which little is known and of how much about the interaction between men, society, and architecture remains to be understood. A tremendous investment in research must be forthcoming if the potential utility of the behavioral sciences to design is to be fully exploited. But the situation is not as impoverished as some critics and skeptics would have us believe. A good deal of empirical research has been undertaken on many problems, and many potentially productive ideas and concepts have been developed. This work, however, is not widely known or easily accessible. It is this fact that constitutes the rationale for this collection of articles, essays, and selections from books and research monographs.

I have tried to assemble some of the most illuminating material in five important areas of converging interest between the social and design disciplines. The first of these areas deals with current research and theory on human anatomy and physiology, on man's sensory apparatus and his behavior in space, and on the requirements that these characteristics generate for the design of buildings. The second area deals with the impact of spatial organization on social interaction and group relationships, as revealed through studies of friendship patterns, communication and privacy. Part Three of the book discusses environmental influences on physical and mental health, with particular attention to the role of housing conditions, noise, esthetic surroundings, urban relocation and overcrowding. A fourth area is concerned with the work that anthropologists, functional sociologists, and psychologists have done in demonstrating the significance of architecture as the expression of social values and the reinforcement for cultural patterns. Part Five includes a series of readings that illustrate the ways in which architects and behavioral scientists are applying a variety of these ideas and approaches to the practical problems of the design process.

The selections have been written primarily by behavioral scientists and designers working in the behavioral science mode. The selections within each part have been arranged to provide an ordered argument or exploration of the general topic with which the part as a whole deals. To facilitate the reader's appreciation of the argument, each selection is preceded by a short prefatory statement. In view of the fact that a single article or preface can hardly be representative of the depth of the literature that has developed around an argument, I have included an annotated bibliography, which is keyed to the selections through the use of subheadings.

The resulting collection is not intended as a manual or handbook to guide design decisions on specific projects, nor is it intended to be just an assemblage of interesting articles dealing with the intriguing issues that arise when the behavioral sciences confront architecture. It has a polemical aim as well: namely, by the selection, organization, and arrangement of the readings and introductory notes, to urge both architects and behavioral scientists to recognize certain features of the phenomena to which their work is addressed. These points can be summarized as follows:

1. Architecture is a legitimate topic of inquiry for the social sciences. It is an element in human culture and social organization to which all people are responding even when they are unaware of it.

2. Architectural phenomena involve a range of properties—from the subtle and elusive features of symbolism and sensual qualities at one end to the utilitarian qualities of measurable space and ambient conditions at the other—and *all* of these properties must be kept in view if one is to achieve a comprehensive understanding of the effect of the built environment on man and society.

3. Sensitivity to the totality of buildings and environments implies, in turn, recognition of the fact that architecture connects with the full range of human qualities, capacities, instincts, feelings, needs, and dispositions, including the measurable needs for light and air, the experimentally observable functions of seeing and hearing, and the experientially observable demands for communication and group membership, as well as the cultural need for strong integrative symbols and the individual need for a sense of place. The latter requirements probably cannot be directly observed or measured, but they can be inferentially determined from the study of human actions and the linguistic and symbolic products of society.

4. Designers and others who are anxious to apply the insights and findings of the behavioral sciences to the creation of built environments must be careful to recognize the variety of interconnections between buildings and men. They should not merely use the findings from a selected sample of studies to justify an approach to architecture that may in its concern for behavioral requirements be just as restrictive as the older design methodology was in its concern for symbolic and esthetic features.

5. Finally, behavioral scientists and architects who collaborate in joint efforts should realize that full appreciation of the behavioral science tradition demands using its critical apparatus not only to consider the spatial organization and building specifications that are appropriate for reinforcing existing behavior patterns and preferences but also to evaluate and, if necessary, to

encourage the reform of the goals and purposes that the existing patterns imply.

This volume grows out of my experience in working with architects, in teaching sociology to architecture students, and in discussing architectural problems with sociologists. I am especially grateful to Peter Cowan, Peter Eisenman, Kenneth Frampton, Robert Geddes, and Robertson Ward Jr. for many valuable discussions about architecture, building, design, and society; to William L. Gum and Irving Kristol for encouraging me to put this volume together; and to Angela G. Irby for her guidance in making available the resources of Princeton University's Urban and Environmental Studies library. The editorial and bibliographical assistance of Barbara Westergaard has been invaluable. My wife, Sonya Rudikoff Gutman, has been a sympathetic critic and reader. I owe a special debt to the late John Madge for his help in getting me to appreciate the sociology of architecture and I would like to dedicate this book to his memory.

R. G.

Princeton, New Jersey
March, 1971

Contents

PART FIVE
The Application of Behavioral Science to Design

PART ONE
Behavioral Constraints on Building Design

The Aesthetics of Function

JAMES MARSTON FITCH

It is common in design circles to claim that architectural phenomena are enormously complex. Usually what this assertion means is that a building is made up of so many different kinds of systems and is subject to such a wide variety of technological, esthetic, and social constraints that it is often exceedingly difficult to resolve a design problem. The notion of architectural complexity, however, also applies to the relations between the built environment and society. Many different aspects of architecture and a variety of human needs and group processes are interconnected. For example, the visual qualities of architecture, its geometrical forms, the environmental control systems of buildings, the sheer provision of two-dimensional surfaces and three-dimensional spaces—all these aspects of architecture may become meaningful to people and influence their behavior. In the other direction, there are a great number of biological, psychological, and cultural needs that architecture and the environment have the capacity to satisfy. At the least, many of these needs can be satisfied through social mechanisms and social forms that architecture can help to organize and regulate. These needs are related to specific characteristics of the human organism, including man's anatomical structure and physiology, his personality and unconscious mental life, his perceptual apparatus, his use of symbol systems for communication, and his dependence upon group interaction for civilized survival.

Fitch's selection is an attempt to provide a conceptual framework that will alert the student of architectural phenomena to the many different ways in which the built environment and man are related. His argument is particularly directed against the traditional emphasis in architectural training and criticism on the visual qualities of buildings. Fitch counters this view by describing the linkages between the human being's response to the environment and his full perceptual mechanism. The full perceptual mechanism includes not only the visual and auditory senses but the gustatory, olfactory, and haptic responses, and the sense of spatial orientation as well. This perspective leads Fitch to a definition of architecture as a "third environment" that mediates between the hazards of the natural world and of civilized society and the internal breathing, feeling, seeing, and hearing processes of man.

Two additional polemical thrusts underlie Fitch's argument. One is the

Reprinted from James Marston Fitch, "The Aesthetics of Function," *The Annals of the New York Academy of Sciences* 128, article 2 (September 27, 1965): 706–714.

view, repeated in several selections in this book, that until basic anatomical and physiological needs are better satisfied through building designs, human societies cannot really afford the luxury of an interest in the esthetic properties of architecture. The second is the demand for an experimental architecture that will also be experiential, that is to say, that will be responsive to the full range of human needs and will call upon the total sensory capacity of the human organism.

☐

A fundamental weakness in most discussions of aesthetics is the failure to relate it to experiential reality. Most literature on aesthetics tends to isolate it from this matrix of experience, to discuss the aesthetics process as though it were an abstract problem in logic.

Art and architectural criticism suffers from this conceptual limitation. This finds expression in a persistent tendency to discuss art forms and buildings as though they were exclusively visual phenomena. This leads to serious misconceptions as to the actual relationship between the artifact and the human being. Our very terminology reveals this misapprehension: we speak of art as having "spectators," artists as having "audiences." This suggests that man exists in some dimension quite separate and apart from his artifacts; that the only contact between the two is this narrow channel of vision or hearing; and that this contact is unaffected by the environmental circumstances in which it occurs. The facts are quite otherwise and our modes of thought should be revised to correspond to them.

Art and architecture, like man himself, are totally submerged in an exterior environment. Thus they can never be felt, perceived, experienced in anything less than multi-dimensional totality. A change in one aspect or quality of the environment inevitably affects our response to, and perception of, all the rest. The primary significance of a painting may indeed be visual; or of a concert, sonic: but perception of these art forms occurs in a situation of experiential totality. Recognition of this is crucial for aesthetic theory, above all for architectural aesthetics. Far from being based narrowly upon any single sense of perception like vision, architectural aesthetics actually derives from the body's *total* response to, and perception of, its external physical environment. It is literally impossible to experience architecture in any "simpler" way. *In architecture, there are no spectators: there are only participants.* The body of architectural criticism which pretends otherwise is based upon photographs of buildings and not actual exposure to architecture at all.

Life is coexistent and coextensive with the external natural environment in which the body is submerged. The body's dependence upon this external environment is absolute—in the fullest sense of the word, *uterine*. And yet, unlike the womb, the external natural environment does not afford optimum conditions for the existence of the individual. The animal body, for its survival, maintains its own special internal environment. In man, this internal environment is so distinct in its nature and so constant in its properties that it has been given its own name, "homeostasis." Since the natural environment is anything but constant in either time or space, the contradictions between internal requirements and external conditions are normally stressful. The body has wonderful mechanisms for adjusting to external variations, e.g., the eye's capacity to adjust to enormous variations in the luminous environment or the adjustability of the heat-exchange mechanism of the skin. But the limits of adaptation are sharp and obdurate. Above or below them, an ameliorating element, a "third" environment, is required.

Before birth, the womb affords this to the foetus. But man, once born into the world, enters into a much more complex relationship with his external environment. Existence now is on two distinct levels, simultaneously and indissolubly connected, the metabolic and the perceptual. (Figure 1–1.) The metabolic process remains basic. It is at once a "preconscious" state and the material basis of consciousness. Many of life's fundamental processes transpire at this level: heart beat, respiration, digestion, hypothalmic heat exchange controls, etc. Metabolic disturbance occurs only when the external environment begins to drop below the minimal, or rise above the maximal, requirements of existence. And sensual perception of the external environment comes into play only *after* these minimal requirements are met. (As a matter of fact, loss of consciousness is one of the body's characteristic responses to environmental stress—drop in oxygen or pressure, extremes of heat and cold, etc.)

Metabolic process then is clearly the precondition to sensory perception, just as sensory perception is the material basis of the aesthetic process. But the aesthetic process only begins to operate maximally, i.e., as a uniquely human faculty, when the impact upon the body of all environmental forces are held within tolerable limits (limits which, as we have said, are established by the body itself). Thus, we can construct a kind of experimental spectrum of stress. The work of psychiatrists like Dr. George Ruff at the University of Pennsylvania establishes the lower end of this spectrum: sensory overloading is destructive, first of balanced judgments, then of rationality itself.[1] But

5

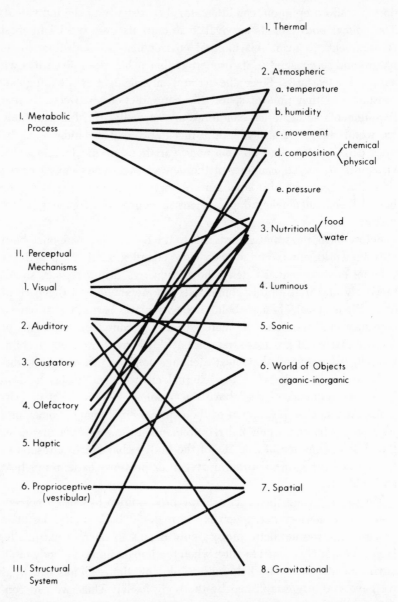

Figure 1–1 The relationship of the metabolic process to its environmental support is literally uterine. And since the process is the substructure of consciousness, sensory perception of changes in the environment in which the body finds itself is totally dependent upon satisfaction of the body's minimal metabolic requirements.

the other end of this spectrum proves equally destructive. Investigations of the effects of sensory deprivation, such as those carried on by Dr. Philip Solomon of the Harvard Medical School, indicate that too little environmental stress (and hence too little sensory stimulation) is as deleterious to the body as too much. Volunteer subjects for Dr. Solomon's experiments were reduced to gibbering incoherence in a matter of a few hours by being isolated from all visual, sonic, haptic and thermal stimulation.[2]

Psychic satisfaction with a given situation is thus directly related to physiologic well-being, just as dissatisfaction must be related to discomfort. A condition of neither too great nor too little sensory stimulation permits the fullest exercise of the critical faculties upon that situation or any aspect of it. But even this proposition will not be indefinitely extensible in time. As one investigator has observed in a recent paper (significantly entitled *The Pathology of Boredom*)[3]: "variety is not the spice of life; it is the very stuff of it." The psychosomatic equilibrium which the body always seeks is dynamic, a continual resolution of opposites. Every experience has built-in time limits. Perception itself has thresholds. One is purely quantitative; the ear cannot perceive sounds above 18,000 cycles per second; the eye does not perceive radiation below 3,200 Angstroms. But another set of thresholds are functions of time: constant exposure to steady stimulation at some fixed level will ultimately deaden perception. This is true of many odors, of "white" sounds and of some aspects of touch.

Of course, even more important facts prevent any mechanistic equating of physical comfort with aesthetic satisfaction. For while all human standards of beauty and ugliness stand ultimately upon a bedrock of material existence, the standards themselves vary astonishingly. All men have always been submerged in the environment. All men have always had the same sensory apparatus for perceiving changes in its qualities and dimensions. All men have always had the same central nervous system for analyzing and responding to the stimuli thus perceived. The physiological limits of this experience are absolute and intractable. Ultimately, it is physiology, and not culture, which establishes the levels at which sensory stimuli become traumatic. With such extremes—high temperatures, blinding lights, cutting edges and heavy blows, noise at blast level, intense concentrations of odor—experience goes beyond mere perception and becomes somatic stress. Moreover, excessive loading of any one of these senses can prevent a balanced assessment of the total experiential situation. (A temperature of 120 degrees F. or a sound level of 120 decibels can render the most beau-

7

tiful room uninhabitable.) But as long as these stimuli do not reach stressful levels of intensity, rational assessment and hence aesthetic judgments are possible. Then formal criteria, derived from personal idiosyncrasy and socially-conditioned value judgments, come into play.

The value judgments that men apply to these stimuli, the evaluation they make of the total experience as being either beautiful or ugly, will vary: measurably with the individual, enormously with his culture. This is so clearly the case in the history of art that it should not need repeating. Yet we constantly forget it. Today, anthropology, ethnology and archaeology alike show us the immense range of aesthetically satisfactory standards which the race has evolved in its history: from cannibalism to vegetarianism in food; from the pyramid to the curtain wall in architecture; from polygamy and polyandry to monogamy and celibacy in sex; from hoopskirt to bikini in dress. Yet we often act, even today, as if our own aesthetic criteria were absolutely valid instead of being, as is indeed the case, absolutely relative for all cultures except our own.

Our aesthetic judgments are substantially modified by non-sensual data derived from social experience. This again can be easily confirmed in daily life. It is ultimately our faith in antiseptic measures that make the immaculate white nurses, uniforms and spotless sheets of the hospitals so reassuring. It is our knowledge of their cost which exaggerates the visual difference between diamonds and crystal, or the gustatory difference between the flavor of pheasant and chicken. It is our knowledge of Hitler Germany which has converted the swastika from the good luck sign of the American Indians to the hated symbol of Nazi terror. All sensory perception is modified by consciousness. Consciousness applies to received stimuli, the criteria of digested experience, whether acquired by the individual or received by him from his culture. The aesthetic process cannot be isolated from this matrix of experiential reality. It constitutes, rather, a quintessential evaluation of and judgment on it.

Once in the world, man is submerged in his natural external environment as completely as the fish in water. Unlike the fish in his aqueous abode, however, he has developed the capacity to modify it in his favor. Simply as an animal, he might have survived without this capacity. Theoretically, at least, he might have migrated like the bird or hibernated like the bear. There are even a few favored spots on earth, like Hawaii, in which biological survival might have been possible without any modification. But, on the base of sheer biological existence, man builds a vast superstructure of institutions, processes and activities: and these could not survive exposure to the natural environment even in those climates in which, biologically, man could.

Thus man was compelled to invent architecture in order to become man. By means of it he surrounded himself with a new environment, tailored to his specifications; a "third" environment interposed between himself and the world. Architecture, is thus *an instrument whose central function is to intervene in man's favor*. The building—and, by extension, the city—has the function of lightening the stress of life; of taking the raw environmental load off man's shoulders; of permitting *homo fabricans* to focus his energies upon productive work.

The building, even in its simplest forms, invests man, surrounds and encapsulates him at every level of his existence, metabolically and perceptually. For this reason, it must be regarded as a very special kind of container. (Figure 1–2.) Far from offering solid, impermeable barriers to the natural environment, its outer surfaces come more and more closely to resemble permeable membranes which can accept or reject any environmental force. Again, the uterine analogy; and not accidentally, for with such convertibility in the container's walls, man can modulate the play of environmental forces upon himself and his processes, to guarantee their uninterrupted development, in very much the same way as the mother's body protects the embryo. Good architecture must thus meet criteria much more complex than those applied to other forms of art. And this confronts the architect, especially the contemporary architect, with a formidable range of subtle problems.

All architects aspire to give their clients beautiful buildings. But "beauty" is not a discrete property of the building: it describes, rather, the client's response to the building's impact upon him. This response is extremely complex. Psychic in nature, it is based upon somatic stimulation. Architecture, even more than agriculture, is the most environmental of man's activities. Unlike the other forms of art— painting, music, dance—its impact upon man is total. Thus the aesthetic enjoyment of an actual building cannot be merely a matter of vision (as most criticism tacitly assumes). It can only be a matter of total sensory perception. And that perceptual process must in turn have adequate biological support. To be truly satisfactory, the building must meet *all* the body's requirements, for it is not just upon the eye but upon the whole man that its impact falls.

From this it follows also that the architect has no direct access to his client's subjective existence: the only channels of communication open to him are objective, somatic. Only by manipulating the physical properties of his environment—heat, air, light, color, odor, sound, sur-

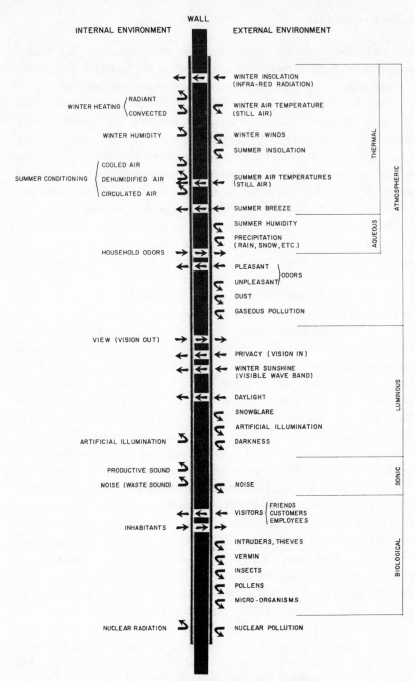

Figure 1–2 The building wall can no longer be considered as an impermeable barrier separating two environments. Rather, it must be designed as a permeable filter, capable of sophisticated response to the wide range of environmental forces acting upon it. Like the uterus, its task is the modulation of these forces in the interests of its inhabitants—the creation of a "third environment" designed in man's favor.

face and space—can the architect communicate with his client at all. And only by *doing it well*, i.e., meeting all man's requirements, objective and subjective, can he create buildings which men may find beautiful.

The matter by no means ends here, however. The architect builds not merely for man at rest, man in the abstract. Typically, he builds for man at work. And this confronts him with another set of contradictions. For work is not a "natural" activity, as Hannah Arendt has brilliantly reminded us.[4] Labor, according to her definition, is "natural" —that is, the use of the whole body to meet its biological needs, to feed it, bathe it, dress it, protect it from attack. Work, on the other hand, is "unnatural"—the use of the hand and the brain to produce the artificial, non-biological world of human artifice (skyscrapers, textbooks, paintings, space ships, highways, symphonies and pharmaceuticals). Both levels of human activity are, of course, fundamental to civilization, and the world of work can only exist as a superstructure on the world of labor. But insofar as we share the world of labor with the beasts, it can fairly be described as both natural and subhuman. Only the world of work, of human thought and artifice, is truly human.

This distinction is not so fine as it might at first appear: it has important consequences for architectural design. For if the architect ever builds for the wholly "natural" man, it will be only in his house, at his biological activities of resting, eating, lovemaking and play. Most other modern building types involve man at work, engaged in a wide spectrum of "unnatural" processes. Each of these involves stress. Stress, as we have seen, comes either from too much or too little stimulation, from sensory "overloading" and "underloading" alike. Biological man requires a dynamic balance, a golden mean between extremes. But modern work knows no such requirements: on the contrary, for maximum output and optimum quality, it sometimes implies environments of absolute constancy (e.g., pharmaceuticals, printing) and often requires extreme conditions never met in nature (e.g., high-temperature metallurgy, cobalt radiation therapy, etc.).

When plotted, these two sets of requirements will seldom lie along the same curve. From this it follows that architecture must meet two distinctly different sets of environmental criteria—those of man at some "unnatural" task, and those of the "unnatural" process itself.

Variety may indeed be the very stuff of man's natural life. But most of our human activities are, to a greater or lesser extent, "unnatural." From the moment we place the young child in kindergarten, we are imposing "unnatural" tasks upon him—placing his eyesight, his pos-

11

ture, his capacity for attention under quite abnormal stress. And this situation grows more acute throughout his education and his normal working life. As an adult, his biological existence is linked to processes which are never completely congruent with his own. Often they involve work which is fractionalized, repetitive and hence often unintelligible to the individual; often, the processes are actually dangerous to him. Only in agriculture does he confront work whose "natural" environment, rhythms and wholeness correspond to his own; but only six out of one hundred American workers are involved nowadays in this work.

The child at school faces a situation not qualitatively different from his father on the job: namely, to accomplish a given amount of work in a given time. Ideally, his physical growth and intellectual development should be steady and parallel. His rate of development should be as high at the end of his school day as at its beginning. In reality, of course, this is impossible. His energies flag as the day advances and nothing but play, food and rest will restore them. The question for architects is how should the classroom intervene in his favor? How to manipulate his external environment so that his learning advances with optimum speed and minimum stress?

It should be immediately apparent that the child's requirements are dynamic and imply a dynamic relationship with his classroom. No classroom should confront the child with a fixed set of day-long environmental norms, e.g., 72°F. air, 50 per cent humidity, 60 foot lamberts at desk top, 45 decibels of sound. Far from being held at some fixed level, the probability is that environmental conditions should be continually changing. *But this change cannot be casual or statistically indeterminate* (if change alone were all that was required, the class could be held in a nearby meadow). It must be a *designed* response to the child's changing requirements. The child may well need less heat at 2 p.m. than at 9 a.m. At day's end he may need less humidity and more oxygen; he may require more light and a different color; he may need a chair that gives a different posture or sound levels higher or lower than the morning. Whatever the requirements are, they could only derive from the child himself, in the experiential circumstances of study. They cannot be met by mechanistic engineers (windowless classrooms, "steady state" controls) nor by formalistic architects who design as though visual perception is the whole of experience.

But the symbiotic relationship between the architectural container and the men and processes contained is nowhere clearer than in the modern hospital. Here we find every degree of biological stress, including that of birth and of death. Here we find a wide range of highly specialized technologies, each with its own environmental requirements. And here we find the narrowest margins for error of any building type: here success or failure are literally matters of life or death. Here, if anywhere, we can observe the integral connections of metabolic function and aesthetic response as shown in Figure 1-1.

The seriously ill patient—above all, the major surgery case—will traverse the full experiential spectrum during his stay at the hospital. Stress will be greatest under surgery. His relationship with his environment can be almost wholly defined in somatic terms. Since he is under total anesthesia, there is no aesthetic aspect to his experience. (It is interesting, in this connection, to note that the two words anesthesia and aesthetic have a common origin in the Greek word meaning "to feel" or "to perceive.")

His gradual process of convalescence—through the recovery room, intensive nursing, regular nursing and ambulatory state, on up to discharge—traverses the full spectrum of experience. Precisely as the metabolic crisis diminishes so will his aesthetic response rise to the front of consciousness. Colors, lights, noises and odors which he was too ill to notice can now become major factors of experience. And their satisfactory manipulation becomes matters of active therapy.

The surgeon and his staff too will meet their greatest period of stress during surgery. At this juncture their requirements will be opposed to those of the patient. Where the latter requires warm moist air (and anti-explosive measures demand even higher humidities), the staff under nervous tension should ideally be submerged in dry, cool air. But since stress for them is of limited duration while any added load might be disastrous for the patient, the room's thermo-atmospheric environment is usually designed in the latter's favor. The staff sweats and suffers and recovers later. On the other hand, the luminous environment of the operating room must be wholly designed in the surgeon's favor (and no contradiction is raised because of the patient's lack of consciousness). The color of the walls, of the uniforms, even of the towels is quite as important to visual acuity of the surgeon as the lighting fixture themselves.

Thus, every decision made in design of the operating room will be based upon functional considerations, objectively evaluated. The very nature of the intervention prohibits any abstractly "aesthetic" considerations. The margin of safety is too narrow to allow the architect the luxury of any formalistic decisions based upon subjective preferences. In varying degrees, this situation will obtain in other specialized areas of the hospital. And it will increase as the hospital comes to be regarded not merely as a container for men and processes but as being itself an actual instrument of therapy. There are many evidences of this tendency already: the hyperbaric chamber where barometric pressure and oxygen content are manipulated in the treatment of both circulatory disorders and gas gangrene; the metabolic surgery suites where body temperatures are reduced to slow the metabolic rate before difficult surgery; the use of saturated atmospheres for serious cases of burn; artificially-cooled, dry air to lighten the thermal stress on cardiac cases; the use of electrostatic precipitation and ultraviolet radiation to produce completely sterile atmospheres for difficult respiratory ailments or to prevent cross-infection from contagious diseases. Here the building is not merely manipulating the natural environment in the patient's favor but actually creating totally new environments with no precedent in nature as specific instruments of therapy.

The exact point in hospitalization at which these environmental manipulations cease to be purely therapeutic and become merely questions of comfort or satisfaction, i.e., the point at which they cease to be functional and become aesthetic problems, is not easy to isolate. Objectionable odors, disturbing noises and lights; uncomfortable beds; lack of privacy; hot, humid atmosphere—all these will work against "beauty" in the hospital room. They may also delay convalescence. We cannot hope to make modern medical procedures "pretty" and the well-adjusted patient will probably want to leave the hospital as soon as possible under any circumstances. All the more reason, then, that every external factor be analyzed as objectively as possible, with a view to removing all unnecessary stress.

All of this suggests the possibility of establishing, much more precisely than ever before, an objective basis for aesthetic decision. It would be mistaken to attach too much importance to aesthetics in hospital design; but it would be equally foolish to minimize it. It cannot, in any case, be avoided. Everything the architect does, every form he adopts or material he specifies, has aesthetic repercussions. His problem is thus not Hamlet's: to act or not to act. It is rather to act wisely, understanding the total consequences of his decision.

If the architect's aesthetic standards are to be placed on a firmer factual basis than the one on which they now stand, he will need the help of physiologists and psychologists to do it. Architecture needs a much more systematic and detailed investigation of man's actual psychosomatic relationship with his environment than has yet been attempted, at least in architecture. It is not at all accidental that we can find the broad lines of such research appearing in the field of aerospace medicine. For man can only penetrate space by encapsulating himself in a container of terrestrial environment. And to accomplish this he must ask fundamental questions: what, actually, *is* this environment? What specifically is its effect upon us? What *is* its relation to human pleasure and delight?

In the design of the space vehicle, for example, it is no longer possible to say where problems of simple biological survival leave off and more complex questions of human satisfaction begin. Clearly, they constitute different ends of one uninterrupted spectrum of human experience. It is very probable that the upper end of this spectrum, involving as it does man's innermost subjective existence, can never be fully explored or understood. But it could certainly be far better understood than it is today, even among architects and doctors.

American society today employs some 270 distinct building types to provide the specialized environments required by its multiform activities. Most of them embody contradictions which must be resolved at two different levels: first between the persons and processes contained and then between their container and the natural environment. Respect for these two conditions is mandatory if the building is to be operationally successful. And yet, respect for these two conditions will often leave the architect with little room in which he can manipulate the building for purely formal, i.e., aesthetic, ends.

Most contemporary failures in architecture (and they are very many) stem either from a failure to understand this situation or else from a refusal to come to terms with it. Of course, no building can grow like an organism. Architects do not work with living tissue, with its powers of cellular division and genetic memory. In this sense, buildings must always be designed by men and these men will always bring to the task preconceived ideas of what forms they ought to assume. As Ernst Fischer, the Austrian philosopher has said, a good honey bee will often put a bad architect to shame. "But what from the very first distinguishes the most incompetent of architects from the best of bees is that the architect has built a cell in his head before he constructs it in wax." [5] Good or bad, beautiful or ugly, the building is always the expression of somebody's creative ambitions. Today, more than ever in history, these ambitions must be contained, structured and disciplined by objectively verifiable terms of reference.

NOTES

1. Lecture. 29 October 1963. School of Architecture, Columbia University, New York.

2. Lecture. 12 November 1963. Sensory Deprivation and Psychological Stress. Columbia University, New York.

3. Heron, Woodburn. 1957. Scientific American. N.Y. 196: 1 (52).

4. Arendt, Hannah. 1959. The Human Condition, Doubleday, New York.

5. Fischer, Ernst. 1963. The Necessity of Art. Pelican Book, New York, p. 17.

Physiology and Anatomy
of Urination

ALEXANDER KIRA

Although Fitch is probably correct in claiming that discussions of architecture have often proceeded as if the only important human or social dimension of architecture was how a building looked to the educated eye, the fact is that buildings, if they are to meet even the minimal requirements of functional adequacy, must necessarily respect the anatomical and physiological characteristics of the organism. Indeed, the importance of human biology as a constraint on design is an ancient architectural notion, having been discussed by Vitruvius, who in the first century A.D. advised practitioners of architectural design to acquire a basic knowledge of medicine. Some architects, for example Leonardo and Alberti in Renaissance Italy and Le Corbusier in our own time, have worked with the idea of basing a formal geometry of design on the dimensions of the human figure.

However, it is possible to conclude that respect for the constraining power of man's biological nature has declined since the Industrial Revolution, and that contemporary architecture, partly because of its technical prowess, has tended to overlook the role of biological factors. As a result, for several decades now, there has been a growing sentiment in architectural and environmental design circles, particularly in schools of design, to reintroduce a deliberate concern for anatomical and biological studies.

This new emphasis on the role of biology in the practice of architecture has taken form in the development of specialized fields of scientific inquiry, such as ergonomics, or human factors engineering, and anthropometrics. Ergonomics is concerned primarily with developing work environments that are compatible with human physiological processes. Anthropometrics compiles anatomical measurements for different age groups and populations, thus providing an objective basis for determining the size of spaces and equipment. Both specialties examine in minute detail the characteristics of the human organism at rest and in movement, often in laboratory environments. These data are then used to design equipment and spaces that will fit the human body, not only in static terms but also when performing the move-

Reprinted from Alexander Kira, "Physiology and Anatomy of Urination," and "Design Considerations for Urination," in *The Bathroom, Criteria for Design* (New York: Bantam Books, 1967), pp. 138–151. © 1966 by Cornell University. Reprinted by permission of Bantam Books, Inc.

ments necessary to the task at hand. These studies have been applied with greatest effect to the design of industrial and military equipment and to the design of highly specialized environments that impose unusual stress on the organism, such as space capsules and submarines.

The significance of Kira's research is that he has applied to a domestic facility, the bathroom, the same careful method of investigating the requirements for comfortable and efficient operation ordinarily used in the study of industrial and military equipment. The selection reprinted deals with the design of equipment for urination within the home. In the book from which it is taken, Kira also analyzes facilities for washing, bathing, and defecation. The study was based on a thorough review of the previous anthropometric and ergonomic literature; a field survey of user attitudes, practices, and preferences; and detailed observations of personal hygiene activities in a laboratory specially constructed for the research.

☐

The Process of Urination

Urination, or micturition, is the process of excreting from the body the waste fluids produced by the kidneys. The kidney is a highly discriminating organ which processes the body's supply of blood. It eliminates varying amounts of waste substances according to the body's needs. The urine, which is the final excretory product, is a composite not only of waste products which may have been in the blood but also of foreign substances and the excess products of the metabolic processes. Because the kidneys function to maintain the constancy of the body's internal environment, the composition of urine may vary considerably from one discharge to another. The quantity of urine which is produced over a 24-hour period varies directly with the amount of fluid intake but generally averages between 1,000 and 1,400 cc. Normal urine has an amber color and a very faint odor unless allowed to stand at room temperature for any length of time. As the urine is produced, it is carried through the ureters, or ducts, to the bladder where it accumulates until discharged from the body through the urethral openings.

Inasmuch as body posture has an effect on blood circulation, it can also affect urine composition and volume. The effect, however, is not significant unless there is considerable change or considerable stress from one posture and there is no evidence to suggest that posture has any appreciable bearing on the act of urination itself, either in terms of comfort or facilitating or hindering the process as is the case for defecation.[1]

Although the process of toilet training with respect to urination does not appear to be as complex and fraught with psychological overtones as defecation, it does, nevertheless, demand a similar period of training and requires a similar degree of neuromuscular differentiation and control. The development of voluntary bladder control is generally not achieved until from 18 to 30 months. Usually nighttime control takes longer. Full control and the ability to void without any assistance is usually not achieved until well into the third or fourth year. Because of the differences in the positioning of the bladder, males generally have greater difficulty in developing proper control since the anal and urethral sphincters are so close together as to require a particularly fine neuromuscular differentiation.[2] In the female the two sphincters are separated by the vagina. While this simplifies the problem of learning to control each of the sphincters separately, the relation of the vagina to the bladder and the urethral sphincter often results in a sympathetic stimulation leading to urination. This is particularly true during the later months of pregnancy when the ever increasing pressure on the bladder results in more and more frequent urges to urinate. It may also be caused by vaginal stimulation prior to, or during, intercourse, especially if the bladder is at all full.

In this connection it may also be noted that the urge to urinate frequently is also very common among the aged. Largely this is due to an atrophying of the kidneys and bladder and a weakening of the sphincter muscles. Another fairly common problem among the aged is incontinence, particularly among prostate patients. This gradual degeneration of body functions may be regarded in some respects as a reversal of the initial developmental processes as, for example, in the loss of neuromuscular controls, which in some instances causes aged men to be as inept at urinating as small boys.

Anatomy

Anatomical differences between the male and female result in certain aspects of the urination process being different for each of the sexes. Aside from the problem of developing controls, the most significant and obvious difference is in the location and nature of the actual urethral openings from which the urine is discharged. In the female, the urethra is located just in front of the vagina, within the labial folds, and well inside the body envelope. As a consequence, for all practical purposes, she has no control over the direction of the urine stream. As we shall see later, this has certain consequences which restrict the posture assumed and the kind of facilities which might be provided. In the male, on the other hand, the urethral opening is located in the penis, thus lying outside the body envelope and permitting control of the urine stream within the entire volume circumscribed by its possible trajectory.

Design Considerations for Urination

DESCRIPTION OF ACTIVITY

Female Urination. The nearly universal custom in Western societies is for females to urinate in a sitting position (or squatting, if no support is available). From a purely physiological viewpoint, females could perform in a standing position as well. Urinating in such a position, however, inevitably results in soiling oneself, both directly and from splash, since the female's urine stream cannot be directed away from its essentially vertical axis. In addition, the complications of present-day clothing present varying degrees of handicap to comfortable, or possible, urinating in any position other than sitting, without virtually disrobing, because of the present tendency for some form of girdle, or otherwise restrictive and elasticized undergarment, to be worn virtually universally and constantly—even by teenagers. In this connection, it may be noted that attempts have been made over the years to provide a "stand-up" urinal for females similar to the standard men's wall-hung urinal, except for a longer projecting basin, primarily with the aim of improving the traffic capacity and particularly the sanitation of public facilities. In using these fixtures, a woman would have to partially disrobe and then straddle the projecting lip of the fixture in more or less a standing position. The practical difficulties of using the fixture in terms of clothing, combined with the psychological resistances to being publicly uncovered, have resulted in relatively little acceptance of it. The problem of exposure has been resolved by placing the fixture in a stall, but this has negated the potential advantages of economy and rapid turnover in use.

It seems obvious, however, that under present circumstances, particularly in the home where the problem of sanitation, compared with public facilities, can be considered for practical purposes to be nonexistent, the most convenient and comfortable position for a woman to assume for urination is a sitting one. If we accept this premise, the problem then is largely one of making appropriate minor modifications

21

in whatever fixtures might evolve for defecation since the basic requirements are very similar. Accordingly, the rest of this discussion, since we are concerned primarily with facilities in the home, focuses on the particular problems posed by male urination which is almost overwhelmingly accomplished from a standing position and which poses major sanitary problems.

Male Urination. Males can urinate equally conveniently and comfortably from either a sitting/squatting, or standing, position. However, the restrictive effects of clothing, the sexual considerations which are involved, and the extreme convenience have caused men to favor the standing position almost universally. In general, men will urinate in a sitting/squatting position only when this activity takes place in conjunction with defecation and they have already assumed a sitting position. Insofar as urination, per se, is concerned, we must regard it as primarily a standing activity.

Because of the male's anatomy and his early learned ability to control the trajectory of the urine stream, there is, in some respects, relatively little problem of any substantial self-soiling in a standing position.[3] The qualification depends upon the nature of the facilities available. That there are serious soiling problems associated with the use of current home facilities may be attested to by any housewife or cleaning woman. The soiled fixtures and the soiled, discolored, and rotted floors and walls, which everyone is familiar with, stem from the use of the water closet, which is completely inadequate for this purpose, instead of a separate "urinal." The key to these problems lies in understanding the particular characteristics of the male urine stream.

Urine passing through the slit-like urethral opening is emitted in the form of a thin sheet which twists and spirals for several inches and then disintegrates into a centrifugal spray. (See Figure 2–1.) Both the point of disintegration and the maximum diameter of the spray are directly proportional to the velocity of the stream, which is a function of the bladder pressure. A low velocity produces an increment (each twist in the integrated phase of the stream) of approximately ⅜ of an inch; extreme velocity an increment of almost 2 inches. Normal velocity produces an increment of approximately 1 inch. In every instance, however, the centrifugal action causes the stream to disintegrate and assume a roughly conical shape. It is this dispersion which is responsible for a substantial share of the soiling both of the self and of the surroundings which can occur when urinating from a standing position, and when the receiving container is not as close as, for example,

Figure 2–1 Typical Dispersion and Splash Pattern of a Simulated Male Urine Stream.

a wall-hung urinal which intercepts the stream before the point of dispersion.

Another aspect which must be considered is the inability of the male to predict, or accurately position, the *initial* point of impact of the urine stream. Although the degree of accuracy is reasonable in most instances, there are a sufficient number of "accidents," or gross distortions, attributable generally to temporary and unnoticed dermal adhesions of the urethral opening. Once the activity has begun, however, most adult males can, by a process of successive corrective maneuvers, exercise fairly accurate control thereafter. The notable exceptions are the ill and intoxicated, the very young, or the very old and infirm.

The normal water closet, however, presents a relatively poor target, particularly because of the psychological resistances involved in its use. Because of the general taboos on the elimination processes, and the particular aversions to being directly and actively aware of elimination taking place, most men will try to avoid urinating into the standing pan water—the easiest and most natural target—in order to avoid the embarrassment of being heard, since the noise, particularly with a full bladder, can be quite considerable and easily identified. Once this decision is made, the choice of target areas is limited to the sides and front and back walls of the bowl. In the majority of water closets the bowl configurations are such that these areas are quite small and difficult to hit with any degree of accuracy. Because of the necessity to stand up close to the front of the bowl to catch the dribble at the end of the action, the possibilities are further limited to the sides and the back. However, since the back wall in most cases is vertical or nearly so, the target area presented is quite small and is useful for only a brief period since the length of the stream trajectory continuously

23

varies. This leaves only the side walls which present a feasible elongated target. Since this area rarely exceeds 2 inches by 7 or 8 inches it becomes obvious that not only is the proper trial and error maneuvering difficult to accomplish successfully, but also half of the stream spray inevitably falls outside the bowl.

Still another problem which arises in the use of the water closet is the back splash which results when the urine stream hits a hard surface. (See Figure 2-1.) This problem will, of course, arise and have to be dealt with in any container. However, it poses a particular problem with respect to use of the water closet since this fixture has obviously been primarily designed to accommodate defecation, and urination has been left to be accomplished as best it can.

Any stream of relatively nonviscous liquid hitting a hard surface (including a body of liquid) will result in a considerable splash. The direction and extent of this rebound, or splash, is determined not only by the force with which the stream strikes the surface, but also, and more importantly, by the configuration of the surface and the angle at which the stream hits the surface. Proper manipulation of this latter factor can appreciably reduce the quantity of splash and can control its direction.

DESIGN CONSIDERATIONS

For a fixture to adequately accommodate male urination from a standing position, the following criteria should be observed. The receiving container must be so positioned, relative to the point of origin, as to intercept the urine stream before the point of appreciable disintegration. The container must be of a size and shape which will present an adequate "target" under a variety of circumstances. Use of the fixture should be relatively noiseless. The internal configuration of the container should be such as to avoid or minimize back splash, and the production of aerosols. The resulting fixture should not be obvious in appearance, and should probably look as little like the urinal found in "men's rooms" as possible.

In order to adequately provide for male urination in the home there are several possible approaches which may be taken. The first, and most obvious, is to provide a standard wall-hung urinal since this satisfies all the necessary functional criteria. It is unlikely, however, to meet with general acceptance, chiefly because of various psychological reasons. In addition, it may be argued on practical grounds that such a fixture would entail too much extra space and expense even if the

24

standard urinal were to be adapted for household tank-type operation. In view of all the evidence, this solution might as well be dismissed for the moment, even though it represents the simplest and most direct one.

A second approach is to try to make appropriate modifications to the water closet. This would offer the advantage of being relatively un-obvious and at the same time relatively inexpensive. Extensive in-vestigation, however, indicates that this is a next to impossible task. This is particularly true with respect to the low water closet since, as will shortly be made clear, the farther the container is from the point of origin, the greater the problem of containment of the stream. As is so often the case, in trying to accomplish several functions, each is compromised. The more the fixture is modified to accommodate urina-tion the poorer it becomes for its primary function of defecation.

A third possibility, which might be mentioned in passing, is that, instead of accommodating the standing male, perhaps things should somehow be so arranged so that he would have to sit. From all prac-tical and psychological viewpoints, this would seem, however, to be totally unworkable. Aside from changing a natural and age-old habit, it is likely to meet with strong resistance, from the aspect of conve-nience, particularly since in recent years the male has become ever more accustomed to the speed and effortlessness of the urinal, which is now almost universal. The idea of having to substantially undress for an operation which is presently so simple would certainly meet with considerable opposition. There is also not much question but that it would encounter a great deal of psychological resistance since it would, in effect, deny the male the free use of his greatest glory and would condemn him to assume the position of a woman.

The final and most logical possibility is to attempt to evolve a totally new fixture which will satisfy all of the criteria described.

Stream Characteristics and Positioning of Container. As pointed out earlier, the major problem posed by the standing male urinating in a water closet is the centrifugal breakup and dispersion of the urine stream which results in considerable soiling of the self and the sur-rounding area.

The behavior of a simulated stream was studied, assuming a point of origin of 29 inches above the floor, relative first, to an intercepting plane at a height of 16 inches (standard water closet), and then to an intercepting plane at a height of 9 inches (point of assumed intercep-tion of a floor mounted urinal and of the proposed squat closet). In

25

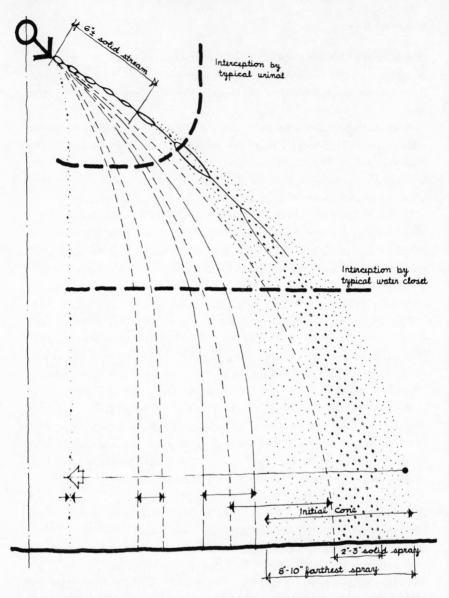

Figure 2–2 **Dispersion and Containment Characteristics of Simulated Male Urine Stream.** The stream at any given moment assumes the form of a warped conical solid which shrinks and shifts its base over a period of time. The size of the receiving container is also directly related to its distance from the point of origin.

every instance, the full extent of the spray indicated in Figure 2–2 could be measured within a 30-second period, the assumed average time of urination. Graus cites 45 seconds as the average time in military situations.[4] This higher figure is undoubtedly due to the opportunities for urination or rather, the lack of them. The actual range, however, is quite considerable and can vary from 10 or 15 seconds up to a minute and a half, or longer, depending on how full the bladder is. It should be noted that these dispersion figures for a simulated stream represent minimums which are rarely achieved in actuality. Depending upon the particular angle of the stream trajectory, there is likely to be a greater dispersion the flatter the trajectory and the greater the pressure. In addition, incidental dermal adhesions can result in an immediate and erratic dispersion of the stream.

When we consider that the stream assumes the form of a warped conical solid with a shifting base, it is obvious, as indicated in Figure 2–2, that the size and shape of the necessary container or enclosure is directly related to its distance from the point of origin in order to completely contain the stream. The closer the container is to the point of origin, the more compact it can be and the less the danger of accidental soiling. In view of the range of heights of adult males, the front lip of the container should be set at a minimum height of 24 inches from the floor, the height at which regular wall-hung urinals are commonly set. At this height, the container needs to have a minimum opening dimension approximately 10 inches by 10 inches.

The container must also be so shaped and positioned that it can be more or less straddled in order to catch the dribble and drip at the conclusion of urination, again, in a fashion similar to existing wall-hung urinals.

Size and Shape of Container. The particular combination of size and shape may vary over a considerable range, so long as the container meets the criteria of presenting an adequate target area and of minimizing and containing back splash as well as dispersion.

In terms of shape, the most crucial point is that the contouring be such as to keep back splash to a minimum. To allow for variable bladder pressures and/or variable stream trajectories, the cross section should be continuously variable so that the surface maintains a constant relationship to the stream. (See Figure 2–3.) The effect of this angular relationship between the stream and the impact surface is shown in Figure 2–3, which reports the results of a series of tests with a simulated vertical stream at maximum pressure (twist length of 2 inches). As indicated, the smaller the angle between the stream and the impact surface the less the resulting splash. In general, it would be desirable to keep this relationship within a 30-degree limit in both a lateral and a longitudinal direction. While a properly designed single warped planar surface can keep splash within reasonable limits, it

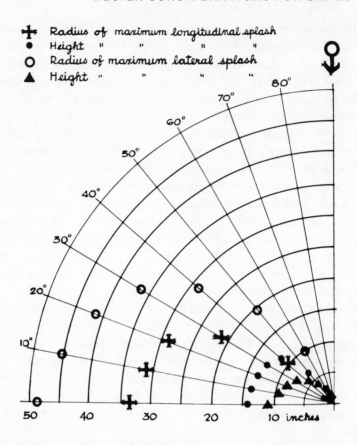

Figure 2–3 Variations in Splash Effects according to Angular Relationship between Stream and Contact Surface.

would obviously be desirable to warp both surfaces. Offhand, this would suggest that a spherical configuration might be the most appropriate. However, if we take into account the effect of the continuously varying angle between the stream and the surface, it becomes apparent that the ideal shape is one which approximates a funnel. (See Figure 2–4.) Such a form would result in a minimum of splash and would direct most of it forward. It is also critical that the axis of the container be set at an appropriate angle. In the course of normal urination the angle formed by a maximum trajectory rarely exceeds 60 degrees from the vertical. Accordingly, the angle at which the container should be set lies in the 40 to 50 degree range. This is the "critical" range in the sense that maximum trajectory equals maximum pressure, which in turn equals maximum dispersion and splash. As the stream trajectory

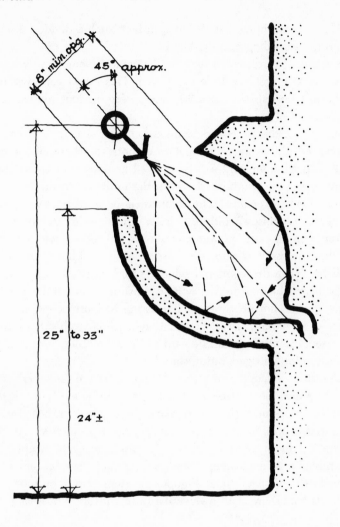

Figure 2–4 Sectional View of Stream Showing Necessary Dimensions and Configurations for Containment.

drops off into the 20 and 10 degree range it begins to form a larger angle with the surface, but the problems at this range are considerably less.

Experiments have also suggested that a single ridge placed in the longitudinal plane of the stream can assist in further reducing the problem of containment since it has the effect of dividing the stream and deflecting it laterally. As a result, it would be possible in some circumstances to provide a smaller container. A divider is likely to be particularly useful in the area of greatest pressure impact. Many models of wall-hung urinals have, in fact, such a divider as a result of the trap protruding into the bowl.

Another feature which may be desirable is something which would serve as a "target" in the critical area. This might conceivably be the ridge just described or possibly some very obvious marker set in the surface.

Insofar as the precise determination of a size for the container is concerned, this is again a function of both the shape of the container and its positioning and can be arrived at only after these other variables have been established within the limits set forth.

Avoidance of Noise. The avoidance of a distinctive and clearly recognizable noise should be a major consideration in any design. Pan water such as exists in water closets is the most obvious thing to be avoided unless it is normally missed as in wall-hung urinals. It may well be that a dry container which is flushed is the best way to cope with this problem, since the noise of flushing, while it meets with some objections, is not nearly so embarrassing to most people as the direct noise of urination.[5] In the event that materials other than chinaware are used, attention should be paid to their denseness, or mass, in terms of drumming and generating sound.

Controls. Since we are considering a fixture intended solely for stand-up use, the controls for flushing should be easily reached from a standing position. This is perhaps best accomplished by a hand operated control located approximately 36 to 48 inches from the floor. A foot operated control unless it is simple to clean is apt to be undesirable from a cleaning standpoint. Again, caution should be observed with respect to ambiguous or dual (hand or foot) operated controls which are both awkward to use and unsanitary as a result.

SUMMARY: DESIGN POSSIBILITIES

In order to illustrate the application of the criteria developed in this paper, one possible approach to a home urinal is shown in Figure 2–5 in outline form. The fixture is assumed to be a funnel-like container which pulls down, or out, from a recess in the wall, much like a pullman lavatory. In order to save space and utilize other existing plumbing it has also been assumed that this fixture would be mounted over the water closet and would use the same tank for flushing, the same vent space, and other features. In the illustration, the urinal is shown in combination with the low-squat water closet suggested and illustrated in a previous section. Use of this water closet assumes that it can be straddled so that the dimensions of the urinal can be kept at a

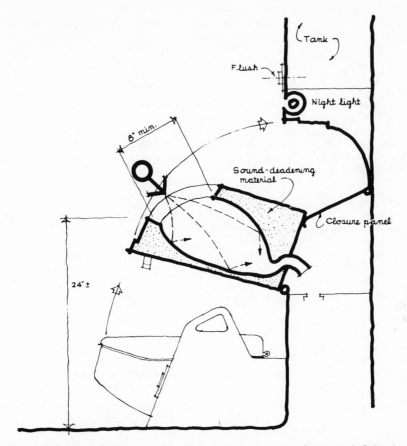

Figure 2–5 Experimental Home Urinal Incorporating Suggested Criteria. One possible approach to the home urinal might be in the form of a pull-down funnel-like fixture set over the toilet.

minimum. It has also been assumed that the fixture would normally be dry and that it might be either manually or automatically flushed when closed up into the wall.

As proposed, this combination of fixtures might also lend itself fairly readily to some form of prefabricated assembly, complete with the necessary electrical controls, night-light, and so forth.

The criteria upon which this particular proposal rests are that: the fixture be available, be functional, and be obvious as to its purpose, but only when needed and in use. Undoubtedly, these same criteria might be met in a variety of other ways. In some instances, it may be preferable to provide a regular separate urinal similar to that illustrated in Figure 2-4.

NOTES

1. Smith, H. W., *The Kidney—Structure and Function in Health and Disease*, New York: Oxford University Press, 1951.

2. Despert, J. L., "Urinary Control and Enuresis," *Psychosomatic Medicine*, Vol. 6, No. 4, 1944, p. 294.

3. On the other hand the relatively minor but inevitable problem which does exist, is still significant enough to have been memorialized in the scatological rhyme familiar to every American male: "No matter how much you jiggle and squeeze, the last drop always goes down your knees."

4. Graus, H., "A Scientific Approach to Military Plumbing Fixture Requirements," *Air Conditioning, Heating and Ventilating*, February 1957, p. 96.

5. Langford, Marilyn, *Personal Hygiene Attitudes and Practices in 1000 Middle-Class Households*, Memoir 393, Ithaca, N.Y.: Cornell University Agricultural Experiment Station, 1965, pp. 29, 30.

3

Cultural Variability in Physical Standards

AMOS RAPOPORT AND NEWTON WATSON

Kira's research into bathroom design provides a good illustration of the difficulties inherent in the methodology of equipment studies, which often assume that information about universal biological characteristics can be used to project new and more efficient environmental designs. What Kira's selection demonstrates is that even when one is dealing with criteria that relate to so called hard information, it is important for the designer to respect the interpretations that different groups of users put on the particular facilities and design forms and the biological activities to which they relate. For example, Kira found it necessary to modify his designs to take account of the clothing styles of Western women, feelings of shame about urinary activity, attitudes toward urine odor, and the high valuation placed on toilet privacy.

The same general principle, but applied to a broader range of environmental situations, is illustrated by Rapoport and Watson's survey of physical standards in Western nations, India, and Japan. Physical and environmental standards are those rules or norms institutionalized in a society that define acceptable levels of daylight, heat, noise, and room and furniture size. They are written down in the form of building codes established by governmental ordinance or are described in handbooks of architectural practice. To some degree these standards have been derived from ergonomic and anthropometric studies carried out by building research organizations in each country, although in large part they also derive from unconscious cultural processes.

Rapoport and Watson make several points about the degree of cultural variability in these standards. (1) The situations for which it is judged necessary to establish standards differ between societies. For example, American charts show a number of activities, such as drinking at a bar or eating at a counter, that are missing in Indian handbooks. (2) Given the fact that a group of countries will have standards applying to similar conditions, the standards will vary widely. This generalization applies not only to space standards, which architects have known for a long time possess "low criticality," but applies as well to standards for heat, light, and noise, which usually have

Reprinted from Amos Rapoport and Newton Watson, "Cultural Variability in Physical Standards," *Transactions of the Bartlett Society,* Bartlett School of Architecture, University College, London 6 (1967–1968): 63–83.

been assumed to be biologically determined and thus to have "high criticality." (3) Finally, Rapoport and Watson point out that standards differ not only across cultures but within them, depending upon the social context in which the facility is used. Standards for tread and riser dimensions in stair design differ for interior, exterior, domestic, and ceremonial staircases.

The authors conclude their selection by asserting that an awareness of the cultural component present in standards that relate to biological factors should be an important aid to architects and designers who practice in different societies.

□

Recent attempts to develop user requirements as a basis for physical design in building reflect the desire for a more rational approach in the light of the increasing complexity of the problems involved in design and the increasing separation between designer and user. In seeking for hard data it is understandable that physical determinants such as anthropometrics and ergonomics, as well as comfort needs with regard to light, heat and sound should until recently have received more attention than topics within the more complex socio-cultural and psychological realms. Recently, however, a growing interest in the socio-cultural and psychological forces involved in the development and use of space organizations has led to work on these aspects in a number of places.

E. T. Hall [1] was among the first to draw attention to the cultural variability of the use of space, the scale of spaces, needs for privacy, tolerance of noise and overcrowding, and the like. Similarly, in his recent work on the bathroom, Alexander Kira [2] has pointed out that while the problems of personal hygiene have remained constant, the ways in which people have coped with them have varied widely depending on the beliefs, fears and values which have motivated them at any particular time and place. He gives many examples of different attitudes to privacy, cleanliness, odors and comfort, and suggests that it is such attitudes rather than mere utility which give insights into, for example, the preference for showers rather than baths and other significant planning decisions regarding personal hygiene.

It is the thesis of this selection that even physical standards which might be regarded as "hard" and quantifiable data are themselves affected by cultural attitudes and social forces prevailing at the time and place of their inception. Such standards, in common with most human activities and institutions, are the result of a combination of constant and variable factors. In the area which we are discussing, the constant aspects which set certain possible ranges and limits are man's physiological and anatomical characteristics, while the variables are *culturally defined choices.* The fact that choice exists is due to what one could term the low *criticality* of architecture [3] since choice plays a major role only where criticality is low. In this paper we will discuss a number of examples of physical standards of apparently high criticality—*anthropometrics, noise, thermal comfort and lighting*—and try to show that they contain a rather important component of choice. It is not, of course, our intention to deny the need for the existence of standards and ranges of acceptability and non-acceptability but rather to suggest that the physical determinants of built form are a more complex and subtle matter than is commonly accepted.

That this is so is better known outside the design professions than it is within them. René Dubos,[4] for example, has pointed out that we respond actively and often creatively to environmental stimuli—we shut out some, modify others through symbolic and other socio-cultural mechanisms and our responses to these stimuli depend on the meaning which we attach to them, depending on our cultural background. Man can therefore use the effects of these stimuli for his own purposes which he selects.

Douglas H. K. Lee has similarly discussed "the role of attitude in response to environmental stress"[5] pointing out that the influence of attitude increases as the severity of the stress decreases, i.e., as the criticality goes down. However, even in highly critical situations the influence of cultural attitudes can be quite striking. For example, it has even been suggested, although not universally accepted, that cultural attitudes "can determine such basic physiological responses as glandular secretions, sexual appetites, the pulse rate, the direction of peristalsis and so on."[6] The fact that responses to pain, whether caused by injury or disease, seem to be affected by cultural attitudes as expressed in child-rearing practices, expectations of roles and the like seems, however, to have been well documented.[7]

Anthropometrics

In establishing a starting-point for physical design, the size of the human body is often considered in relation to the equipment which it uses and the swept volumetric zones which it occupies when in movement. It is known that there are variations of human size due to heredity. A

35

comparison of the body sizes of American Whites and Negroes with Japanese (for example) shows the following differences:

	Mean Height	Mean Weight
American Whites	68.4 in.	155 lb. (11 st. 1 lb.)
American Negroes	68.0 in.	152 lb. (10 st. 12 lb.)
Japanese	63.5 in.	121 lb. (8 st. 9 lb.)[8]

These variations concern the manufacturers of "off-the-peg" clothing for civilian and military use. NATO, for example, was forced into making comparative anthropometric studies of American and Southeast European troops from Italy, Greece and Turkey in order to establish ranges of equipment sizes which would be required.[9] This variability of the human body has been taken seriously by services supply branches in spite of the jokes about ill-fitting clothing which surround quartermasters' stores. The variation within groups has been considered along a normal curve and the stress has been on establishing ranges of dimensions and tolerance limits rather than precise data.[10] Less commonly considered has been variability over time. It has recently been pointed out that US soldiers in World War II were 0.7 in. taller and 13 lb. heavier on average than World War I GIs (67.7 in. compared with 68.4, 142 lb. compared with 155).[11] The changes in size among the Japanese since the end of the war have also received attention. While these increases over time have been attributed to improved diet, fashion probably also plays a part. A comparison of the ideals of feminine beauty as revealed in paintings and advertising are a clear indication of this; compare, for example, the currently fashionable slim and boyish figures with those of Rubens, or the deliberately distorted feet, ears, lips, head shapes and degree of obesity of various cultures.

Variations in size and body shape between different sub-cultural groups within a single culture is another aspect which has recently been discussed. There are the rather obvious differences between military and civilian populations due to the selection process involved and there are even variations between different branches of the armed forces.[12] A curious difference, more difficult to explain, is that, for example, between American lorry drivers and research workers; as a group the former average 68.5 in. and 167 lb. while the latter average 70.6 in. and 167 lb.—with consequent very different body proportions.[13]

All these variations in body size suggest the fallacy of the "average man" concept. But the influence of anthropometrics on design is made even more complex by the effects of the way man moves and uses equipment. Since motor habits and gestures vary considerably with culture,[14] we may well expect this to introduce further variations into anthropometric data leading to variations in the types, sizes and arrangements of anthropometric space requirements. That this is indeed the case is shown by the differences between the recommended space standards for certain basic and similar activities as well as the great number of activities found in certain cultures and not in others. For example, American standards recommend a minimum width of 5 ft. 4 in. for two people facing each other in a dining booth. This dining pattern is not shown at all in Indian data, but for two people facing each other across a dining *table* the American dimension is 6 ft. 2 in., while in India it is 5 ft. 6 in. (i.e., 8 in. less). The Indian data show additional requirements for eating in a squatting position (6 ft. 6 in.) and also distinguish between informal and formal situations with different dimensions, both for dining at a table and in a squatting position [15] (see Figures 3–1 and 3–2).

The American charts also show a number of activities which are missing in the Indian examples (drinking at a counter, drinking at a bar, etc.), while the Indian charts show many examples missing in Western charts (squatting for both toilet and eating, meditation positions, Yogi exercise position, braiding hair, worshipping positions, receiving various vendors at the door, story-telling to a group of many children, etc.). For any given activity the variety of positions in India seems greater, involving formal and informal situations, different types of furniture (traditional and Western) and other variations. Food preparation, washing and toilet activities are totally different because the ways of doing things and equipment used differ. For example, double beds in India are 4 ft. 9½ in. × 6 ft. 2½ in., in Britain 4 ft. 6½ in. × 6 ft. 6 in. Kitchen counters in India are 2 ft. 4 in. for traditional equipment, 2 ft. 9 in. for Western equipment, and in the US 3 ft. 0 in. While these differences are perhaps to be expected between Eastern and Western cultures, they are also found *within* Western cultures. For example, in Germany we find anthropometric data for a woman beating out a rug outdoors [16] which, not surprisingly, is missing in US data. There are also marked differences between the standards recommended for similar activities between more comparable ways of life.

For example, the domestic WC cubicle is usually reduced to a mini-

37

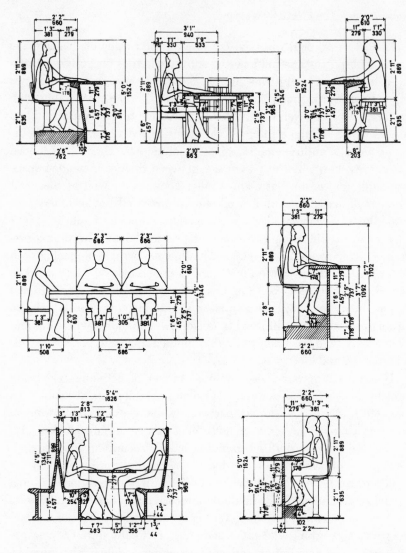

Figure 3–1 American Anthropometric Standards. Source: Timesaver Standards (New York: McGraw-Hill, 4th ed., 1966), p. 15.

mum, and any oversizing by the designer is regarded as waste space. Yet we find a variation of 20 cm. (8 in.) between the widths recommended by German, US and British standards which amounts to about 25% of the width.

British	70-75 cm.	(*Space in the Home*. London: HMSO, 1968.)
	2 ft. 3¼ in.-2 ft. 5¼ in.	
US	80-90 cm.	(*Timesaver Standards*. New York: McGraw-Hill,
	2 ft. 7¼ in.-2 ft. 11 in.	4th ed. 1966.)
Germany	80 cm.	(Rainer Wolff, *Das Kleine Haus*. Munich:
	2 ft. 7¼ in.	Callway, 1959.)

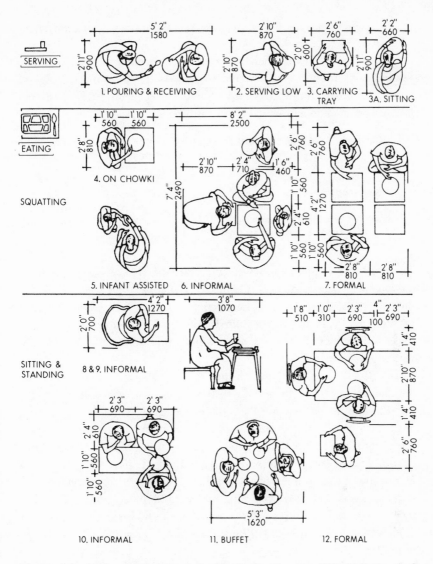

Figure 3–2 Indian Anthropometric Standards. Source: CIB Bulletin, 1, 2 (1966):16.

Even between England and Scotland we find differences, for example, in the recommended volumes for linen storage:

Scotland	0.9 m.^{3} (31.9 cu. ft.)
England	0.4-0.6 m.^{3} (14.1-21.2 cu. ft.)
Sweden	0.14-0.33 m.^{3} (4.9-11.6 cu. ft.)[17]

One wonders why the thrifty Scots collect so much linen!

Stairs might be thought to represent an area of particularly high criticality yet even here we commonly find rather considerable variations. In the United States 2 storeys is the maximum allowed for walking up, as it is in the UK (where 3 is allowed for maisonettes), while in France 4–5 storeys is still commonly used. If we examine rules of thumb formulae, handbooks and regulations regarding tread-riser relationships, we find a great variability and possible range.

Common rule of thumb (in Britain)	riser × tread = 66 in.
	2 riser + tread = 23 in.
Britain (*Specification*, 1968, Vol. 1, p. 252)	2 riser + tread = 22½-25 in.
Germany (Neufert, op. cit.)	2 riser + tread = 23.8-25 in. (norm 24.4 in.)
US (NY City Code and National Board of Fire Underwriters cited in *Timesaver Standards*)	riser × tread = 70-75 in.

None of these suggest optima but give "acceptable" ranges which vary a good deal. If maxima and minima for both riser and tread are fixed, the range is still great. For R between 7–9 in. and T between 8½–11½ in. there are 35 configurations possible using ½ in. intervals only, and these recommended maxima and minima themselves can be seen to vary a great deal.

Alberti (Book 1 ch. 3) was quite specific when he stated that the number of steps had to be odd so that "we always set our right foot into the temple first" saying that "the best architects never put above 7 or at most 9 steps together in one flight; imitating I suppose the number of either the planets or the heavens . . ." but his recommendations as to height of steps were more liberally defined "never higher than 9 in. nor lower than 6 in." Figure 3–3 shows the spread of recommended stairs and was prepared from data published in *Specification* (Britain), 1968, Vol. 1, Neufert's *Bauentwurfslehre* (Germany), *Timesaver Standards* (USA) and the *Uniform Building Regulations* (State of Victoria, Australia).

It is interesting to note that while the English *normal* stair has a rise of 19 cm. (7.4 in.) and a tread of 21 cm. (8.2 in.), in Germany a rise of 20 cm. (7.8 in.) and tread of 22 cm. (8.5 in.) is regarded as too steep and a *normal* stair in Germany (Rainer Wolff, *Das Kleine Haus*) has a rise of 17 cm. (6.6 in.) and a tread of 28 cm. (10.7 in.).

In testing and questioning English people about stairs no optimum was found. The stairs preferred were, surprisingly, *not* those which used the least energy but rather those which were "comfortable" (a subjective measure) and gave safe support to the shoe. There were variations between men and women regarding stairs using the least amount of energy, and stairs preferred, and there were also variations within these groups even for the limited sample tested.[18]

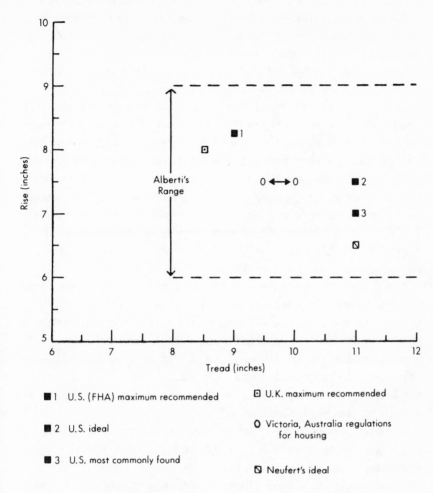

Figure 3–3 Chart Showing Variation in Recommended Proportions of Stairs in the U.K., U.S., and Australia.

In the various designers' guides to staircase design the suggested proportions change depending on whether stairs are interior or exterior, domestic or "grand," which suggests that the limits set are not *physical* but *contextual*.

Noise

We have already referred to Hall's point that the tolerance of noise varies with culture. There seems to be evidence that some cultures may actually prefer high noise levels, and Hall suggests that Italians in general, and southern Italians in particular, prefer rather high noise levels whereas Germans have stringent requirements for quiet. On that scale Americans come somewhere between.

Beranek has pointed out that European standards for noise control tend to be rather higher than American ones. He attributes this both to the greater experience of flat dwelling in Europe and also to a greater stress on the quality of life rather than on gadgets.[19] Countries such as the Netherlands, the Soviet Union, Sweden and Germany have well developed codes; Britain has only "recommended" standards but these are still higher than those of the proposed New York City code—the only one being considered by any American city. For airborne sound the Dutch code requires a 54 dB reduction at 2,000 cycles; the British recommendation is 56 dB for grade I and 54 dB for grade II, while New York proposes 45 dB at the same frequency. Figure 3–4 shows some comparative curves derived from various sources.

The current noise-reduction performance of buildings in New York and other American cities is worse still. Part of the difficulty in setting better standards is political—the number of jurisdictions with their own codes and the like. It is also interesting to note that the concern with noise control in the US began as a result of an insurance claim—an example of the point made by Boris Pushkarev that insurance requirements and frequent law-suits are important design constraints and form determinants in the United States.[20]

If we consider the 1963 recommendations on noise reduction by the Federal Housing Administration we find that, for structure-borne sound, the range of recommendations for reduction among the codes considered is rather sizable.[21] Figure 3–5 shows the FHA recommendations, the range of recommendations in the overseas codes considered, and some specific European curves which we have superimposed. It is clear that there is agreement only within fairly wide limits, and that once again, the specific standards seem to be related to attitudes and choices rather than any definite physical needs.

Temperature

Thermal comfort, the *raison d'être* for heating and other environmental controls is also variable. Not only does it vary due to adaptation, as experiences with people moving to both tropics and arctic conditions have shown, but it also seems to have different values in different cul-

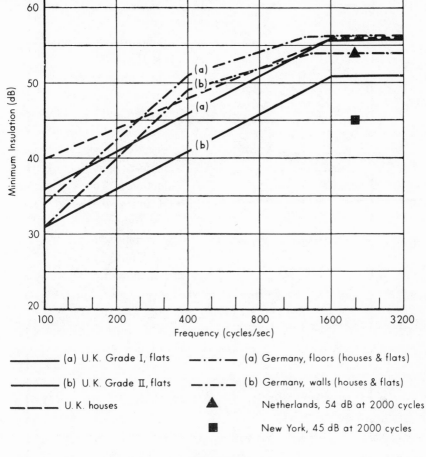

Figure 3–4

tures. Consider, for example, the case of Australian airmen training in Canada during World War II. One would have expected that Australians, unused to cold weather, would suffer from the cold. The main problem, however, was the "overheated" atmosphere in the barracks. There are possibly apocryphal stories of airmen in Alberta in midwinter breaking fixed windows to reduce temperatures in barracks with uncontrolled radiators.

There are figures relating to the comfort zones for different groups which clearly show these differences. In light industry in Great Britain the optimum in the summer is about 63° F. (ET) [22] with a range be-

43

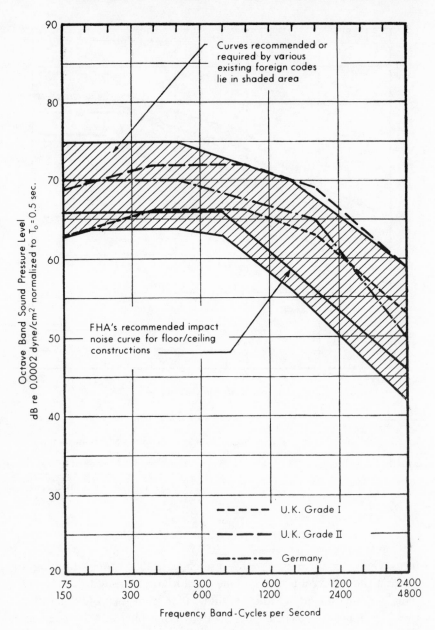

Figure 3–5

tween 57–63° F. (ET). The corresponding comfort zones for American workers are 65–69° F. (ET) for winter and 69–74° F. (ET) for summer with the optimum somewhere around 67° F. (ET) for winter and 71° F. (ET) for summer.[23]

Great Britain	sedentary work	65° F. (60-68° F. range)
	light work	60° F. (60-65° F. range)
	heavy work	55° F. (55-60° F. range)
South Africa	sedentary work	68-70° F.
	light work	65-68° F.
	heavy work	60-65° F. [24]

In Australia the figure for office workers is 80–82° F. (DBT) with a range between 77–90° F.[25]

Even within one country there are differences between groups. In Australia, for example, outdoor manual workers were comfortable at 87° F. compared with 80–82° F. for office workers. In the US there are differences between men and women (due, in part, to the clothing worn), age groups, geographic location, winter and summer seasons, diet, etc. Winter comfort in the US at 66° F. rises to 73° F. (ET) in summer, although the range in that case is 69–73.[26]

As one would expect, the difference in temperatures at which people are comfortable result in different recommendations for temperatures to be maintained. Within the figures given (see Table 3–1), comparing Great Britain, the United States and Germany, it is noticeable that there are particularly great differences for certain spaces. For example, bedrooms in Britain are kept colder than American bedrooms by a greater amount than other spaces, and the differences generally are greater for houses than for other building types. This is also reflected in the differentiation between different parts of the house in the United Kingdom but *not* in the United States. The generally higher American temperatures are due not only to higher comfort zones generally but also because American design temperatures are largely for women who tend to be more lightly dressed than men and are dominant in the design requirements, unlike Britain until very recently. Standards in Britain are also going up, as they tend to do with the growth of affluence and technology [27]—possibly as status symbols and partly influenced by advertising.

For example, the need for air conditioning in summer may not always be due to physiological needs but rather to the living standards which society expects. This is shown by the new hotels and motels in the San Francisco Bay Area which need to be air conditioned if rooms are to be let, although the climate certainly does not require it. Similar points have also been made regarding the cleanliness of bathrooms [28] and also light levels (which are discussed in the next section).

TABLE 3-1

Comparative Recommended Temperatures (°F.) in UK, USA and Germany

	UK (IHVE guide 1965)	Germany	USA (ASHRAE guide 1963)	
Living Room	65°	68°		*Homes** Note:
Bedroom	60°	68°		*(a)* no
Bed-Sitting Room	65°		73-75°	differentiation
Kitchen	60°	68°		*(b)* major
Bathroom	60°	71.6°		difference with UK, especially bedrooms
School: Assembly Halls	65°		68-72°	
Gymnasium	55°	59°	55-65°	
Teaching Rooms	65°	68°	72-74°	
Changing Rooms		71.6°	65-68°	
Hotels: Bedrooms	60°		75°*	
Ballroom	65°		65-68°	
Dining Room	65°		72°	
Theatre Auditorium	65°		68-72°	
Hospital:	65°		72-74°	
Operating Room	65-70°		70-95°	
Shops, Stores	65°		65-68°	
Offices: Conference Rooms		64.4°		
Typing Rooms		68°		
Circulation		59°		

*Indicates major differences.

Sunlight, Daylight and Artificial Light

SUNLIGHT

The lighting committee of the Building Research Board have pressed for a minimum standard with regard to sunlighting "because there is an evident desire of people to have it." [29] It has been suggested that past regulations were "framed to allow excessively easy legislative control and/or to allow for inadequate education of the designer with the result that *the underlying functional principles have been completely obscured.*" [30] The authors of this selection draw attention to the pseudo-functional status given to abstracted standards in design manuals and criticize the tendency of designers to derive functional criteria from "relatively imprecisely defined data." They go on to consider a standard of sunshine from which the "designer can find the penalty for not orientating the room in the preferred direction"; this penalty being, of

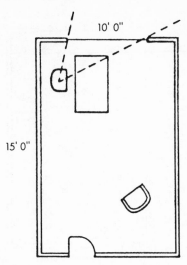

Figure 3–6   Room Layout as Designed—Furniture Turned to Light, Sun, and View.

course, the partial or total deprivation of sunlight. This assumes that sunshine in rooms is a desirable feature in northern temperate climates, although there is in fact, little scientific evidence to show that behavior in buildings is affected by sunlight in temperate zones.

A recent study carried out in the Bartlett School of three large London "tower" office blocks examined precisely this point—the effect which sunlight (and view) might have on the way office workers in single rooms arranged their furniture.[31] Similar rooms were studied for each orientation, in which the designers had intended the occupant to arrange himself as in Figure 3–6 so that he could enjoy sun and view. From the results of the survey there would seem to be stronger influences than environmental factors at work in these particular rooms. The most commonly found arrangement was that shown in Figure 3–7 in which the occupant had positioned his desk diagonally across the corner of the room. The reasons for this might be twofold: (a) it seems critical for the user of the room to have complete visual coverage of the door so that anyone entering may be immediately recognized, (b) it seems important to establish a public zone and a private one which the "intruder" rarely penetrates. These considerations were dominant to the extent of some occupiers sitting with their back to view and sun. It is possible that if the same study was replicated in other cultures other patterns of space organizations might be found based on other criteria—possibly even giving priority to sun and view.

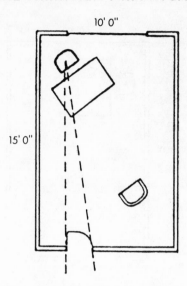

10' 0"

15' 0"

Figure 3–7   Room Layout as Used—Furniture Turned to Give Visual Control of the Door and to Create a Private Zone.

DAYLIGHT

In England, daylight standards have been given more importance than in most countries. A school designer, for example, has to comply with a statutory requirement which states that a minimum daylight factor of 2% must be provided on the working plane—the daylight factor being expressed as a percentage of sky brightness. The intention behind this regulation was to ensure that, in addition to receiving adequate daylight to work by, children and teachers were given the opportunity of viewing the world outside. The regulations, in fact, assumed that adequate daylight and view were inextricably linked.

Earlier regulations presumably relate to then current teaching techniques, economic conditions and cultural attitudes. In 1863 it was recommended that windows be placed so that "full light" should fall on the *faces* of the children and teacher, no doubt indicating the great importance placed on verbal communication and discipline at that time and also related to the static conditions with positions of both teachers and pupils fixed. In 1888 the regulations required classrooms to be lit from two sides—an indication of a felt need for cross ventilation, possibly as part of the "healthy mind in a healthy body" trend linked with the then current interest in improved public health. 1901 saw the regulations requiring no desk to be more than 20 ft. from a window and related the area of window to floor space (⅕ was required). At that time there was clearly much more desk work involved.

The 1945 post-war regulations established a 2% minimum daylight factor, but 5% was "preferred." As a result of this, schools were over-glazed and classrooms became overheated in summer from solar gain and were cold in winter due to rapid heat loss.[32] The present regulations, in force since 1951, dropped the references to 5% because of this tendency to overglaze.

We are at present seeing further changes in teaching techniques: the greater freedom shown to children in primary education and "involvement teaching" are currently fashionable attitudes which are finding their way into secondary education. The formal classroom seems to be on its way out, and educational methods now call for more open spaces and, as a result, deeper plans in which it is impossible to achieve the statutory daylight factors by sidelighting alone. Designers are employing techniques of top-lighting and permanent artificial supplements to achieve the recommended levels. Social, cultural and economic determinants may soon cause a further change in our approach to daylighting standards in this country, although it is unlikely that total daylight exclusion, already tried in the US where there have been a number of windowless schools built, will be accepted in England—another example of differences based on cultural attitudes rather than any clear objectively established needs.

It is, in fact, varying cultural needs which seem to lead to standards. "The establishing of levels [of daylight] depends upon the indigenous culture. If the current fashion is for 'picture windows' and for a seeking after outdoor life, the standard of daylight considered necessary for amenity will be far higher than in a society which considers the outdoor elements to be cruel and inimical to human well-being. Hence an arrangement of windows which may appeal to one may be disliked by another, depending on his training or upon the *environmental culture from which he springs*."[33]

ARTIFICIAL LIGHT

Standards for artificial light seem to have been rising constantly since the English optometrist Trotter wrote in 1908: "one foot-candle is a very convenient and comfortable illumination . . . and more than 3 foot-candles is seldom obtained in artificial illumination." The output of a 5 ft. fluorescent tube is now around 4,500 lumens and it seems reasonable to suppose that mechanical efficiency will increase. Although designers recognize that good lighting is not just the provision of ever higher lighting levels it seems that increasing wealth, advertising and changing cultural habits of a particular country bear more closely on the recommended artificial lighting than "real" psycho-physiological needs.

By its nature artificial lighting can be designed to finer tolerances than can daylighting and most countries specify precise values in lux

TABLE 3-2

	U.S.A.[1]	Great Britain[2]	France[3]
	lux	lux	lux
Most Difficult Seeing Tasks Finest precision work. Involving: finest detail; poor contrasts; long periods of time. Such as: extra-fine assembly; precision grading; extra-fine finishing.	10000-20000	1500-3000	1500-3000
Very Difficult Seeing Tasks Precision work. Involving: fine detail; fair contrasts; long periods of time. Such as: fine assembly; high-speed work; fine finishing.	5000-10000	700-1500	700-1500
Difficult and Critical Seeing Tasks Prolonged work. Involving: fine detail; moderate contrasts; long periods of time. Such as: ordinary benchwork and assembly; machine shop work; finishing of medium-to-fine parts; office work.	1000-5000	300-700	300-700
Ordinary Seeing Tasks Involving: moderately fine detail; normal contrasts; intermittent periods of time. Such as: automatic machine operation; rough grading; garage work areas; switchboards; continuous processes; conference and life rooms; packing and shipping.	500-1000	150-300	150-300
Casual Seeing Tasks Such as: stairways; reception rooms; washrooms, and other service areas; inactive storage.	200-300	70-150	70-150
Rough Seeing Tasks Such as: hallways; corridors-passageways; inactive storage.	100-200	30-70	30-70

1 footcandle = 1 lm/sq. ft. = 10.8 lux

SOURCE: From Leslie Larson, *Lighting and Its Design*, New York, Whitney Library of Design, 1964, p. 22. © 1964 Whitney Library of Design, New York, N.Y.

[1] I.E.S. Handbook 1959, Table 9-53, pp. 9-76 to 9-84.

[2] I.E.S. Code 1961, Interior Lighting, p. 41.

[3] L'Ass. Française des Eclairagistes, Recomm. 1961, p. 33.

for a range of seeing tasks. In spite of this precision in the recommended levels there are considerable variations between countries (see Table 3–2). For example, for machine shop and office routines, the ratio between recommended levels in Switzerland, Great Britain and the United States is 1:3:9. While there may be minor physiological differences between the inhabitants of these countries, as we have discussed earlier in this selection, these differences alone would not ac-

TABLE 3-2 *(continued)*

Germany[4]	Sweden[5]	Finland[6]	Belgium[7]	Switzer-land[8]	Australia[9]
lux	lux	lux	lux	lux	lux
4000	1000-2000	1000-2000		over 1000	over 2000
600-1000	300-500	500	500-1000	300-1000	700-1500
250-500	300	300	250-500	150-300	300-700
120-250	150	150	100-250		150-300
60	40-80	80	50-80	40-80	70-150
30	20	40	20-30		50-70

[4] Deutsche Industrie Normen. Blatt 5053, Table 1, 1953.
[5] Svenska Belysningssälskapet, Lux table 1949.
[6] Proceedings, C.I.E. Stockholm 1951, report 62b, p. 31.
[7] Com. Nat. Belge de l'Eclairage, Code preliminaire 1951, p. 12.
[8] Schw. Elektr. Verein, Leitsätze 1947, S. 6.
[9] Australian Standard Code No. CA. 30-1957.

51

count for variations of this magnitude. The range of levels considered desirable must be related to economic and cultural factors. American standards are invariably the highest for all the tasks in the table. What the table does not show are the *attitudes towards* artificial lighting design. In England, in spite of pressure from certain quarters for continual increases in light levels, a good deal of effort has gone into the introduction of qualitative standards such as the "glare index" which to some extent controls the design of fittings. In the US no such controls exist and the trend is for higher levels *per se*. There are also differences among various countries in the preference for fluorescent versus incandescent light, and other variations in lighting design—all linked, it would seem, to cultural factors.

Conclusion

In this selection we have sought to show that even physical standards (supposedly the only "hard" information designers possess) are greatly affected by values and culturally based choice. The study of comparative standards, their relation to physiological and psychophysical experiments in different cultures and to differing value systems may help to define those areas of requirements which are based on constant needs, i.e., the ranges of feasibility and criticality, while the variations for different cultures would enable standards to be compared and would also help designers working in other cultures, especially in the developing countries. A monitoring of the rate of change would enable forecasts to be made of possible developments in standards and also to isolate these aspects of change which are due to real improvements in environmental quality, due to rising standards of wealth and demand, and those which are due to changing fashion and the impact of advertising and hard-pressure salesmanship. This would seem to be an essential component in the development of a meaningful understanding of user requirements and the relation of man to his environment.

NOTES

1. E. T. Hall, *The Silent Language.* Garden City, N.Y.: Doubleday, 1959. *The Hidden Dimension.* Garden City, N.Y.: Doubleday, 1966.
2. Alexander Kira, *The Bathroom.* New York: Bantam Books, 1967.
3. This concept is described in Amos Rapoport, *House Form and Culture.* Englewood Cliffs, N.J.: Prentice-Hall, 1969.
4. René Dubos, *Man Adapting.* New Haven: Yale University Press, 1966; "Humanistic biology," *American Scientist,* 53, 1965, pp. 4–19.

5. *Journal of Social Issues*, Vol. XXII, No. 4, 1966, pp. 83–91.

6. See Harry C. Bredemeier and Richard M. Stephenson, "The analysis of culture," in Peter I. Rose (ed.), *The Study of Society*. New York: Random House, 1967, p. 120.

7. See Mark Zborowski, "Cultural components in responses to pain," *Journal of Social Issues*, 8, 1953, pp. 16–31. For a review of the literature on this topic see B. B. Wolff and S. Langley, "Cultural factors and response to pain: a review," *American Anthropologist*, Vol. 70, No. 3, June 1968, pp. 494–501.

8. A. Damon, H. W. Stoudt and R. A. McFarland, *The Human Body in Equipment Design*. Cambridge, Mass.: Harvard University Press, 1966, pp. 10 ff.

9. Ibid., p. 11.

10. Ibid., p. 38.

11. Ibid., p. 11.

12. Ibid., p. 11.

13. Ibid., p. 11.

14. Clyde Kluckhohn, "Culture and behavior," in G. Lindzey (ed.), *Handbook of Social Psychology*, Vol. 2. Cambridge, Mass.: Addison-Wesley, 1954.

15. For American data, see *Timesaver Standards*. New York: McGraw-Hill, 4th ed., 1966, p. 15; for Indian data see *CIB Bulletin*, 1–2, 1966, p. 16.

16. Ernst Neufert, *Bauentwurfslehre*. Ullstein Fachverlag, 1962, p. 169.

17. *A.J. Metric Handbook*, para. 17.42 and Table X.

18. J. S. Ward and P. Randall, "Optimum dimensions for domestic stairways," *Architects' Journal*, 5 July 1967, pp. 29–34.

19. Leo L. Beranek, "Noise," *Scientific American*, December 1966, pp. 66–76.

20. Boris Pushkarev in J. B. Holland (ed.), *Who Designs America?* Garden City, N.Y.: Doubleday, 1966, pp. 113–15.

21. *Impact Noise Control in Multifamily Dwellings*, FHA No. 750, Washington, D.C., January 1963.

22. Within the range of 20–60° relative humidity at the hot time of day the dry-bulb temperature can be used interchangeably with effective temperature. See W. V. McFarlane, *Tropical Building Studies*, Vol. 1, No. 2, 1962 (University of Melbourne), p. 102.

23. Van Straaten, *Thermal Performance of Buildings*. Amsterdam: Elsevier, 1967, p. 32.

24. Ibid.

25. McFarlane, op. cit., Vol. 1, No. 4, 1962, p. 7.

26. T. S. Rogers, *Thermal Design of Buildings*. New York: Wiley, 1964, p. 4.

27. See Douglas H. K. Lee, op. cit., p. 86, where he points out that the acceptable indoor winter temperature has gone up from 68° F., still beloved by the British [*sic*—see Table 3–1], to 72° F., 74° F. and now even 78° F.

28. Ibid.

29. "Sunlight in building," *Proc. CIE International Conference*, 5–9 April 1965, Newcastle-on-Tyne: Paper 1, R. G. Hopkinson, "The Psychophysics of sunlighting."

30. Ibid. Paper 4, J. H. Ritchie and J. K. Page, "Sunshine and sun control standards."

31. Duncan Joiner and Newton Watson. This forms part of a Ph.D. thesis not yet published.

32. R. G. Hopkinson, P. Petherbridge, J. Longmore, *Daylighting*. London: Heinemann, 1966, p. 401.

33. Ibid., p. 404 (our italics).

4

Invasions of Personal Space

NANCY JO FELIPE AND ROBERT SOMMER

Previous selections have indicated that data drawn from human biology become fully useful to designers only when they are interpreted in terms of the cultural context in which men live. A respect for the importance of suprabiological factors in design is now showing itself in other ways, too, especially in the interest that architects and planners have evinced in understanding the psychological roots of environmental response. This new interest goes beyond the architect's traditional concern with the psychology of perception and is focused instead on the areas of psychology dealing with the dynamics of personality functioning.

In attending to the implications of depth psychology for environmental design, two questions are, in effect, being asked. The first is whether or not there are any personality needs that are specifically environmental, in the sense that they are best satisfied by the provision of a physical object rather than a social pattern. The second issue is to determine whether or not such needs, if they exist, are universal, that is to say, characteristic of the human organism, regardless of the cultural or social setting in which he lives.

One of the few such personality needs to have been successfully identified thus far is the need for personal space. Personal space is usually defined as an area with invisible boundaries surrounding a person's body into which no one may intrude. It is sometimes described metaphorically as an invisible snail shell, a soap bubble, or breathing room. The need to maintain such a space is apparently deeply rooted in the human personality, even though the volume of space varies between cultures and for different persons and situations in the same culture.

The concept of personal space was first formulated by Simmel in the early 1900s and was investigated empirically by social psychologists in the 1930s, but it has received its most extensive development much more recently. In the following selection Felipe and Sommer discuss one of the many ways in which the existence of the need has been inferred experimentally. Their method was to approach naïve subjects living in mental hospitals or studying in library reading rooms and to observe the subjects' reactions to the invasion of their personal space. Most of the subjects first tried to accommodate themselves to the intruder, but eventually most fled, even though in the case

Reprinted from Nancy Jo Felipe and Robert Sommer, "Invasions of Personal Space," in Social Problems 14, no. 2 (1966): 206–214. Reprinted by permission of The Society for the Study of Social Problems.

of the students using the reading rooms, this meant interrupting their work. The authors conclude their article by relating their findings to studies of animal behavior and by speculating about the variety of factors likely to modify the human response to the invasion of personal space.

It should be noted that the concept of personal space has been utilized in the design of many types of small-scale, intimate environments, including dormitory rooms, school classrooms, mental hospital wards, subway car seating, dining tables, and park benches.

☐

The last decade has brought an increase in empirical studies of deviance. One line of investigation has used the case study approach with individuals whom society has classified as deviants—prostitutes, drug addicts, homosexuals, mental patients, etc. The other approach, practiced less frequently, has involved staged situations in which one individual, usually the investigator or one of his students, violates the norm or "routine ground" in a given situation and observes the results.[1] The latter approach is in the category of an experiment in that it is the investigator himself who creates the situation he observes and therefore has the possibility of systematically varying the parameters of social intercourse singly or in combinations. From this standpoint these studies have great promise for the development of an experimental sociology following the model set down by Greenwood.[2] With topics such as human migration, collective disturbance, social class, the investigator observes events and phenomena already in existence. Control of conditions refers to modes of observations and is largely on an *ex post facto* statistical or correlational basis. On the other hand, few staged studies of deviance have realized their promise as experimental investigations. Generally they are more in the category of demonstrations, involving single gross variations of one parameter and crude and impressionistic measurement of effect without control data from a matched sample not subject to the norm violation. Of more theoretical importance is the lack of systematic variation in degree and kind of the many facets of norm violation. The reader is left with the impression that deviancy is an all-or-none phenomenon caused by improper dress, impertinent answers, naïve questions, etc. It cannot be denied that a graduate student washing her clothes in the town swimming pool is breaking certain norms. But we cannot be sure of the norms that are violated or the sanctions attached to each violation without some attempt at isolating and varying single elements in the situation.

The present selection describes a series of studies of one norm violation, sitting too close to another individual. Conversational distance is affected by many things including room density, the acquaintance of the individuals, the personal relevance of the topic discussed, the cultural backgrounds of the individuals, the personalities of the individuals, etc.[3] There are a dozen studies of conversational distance which have shown that people from Latin countries stand closer together than North Americans,[4] eye contact has important effect on conversational distance,[5] introverts stand farther apart than extraverts,[6] friends place themselves closer together than strangers,[7] and so on, but there is still, under any set of conditions, a range of conversational distance which is considered normal for that situation. Several of these investigators, notably Birdwhistell,[8] Garfinkel,[9] Goffman,[10] and Sommer [11] have described the effects of intruding into this distance or personal space that surrounds each individual. The interest shown in the human spacing mechanisms as well as the possibilities of objective measurement of both norm violation and defensive postures suggests that this is an excellent area in which to systematically study norm violations.

The present selection describes several studies of invasions of personal space that took place over a 2-year period. The first was done during the summer of 1963 in a mental hospital. At the time it seemed that systematic studies of spatial invasions could only take place in a "crazy place" where norm violation would escape some of the usual sanctions applied in the outside world. Though there is a strong normative control system that regulates the conduct of mental patients toward one another and toward staff, the rules governing staff conduct toward patients (except cases of brutality, rape, or murder), and particularly higher status staff, such as psychiatrists, physicians, and psychologists, are much less clear. At times, it seems that almost anything can be done in a mental hospital provided it is called research, and one can cite such examples as psychosurgery, various drug experiments, and recent investigations of operant conditioning as instances where unusual and sometimes unproven or even harmful procedures were employed with the blessings of hospital officialdom. To call a procedure "research" is a way of "bracketing" it in time and space and thus excluding it from the usual rules and mores. This is one reason why we supposed that spatial invasions would be more feasible inside a mental hospital than outside. We had visions of a spatial invasion on a Central Park bench resulting in bodily assault or arrest on a sex deviant or "suspicious character" charge. It seemed that some studies of norm violation were deliberately on a one-shot basis to avoid such difficulties. After the first study of spatial invasions in a mental hospital had been completed, however, it became apparent that the method could be adapted for use in more typical settings. We were then able to undertake similar intrusions on a systematic basis in a university library without any untoward consequences, though the possibilities of such problems arising were never far beyond the reaches of consciousness in any of the experimental sessions.

Method

The first study took place on the grounds of Mendocino State Hospital, a 1500-bed mental institution situated in parklike surroundings. Most wards were unlocked and many patients spent considerable time outdoors. In wooded areas it was common to see patients seated underneath trees, one to a bench. Because of the easy access to the outside as well as the number of patients involved in hospital industry, the ward areas were relatively empty during the day. This made it possible for the patients to isolate themselves from other people by finding a deserted area on the grounds or remaining in the almost empty wards. The invasions of personal space took place both indoors and outdoors. The victims were chosen on the basis of these criteria: the victim would be a male, sitting alone, and not engaged in any clearly defined activities such as reading, card playing, etc. All sessions took place near the long stay wards, which meant that newly admitted patients were largely omitted from the study. When a patient meeting these criteria was located, E walked over and sat beside the patient without saying a word. If the victim moved his chair or moved farther down the bench, E would move a like distance to keep the space between them about 6 inches. There were two experimental conditions. In one, E sat alongside a patient and took complete notes of what ensued. He also jiggled his keys occasionally and looked at the patient in order to assert his dominance. In the second experimental condition, E simply sat down next to the victim and, three or four times during the 20-minute session, jiggled his keys. Control subjects were selected from other patients seated at some distance from E but still within E's visual field. To be eligible for the control group, a patient had to be sitting by himself and not reading or otherwise engaged in an activity as well as be visible to E.

Each session took a maximum of 20 minutes. There were sixty-four individual sessions with different patients, thirty-nine involved the procedure in which E took notes and twenty-five involved no writing.[12] One ward dayroom was chosen for additional, more intensive observations. During the daylight hours this large room was sparsely populated and the same five patients occupied the same chairs. These patients would meet Esser's criteria of territoriality in that each spent more than 75 per cent of his time in one particular area.[13]

Results

The major data of the study consist of records of how long each patient remained seated in his chair following the invasion. This can be compared with the length of time the control patients remained seated. Figure 4-1 shows the cumulative number of patients who had de-

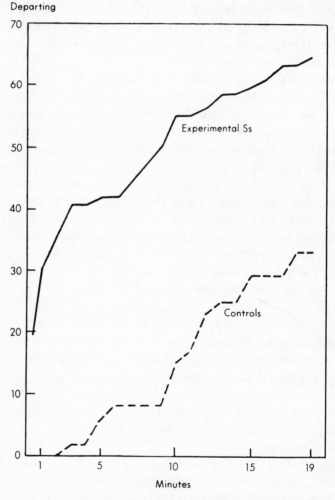

Figure 4–1 Cumulative Percentage of Patients Having Departed at Each 1-Minute Interval.

parted at each 1-minute interval of the 20-minute session. Within 2 minutes, all of the controls were still seated but 36 per cent of the experimental subjects had been driven away. Within 9 minutes fully half of the victims had departed compared with only 8 per cent of the controls. At the end of the 20-minute session, 64 per cent of the experimental subjects had departed compared with 33 per cent of the controls. Further analysis showed that the writing condition was more potent than the no-writing condition but that this difference was significant only at the .10 level ($\chi^2 = 4.61$, df $= 2$). The patient's actual departure from his chair was the most obvious reaction to the intrusion. Many more subtle indications of the patient's discomfort were evident. Typically the victim would immediately face away from E, pull in his shoulders, and place his elbows at his sides. Mumbling, irrelevant laughter, and delusional talk also seemed to be used by the victim to keep E at a distance.

Repeated observation of the same patients took place on one particular ward where the patients were extremely territorial in their behavior. Five patients generally inhabited this large room and sat in the same chairs day after day. There were gross differences in the way these particular territorial patients reacted to the writer's presence. In only one case (S_3) was E clearly dominant. At the other extreme with S_1 and S_2, it was like trying to move the Rock of Gibraltar. E invariably left these sessions defeated, with his tail between his legs, often feeling the need to return to his colleagues and drink a cup of coffee before attempting another experimental session. S_5 is a peculiar case in that sometimes he was budged but other times he wasn't.

Study Two

These sessions took place in the study hall of a university library, a large room with high ceilings and book-lined walls. The room contains fourteen large tables in two equal rows. Each table is 4×16 feet, and accommodates six chairs on each long side. Because of its use as a study area, students typically try to space themselves as far as possible from others. Each victim was the first female sitting alone in a pre-determined part of the room with at least one book in front of her, two empty chairs on either side (or on one side if she was at the end of the table), and an empty chair across from her. An empty chair was also required to be across from E's point of invasion. The second female to meet these criteria and who was visible to E served as a control. The control was observed from a distance and no invasion was attempted. Sessions took place between the hours of 8–5 on Mondays through Fridays; because of time changes between classes and the subsequent turnover of the library population, the observations began between 5 and 15 minutes after the hour. There were five different experimental conditions.

Condition I: E walked up to an empty chair beside an S, pulling the chair out at an angle, and sat down, completely ignoring S's presence. As E sat down, she unobtrusively moved the chair close to the table and to S, so that the chairs were approximately within 3 inches of one another. The E would lean over her book, in which she surreptitiously took notes, and tried to maintain constant shoulder distance of about 12 inches between E and S. To use Crook's terms, E tried to maintain the arrival distance, and to keep the S from adjusting to a settled distance.[14] This was sometimes difficult to do because the chairs were 18½ inches wide and an S would sometimes sit on the other half of her chair, utilizing its width as an effective barrier. However, E tried to get as close to the Ss as possible without actually having any physical contact. If the S moved her chair away, E would follow by pushing her chair backward at an angle and then forward again, under the pretense of adjusting her skirt. At no time did she consciously acknowledge S's presence. In this condition E took detailed notes of the S's behavior, as well as noting time of departure.

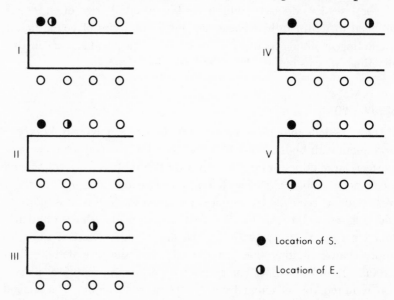

Figure 4–2 Seating of Intruder Vis-à-vis Victim in Each Experimental Condition.

Condition II: E went through the same procedure, except instead of moving the adjacent chair closer to S, E sat in the adjacent chair at the expected distance, which left about 15 inches between the chairs or about 2 feet between the shoulders of E and S.

Condition III: One empty seat was left between E and S, with a resulting shoulder distance of approximately 3½ feet.

Condition IV: Two empty seats were left between E and S with a resulting shoulder distance of about 5 feet.

Condition V: E sat directly across from S, a distance of about 4 feet.

In all conditions E noted the time of initial invasion, the time of the S's departure (or the end of the 30-minute session, depending on which came first), and any observable accommodation to E's presence such as moving books or the chair. For the controls E noted the time the session began and the time of the C's departure if it occurred within 30 minutes after the start of the session.

Results

Figure 4–3 shows the number of subjects remaining after successive 5-minute periods. Since there was no significant difference between the scores in Conditions II–V, these were combined in the analysis. At the end of the 30-minute session, 87 per cent of the controls, 73 per cent of the Ss in the combined conditions remained, compared to only 30 per cent of the experimental Ss in Condition I. Statistical analysis shows that Condition I produced significantly more flight than any of the other conditions, while there was a slight but also significant difference between the combined conditions (II to V) and the control condition. Although flight was the most clearly defined reaction to the invasion, many more subtle signs of the victim's discomfort were evident. Frequently an S drew in her arm and head, turned away from E exposing her shoulder and back, with her elbow on the table, her face resting on her hand. The victims used objects including books, notebooks, purses, and coats as barriers, and some made the wide chair into a barrier.

Discussion

These results show clearly that spatial invasions have a disruptive effect and can produce reactions ranging from flight at one extreme to agonistic display at the other. The individual differences in reacting to the invasion are evident; there was no single reaction among our

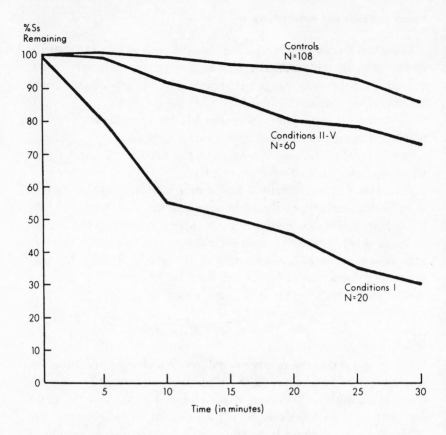

%Ss
Remaining

Figure 4–3 Per cent of Victims Remaining at Each 5-Minute Interval after the Invasion.

subjects to someone "sitting too close." The victim can attempt to accommodate himself to the invasion in numerous ways, including a shift in position, interposing a barrier between himself and the invader, or moving farther away. If these are precluded by the situation or fail because the invader shifts positions too, the victim may eventually take to flight. The methods we used did not permit the victim to achieve a comfortable *settled distance*. Crook studied the spacing mechanisms in birds, and found three component factors that maintain individual distance, which he defined as the area around an individual within which the approach of a neighboring bird is reacted to with either avoidance or attack.[15] A number of measurements may be taken when studying individual distance—the arrival distance (how far away from settled birds a newcomer will land), settled distance (the resultant distance after adjustments have occurred), and the distance after departure. The conditions in Study One and in Condition I of the second study called for E to maintain the arrival distance, and to keep the victim from adjusting to a settled distance. In these conditions, the victim was unable to increase the arrival distance by moving away (since the invader followed him down the bench in Study One and moved her chair closer in Study Two), and the greatest number of flight reactions was produced by these conditions. McBride, who has studied the spatial behaviors of animals in confinement, has found that avoidance movements and turning aside are common reactions to crowding,[16] particularly when a submissive animal is close to a dominant animal. Literally the dominant bird in a flock has more space and the other birds will move aside and look away when the dominant bird approaches. Looking away to avoid extensive eye contact was also a common reaction in the present studies. This probably would not have occurred if a subordinate or lower status individual had invaded the personal space of a dominant or higher status individual. There was also a dearth of direct verbal responses to the invasions. Only two of the mental patients spoke directly to E although he sat right beside them, and only one of the eighty student victims asked E to move over. This is some support for Hall's view that "we treat space somewhat as we treat sex. It is there but we don't talk about it." [17]

We see then that a violation of expected conversational distance produces, first of all, various accommodations on the part of the victim. The intensity of his reaction is influenced by many factors including territoriality, the dominance-submission relationship between invader and victim, the locus of the invasion, the victim's attribution of sexual motives to the intruder (in this case all victims and intruders were like-sex individuals), etc. All of these factors influence the victim's definition of the situation and consequently his reaction to it. In the present situation the first reaction to the invasion was accommodation or adaptation: the individual attempted to "live with" the invasion by turning aside, interposing a notebook between himself and the stranger, and pulling in his elbows. When this failed to relieve the tension produced by the norm violation, flight reactions occurred.

There are other elements in the invasion sequence that can be varied systematically. We have not yet attempted heterosexual invasion sequences, or used invaders of lower social standing, or explored more than two unusual and contrasting environments. We are making a start toward using visual rather than spacial invasions, in this case staring at a person rather than moving too close to him. Preliminary data indicate that visual invasions are relatively ineffective in a library where the victims can easily retreat into their books and avoid a direct visual confrontation. There are many other types of intrusions, including tactile and olfactory, that have intriguing research potentialities. It is important to realize that the use of staged norm violations permits these elements to be varied singly and in combination, and in this sense to go beyond the methods of *ex post facto* or "natural experiments" or single-point demonstrations. It is noteworthy that the area of norm violation provides one of the most fruitful applications for the experimental method.

NOTES

1. See for example Harold Garfinkel, "Studies of the Routine Grounds of Everyday Activities," *Social Problems*, 11 (Winter, 1964), pp. 225–250.
2. Ernest Greenwood, *Experimental Sociology*, New York: Kings Crown Press, 1945.
3. Edward T. Hall, *The Silent Language*, Garden City, N.Y.: Doubleday, 1959.
4. Edward T. Hall, "The Language of Space," *Landscape*, 10 (Autumn, 1960), pp. 41–44.
5. Michael Argyle and Janet Dean, "Eye-Contact, Distance, and Affiliation," *Sociometry*, 28 (September, 1965), pp. 289–304.
6. John L. Williams, "Personal Space and its Relation to Extraversion-Introversion," unpublished M.A. thesis, University of Alberta, 1963.
7. Kenneth B. Little, "Personal Space," *Journal of Experimental Social Psychology*, 1 (August, 1960), pp. 237–247.
8. Birdwhistell, R. L. *Introduction to Kinesics*, Washington, D.C.: Foreign Service Institute, 1952.
9. Garfinkel, *op. cit.*
10. Erving Goffman, *Behavior in Public Places*, New York, N.Y.: The Free Press, 1963.
11. Robert Sommer, "Studies in Personal Space," *Sociometry*, 22 (September, 1959), pp. 247–260.
12. Four incomplete sessions are omitted from this total. On two occasions a patient was called away by a nurse and on two other occasions the session was terminated when the patient showed signs of acute stress. The intruder in Study One was the junior author, a 35-year-old male of slight build. It is likely that invasions by a husky six-footer would have produced more immediate flight reactions.
13. Aristide H. Esser, *et al.*, "Territoriality of Patients on a Research Ward," *Recent Advances in Biological Psychiatry*, Vol. 8, in Joseph Wortis, ed., New York: Plenum Press, 1965.
14. J. H. Crook, "The Basis of Flock Organization in Birds," in W. H. Thorpe and O. L. Zangwill (eds.), *Current Problems in Animal Behaviour*, Cambridge: Cambridge University Press, 1961, pp. 125–149.
15. Crook, *op. cit.*
16. Glen McBride, *A General Theory of Social Organization and Behaviour*, St. Lucia: University of Queensland Press, 1964; also McBride, *et al.*, "Social Forces Determining Spacing and Head Orientation in a Flock of Domestic Hens," *Nature*, 197 (1963), pp. 1272–1273.
17. Hall, *The Silent Language, op. cit.*

5

Territoriality: A Neglected
Sociological Dimension

STANFORD M. LYMAN AND MARVIN B. SCOTT

Territoriality, defined as the need of individuals and groups to claim some geographical area as their own, is another need of the human personality that can best be satisfied through the provision of specific environmental or spatial conditions. The specific environmental condition that can fulfill this need is the availability of a fixed, circumscribed area, which the individual or group has the capacity to control. A territory, because it is a fixed area, can be said to exist even when the individual identified with it is not physically present. Territory thus differs from personal space, which is something an individual carries around with him. (Personal space is sometimes referred to as portable territory.)

Most discussions of the concept of territoriality note that it was first developed to explain the spatial behavior of animals. As a consequence, the application of the concept to human behavior has usually proceeded by crude analogy, and thus people have tended to overlook the fact that concern for territory and the response to its invasion are linked to the symbolic and cultural dimensions of human psychology as well as to the biological. The great merit of the selection by Lyman and Scott is that it makes these connections clear. Territoriality is by definition a spatial phenomenon, but the way its boundaries are defined, the uses to which it is put, the manner in which groups cope with invasions, and the consequences of territorial deprivation for social order are all highly variable. The authors, for example, distinguish four different types of human territories (public territories, home territories, interactional territories, and body territories); three types of territorial encroachment (violation, invasion, and contamination); and three types of reaction to encroachment (turf defense, insulation, and linguistic collusion).

Lyman and Scott's discussion is redolent with implications for housing and urban design. Especially interesting is the distinction they make between public territories, which are accessible to all citizens but in which users are under public scrutiny and must conduct themselves according to official norms, and home territories, which are private areas in which users are relatively free to behave in their own individual fashion. Both types of territory serve a purpose in cities. They mention that the need for a home

Reprinted from Stanford M. Lyman and Marvin B. Scott, "Territoriality: A Neglected Sociological Dimension," in *Social Problems* 15, no. 2 (1967): 236–249. Reprinted by permission of the Society for the Study of Social Problems.

territory can be met through erecting walls and doors, but that invaders can also be excluded by the confusion of odd gestures, strange ethnic dialects, and other manifestations of linguistic collusion. Designers presumably must be sensitive to the possibility that these insulating and defensive mechanisms can operate at the urban scale.

☐

All living organisms observe some sense of territoriality,[1] that is, some sense—whether learned or instinctive to their species—in which control over space is deemed central for survival.[2] Although man's domination over space is potentially unlimited, in contemporary society it appears that men acknowledge increasingly fewer *free* territories for themselves.[3]

Free territory is carved out of space and affords opportunities for idiosyncrasy and identity. Central to the manifestation of these opportunities are boundary creation and enclosure. This is so because activities that run counter to expected norms need seclusion or invisibility to permit unsanctioned performance, and because peculiar identities are sometimes impossible to realize in the absence of an appropriate setting.[4] Thus the opportunities for freedom of action—with respect to normatively discrepant behavior and maintenance of specific identities—are intimately connected with the ability to attach boundaries to space and command access to or exclusion from territories.

In American society where territorial encroachment affects nearly all members of society, certain segments of the population are particularly deprived, namely, Negroes, women, youth, and inmates of various kinds. With these categories in mind, this selection re-introduces a neglected dimension of social analysis important to understanding deprived groups.

Our strategy is twofold: first, to bring together under a new set of organizing concepts the notions of types of territory, types of territorial encroachment, and types of responses to encroachment; and second, to specify the reactions of spatially deprived groups.

The Types of Territories

We can distinguish four kinds of territories, namely, *public territories, home territories, interactional territories* and *body territories.*

PUBLIC TERRITORIES

Public territories are those areas where the individual has freedom of access, but not necessarily of action, by virtue of his claim to citizenship.[5] These territories are officially open to all, but certain images and expectations of appropriate behavior and of the categories of individuals who are normally perceived as using these territories modify freedom. First, it is commonly expected that illegal activities and impermissible behavior will not occur in public places. Since public territories are vulnerable to violation in both respects, however, policemen are charged with the task of removing lawbreakers from the scene of their activities and restricting behavior in public places.[6]

Second, certain categories of persons are accorded only limited access to and restricted activity in public places. It is expected, for instance, that children will not be playing in public playgrounds after midnight; that lower-class citizens will not live—although they might work—in areas of middle-class residence; and that Negroes will not be found leisurely strolling on the sidewalks of white neighborhoods, though they might be found laying the sewer pipe under the streets.

Since the rights of such discrepant groups to use these territories as citizens sometimes contradicts the privileges accorded them as persons, such territories are not infrequently the testing grounds of challenges to authority. The wave of sit-ins, wade-ins, and demonstrations in racially segregated restaurants, public beaches, and schools constitutes an outstanding recent example. Informal restrictions on access to public territories often violate unenforced or as yet untested rights of citizens. Since the informal delineation of some of these territories implies the absence of certain persons, their presence stands out. Policemen frequently become allies of locals in restricting citizenship rights when they remove unseemly persons from territories which they do not regularly habituate, or when they restrict certain categories of persons to specific areas.[7]

Public territories are thus ambiguous with respect to accorded freedoms. First, the official rights of access may be regularly violated by local custom. Second, status discrepancy may modify activity and entrance rights. For example, the ambiguity in the distinction between minors and adults is a source of confusion and concern in the regulation of temporal and access rights to those whose status is unclear. Finally, activities once forbidden in public may be declared permissible, thus enlarging the freedom of the territory; or activities once licit may be proscribed, thus restricting it. Hence display of female breasts is now permitted in San Francisco nightclubs, but not on the streets or before children. Nude swimming enjoys police protection at certain designated beaches, but watching nude swimmers at these same beaches is forbidden to those who are attired.

HOME TERRITORIES

Home territories are areas where the regular participants have a relative freedom of behavior and a sense of intimacy and control over the area. Examples include makeshift club houses of children, hobo jungles, and homosexual bars. Home and public territories may be easily confused. In fact "the areas of public places and the areas of home territories are not always clearly differentiated in the social world and what may be defined and used as a public place by some may be defined and used as a home territory by others." [8] Thus, a home territory that also may be used as a public one is defined by its regular use by specific persons or categories of persons and by the particular "territorial stakes" or "identity pegs" that are found in such places. The style of dress and language among the patrons at a bar may immediately communicate to a homosexual that he has arrived in home territory, while a heterosexual passerby who pauses for a drink may be astonished or outraged when he is accosted for sexual favors by the stranger seated next to him. Large-scale clandestine brotherhoods indoctrinate their members in secret codes of dress and demeanor so that regardless of their later travels they can unobtrusively communicate their fraternal identity and ask for assistance from one another in otherwise public places. Home territories sometimes enjoy a proactive status, beyond the presence of their inhabitants, in the form of reserved chairs, drinking mugs, signs or memorabilia that serve to indicate special and reserved distinctions.

Home territories may be established by "sponsorship" or "colonization." An example of the former is found in the merchant emigrants from China who established caravansaries in certain quarters of Occidental cities which served as public trading establishments but also as living quarters, employment agencies, meeting places, and courts for their *Landsmänner*.[9] Colonization occurs when a person or group lays claim to a formally free territory by virtue of discovery, regular usage, or peculiar relationship. Thus certain restaurants become home territories to those who are impressed with their first meal there; to those who eat there on specific occasions, such as luncheons, birthdays, or after sporting events; and to those who are intimate with the waitress.

Loss of home status may be occasioned by the death or resignation of a sponsor, by violation of the previously established usages, by rejection, or by conquest. Erstwhile "regulars" at a bar may discover they are no longer warmly greeted nor eligible for a free drink when the proprietor dies or when their patronage becomes irregular. Homosexuals may desert a "queer bar" when it becomes a place which heterosexuals frequent to observe deviant behavior.

It is precisely because of their officially open condition that public areas are vulnerable to conversion into home territories. The rules of openness are sufficiently broad and ambiguous so that restrictions on time, place, and manner are difficult to promulgate and nearly impossible to enforce. Armed with a piece of chalk children can change the public sidewalk into a gameboard blocking pedestrian traffic. Despite building codes and parental admonitions youngsters convert abandoned buildings or newly begun sites into forts, clubs, and hideaways.[10]

But children are not the only colonizers on the public lands. Beggars and hawkers will stake out a "territory" on the sidewalks or among the blocks and occupy it sometimes to the exclusion of all others similarly employed. The idle and unemployed will loiter on certain streetcorners, monopolizing the space, and frightening off certain respectable types with their loud, boisterous, or obscene language, cruel jests, and suggestive leers. Members of racial and ethnic groups colonize a portion of the city and adorn it with their peculiar institutions, language, and rules of conduct.[11] Ethnic enclaves, like certain notorious homosexual bars and prisons on open-house day, are often "on display" to non-ethnics who thus grant legitimacy to the colony's claim for territorial identity.

Among the most interesting examples of colonizing on the public lands are those attempts by youths to stake out streets as home territories open only to members of their own clique and defended against invasion by rival groups. Subject always to official harassment by police and interference by other adults who claim the streets as public territories, youths resolve the dilemma by redefining adults as non-persons whose seemingly violative presence on the youth's "turf" does not challenge the latter's proprietorship. Streets are most vulnerable to colonizing in this manner and indeed, as the early studies of the Chicago sociologists illustrated so well, streets and knots of juxtaposed streets become unofficial home areas to all those groups who require relatively secluded yet open space in which to pursue their interests or maintain their identities.[12]

INTERACTIONAL TERRITORIES

Interactional territories refer to any area where a social gathering may occur. Surrounding any interaction is an invisible boundary, a kind of social membrane.[13] A party is an interactional territory, as are the several knots of people who form clusters at parties. Every interactional territory implicitly makes a claim of boundary maintenance for the duration of the interaction. Thus access and egress are governed by rules understood, though not officially promulgated, by the members.

Interactional territories are characteristically mobile and fragile. Participants in a conversation may remain in one place, stroll along, or move periodically or erratically. They may interrupt only to resume it at a later time without permanently breaking the boundary or disintegrating the group. Even where "settings" are required for the interaction, mobility need not be dysfunctional if the items appropriate to the setting are movable. Thus chemists may not be able to complete a discussion without the assistance of a laboratory, but chess players may assemble or disassemble the game quite readily and in the most cramped quarters. Similarly, so long as Negroes were chattel slaves slaveholders might move them anywhere their services or appearance were needed.

The fragility of interactional territories is constantly being tested by parvenus and newcomers. The latter, even when they possess credentials entitling them to entrance into the interactional circle, break down ongoing interaction and threaten it by requiring all to start over again, end it instead, and begin a new subject of common interest, or disintegrate.[14] Parvenus are a greater threat since their presence breaks the boundaries of the interaction and challenges the exclusiveness of the group. They may be repulsed, or accepted fully, though the latter is less likely than the granting of a "temporary visa," i.e., rights to interact for the instant occasion with no promise of equal rights in the future.

BODY TERRITORIES

Finally, there are body territories, which include the space encompassed by the human body and the anatomical space of the body. The latter is, at least theoretically, the most private and inviolate of territories belonging to an individual. The rights to view and touch the body are of a sacred nature, subject to great restriction. For instance, a person's rights to his own body space are restricted where norms govern masturbation, or the appearance and decoration of skin. Moreover, rights of others to touch one's body are everywhere regulated, though perhaps modern societies impose greater restrictions than others.[15]

Body territory is also convertible into home territory. The most common method is marriage in a monogamous society in which sexual access to the female is deemed the exclusive right of the husband so long as he exercises propriety with respect to his status. Ownership, however, is not necessarily or always coterminous with possession, so that sexual rivalry might continue illegitimately after a marital choice has been made and erupt in trespass on the husband's sexual property.[16] Under situations where women are scarce, such as nineteenth-century overseas Chinese communities in the United States, sexual property was institutionalized through organized prostitution, and the few Chinese wives among the homeless men were carefully secluded.[17]

Body space is, however, subject to creative innovation, idiosyncrasy, and destruction. First, the body may be marked or marred by scars, cuts, burns, and tattoos. In addition, certain of its parts may be inhibited or removed without its complete loss of function. These markings have a meaning beyond the purely anatomical. They are among the indicators of status or stigma. They can be signs of bravado as was the dueling scar among German students, or of criminality as is a similar scar on Italians and Negroes in America. Loss of an eye may prevent one's entrance into dental school, but at least one clothing manufacturer regards one-eyed men as status symbols for starched shirts. Tattoos may memorialize one's mother or sweetheart as well as indicate one's seafaring occupation.

The human organism exercises extraterritorial rights over both internal and external space. In the latter instance the space immediately surrounding a person is also inviolate.[18] Thus conversations among friends are ecologically distinguishable from those between acquaintances or strangers. A person who persists in violating the extraterritorial space of another of the same sex may be accused of tactlessness and suspected of homosexuality, while uninvited intersex invasion may indicate unwarranted familiarity.[19] Moreover, eye contact and visual persistence can be a measure of external space. Thus two strangers may look one another over at the proper distance, but as they near one another, propriety requires that they treat one another as non-persons unless a direct contact is going to be made.[20]

Control over "inner space" is the quintessence of individuality and freedom. Violations of "inner space" are carried out by domination, ranging in intensity from perception of more than is voluntarily revealed to persuasion and ultimately hypnosis.[21] Demonstration of idiosyncrasy with respect to "inner space" is exemplified by the modifications possible in the presentation of self through the uses of the several stimulants and depressants.

Territorial Encroachment

We can distinguish three forms of territorial encroachment: violation, invasion, and contamination.

Violation of a territory is unwarranted use of it. Violators are those who have repulsed or circumvented those who would deny them access. Violators are also, by virtue of their acts, claimants in some sense to the territory they have violated. Their claim, however, may vary in scope, intensity, and objective. Children may violate the graves of the dead by digging "for treasure" in the cemetery, but unlike ghouls, they are not seeking to remove the bodies for illicit purposes. Some territories may be violated, however, merely by unwarranted entrance into them. Among these are all those territories commonly restricted to categorical groups such as toilets, harems, nunneries, and public baths —areas commonly restricted according to sex. Other territories may not be necessarily violated by presence but only by innovative or prohibited use. Thus some parents regard family-wide nudity as permissible, but hold that sexual interest or intercourse among any but the married pair is forbidden. Interactional territories are violated when one or more of the legitimate interactants behaves out of character.[22]

Invasion of a territory occurs when those not entitled to entrance or use nevertheless cross the boundaries and interrupt, halt, take over, or change the social meaning of the territory. Such invasions, then, may be temporary or enduring.

Contamination of a territory requires that it be rendered impure with respect to its definition and usage. Cholera may require that a portion of the city be quarantined. In a racial caste society the sidewalks may be contaminated by low caste persons walking upon them. Home territories may be contaminated by pollution or destruction of the "home" symbols. Orthodox Jews may destroy their dinnerware when an unwary maid has accidentally mixed the milk and meat dishes. Heterosexuals who regularly congregate at a bar sometimes discontinue their patronage when known homosexuals begin frequenting the bar. (This example illustrates a continuum in the process of territorial encroachment from invasion to contamination.) Interactional territories may be contaminated by sudden odors, especially if they emanate from one of the interactants, or by indiscreet language, e.g., obscenity, among those for whom identification with such language constitutes a loss of face or a reduction in status.[23]

Contamination of bodily territories occurs whenever the immediate space of or around the body is polluted. The removal by bathing of

material involuntarily attached to the skin constitutes a ritualized puri-
fication rite of considerable importance in industrial societies.[24] However, body space may be contaminated in many ways, by smell, look,
touch, and by proximity to contaminated persons or things. The sensitivity with respect to touch illustrates the complex nature of this contamination and also its peculiarly social character. The rules regarding
touch are highly developed in American society and are clear indicators
of social distance between individuals and groups.[25] Typically, older
people can touch younger ones, but suspicions of sexual immorality
modify such contacts. Women who are friends or relatives may greet
one another with a light kiss (commonly called a "peck") on the cheek,
but not on the lips. Men who are long absent may be greeted by male
friends and relatives with a hearty embrace and a touching of the
cheeks, but the embrace must not be overlong or tender. Indeed,
"rough-housing," mock-fighting, and pseudo-hostility are commonly
employed in masculine affective relationships. Touch which would
otherwise be contaminating is exempt from such designation when it
takes place in situations of intense social action, e.g., on a dance floor,
or in situations when the actors are not privileged to interact, e.g.,
crowded buses. At other times bodies contaminated by impermissible
contacts are restored to their pure state by apologies.

Body space may be contaminated by a kind of negative charismatic
contact whereby objects, though neutral in themselves, carry a contaminating effect when transferred directly to the body. Thus a comb
or toothbrush may not be lent or borrowed in certain circles since
to use someone else's tools of personal hygiene is to contaminate
oneself. Typically, when clothing, especially clothing that will directly
touch the skin, is lent, it is proper for the lender to assure the bor-
rower that the apparel is clean, and that it has not been worn by anyone since its last cleaning.[26] A more striking example involves the rule
of some shops forbidding Negroes from trying on clothes—their skin
being regarded as a source of pollution. Similarly, drinking from the
same glass as another is discouraged as a matter of hygiene among
the middle class and as a source of pollution if it occurs among persons
of different races or castes.

Reaction to Encroachment

We have already suggested that something of a reciprocal relation
exists between the territorial types. For example, a public swimming
pool—while officially open to all persons—might be conceived by cer-

tain regular users as an exclusive area. Strangers seeking access by virtue of their diffuse civic rights might be challenged by those whose sense of peculiar propriety is thus violated. Such a confrontation (sometimes called "when push meets shove") could result in retreat on the part of the party seeking admittance, flight on the part of those favoring denial, or strategy and tactics on the part of the contending parties to expand the area of legitimate access on the one hand, and withhold entirely or restrict the meaning of entry on the other.

Of course, the occupants of a territory may extend its use to others whose presence is not regarded as a threat. The most common situation is that in which common usage will not destroy or alter the value of the territory.[27] When public territories have been colonized by users who do not fully monopolize the space, who embroider it by their presence, or whose occupancy still allows for other public and colonizing usages, the colonists will not be seriously opposed. Delinquent gangs who often define the streets of a neighborhood as a home territory do not usually regard the presence of local adults and children as an encroachment on their own occupancy. Unwarranted intrusion on interactional territories may be countenanced if the unwelcome guest indicates his willingness to be present on this occasion alone with no future rights of reentry, or to listen only and not to interrupt the proceedings. Bodies usually invulnerable to feel and probe by strangers may be violated if circumstances render the act physically safe, socially irrelevant, or emotionally neutral. Thus female nurses may massage their male patients with mutual impunity, and striptease dancers may perform unclothed upon a raised stage out of reach of the audience.[28] However, all such contacts will tend to be defined as territorial encroachment when the claimants threaten obliteration, monopoly, or fundamental alteration of a territory. Under these conditions, the holders of territory are likely to react to unwelcome claimants in terms of *turf defense, insulation,* or *linguistic collusion.*

TURF DEFENSE

Turf defense is a response necessitated when the intruder cannot be tolerated. The animal world provides a multitude of examples which are instructive with respect to the human situation.[29] Here we may be content however, to confine ourselves to the human scene. When Chinese merchants sought "colonizing" rights among the urban merchants of San Francisco, they were welcomed and honored. A few years later, however, the appearance of Chinese miners in the white

Americans' cherished gold fields called forth violent altercations and forced removals.[30] In contemporary American cities delinquent gangs arm themselves with rocks, knives, tire irons, and zip guns to repel invaders from other streets.[31] Among the "primitive" Kagoro the choice of weapons is escalated in accordance with the social distance of the combatants; poison spears and stratagems are employed exclusively against hostile strangers and invaders.[32]

Turf defense is an ultimate response, however. Other more subtle repulsions or restrictions are available to proprietors wishing to maintain territorial control.

INSULATION

Insulation is the placement of some sort of barrier between the occupants of a territory and potential invaders. The narrow streets, steep staircases, and regularized use of Cantonese dialects in Chinatowns serve notice on tourists that they may look over the external trappings of Chinese life in the Occidental city but not easily penetrate its inner workings. Distinct uniforms distinguishing status, rights, and prerogatives serve to protect military officers from the importunities of enlisted men, professors from students, and doctors from patients.[33] Bodily insulation characteristically takes the form of civil inattention and may be occasioned by a subordinate's inability to repel invasion directly. Another common form of insulation involves use of body and facial idiom to indicate impenetrability. It may be effected by the use of sunglasses,[34] or attained accidentally, by dint of culturally distinct perceptions of facial gestures, as, for example, often happens to orientals in Western settings.[35] It can also be attained by conscious efforts in the management and control of the mouth, nostrils, and especially the eyes.[36]

LINGUISTIC COLLUSION

Linguistic collusion involves a complex set of processes by which the territorial integrity of the group is reaffirmed and the intruder is labeled as an outsider. For example, the defending interactants may engage one another in conversation and gestures designed to so confuse the invader that he responds in a manner automatically labeling him eligible for either exclusion from the group or shameful status diminution. In one typical strategy the defending interactants will speak to one another in a language unfamiliar to the invader. Ethnic enclaves provide numerous examples. Jewish and Chinese storekeepers will speak Yiddish and Cantonese respectively to their clerks when discussing prices, bargaining rights, and product quality in the presence of alien customers. Negroes may engage one another in a game of "the dozens" in the presence of intruding whites, causing the latter considerable consternation and mystification.[37] And teenagers develop a peer group argot (frequently borrowed from Negro and jazz musician usages) which sets them apart from both children and adults, and which, incidentally, is most frequently cited as proof for the claim that a distinctive youth culture does exist in the United States.

In another recognizable strategy, the participants continue to engage in the same behavior but in a more exaggerated and "staged" manner. Mood and tone of the voice are sometimes regulated to achieve this effect. Thus persons engaged in conversation may intensify their tone and include more intra-group gestures when an outsider enters the area. Professors may escalate the use of jargon and "academese" in conversations in the presence of uninvited students or other "inferiors." Homosexuals engaged in flirtations in a "gay" bar may exaggerate their femininity when heterosexuals enter the establishment. Such staged displays call attention to the exclusive culture of the interactants and suggest to the outsider that he is bereft of the cards of identity necessary to participate.

Reaction to the Absence of Free Space

There are some segments of society that are systematically denied free territories. One outstanding example is that of lower-class urban Negro youth. Their homes are small, cramped, and cluttered and also serve as specialized areas of action for adults; their meeting places are constantly under surveillance by the agents of law enforcement and social workers; and, when in clusters on the street, they are often stopped for questioning and booked "on suspicion" by the seemingly ever-present police.[38]

What is the condition of Negro youth in particular appears to be an exaggerated instance of the trend with respect to denial of freedom among youth in general. Thus it has been suggested that youth are adrift somewhere between humanism and fatalism, i.e., between situations in which they feel they have control over their destinies and those in which such control is in the hands of forces outside youth's individual direction and influence.[39] In such a situation one response is to seek to maximize the area of freedom, the situations in which one can exercise liberty and license, the times one can be cause rather than effect. Among lower-class youth the carving of home territories out of the space provided as public ones is common and has already been noted. Note also, however, the frequency with which youth-created home territories are subject to invasion, violation, and contamination and the relative vulnerability of youth home territories to such encroachments.

Exercising freedom over body territory provides a more fruitful approach to those for whom public territories are denied and home territories difficult or impossible to maintain. The body and its attendant inner and external space have an aura of ownership and control about them that is impressed upon the incumbent. The hypothesis we wish to suggest here is that as other forms of free territory are perceived to be foreclosed by certain segments of the society, these segments, or at least those elements of the segments not constrained by other compelling forces, will utilize more frequently and intensively the area of body space as a free territory. Three forms of such utilization are prominent: *manipulation, adornment,* and *penetration.*

Manipulation rests upon the fact that the body is adjustable in a greater number of ways than are positively sanctioned and that by modifying the appearance of the self one can establish identity, and flaunt convention with both ease and relative impunity. Thus children, separated from one another for being naughty and enjoined from conversation, may sit and "make faces" at one another, conforming to the letter of their punishment but violating its principle. Teenagers, denied approval for the very sexual activity for which they are biologically prepared, and also enclosed more and more from private usage of public territories for such purposes, have developed dance forms which involve little or no body contact but are nevertheless suggestive of the most intimate and forbidden forms of erotic interaction. Further, male youth—enjoined from verbal scatological forms by customs and by rules of propriety—have developed a gesture language by which they can communicate the desired obscenity without uttering it.

Adornment of the body is another response.[40] By covering, uncovering, marking, and disfiguring the body individuals can at least partly overcome whatever loss of freedom they suffer from other encroachments. Both the French "bohemians" of the nineteenth century and the disaffected American Negro youths of the twentieth have exhibited themselves as "dandies," [41] while the ascetic Doukhobors of British Columbia disrobe entirely and in public when challenged by authority.[42] Body space may also be attended by filling in the apertures in nose, mouth and ears by rings, bones, and other emblematic artifacts; by marking upon the skin with inks and tattoos; and by disfigurements, scars, and severance of non-vital members. An alternative mode of adornment, that appears to be directed definitely against elements of the core culture, is the refusal to use instruments of personal hygiene. We have already noted how these instruments acquire a peculiar aspect of the personal charisma of the user so that people do not customarily borrow the comb, toothbrush, and razor of another unless the contamination that occurs thereby is neutralized. Here, however, adornment occurs by simply *not* washing, combing, shaving, cutting the hair, etc. Like public nudity this form of assertiveness and reaction to oppression has the advantage of inhibiting a like response among those who are offended by the appearance created thereby, but, unlike stripping in public, has the added advantage of being legal.

Penetration refers to the exploitation and modification of inner space in the search for free territory. One might hypothesize that the greater the sense of unfreedom, the greater the exercise of body liberty so that penetration is an escalated aspect of manipulation and adornment. There is, as it were, a series of increasing gradations of body space. The ultimate effort is to gain freedom by changing one's internal environment. The simplest form of this is cultivating a vicarious sense of being away, of transporting the self out of its existential environment by musing, daydreaming, or relapsing into a reverie.[43] However, voluntary reorganization of the inner environment can be assisted by alcohol and drugs. Contemporary college youth sometimes partake of hallucinogenic and psychedelic drugs in order to make an inner migration (or "take a trip" as the popular idiom has it).

Conclusion

The concept of territoriality offers a fruitful approach for the analysis of freedom and situated action. Although the early school of ecology in American sociology provided a possible avenue for this kind of exploration, its practitioners appear to have eschewed the interactionist and phenomenological aspects of the subject in favor of the economic and the biotic. Nevertheless, much of their work needs to be examined afresh for the clues it provides for understanding the nature and function of space and the organization of territories. Similarly the work done by the students of non-human animal association provides clues to concept formation and suggestions for research. Here we may mention several potentially fruitful areas. The first involves cross-cultural studies of territoriality. Such studies would attempt to describe in greater specificity the constituent features of types of territoriality, the ways in which they vary, and their interrelationships. Using a cross-cultural perspective would also serve to specify generic forms of reactions to territorial encroachment and to establish how certain contexts predispose one type of response rather than another. A second area of research would focus on a variety of deviant behaviors (e.g., crime, juvenile delinquency, drug addiction) with the purpose of understanding the part the territorial variable plays in the etiology of such behaviors. Finally, we may suggest that micro-sociological studies of territoriality—which are perhaps more amenable to rigorous research design—may be extrapolated to an analysis of macro-sociological inquiries, especially in the realm of international affairs.

NOTES

AUTHOR'S NOTE: We are grateful to Donald Ball and Edwin Lemert for their critical reading of the manuscript.

1. The concept of territoriality was introduced into sociological analysis in the twenties under the label of "the ecological school." For an early statement see Robert E. Park, Ernest W. Burgess, and R. D. McKenzie, *The City*, Chicago: University of Chicago Press, 1925. For a summary and bibliography of the school see Milla Aissa Alihan, *Social Ecology*, New York: Columbia University Press, 1938. An updated version of this school is found in James A. Quinn, *Human Ecology*, New York: Prentice-Hall, 1950 and Amos H. Hawley, *Human Ecology, A Theory of Community Structures*, New York: The Ronald Press, 1950.

Originating in animal studies, "territoriality" still looms large as an organizing concept in ethology. For a summary statement see C. R. Carpenter, "Territoriality: A Review of Concepts and Problems," in A. Roe and G. Simpson, eds., *Behavior and Evolution*, New Haven, Conn.: Yale University Press, 1958, pp. 224–250.

For a challenging argument that sociological investigation can fruitfully employ the techniques of comparative ethology—especially to such subjects as territoriality —see Lionel Tiger and Robin Fox, "The Zoological Perspective in Social Science," *Man*, I., 1, (March, 1966), esp. p. 80.

Only very recently have sociologists revived ecological thinking to include a truly *interactional* dimension. The outstanding contributor is, of course, Edward T. Hall. See his *The Silent Language*, Garden City, New York: Doubleday and Co., 1959, and *The Hidden Dimension*, Garden City, New York: Doubleday and Co., 1966. For a masterful application of the concept of territoriality in interactional terms see Erving Goffman, *Asylums*, Garden City, New York: Doubleday and Co., Anchor Books, 1961, pp. 227–248. In a slightly different vein see the interesting efforts of Robert Sommer, "Studies in Personal Space," *Sociometry*, 22 (September, 1959), pp. 247–260, and the writings of Roger Barker, especially his "Roles, Ecological Niches, and the Psychology of the Absent Organism," paper presented to the conference on the Propositional Structure of Role Theory, University of Missouri, 1962.

2. For the argument that human territoriality is a natural rather than a cultural phenomenon see Robert Ardrey, *The Territorial Imperative*, New York: Atheneum, 1966, pp. 3–41.

3. The idea of "free territory" is derived from Goffman, *loc. cit.*

4. See Erving Goffman, *The Presentation of Self in Everyday Life*, Garden City, New York: Doubleday and Co., Anchor Books, 1959, p. 22.

5. The term "citizenship" is used in a sense similar to that employed by T. H.

Marshall in *Class, Citizenship and Social Development*, Garden City, New York: Doubleday and Co., Anchor Books, 1965, esp. pp. 71–134.

6. See Harvey Sacks, "Methods in Use for the Production of a Social Order: A Method for Warrantably Informing Moral Character." Center for the Study of Law and Society, University of California, Berkeley, 1962; and Aaron Cicourel, *The Social Organization of Juvenile Justice,* unpublished manuscript.

7. See Jerome Skolnick, *Justice Without Trial,* New York: John Wiley, 1966, pp. 96–111 *et passim;* and Sacks, *op. cit.*

8. Sherri Cavan, "Interaction in Home Territories," *Berkeley Journal of Sociology,* 5 (1963) p. 18.

9. See Stanford M. Lyman, *The Structure of Chinese Society in Nineteenth Century America,* unpublished, Ph.D. dissertation, Berkeley: University of California, 1961.

10. Indeed, children are among the most regular and innovative creators of home territories from the space and material available to the public in general. Speaking of their peculiar tendency to violate the rules governing trespass, William Prosser has aptly observed, "Children, as is well known to anyone who has been a child, are by nature unreliable and irresponsible people, who are quite likely to do almost anything. In particular, they have a deplorable tendency to stray upon land which does not belong to them, and to meddle with what they find there." "Trespassing Children," *California Law Review* (August, 1959), p. 427.

11. Ethnic groups in the process of assimilation sometimes discover to their astonishment that the isolated slum wherein they have traditionally and unwillingly dwelt is in fact a home territory possessed of cherished values and irreplaceable sentiments. A militant Negro thus writes: "For as my son, Chuck, wrote me after exposure to the Negro community of Washington: 'I suddenly realized that the Negro ghetto is not a ghetto. It is home.'" John Oliver Killens, *Black Man's Burden,* New York: Trident Press, 1965, p. 94.

12. Harvey W. Zorbaugh, *The Gold Coast and the Slums,* Chicago: University of Chicago Press, 1929. See also Jane Jacobs, *The Death and Life of Great American Cities,* New York: Vintage Books, 1961, pp. 29–142.

13. See Erving Goffman, *Behavior in Public Places,* New York: The Free Press, 1963, pp. 151–165 *et passim.*

14. An excellent illustration of the several facets of this process and attendant issues in social gatherings is found in David Riesman, *et al.,* "The Vanishing Host," *Human Organization,* (Spring, 1960), pp. 17–27.

15. Talcott Parsons notes that "the very fact that affectionate bodily contact is almost completely taboo among men in American society is probably indicative of [the limited nature of intra-sex friendship] since it strongly limits affective attachment." *The Social System,* Glencoe, Ill.: The Free Press, 1951, p. 189. For an empirical study and analysis of touching relations see Erving Goffman, "The Nature of Deference and Demeanor," *American Anthropologist,* 58 (June, 1956), pp. 473–502.

16. See Kingsley Davis, *Human Society,* New York: Macmillan, 1948, pp. 19–193.

17. Lyman, *op. cit.,* pp. 97–111.

18. The perceptions of Simmel on this subject surpass all others and we are indebted to his work. Thus Simmel has noted:

In regard to the "significant" [i.e., "great"] man, there is an inner compulsion which tells one to keep at a distance and which does not disappear even in intimate relations with him. The only type for whom such distance does not exist is the individual who has no organ for perceiving distance. . . . The individual who fails to keep his distance from a great person does not esteem him highly, much less too highly (as might superficially appear to be the case); but, on the contrary, his importune behavior reveals lack of proper respect. . . . The same sort of circle which surrounds a man—although it is value-accentuated in a very different sense —is filled out by his affairs and by his characteristics. To penetrate this circle by taking notice, constitutes a violation of personality. Just as material property is, so to speak, an extension of the ego, there is also an intellectual private property, whose violation effects a lesion of the ego in its very center.

[Georg Simmel, "Secrecy and Group Communication," reprinted in T. Parsons, *et al., Theories of Society,* New York: The Free Press, 1961, p. 320.] For an updated statement of Simmel's point see Goffman, *Behavior in Public Places, op. cit.*

19. An interesting dilemma in this respect arises for the deaf and myopic. In attempting to appear as "normals" they may overstep another's territorial space and thus call attention to the very stigma they wish to conceal. On the problems of those who are stigmatized see Goffman, *Stigma,* Englewood Cliffs, New Jersey: Prentice-Hall, 1963.

20. Goffman refers to this as "civil inattention." See *Behavior in Public Places, op. cit.*

21. Compare the remarks by Simmel, *op. cit.,* p. 321.

In the interest of interaction and social cohesion, the individual must know certain things about the other person. Nor does the other have the right to oppose this knowledge from a moral standpoint, by demanding the discretion of the first: he cannot claim the entirely undisturbed possession of his own being and consciousness, since this discretion might harm the interests of his society. . . . But even in subtler and less unambiguous forms, in fragmentary beginnings and unexpressed notions, all of human intercourse rests on the fact that everybody knows somewhat more about the other than the other voluntarily reveals to him; and those things he knows are frequently matters whose knowledge the other person (were he aware of it) would find undesirable.

See also Goffman, *The Presentation of Self in Everyday Life, op. cit.,* pp. 1–16.

22. The structural properties and parameters of interactional territories in unserious gatherings have been admirably presented by Georg Simmel. See his "The Sociology of Sociability," *American Journal of Sociology,* (November, 1949), pp. 254–261. Reprinted in Parsons, *et al., Theories of Society, op. cit.,* pp. 157–163.

23. Here perhaps it is worth noting that language has a "tactile" dimension, in the sense that to be "touched" audially by certain terms is to be elevated or reduced in status. For Southern Negroes to be publicly addressed as "Mr.," "Miss," and "Mrs.," and by last names is considered so relevant for removal of caste barriers that legal action to require these usages has been undertaken. We may also note that genteel persons are polluted by audial contact with slang, obscenity, and, on occasion, idiomatic expression.

24. See Horace Miner, "Body Ritual Among the Nacirema," *American Anthropologist,* 55, 3 (1956).

25. Note such phrases as "I wouldn't touch him with a ten-foot pole," "She's under my skin," "He's a pain in the neck," and "Look, but don't touch." For the rules regarding touch see Erving Goffman, "The Nature of Deference and Demeanor," *op. cit.*

26. Robin Williams has shown that one test of social distance among the races in America is their unwillingness to try on clothing at an apparel shop when they have witnessed that clothing tried on and rejected by members of another—and supposedly inferior—race. Robin Williams, *Strangers Next Door,* Englewood Cliffs, New Jersey: Prentice-Hall, 1964, pp. 125–130.

27. Our usage is similar to that employed in describing the relationships in plant-communities.

The majority of individuals of a plant-community are linked by bonds other than those mentioned—bonds that are best described as commensal. The term commensalism is due to Van Beneden, who wrote "Le commensal est simplement un compagnon de table," but we employ it in a somewhat different sense to denote the relationship subsisting between species which share with one another the supply of food-material contained in soil and air, and thus feed at the same table.

[Robert E. Park and Ernest W. Burgess, *Introduction to the Science of Sociology,* Chicago: University of Chicago Press, 1921, p. 175. (Adapted from Eugenius Warming, *Oecology of Plants,* London: Oxford University Press, 1909, pp. 12–13, 91–95.)]

28. Ann Terry D'Andre, "An Occupational Study of the Strip-Dancer Career," paper delivered at the annual meetings of the Pacific Sociological Association, Salt Lake City, Utah, 1965.

29. See Ardrey, *op. cit.*, p. 210, who writes: "Biology as a whole asks but one question of a territory: Is it defended? Defense defines it. Variability becomes the final description." See also Konrad Lorenz, *On Aggression*, New York: Harcourt, Brace and World, 1966, pp. 33–38 *et passim*.

30. See Mary Coolidge, *Chinese Immigration*, New York: Henry Holt, 1909, pp. 15–26, 255–256.

31. See Lewis Yablonsky, *The Violent Gang*, New York: Macmillan, 1962, pp. 29–100 for a good ethnography of urban gangs. For an analytical treatment see Frederic M. Thrasher, *The Gang*, Chicago: University of Chicago Press, 1927, pp. 97–100, 116–129.

32. See M. G. Smith, "Kagoro Political Development," *Human Organization*, (Fall, 1960), pp. 137–149.

33. It is now a commonplace of sociological irony that persons thus insulated are vulnerable once the insulating material is removed or ubiquitously available. Thus non-coms will insult officers in clubs when both are out of uniform, psychiatrists will be mistaken for patients at dances held in the recreation room of an insane asylum, and students will adopt an inappropriate familiarity with professors not wearing a coat and tie.

34. See Goffman, *Behavior in Public Places, op. cit.*, p. 85 for a succinct account of the elements of this process as a form of civil inattention.

35. Kathleen Tamagawa, *Holy Prayers in a Horse's Ear*, New York: Long, Smith, Inc., 1932, pp. 144–151 *et passim*. André M. Tao-Kim-Hai, "Orientals are Stoic," in F. C. Macgregor, *Social Science in Nursing*, New York: Russell Sage, 1960, pp. 313–326.

36. See Georg Simmel, "The Aesthetic Significance of the Face," in Kurt H. Wolff, ed., *Georg Simmel 1858–1918*, Columbus, Ohio: Ohio State University Press, 1959, pp. 280–281.

37. The usual situation is quite the reverse, however. The "dozens" and other verbal contest forms are most frequently used by Negroes within the ethnic enclave out of earshot and view of whites. See Roger D. Abrahams, *Deep Down in the Jungle*, Hatboro, Penn.: Folklore Associates, esp. pp. 41–64.

38. See Carl Werthman, *Delinquency and Authority*, M.A. Thesis, Berkeley: University of California, 1964.

39. David Matza, *Delinquency and Drift*, New York: John Wiley, 1964.

40. Many suggestive essays on this subject can be found in *Dress, Adornment, and the Social Order*, M. E. Roach and J. B. Eicher, eds., New York: John Wiley, 1965.

41. See Cesar Grana, *Bohemian vs. Bourgeois*, New York: Basic Books, 1964, and Harold Finestone, "Cats, Kicks, and Color," *Social Problems*, 5, 1 (1957), pp. 3–13.

42. See Harry B. Hawthorn, ed., *The Doukhobors of British Columbia*, Vancouver, B.C.: The University of British Columbia and Dent & Sons, 1955.

43. Goffman, *Behavior in Public Places, op. cit.*, pp. 69–75.

6

The Physical Environment: A Problem for a Psychology of Stimulation

JOACHIM F. WOHLWILL

There has been growing interest among architects and other students of environmental phenomena in the question of whether or not complex, ambiguous, noisy, and otherwise stimulating urban environments are beneficial or harmful. In some cases designers and planners have urged that noise levels and population densities be reduced on the grounds that sensory overloads are causing apathy and personality decay; at the same time other members of the same professions have been arguing that urban landscapes are harmfully monotonous and that there is a need for greater diversity in the urban landscape, for an architecture that is more complex and contradictory.

It is difficult to assess the validity of these points of view, in large part because the concepts being used are poorly defined, but even when they are more clearly defined, they deal with phenomena that are not really comparable. Nevertheless, discussion of this issue is at least potentially capable of greater clarification, because it is obviously related to serious research now taking place in psychology to identify and define the need for sensory stimulation and the function of sensory arousal in the development of a healthy personality.

Wohlwill's selection is an attempt to summarize current data and theory on the psychology of stimulation and to discuss the implications of this material for environmental design, in terms of three important but unresolved issues. The first issue is: which dimensions of stimulation are most important for arousing the organism and maintaining its curiosity? Many stimulus characteristics have been investigated, including intensity, novelty, complexity, temporal change, and surprisingness, but no experimental means have yet been found for establishing the relative significance of these dimensions. The second issue is: for a particular group, is there an optimal level of stimulation, and if so, how can it be determined operationally? Most interesting in this regard is the theory that an individual establishes an adaptation level for himself and that deviations from the level in either direction are

Reprinted from Joachim F. Wohlwill, "The Physical Environment: A Problem for a Psychology of Stimulation," *Journal of Social Issues* 22, no. 4 (1966): 29–38. © The Society for the Psychological Study of Social Issues.

evaluated positively within a certain range, whereas outside this range stimuli are experienced as unpleasant. Although it is not specifically discussed in Wohlwill's selection, there has been some experimental effort to explain the popularity of the golden section as a measure of architectural proportion in terms of a similar theoretical proposition. The final issue is the relation between short-run and long-run effects. Even when an individual seems to have adjusted successfully to a particular level of sensory stimulation, there may be a long-run damage that he is not aware of.

It is obvious, as Wohlwill points out, that a good deal more research must be done on the effects of sensory stimulation or deprivation before answers can be found that can be applied to the problems of environmental design. Indeed, a similar conclusion is justifiable with respect to the other two psychological needs discussed in this section—personal space and territoriality.

☐

Introduction

As a psychologist this writer has been struck by a curious paradox. Psychologists never tire to point out the importance of stimulus factors as a determinant of behavior, and of the role of environmental influences in behavior. Yet, as a group they have had relatively little to say on the important problems relating to man's response to his physical environment. We may hope that the valuable contributions now being made to this area by many psychologists portend a change in this state of affairs in the foreseeable future. Meanwhile it may be instructive to examine briefly, at the outset, some of the likely reasons for this seeming lack of attention given to these problems by psychologists; our primary aim, however, is to point more positively to some recent developments in the experimental psychology of motivation which appear to have interesting implications for the study of the impact of the physical environment on behavior and for approaches to environmental design.

That child psychologists, personality psychologists and social psychologists with an environmentalist bias should have neglected the role of the physical environment in behavior is readily understandable. For the most part they have been interested in the interpersonal, social and cultural aspects of the environment, in line with the prevalent drive theory of motivation, built on the concepts of appetitive and aversive reinforcement, which has featured much of their thinking. According to this conception, it is *people* who administer rewards and punishments; the natural and artificial surroundings in which people live thus have little power to influence behavior. Not surprisingly, this has been true of those working outside of a stimulus-response reinforcement model, notably within a field-theoretical framework. Yet even here, where the vocabulary of boundaries, barriers and field forces might seem to favor attention to variables of the physical environment, primary interest has remained in the analysis of interpersonal interaction, social encounters, and the like.

Turning now to the side of experimental psychology, ever since the appearance in 1949 of Hebb's influential *The Organization of Behavior*, the role of sensory stimulation from the environment, not only for the normal development of perceptual and cognitive functions but for motivational processes as well, has become of increasing concern. Yet, starting from the premise that stimulation is good, indeed essential for the development and maintenance of normal behavior, most of the efforts of workers in this area have been devoted to demonstrating the deleterious effects of drastic reductions in level of stimulation, whether as a short-term condition with human adults (cf. the work on "sensory deprivation," [10]) or as a more prolonged condition of the early experience of animals (e.g., 11, 1961). Where attempts have been made to enhance the behavioral effectiveness of animals, e.g., their problem-solving ability, by providing for "enriched" stimulus environments, the research has typically started from a straightforward "the more, the better" assumption. The success of such efforts is not surprising, if one bears in mind the impoverished level of stimulation provided by the typical laboratory environment used as the base of comparison for most of these studies, but its relevance to the living conditions under which modern man operates is doubtful.

A recent extension of this stimulus-enrichment approach to the study of "imprinting" in newly hatched chicks, that is, the development of the following response to the mother, is particularly instructive in revealing the psychologists' conception of an optimal set of stimulus conditions. The authors describe the treatment to which the experimental animals were subjected immediately after hatching as follows:

> *The complex environment . . . consisted of a black-walled enclosure with random stripes and blotches of white paint. Above was a bank of six 200-w light bulbs which flashed on and off at 1-sec. intervals. Two metronomes produced a constant ticking. A radio, tuned to a local AM station, played constantly at high volume. Every 30 min. E stroked each chick's back with a foam rubber brush and with a whisk broom for 15 sec., rang a bicycle bell for 2 min., and gave a gentle puff of air from an air compressor (5, p. 654).*

Let it be recorded that this treatment apparently worked wonders on the imprinting response of these chicks, which developed both earlier and more strongly than did chicks who started life amidst more humdrum environmental conditions. Yet this positive result will not be altogether reassuring to some who may see in the treatment described above only a slight caricature of the frenetic bombardment from stimuli of all kinds encountered in certain urban environments. After all, newborn chicks, even of the Vantress Broiler variety used in this study, are not to be equated to human beings, and the imprinting response hardly constitutes a valid model of human behavior and adjustment. Such doubting Thomases could derive support for their skepticism, moreover, by pointing to the case of the typical "culturally deprived" child from the slums, who is apt to grow up under just such conditions of overstimulation, without great profit to his general intellectual development or emotional well being.

A whole host of questions arise at this point: Is there a particular level of stimulation conducive to optimal development? Does patterned stimulation differ in its effects on development from unpatterned (e.g., noise)? Above all, what is the role of meaning (as invested in language and in object stimuli) in modulating the effects of stimulation on development, and what conditions promote the sifting out of meaningful from meaningless stimuli by the child? Though some research with animals has been carried out relative to the first of these questions, the others have remained virtually untouched, so that in the aggregate the evidence available thus far is probably of limited significance for an understanding of the effects of the stimulus conditions characterizing our typical physical environments on the development of the individual.

Once we turn away from the study of the effects of stimulus experience on development, however, we find a considerable body of recent work that is of direct relevance for us, dealing with the stimulus correlates of the arousal of human attention and with human activity involving the seeking out of stimulation. Psychologists have come to recognize what persons in the amusement and recreation industries —to say nothing of observant parents—have known all along: that a large part of the everyday activity of the human (or of the animal, for that matter) has as its aim not to *reduce* unpleasant tensions, e.g., from the hunger or sex drives, but rather to heighten the level of incoming stimulation, by voluntary exposure to stimulus objects or situations that are novel, incongruous, surprising or complex. Man, it seems, is ever curious, ever eager to explore, and unlike the proverbial cat, appears generally to thrive on such activity.

This is not the place to review the extensive literature in this area, dealing with the motivational and arousal properties of stimulation, or to enter into a discussion of the complex theoretical issues raised by this work (1, 3, 4, 13). Let us rather examine its possible relevance to problems of man's response to his physical environment, and some of the questions raised by an attempt to apply such notions to this problem area. We will confine ourselves to a discussion, necessarily oversimplified, of three main questions.

Dimensions of Stimulation

What are the chief dimensions of stimulation that are of concern to the student of environmental psychology? Those most frequently discussed by psychologists include simple intensity, novelty, complexity, and temporal change or variation; to these we may add surprisingness and incongruity, which have been more specifically emphasized by Berlyne (1). If only in an illustrative sense, all of these can be shown to touch on important aspects of our physical environment. To start with intensity, questions of level of noise and illumination have been of concern to industrial designers, architects and planners for some time, although outside of an industrial context there has been little systematic research on the effects of different levels of auditory or visual intensity on behavior. The importance of *novelty* is well known to observers of that favorite pastime, sightseeing, a facet of behavior which can play an important role in questions of urban design (e.g., the role of San Francisco's cable-cars), as well as in the administration of our natural recreation areas. *Complexity* of stimulation may well be a major factor in differential evaluation of urban, suburban and rural environments, as it is in the response to more particular features of our environment, e.g., samples of modern architecture or highway layouts. *Variation* in the stimulus input enters into diverse problems in environmental design that in one way or another have concerned the need to reduce boredom or monotony, from the subtle variations in design introduced into the construction of housing à la Levittown to the layout of highways, e.g., the avoidance of long, straight stretches.[1]

Surprisingness and *incongruity* are likewise of interest to us, notably in architecture and landscape design. As an example, the pleasing effect of surprise in the exploration of a building complex is nicely brought out by Nairn in his perceptive analysis of the layout of the

87

entrance to the Wellesley College campus (8, p. 33ff). The same author lays a good deal of stress on the role of incongruity, though mainly in a negative sense, i.e., by bringing out the jarring effect of the juxtaposition of different structures lacking in any relationship to one another. Whether some degree of incongruity may nevertheless serve a positive function (in the sense of heightening our attention, if not necessarily our affective evaluation of a scene) must remain an unanswered question at this time. (We may note, in any event, that some degree of incongruity in our environment is inevitable, if only because architectural styles change—cf. the contemporary look of the area around Harvard Square.)

While it may thus be easy to illustrate the relevance of these "collative" variables (as Berlyne calls them) to our response to the physical environment, systematic research in this area will have to come to grips with the problems of operational definition and measurement of these variables, in situations not permitting their control or manipulation by the investigator. Even in the laboratory air-tight definitions allowing for consistent differentiation of the effects of novelty from surprise, on the one hand, or temporal variation on the other are difficult to formulate. Similarly the measurement of novelty (particularly in the long-term sense) and of complexity poses considerable problems. All of these are of course greatly magnified when dealing with ready-made stimuli taken from the actual physical environment, such as landscapes, or urban scenes. In such a situation it may be necessary to compromise to a certain extent with scientific rigor, but this is no reason to shy away from research in such real-life settings. If it is impossible to manipulate variables independently, their relative contributions can generally still be assessed through techniques of statistical control and multivariate analysis.

A more critical problem is that of the measurement of these variables, in the absence of systematic, controlled manipulation. Here we will have to resort to indirect methods based on ratings or other subjective scaling methods. It is worth noting in this connection, that a recent study utilizing judges' ratings to assess complexity of landscapes, still showed consistent relationships between this variable and the relative interest (i.e., fixation times) of these stimuli (7). More recent developments in the area of stimulus scaling techniques, some of which allow for the construction of a metric scale even with purely subjective judgments, lessen the need for independent, objective measures of the physical stimulus (12).

Joachim F. Wohlwill

The Concept of an Optimal Level of Stimulation

A number of psychologists working in this area have advanced an optimal-level hypothesis, postulating an inverted-U shaped relationship between magnitude of stimulation along the dimensions considered above and the arousal value of, interest in, or preference for a given stimulus. Except for variables representing continua of stimulus intensity, systematic evidence on this point is actually fairly meager.[2] Nevertheless the concept deserves our consideration, in view of its patent relevance to man's response to the wide range of stimulation encountered in the physical environment. It ties in directly, furthermore, with Helson's Adaptation-level theory, which represents a much more general framework for the study of the most diverse responses to any stimuli varying along some assumed dimension (6). In a nutshell, this theory maintains that for any specified dimension of stimulus variation the individual establishes an AL (adaptation-level) which determines his judgmental or evaluative response to a given stimulus located on that dimension. In particular, with reference to an evaluative response, the principle is that deviations from the AL in either direction are evaluated positively within a certain range, while beyond these boundaries they are experienced as unpleasant.

Let us try to apply this hypothesis to a person's choice of a vacation spot. To this end, let us conceive of a hybrid dimension of "closeness to civilization," which probably represents a composite of such variables as intensity, complexity, temporal variation and novelty. Take a person living in a small eastern city, so that his AL may be assumed to be somewhere in the middle of our dimension. Where will he go for his vacation? He may either be drawn to the kaleidoscopic attractions of a big metropolis like New York, or, alternatively, to the restful vistas of Vermont or the Cape Cod seashore. However, in accordance with the notion that beyond a certain range marked discrepancies from the AL are no longer experienced as pleasant or desirable, we may hypothesize that, in the first case, our vacationer will tend to avoid or be repelled by places representing the more extreme levels of stimulation to be found in the big city (e.g., Times Square at New Year's Eve; the subway during rush hour).[3] If, on the other hand, he chooses the open country, he is apt to want a motel room with TV, or to stick to the more populated resort areas.

This would seem to represent a plausible research hypothesis,

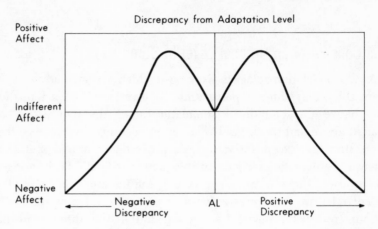

Figure 6–1 Changes in Affective Response to Stimuli as a Function of Extent of Deviation from Adaptation Level (after Helson, H., Adaptation-Level Theory, New York: Harper & Row, 1964).

though there are bound to be exceptions from this norm, e.g., hardy souls preferring a more nearly total isolation from civilization, or on the contrary a more intensive immersion in the stimulation offered by the big city. If so, this would show that not only the AL itself, but the degree of departure from it that would be experienced as pleasurable may vary considerably from one person to the next. This would admittedly make life more complex for the researcher investigating these problems, but would not pose any insuperable difficulties, provided independent measures of these parameters were available. It may also be noted that our model implies that such wilderness-fanciers would be least likely to come from a big metropolitan area; conversely, among those most strongly attracted to the excitement of the bustling metropolis, we should expect to find the visitor from a small town relatively underrepresented.

The Question of Long-Term Adaptation Effects

The concept of adaptation-level itself brings up a further question: What are the long-range effects of exposure to a given environment featured by a particular level of intensity, complexity, incongruity, etc., of stimulation? (In the very nature of the case, if the environment remains constant, novelty and surprisingness effectively cease to be relevant variables.) According to AL theory, the individual's AL will be shifted to a value corresponding more nearly to that environment.[4] This is of course no more than an expression of the fact of adaptation. The question arises, however, whether in spite of the individual's capacity to adapt to an astonishingly wide range of environmental conditions, such prolonged exposure to stimulus environments falling near the extreme of the complexity or intensity dimension, for instance, may not leave its mark nevertheless. That is, it is possible that the arousal value or the subjective evaluation of the stimulus environment by the individual may become assimilated to some normal range, and his behavior become effectively adapted to it; yet more subtle long-term effects on behavior may nevertheless occur. For instance, a commuter subjected morning and evening to rush-hour traffic conditions on the New York subways may come to experience them as no more arousing than would his wife taking a quiet, uncrowded bus ride through suburban streets (though his evaluation of the experience is apt to remain rather more negative). He may even develop the knack of reading and assimilating "all the news that's fit to print," unaware of the din and shoving around him. Yet the cumulative effect of the exposure to these conditions may still leave a residue detectable in his behavior, which might take the form of heightened arousal thresholds, lessened frustration tolerance, or the like, representing the price being paid for this surface adaptation. Or take the child growing up among a steady backdrop of high-intensity TV signals, rattling subway trains and yells from neighbors: he may well adapt to these conditions of noise, but perhaps only by shutting out from awareness much of the input—notably speech—to which in fact he needs to become sensitized for his optimal development.

Admittedly we are operating largely on hunches in our estimates of such long-term behavioral effects of exposure to particular levels of stimulation, but their possible reality can hardly be discounted, especially in view of the considerable evidence in this respect uncovered at the physiological level (2). There are, furthermore, undoubtedly large individual differences in tolerance of or adaptability to extreme levels of stimulation; for example, much migration behavior may be interpretable as an individual's response to his experienced level of stress emanating from the physical as well as the social environment (14).

Conclusion

In closing, we may express the hope that ultimately attention to questions such as these will lead to the creation of a science of environmental esthetics as a branch of psychology concerned with man's effective response to the qualitative and quantitative features of the world of natural and man-made stimuli surrounding him. Esthetics, to be sure, has not been a particularly flourishing branch of psychology in the past, no more than it has, until recently, represented an area of concern in our social, political and economic life. But it is perhaps not an entirely fortuitous coincidence that the attention which leaders in our public life have most recently been giving to the beautification of our artificial environment, as well as to the preservation of natural beauty, comes at the very time that the "new look" in the field of motivation is bringing psychologists ever closer to the realm of esthetics. (It is significant that the two books which are the primary sources with respect to this "new look," i.e., Berlyne (1); Fiske and Maddi (3), both include a chapter on esthetics.) The time would thus seem most auspicious for experimental psychologists to take their place alongside their colleagues in social psychology, sociology, geography, architecture, planning, etc., in a broadside attack on the problems facing us in improving the quality of our environment.

NOTES

1. Other ways in which the variable of temporal change, as well as of complexity of the stimulus input affect our perception of and locomotion within our geographical environment are brought out succinctly by A. E. Parr (9). Many of the points made in his paper are quite apposite to the kind of analysis of the stimulus properties of our environment being presented here.

2. As Fiske and Maddi (3, p. 9) note, most of their book is concerned with understimulation, rather than overstimulation, which they identify with stress. But in view of the emphasis given in their own formulation to the concept of an optimal level of activation, their readiness to dismiss the problem of overstimulation as unimportant is difficult to understand.

3. Though this proposition might seem to lack surface plausibility, it derives some limited support from the results of a pilot study carried out by two Clark undergraduates, Kenneth Holm and Harlan Sherwin, who interviewed tourists at Penn. Station to obtain their reactions to New York City. Of those who lived in suburban districts, one-third expressed some degree of positive reaction to the New York subways, whereas less than 10% of those residing in either small-town or country areas or in a metropolitan area gave any positive responses. It is also interesting to note that, in another sample of suburbanites, only 40% picked the crowds and noise as the aspects they disliked most about New York City, whereas 80% of the country-, small-town- or city-dwellers chose these aspects. (The suburbanites responded almost as frequently to the *dirt* of the city.)

4. It should be noted that for environmental settings characterized by either very low or very high levels of stimulation, the AL should be expected to fall considerably short of this extreme value, since the effects of exposure to a given environment on the AL are superimposed on factors of a more intrinsic sort, relating to the individual's assumed needs for a certain modal level of stimulation lying within some intermediate range.

REFERENCES

1. Berlyne, D. E. *Conflict, Arousal and Curiosity*. New York: McGraw-Hill, 1960.

2. Dubos, R. *Man Adapting*. New Haven: Yale University Press, 1965.

3. Fiske, D. W. and S. R. Maddi, eds. *Functions of Varied Experience*. Homewood, Ill.: Dorsey Press, 1961.

4. Fowler, H. *Curiosity and Exploratory Behavior*. New York: Macmillan, 1965.

5. Haywood, H. C., and D. W. Zimmerman. Effects of early environmental complexity on the following response in chicks. *Percept. mot. Skills*, 1964, **18**, 653–658.

6. Helson, H. *Adaptation-Level Theory*. New York: Harper & Row, 1964.

7. Leckart, B. T. and P. Bakan. Complexity judgments of photographs and looking time. *Percept. mot. Skills*, 1965, **21**, 16–18.

8. Nairn, I. *The American Landscape*. New York: Random House, 1965.

9. Parr, A. E. Psychological aspects of urbanology. *Journal of Social Issues*, 1966, **22**, no. 4, 39–45.

10. Solomon, P., et al., eds. *Sensory Deprivation*. Cambridge: Harvard University Press, 1961.

11. Thompson, R. W. and T. Schaefer, Jr. "Early environmental stimulation." In *Functions of Varied Experience*. D. W. Fiske and S. R. Maddi, eds. Homewood, Ill.: Dorsey Press, 1961, 81–105.

12. Torgerson, W. S. *Theory and Methods of Scaling*. New York: John Wiley and Sons, 1958.

13. White, R. W. "Motivation reconsidered: the concept of competence." In *Functions of Varied Experience*. D. W. Fiske and S. R. Maddi, eds. Homewood, Ill.: Dorsey Press, 1961, 278–325.

14. Wolpert, Julian. Migration as an adjustment to environmental stress. *Journal of Social Issues*, 1966, **22**, no. 4, 92–102.

PART TWO
Spatial Organization and Social Interaction

7

The Psycho-Social Influence of Building Environment: Sociometric Findings in Large and Small Office Spaces

B. W. P. WELLS

One of the principal interests of environmental designers today is the role that architecture can play in fostering social interaction. When architecture is considered in terms of this goal, the aspect of the built environment that is usually examined is spatial organization. What is the horizontal distribution of people and activities across the plane of the earth, as in a site plan or floor plan, or, in a vertical structure, the distribution of rooms and activities from floor to floor? In such discussions spatial organization is measured in terms of the physical and functional distance between persons, groups, and activities.

That architecture does have some influence on social interaction cannot be disputed. A building, or a group of buildings, has the capacity to serve as a communications network. The arrangement of rooms, walls, doors, partitions, driveways, and streets does affect the opportunities people have to see and hear each other and thus to respond to one another. By the location of barriers, apertures, and paths, physical arrangements can provide opportunities for communication, or hinder it. It is only a short step from the chance to communicate to the act of communicating, and therefore, to social interaction.

Wells' study of the formation of cohesive work groups in an office building illustrates the effect of spatial arrangements on communications networks. His measure of the existence of cohesive work groups is the degree of reciprocity in friendship choices among the workers in an insurance company office in Manchester, England. Wells collected data from 295 office workers on one floor about which clerks they preferred to work next to. Of the respondents 214 worked in a large open area, while 81 worked in 1 of 3 smaller enclosed areas. Wells' findings were (1) that choices were directly related to the distances between employees, with both men and women preferring office mates who already were working next to or close to them; (2) that workers in the smaller partitioned areas were likely to prefer office

Reprinted from B. W. P. Wells, "The Psycho-Social Influence of Building Environment: Sociometric Findings in Large and Small Office Spaces," in *Building Science* 1(1965): 153–165.

mates from their own section; and (3) that the percentage of individuals who were not chosen by any of their colleagues, that is who were social isolates, was larger in the smaller work spaces. Wells concludes that internal group cohesion in the smaller areas was greater than in the open plan sections, even though the smaller areas included more isolates and had fewer links with those outside the small area.

It should be noted that Wells' research, although it deals with a general issue in the relation of architecture to behavior, was undertaken in response to a practical design problem. Deep office blocks of the kind discussed in his selection are becoming increasingly common because they are less expensive to construct. However, since most workers prefer daylight and an outside view, deep blocks require large, open plan offices. In his concluding discussion, Wells raises the issue of how the designer and client can achieve a proper balance between the presumed advantages in morale of the more cohesive groups in the smaller spaces and the greater building efficiency and broader departmental ties of the open plan.

□

The approach made in this study is that of sociometry—a complex methodology but one yielding utterly simple data—consisting merely of the preferences or rejections expressed by members of a given group towards other members of that group. These are termed socioprefer-ential choices and are usually written down in reply to a highly specific question about the circumstances of the choice. The method has proved extremely interesting in connection with the sort of research that psychologists may come to use extensively on architectural problems, and with this justification, the methodology has been presented in detail.

However, before describing the experimental work so far completed, a consideration of the background to the psycho-social component of environmental studies would be in order.

Background of Theory and Research

In 1963 John Noble (1) wrote an article in the *Architects' Journal* entitled "The How and Why of Behaviour: Social Psychology for the Architect" in which he wrote "as architects we help to shape people's future behaviour by the environment we create." This is a belief very widely held amongst architects and one, if true, of very great importance not only to architects, but also to the public in general and the human sciences in particular. However, at the present time, the empirical evidence for such a belief (except in the most trivial sense) is sparse indeed: the influence of the building environment remains very much an unknown quantity.

Psychologists spend a great deal of time defining and examining the concept of "environment" and in describing the influence of the environment on the human being. The clearly defined aspects of physical environment such as heat, light and sound; the internal physical environmental features such as hormonal function; the family and the larger social environments, are all matters of the deepest concern to the psychologist. It is, however, an extremely curious fact that the most prominent and obvious feature of our environment, the very buildings, towns and cities in which we act out our entire lives have so far attracted scarcely any attention whatsoever.

At any point *lower* than man on the phylogenetic scale, the biological scientist would regard habitat as a fundamentally important feature in determining an animal's behavior. However, at the level of man, the psychologist and other behavioral and social scientists concentrate their attention on learning and the acquired behavior patterns which have given man a large measure of mastery of his environment. He creates the conditions he feels he needs or wants and is no longer so much influenced by his physical environment. Instead, the greater environmental pressures are applied by the social milieu and organization created from his relative freedom from instinctive behavior patterns. This not to say that there is a complete, or anything like complete, freedom from the influence of the created physical environment. The influence of habitat may be relatively smaller in the case of man, but it may still be a potent factor in influencing certain types of behavior.

Where environmental studies *have* been made, though, they have rather tended to be concerned with the most simple—and probably least influential—aspects. That is, discrete studies of optimal heating, lighting and ventilation, and acoustical conditions. It has further been felt that these factors, taken collectively and in conjunction with subjective preferences for layout and finish, exhaust the topic of the internal environment of buildings—at least so far as the designer is concerned.

However, it is the thesis of this paper that the *social* factors of environment are amongst the most important, and that these are very much the concern of designers where their designs affect the way in which space may be used. This, of course, would be so in almost every case.

One way of thinking about a building is as a catalyst; that is, a relatively inert agent, but one vital to a particular process—in the present context the work of an office. However, if the building *is* a catalyst, it is one which differs in a very important respect from the catalytic agents of chemistry. They facilitate only *one* kind of reaction between substances. The building, on the other hand, may facilitate *many* reactions. For example, common entrances to different departments mean that there are many more opportunities for inter-departmental contacts than if there were separate ones. The results of these interactions must be studied both from the personal-social and from the company point of view. The individual's potential social world is perhaps widened, and it may well be that inter-departmental working is facilitated by such informal contacts. The size of the rooms themselves also sets the limits and range of working, and therefore, social intercourse. Another consequence of room size may follow from the introduction of very large clerical areas which would seem to offer chances for the introduction of more autocratic measures in supervision and management.

The sort of questions which arise in relation to room size are, what happens when a clerk moves from a small office setting to the large open one? In what way do his group sentiments change *vis à vis* both the group and the department or company as a whole? Which group sizes tend to have cohesive and which disintegrative effects on social and working groups? Are they affected at all? How does the individual's concept of himself change; does the worker regard himself as reduced in stature by being given less obvious prominence in a larger group? Does he feel more or less ambitious in the new setting? Are there more far-reaching social consequences? No such systematic work on the influence of office size on the clerical worker has yet been done, and it is some aspects of this fundamentally important problem which will be considered by means of the sociometric approach.

The methods of judging the social conditions within open plan offices are often questionable in the extreme and thus many of the conclusions which are derived must be treated with some caution.

The literature on the open plan design is replete with comment which, in the absence of good supportive evidence, can only be regarded as an attempt on the part of the writer to identify with the clerical worker. The very terms used in stating the problem are heavily weighted with the attitudes of their authors. In an address to the Association of Industrial Medical Officers, McGirr (2) referring to the open plan offices, spoke of "herding clerical staff into them" and described them as "soulless subtopia of impersonalization." He rejected the counter-evidence of their acceptance in America on the grounds that open planning is congruent with the American national aim of "togetherness," whereas it is a "principle fundamentally at variance with our national concepts of individuality and personal privacy."

McGirr's position has clearly been derived from reference to his own standards. His beliefs in the need for individuality and personal privacy are middle class sentiments which are not necessarily relevant to the majority of workers in the large clerical organizations. As Lockwood (3) has pointed out, recent social and economic forces have created paperwork industries manned not by the nonprofessional members of the middle classes, but mainly by members of lower socio-economic groups. The nature of the work is also different: it has been mechanized and de-skilled and is now largely in the hands of young female workers. It has currently more in common with light industrial assembly work than with the clerical work of a generation ago. It may very well be then that the sentiments expressed by McGirr are not those of the modern office worker, but only research will settle the issue.

Unfortunately, the research has usually not been done before the conclusions are anticipated. Even such respected figures as McGirr (who was a member of the Institute of Directors' Main Committee in the publication of "Better Offices" 1962) (4) reach far beyond the evidence when discussing open office planning. For example, later in the paper already referred to, he went on to say:

> . . . by neglecting the social studies already existing in small group performances, these gentleman (i.e. methods engineers and business efficiency experts), may be sowing the seeds of future frustration and breakdown. I believe that as doctors in commerce and industry we have a duty to protect those entrusted to our care against the potential evils of an entirely mechanistic approach by work study.

This, of course, constitutes a clarion call for industrial medical officers to oppose innovation on exceedingly slender evidence and grounds. Almost nothing is known of the consequences of open plan organization and it is premature to claim that it may be the cause of future frustration and breakdown. However, because the chain of evidence is not a strong one, and is probably colored by personal feelings, one certainly cannot disregard McGirr's apprehensions; indeed they are shared by many planners, managements, and their staffs.

McGirr concluded his paper by saying:

> We must make ourselves familiar with studies in group dynamics and breakdown; if satisfied that the human element is being neglected for a

wholly mechanical approach to work, we ought to be fearless in our denunciations.

This is, of course, a sentiment with which few people would disagree, but the links connecting human happiness and psychic balance with space utilization and staff deployment have yet to be shown. The whole question is so important from not only a personal point of view, but also from that of management and designers, that prompt research into the subject is clearly necessary.

Of the little objective research which has been done in connection with building design, perhaps the most celebrated attempt to apply the methods of social psychology has been that of Festinger *et al.* (5). They studied sociometrically the effects of different types of housing and spatial relationship upon group and friendship formation, and concluded that:

> *the relationship between ecological and sociometric structures is so very marked that there can be little doubt that in these communities passive contacts are a major determinant of friendship and group formation.*

Similarly, Gullahorn (6) showed in an office setting that frequency of social interaction and friendship choice were closely related to spatial relationships. This raises the question of whether, in an organization such as the one in which this research was done,[1] and where departments are broken into smaller sections working side by side, informal groups arise more easily between individuals assigned to different formal (i.e. working and administrative) groupings. The study to be described contrasts some of the friendship patterns found in open working areas with those of some relatively small and enclosed ones.

In view of the research findings on the social consequences of spatial contiguity, one might expect a number of important managerial consequences from the decision to adopt either the open or the closed office plan. One might, for example, expect that the single section occupying a small office would offer the greatest opportunity for the formation of a stable work group. In a small office, cohesive forces would derive from the fact that each member of the primary, or face to face, group shares the common working objectives of that group. The small office area produces a closeness of the group determined not only by the physical distances between working spaces, but also by functional distances involved. That is, people are brought close together by the passive interactions taking place as a result of using a common entrance and common circulation space, and also by the non-business interactions at such foci as the filing cabinets, postal trays, and telephones. Unlike the open office, all these interactions will take place on a working unit basis. Thus the small office arrangement produces the best possibility for the formation of a group with a clear identity and concept of itself as a discrete and simple entity.

On the other hand, the open plan office allows for more *possibilities* of interpersonal contact and group formation. Common entrances and circulation spaces will increase the number of inter-group contacts (that is, contacts between different working groups). Without partitions, both the physical and functional distance between groups is reduced and one might expect, from the research findings previously referred to, that the number of intergroup friendships would increase. The individual may then find himself a member of two groups—the formal group of his work section, and an informal friendship group composed of members of *different* sections.

The existence of large numbers of intra-group friendships (i.e. friendships existing within the formal work unit), is a factor which has been shown to be related to group effectiveness and morale (7, 8). However, unlike the small office, the open plan area allows for the easy formation of between section friendships. If these are made at the expense of the within section ones, then one might expect on theoretical grounds that the morale and effectiveness of the work unit might suffer.

The proliferation of friendship groups between work units is also a potential force working against managerial control. The status roles, lines of communication, and group loyalties intended to operate within a working group may well be undermined by the competing claims of the informal group. The influences exerted by the immediate primary group can be very strong indeed, influencing the attitudes, expectations, and behavior of not only the pliable individual, but also the average and strong personality (9–12). An appraisal of these effects should therefore be a prerequisite to the management decision of whether to adopt the open plan: whether the advantages are outweighed by the disadvantages. But this first requires that the research should be done in order to establish the *actual* influence of office size.

THE STATUS OF THE HYPOTHESES

The present investigation of the psycho-social consequences of large and small office areas started with a few specific hypotheses which were derived from the previously referred to literature. They were of the kind that there would be more mutual friendship choices in small areas than large, and that there would be more friendship choices directed outside of people's own formal work group in the large area than in the small. These were, though, only conceptual guide lines: the study was much more empirical and exploratory than it was theoretical and so the hypotheses are relatively unimportant compared with the findings as no existing theoretical issues were being critically tested.

POPULATION AND SAMPLES USED

As has already been referred to, the investigation took place within the head office building of an insurance company. The experimental area was limited to a single floor of 36,000 sq. ft., containing more than three hundred clerks, supervisors and managers.

The floor taken as the experimental one was selected as being the only one which met the criteria of having both large and small work areas with personnel who were closely comparable in terms of their supervision, formal group membership and nature of the work. There were only general clerical areas on the floor—no typing pools or machine rooms—thus there was considerable homogeneity amongst the clerical workers. This homogeneity was increased by the fact of the whole floor being part of the same department: little internal partitioning was used—just sufficient to mark the boundaries of the three sub-departments. These open areas were vast (of the order of one hundred clerks within partition lines which themselves were not wall to wall).

Three small working areas (of approximately thirty clerks) were taken as ones to contrast with the remaining open ones. They were fairly well defined from the open areas as they were sited between partition walls and the walls of enclosed stair wells. All the desks in the small areas faced the window wall and thus the clerks had little opportunity for even visual contact with other members of their department although they were occupied on similar work.

All of the people working on the experimental floor were invited to participate in the study and, with the exception of those away sick or on holiday, all did. They composed 295 general clerks in the grades below section clerk (or supervisor). The sample was therefore fairly homogeneous as it did not include any other such categories as machine operators, typists, managers or supervisors.

Of the 295 respondents, 214 worked in the large open areas, and 81 in the smaller enclosed areas referred to above: age and sex categories were comparable. The youngest group of 15–19 year olds composed 43 per cent of the population, and older workers, the age groups over 40, accounted for 21 per cent. The age groups between 20 and 39 were fairly evenly distributed minorities. The ratio of females to males was of the order 2:1. These proportions are closely similar to the overall distribution of the company's staff.

METHOD OF INVESTIGATION

The method of collecting the sociometric data was dependent, to some extent, upon the need to use the experimental opportunity to collect other material about the attitudes and feelings of the subjects towards large and small offices.[2] This latter material involved the presentation of verbal and visual material (tape recorded instructions and slide projections), the responses to which were to be written in a reply booklet. It was decided to include the sociometric item with this other, less emotionally toned, material.

The experimental setting of the study was a recreation hall which had been made available by the company, and in which there were facilities for projecting slides and presenting tape recorded instructions.

The total sample of 295 was divided into 4 groups of approximately 75; each group taking just under half an hour to process. By taking the subjects as groups and carefully dispersing them within the experimental room it was possible to deal with them as aggregates rather than groups, giving essentially isolated conditions for the individual (thus avoiding interpersonal influence), and having the advantage of processing large numbers at one time. The data collection was completed by lunch time and thus the dangers inherent in subjects discussing experiments were greatly reduced.

ANALYSIS OF DATA

From the point of view of construction, devising a sociometric reply sheet is a perfectly common-sense procedure. Moreno (13) who was principally responsible for the development of the sociometric method, gives a general background to the preparation of such a document in his book "Who shall survive?" The most fundamental prerequisite in using such a technique is, of course, having the confidence of the respondents. In the present instance, the request for sociometric data came as the culmination of a 2-year research project within the company. The investigator was therefore very well known to the respondents and on good personal terms with many of them, having spent a great deal of time working on the floor in question and mixing socially in the coffee lounges and recreation rooms. One might also expect that the study

105

would derive a certain amount of acceptance from the fact that it was supported by the trade union, of which every employee was a member. At all stages in the project great care had been taken to promote the goodwill of the union so that it should continue to recommend the investigations to its members.

As Moreno, and many others since, have pointed out, it is essential to be specific about the conditions under which the preference choice is to be made. That is, whether the choice is a work choice, a dining choice, a choice of sports companion, or what. One must also specify the population from which the choices may be drawn if the pattern of interactions is to be interpretable. The criterion of the sociopreferential choice for this study was the people beside which the respondent would like to work. The universe of choice was limited to those people also working on the same floor. In this case, taking the whole of one floor allowed for most of the possible face to face social interactions which occur during working hours as most between-floor communication must take place either by means of the telephone or the document conveyor.

Selltiz *et al.* (14) have drawn attention to the desirability of stating, where feasible, that the investigator will arrange for the individual's preferences to be met if possible. This was not possible in the present case, and instead the experimenter took the alternative course recommended by Bjerstedt (15).

It may therefore often be advantageous to make the situation cognitively experimental, to stress that nothing will happen as a result of the findings. If there is no need for report-distortion the subject is likely to give a true answer that is after all, most natural and least laborious.

As well as having the general goodwill and support of the subjects, it is also absolutely vital that they be reassured of their anonymity and the fact that their reply forms will be treated in an absolutely confidential manner. The written and spoken instructions made this abundantly clear, and also that the data was to be coded and transferred to punched cards and the questionnaires immediately destroyed. It is though, the investigator's belief that the greatest reassurance came not from promises made at the time, but from people's experience of the way in which other confidences, derived from 2 years of contact, had been maintained.

No limit was set to the number of choices that a respondent could make. Preferences were to be given in ranked order, and spaces were allowed for up to ten names on the reply form. As an additional motivator to the hesitant, the tape recorded instruction "Please try to list at least three people" was given half a minute after the first set of instructions. A total of 2 minutes was allowed to list the preferential choices, and one further minute to complete the additional information about friendships with people on other floors.

FORM OF ANALYSIS OF DATA

The sociometric method is used principally as a tool for the examination of the social structure of groups of less than about forty people, and more usually still, for smaller ones. The techniques of analysis are therefore most developed for the small group. The original method described by Moreno (13) and still the most popular, entails drawing a diagram in which preferences or rejections are represented by lines between the individuals forming the group. (See Figure 7–1.)

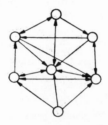

Figure 7–1   Simple Sociometric Diagram.

7 subjects   2 stars
21 preference choices   1 isolate
6 mutual preferences

The diagram is then rearranged in such a way as to make it perceptually more simple. It then remains to look for any trends; to establish who are the isolates in a group, and who are the "stars." The procedures involved are not systematic and the pattern tends to be exceedingly difficult to comprehend with large numbers. (See Figure 7–2.)

To simplify the analysis, methods were developed in which the diagram was replaced by the matrix. Forsyth and Katz (16) developed a method in which the individuals of the group were listed in the same order down the rows and along the columns.

The matrix was completed by entering the choices made by individuals in the row bearing his name and in the column of the person receiving that choice. This gave a picture almost as complicated as the diagram, but it could be simplified by rearranging the order of the columns and rows so that the entries in the matrix clustered as closely as possible about the main diagonal. The diagonal is, of course, composed

107

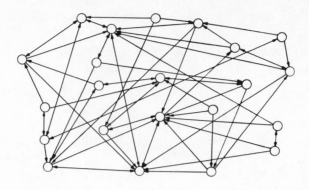

Figure 7–2   More Complex Sociometric Diagram.

22 subjects   3 stars
66 preferences (3 each)   1 isolate
16 mutual preferences

of empty cells as it is formed by the point at which the individual's name appears in both the column and the row. The arrangement shows, in the clusters, those people who have chosen one another relatively frequently. The well separated entries represent the people who have not chosen one another. (See Figure 7–3.)

However, the method of matrix analysis so far described is, as Festinger (17) pointed out, most useful for establishing changes within a group from one time to another and is of little value in demonstrating the existence of subgroups or for comparing two groups. Festinger's own special contribution was to suggest a technique to allow for the determination of cliques within a group.

The above represent the three main types of analysis applied to sociometric data. There are almost innumerable variations of them, but none allows for a comparison of the social organization of physically separated groups, both of which form part of the same universe of choice. The usual situation involves taking two groups, each of which represents a separate universe, and comparing their internal sociometric structures. However, the present study is specifically concerned with the between group relationships and so it must be possible for the respondent to express his choices within his actual universe of choice, rather than an arbitrarily limited one. Therefore the results for the entire floor were treated together, with a corresponding gain in the validity of the data and loss in the rigor of the analytic techniques available.

The main objectives of the analysis were threefold. In the first place to establish the number of choices directed outside of the section in

Subject	1	2	3	4	5	6	7	8	9	10	11	12	13	14	15	16	17	18	19	20	Total Given
1		1									1								1		3
2	1			1												1					3
3		1		1		1															3
4	1			1				1													3
5			1	1			1														3
6							1	1			1										3
7				1		1							1								3
8						1			1	1											3
9											1	1	1								3
10											1	1	1								3
11			1						1	1											3
12					1								1				1				3
13								1				1		1							3
14	1							1								1					3
15													1				1	1			3
16								1						1		1					3
17								1								1		1			3
18																1	1		1		3
19								1	1											1	3
20								1									1	1			3
Total Received	3	2	2	2	3	3	2	8	3	3	4	3	5	0	2	4	4	3	2	2	60

Figure 7–3   Example of a Sociometric Matrix.
20 Individuals   1 Star
60 Preferences (3 each)   1 Isolate
9 Mutual Preferences

which they were made. Secondly, to compare the number of reciprocated choices [3] made within the open areas and the three smaller partitioned ones. Thirdly, to compare the numbers of isolates found in the open and the partitioned areas.[4]

Results

The analysis of results was undertaken in two stages: the first to determine the effect on preference choices of personal variables: the second to determine the effect of the spatial ones, though much of the data for each is given in both stages.

STAGE 1: THE EFFECT OF PERSONAL VARIABLES

The initial task in the analysis was the manual cross-tabulation of the total number of sociometric preferences made by each sex and age group. In the course of the cross-tabulation it was found that 18 per cent of the respondents completing the rest of the reply form had left this particular item blank. They were therefore not included in the analysis, though their number is shown in column 4 of Table 7-1. Their names were also excluded from the preferences made by other people; thus they effectively cease to exist as members of the population studied.

Against the left hand column of Table 7-1 is summarized the number and proportion of preference choices made and received by each sex and age group, and thus the influence of these variables as determinants of choice. It is therefore convenient to consider separately the influence of each.

(1) *Sex as a determinant of preference choice*—Column 3 shows that the average number of choices made by men and women is approximately the same (i.e. 4.4 to 4.2) though columns 4 and 5 show that the men are more likely to refuse to record their preferences than are the women.

It was found that the men, who represent 31 per cent of the sample, in fact received 36 per cent of all the stated preferences; whereas the women, who represent 69 per cent of the sample, received 64 per cent of the total choices made. However, as columns 6 and 7 show, the great majority of choices made by a given sex were directed towards members of the same sex. This held for the entire range of age groups, and it therefore appears that sex is an important determinant of choice pattern. This is not, of course, a novel or unexpected finding; indeed one would have been surprised at any other result. The value of the findings is not therefore intrinsic but they do establish the relative amount of weight to be given to the sex variable when considering the influence of other determinants.

(2) *Age as a determinant of preference choice*—The youngest age group, the 15 to 19 year olds, composed the numerically largest group and made the greatest absolute number of choices. In all, they made 48 per cent of the total preference choices recorded, but they received only 35 per cent of the total choices themselves. Conversely, with the exception of the over 40 age group, all other groups received more choices than they made. It appears therefore that older working companions are generally more acceptable than younger ones.

110

Summary Table of Sociometric Preferences Cross-Tabulated by Age Group and Sex

Age Groups and Sex	(1) Number of Respondents Completing Form	(2) Number of Named Preferences Given	(3) Average Number of Named Preferences Given	(4) Number of Respondents Not Replying	(5) Percentage of Respondents Not Replying (of cols. 1+4)	(6) Choices to Males Number	(6) Percentage (of col. 2)	(7) Choices to Females Number	(7) Percentage (of col. 2)	(8) Choices to 15-19 Year Group Number	(8) Percentage (of col. 2)	(9) Choices to 20-24 Year Group Number	(9) Percentage (of col. 2)	(10) Choices to 25-29 Year Group Number	(10) Percentage (of col. 2)	(11) Choices to 30-34 Year Group Number	(11) Percentage (of col. 2)	(12) Choices to 35-39 Year Group Number	(12) Percentage (of col. 2)	(13) Choices to 40+ Age Group Number	(13) Percentage (of col. 2)
15-19 Years																					
Male	21	91	4.3	2	8.7	64	70.3	27	29.7	48	52.7	19	20.9	14	15.4	2	2.2	5	5.5	3	3.3
Female	95	378	4.0	9	8.7	53	14.0	325	86.0	227	60.1	103	27.2	9	2.4	8	2.1	10	2.6	21	5.6
Totals	116	469	4.0	11	8.7	117	24.9	352	75.1	275	58.6	122	26.0	23	4.9	10	2.1	15	3.2	24	5.1
20-24 Years																					
Male	21	103	4.9	1	4.5	76	73.8	27	26.2	23	22.3	50	48.5	17	16.5	4	3.9	5	4.9	4	3.9
Female	36	158	4.4	6	14.3	22	13.9	136	86.1	52	32.9	74	46.8	5	3.2	9	5.7	7	4.4	11	7.0
Totals	57	261	4.6	7	10.9	98	37.5	163	62.5	75	28.7	124	47.5	22	8.4	13	5.0	12	4.6	15	5.7
25-29 Years																					
Male	3	18	6.0	1	25.0	14	77.8	4	22.2	2	11.1	3	16.7	5	27.8	6	33.3	0	0.0	2	11.1
Female	9	45	5.0	3	25.0	11	24.4	34	75.6	5	11.1	9	20.0	9	20.0	9	20.0	6	13.3	7	15.6
Totals	12	63	5.3	4	25.0	25	39.7	38	60.3	7	11.1	12	19.0	14	22.2	15	23.8	6	9.5	9	14.3
30-34 Years																					
Male	6	27	4.5	2	25.0	23	85.2	4	14.8	0	0.0	1	3.7	6	22.2	15	55.5	1	3.7	4	14.8
Female	3	21	7.0	1	25.0	6	28.6	15	71.4	0	0.0	1	4.8	5	23.8	9	42.9	2	9.5	4	19.0
Totals	9	48	5.4	3	25.0	29	60.4	19	39.6	0	0.0	2	4.2	11	22.9	24	50.0	3	6.2	8	16.7
35-39 Years																					
Male	5	21	4.2	3	37.5	17	81.0	4	19.0	0	0.0	2	9.5	1	4.8	6	28.6	6	28.6	6	28.6
Female	4	13	3.3	1	20.0	0	0.0	13	100.0	1	7.7	1	7.7	0	0.0	3	23.1	2	15.4	6	46.2
Totals	9	34	3.8	4	30.8	17	50.0	17	50.0	1	2.9	3	8.8	1	2.9	9	26.5	8	23.5	12	35.3
40 or More																					
Male	19	69	3.6	12	38.7	58	84.1	11	15.9	2	2.9	6	8.7	1	1.4	8	11.6	21	30.4	31	44.9
Female	19	76	4.0	13	40.6	27	35.5	49	64.5	1	1.3	7	9.2	3	3.9	14	18.4	14	18.4	37	48.7
Totals	38	145	3.8	25	39.7	85	58.6	60	41.4	3	2.1	13	9.0	4	2.8	22	15.2	35	24.1	68	46.9
All Age Groups Combined																					
Male	75	329	4.4	21	21.9	252	76.6	77	23.4	75	22.8	81	24.6	44	13.4	41	12.5	38	11.6	50	15.2
Female	166	691	4.2	33	16.6	119	17.2	572	82.8	286	41.4	195	28.2	31	4.5	52	7.5	41	5.9	86	12.5
Grand Totals	241	1020	4.2	54	18.3	371	36.4	649	63.6	361	35.4	276	27.0	75	7.4	93	9.2	79	7.7	136	13.3

It is interesting to note from columns 6 and 7 that there is a tendency for the proportion of men being chosen by women to rise with the women's age group. On the other hand, the proportion of women chosen by men declines with the older age groups. The reasons for this are not apparent from the results and so one must postulate some other factor; for example, differences in the relative attractiveness of the two sexes for one another at different ages.

Inspection of the blocked-off cells in the center of the table shows that each age group tends to choose predominantly from the members of its own age group. This is most marked for the numerically larger age groups: members of the smaller ones presumably being more cut-off from members of their own age group. With the single exception of the 30–34 year age group it is members of the adjacent age group who are next most frequently chosen. That is, the ones to the immediate left or right of the blocked-off diagonal. In fact, the percentage of choices made to members of the same age group plus those immediately adjacent are as follows:

15-19 years	85 per cent	30-34 years	79 per cent
20-24 years	80 per cent	35-39 years	85 per cent
25-29 years	65 per cent	40 or more	71 per cent

As in the case of the sex variable, it is clear that age group also is a very potent factor in determining the preference choices. Again, the finding is neither novel nor unexpected, but a necessary step in evaluating the factors responsible for preference choices.

STAGE 2: THE EFFECT OF SPATIAL VARIABLES

Tables 7–2 and 7–3 are concerned with the sheer effect of physical distance on the different age and sex groups and are therefore more clearly connected with the designers' and clients' interests. They were prepared by measuring, on a scale floor plan, the distance between the person making the preference choice and the person receiving it. The name of every individual participating had previously been written against his desk position on the plan in order to facilitate such cross-referencing.

The Totals row of Table 7–2 shows a very clear pattern: the number of sociopreferential choices decreases steadily with distance. The only exception to the trend is the case of distances of more than 36 ft., where the number is slightly above that for the 25–36 ft. group, and is

112

Distance of Respondents from Sociometric Choice Cross-Tabulated with Age Group

| | (1) Number of Choices Made by Group | Distance of Respondent from Choice | | | | | | | | | |
| | | (2) 12 Ft. or Less | | (3) 13-18 Ft. | | (4) 19-24 Ft. | | (5) 25-36 Ft. | | (6) More Than 36 Ft. | |
Age Group		Number	Percentage (of col. 1)	Number	Percentage (of col. 1)	Number	Percentage (of col. 1)	Number	Percentage (of col. 1)	Number	Percentage (of col. 1)
15-19	469	187	39·9	129	27·5	64	13·6	41	8·7	48	10·2
20-24	261	111	42·5	78	29·9	34	13·0	22	8·4	16	6·1
25-29	63	20	31·8	12	19·0	12	19·0	11	17·5	8	12·7
30-34	48	18	37·5	10	20·8	12	25·0	4	8·3	4	8·3
35-39	34	12	35·3	6	17·6	7	20·6	4	11·8	5	14·7
40 or More	145	46	31·8	28	19·1	19	13·1	19	13·1	33	22·8
Totals	1020	394	38·6	263	25·8	148	14·5	101	9·9	114	11·2

TABLE 7-3

Distance of Respondents from Sociometric Choice Cross-Tabulated with Sex

| | (1) Number of Choices Made by Group | Distance of Respondent from Choice | | | | | | | | | |
| | | (2) 12 Ft. or Less | | (3) 13-18 Ft. | | (4) 19-24 Ft. | | (5) 25-36 Ft. | | (6) More Than 36 Ft. | |
Sex		Number	Percentage (of col. 1)	Number	Percentage (of col. 1)	Number	Percentage (of col. 1)	Number	Percentage (of col. 1)	Number	Percentage (of col. 1)
Male	329	114	34·7	75	22·8	63	19·1	40	12·2	37	11·2
Female	691	280	40·5	188	27·2	85	12·3	61	8·8	77	11·1
Totals	1020	394	38·6	263	25·8	148	14·5	101	9·9	114	11·2

TABLE 7-4

Summary Table of Sociometric Choices Made and Reciprocated within Sections and Departments, Including the Number of Isolates in Each

	(1)	(2)	(3)	(4)	(5)
	Number of Respondents Completing Form	Number of Named Preferences Given	Average Number of Preferences Given	Number of Respondents Not Replying	Percentage of Respondents Not Replying (of cols. 1 + 4)
Type of Office Space					
Open Areas	174	779	4·5	40	18·7
Small Areas (X, Y and Z)	67	241	3·6	14	17·3
Totals	241	1020	4·2	54	18·3

*The percentage is calculated from twice the actual number of reciprocated choices. in column 2.

presumably a consequence of grouping together several possible distance categories.

One interesting effect apparent from the results in column 2 is that the younger age groups choose the highest proportion of people from those within one desk distance, and the general trend is for this proportion to fall with age. Conversely, inspection of column 6 shows that there is a general trend for older groups to select a higher proportion of their workmate choices from the over 36 ft. distance. This is an effect that one might expect from the tendency, already demonstrated, for choices to be made from members of the same age group. As the older age groups are in a minority, the individuals composing them must be relatively more isolated from one another, and thus the number of choices to greater distances relatively higher.

Table 7–3 compares the distances involved in the preference choices made by men and women. The frequency distribution of choices at various distances is broadly the same, but there is a slight tendency for men to draw a higher proportion of their choices from further away. As with the older age groups, men being a minority, are relatively more isolated from one another. Sex, having been shown to be an important determinant of sociopreferential choice, would therefore be expected to result in choices being made over somewhat greater distances.

114

TABLE 7-4 *(continued)*

(6)		(7)		(8)		(9)		(10)	
Choices to Members of Respondent's Own Section		Choices to Members of Respondent's Own Department		Reciprocated Choices within Single Section		Reciprocated Choices within Single Department		Unchosen Individuals (Isolates)	
Num-ber	Percen-tage (of col. 2)	Num-ber	Percen-tage (of col. 2)	Num-ber	Percen-tage (of col. 2)*	Num-ber	Percen-tage (of col. 2)*	Num-ber	Percen-tage (of col. 1)
498	63·9	710	91·1	147	37·7	207	53·1	8	4·6
195	80·9	229	95·0	80	66·4	84	69·7	6	9·0
693	67·9	939	92·1	227	44·5	291	57·1	14	5·8

This was done because each reciprocal choice involves two choices taken from the total

Workmate choice seems, therefore, to be a result of the simultaneously acting influences of age, sex and physical distance.

Table 7–4 summarizes the sociometric choices made and reciprocated within sections and departments, and the number of isolates found in each. The data from the small partitioned areas is compared with that from the remainder of the floor. Column 1 shows the number of subjects who completed the sociometric question; column 4 shows the number of those who did not. Column 5 shows that the percentage of workers in the large and small areas who did not state their preferences was almost identical.[5] Column 3 shows that there exists a very substantial difference between the average number of choices made by workers in the open areas and those in the small. People working in the larger office spaces produced the greater outgoing choice volume: in sociometric terms exhibiting a higher level of "expansivity" than workers in the small areas.

Columns 6 and 7 show that the preference choices of workers in the small areas are very much more frequently made from amongst members of their own section, and somewhat more frequently from members of their own department, than are those of the open area personnel. Columns 8 and 9 show that this greater proportion of choices made within a single section or department is also paralleled by a much greater proportion of choices reciprocated within them. That the pro-

115

portion of within-department reciprocated choices is much higher for workers in the small areas than for those in the large is, though, a consequence of the great number of within-section reciprocated choices. In fact, the number of reciprocated choices with members of the same department, other than members of the same section, is very much lower.

The results therefore show that there exists a much greater degree of internal cohesion amongst the members of the sections working within the smaller areas than amongst those working in the open ones. However, the number of isolates is greater. Column 10 shows that, though their numbers are small, there are proportionately almost twice as many in the small areas. If spatial relationships *are* important factors in determining the sociopreferential choice, then one might anticipate such a result because a higher proportion of workers in a small area must perforce be relatively physically isolated by working in a corner or beside a wall.

To summarize the results, it was found that both age and sex were important determinants of sociopreferential choice but, allowing for this, they tend to operate within the framework of spatial relationships. As the sections working in both the open and the small areas were essentially similar in respect of the nature of the work and composition of the subsamples, differences in sociometric pattern must be attributable to differences in the size of area in which they worked.

It was found that the social organization of the sections working in small areas was internally more cohesive, though the proportion of isolates was higher, and the number of wider links with other members of the same department much smaller.

The higher average number of preference choices made by members of the open areas, coupled with the lower proportion of reciprocations, shows that the social-occupational network existing in the two types of area are fundamentally different. In the small areas there exists a fairly tight social group, whereas the social links connecting people in the open areas are much less tightly knit.

Discussion of Results and Conclusions

Objective differences have been shown to result from locating working sections in large and small areas, and the existence of these differences now raises the management question of which one is to be preferred. The internal cohesiveness of the sections in the small area meets many of the criteria for small group effectiveness. On the other hand, the sections in the open areas have better interconnections with other parts of the department and may therefore constitute a more effective total working unit than the sum of individual sections.

It may be that individuals working in small areas enjoy better morale as a result of their internal cohesiveness or, alternatively, that they inbreed greater tensions as a result of the relative lack of contact with a wider working group. Managements may wish to promote small and exclusive work groups of high morale and efficiency, and this may prove to be one way of doing it. On the other hand, they may wish to promote the department as the more important work unit, to encourage cooperation between the subunits rather than competition. All of these different alternatives are possible results of different types of spatial arrangements. The exact results of particular arrangements cannot yet be predicted, but it *is* clear that they must be investigated as a part of management's effective method of control. Thus, because of the relationship between the spatial organization of the building and socio-occupational relationships, organizational and man-management problems might be expected to become a more substantial part of the architectural and design problem.

Earlier in this paper, the possible psychological factors influencing the decision to opt for deep block and open office design were discussed, and it has since been shown that the social milieu, and thus the psychological climate, of large and small offices are in fact radically different.

Having established an empirical basis for these psycho-social differences, it now remains to examine further McGirr's assumptions about the possible medico-psychological consequences of the deep and open office. If undesirable effects are found, then clearly the arguments for and against different types of accommodation must ultimately be measured against the criterion of human needs. This may also be so even though the psycho-social effects are nonclinical but are influential on morale and job performance. As yet, no such information is available but the appropriate research has already begun in the Department of Building Science, in Liverpool.

In conclusion, and by way of a justification for having dealt with the techniques of sociometry in such detail, it should be stressed just what promise they hold. They offer the chance to extend beyond the physical and simpler psychological studies to a point much closer to the understanding and control of the *total environment*—a concept which neces-

117

sarily includes a substantial psycho-social component. With the increasing professional interaction of behavioral and building scientists, sociometry will come to be applied not only to offices and factories but to building complexes such as in town planning and neighborhood design. This selection will have fulfilled its purpose if it has adequately introduced the subject.

NOTES

1. The head office of a large insurance company, housed in new office block.
2. The attitudinal study does not form part of this selection.
3. A reciprocated choice is where two individuals mutually choose one another.
4. An isolate is defined as a person unchosen, on the criterion of the test, by any of the other members of his group.
5. Many of the refusals were of the form "no particular preference," or "I get along quite well with most people." They are not, therefore, necessarily a refusal to co-operate but may reflect a genuine lack of strongly held preferences.

REFERENCES

1. J. Noble, The how and why of behaviour: social psychology for the architect. *Architects' J.*, **137**, 531–546 (1963).
2. P. O. M. McGirr, Environmental targets in offices and commercial premises. *Trans. Ass. Industr. Med. Offrs.*, Vol. 9, No. 3 (1959).
3. D. Lockwood, *The black-coated worker.* London: Allen & Unwin, 1958.
4. *Better Offices.* London: An Institute of Directors Publication, 1962.
5. L. Festinger, S. Schachter and K. Back, *Social pressures in informal groups: a study of human factors in housing.* London: Tavistock Publications, 1963.
6. J. T. Gullahorn, *Distance and friendship as factors in the gross interaction matrix.* In the Sociometry Reader, ed. J. L. Moreno. Glencoe: The Free Press, 1960.
7. D. M. Goodacre, Group characteristics of good and poor performing combat units. *Sociometry*, **16**, 168–178 (1953).
8. D. Cartwright and M. Herwitz, A projective method for the diagnosis of group properties. *Hum. Relat.*, **6**, 397–410 (1953).
9. M. Sherif, A study of some social factors in perception. *Arch. Psychol.*, **27**, 187 (1935).
10. M. Sherif, *The psychology of social norms.* New York: Harper & Row, 1936.
11. S. E. Asch, *Effects of group pressure upon the modification and distortion of judgments.* In Readings in Social Psychology, eds. E. E. Maccoby, T. M. Newcomb and E. L. Hartley. London: Methuen, 1959.
12. F. J. Rothlisberger and W. J. Dickson, *Management and the worker:* an account of a research program conducted by the Western Electric Company, Hawthorne Works, Chicago. Cambridge, Mass.: Harvard University Press, 1939.
13. J. L. Moreno, Who shall survive? A new approach to the problem of human interrelations. *Nervous and Mental Disease Monograph,* Washington. Series No. 58 (1934).
14. C. Selltiz, M. Jahoda, M. Deutsch and S. W. Cook, *Research methods in social relations.* London: Methuen, 1959.

15. A. Bjerstedt, The methodology of preferential sociometry. *Sociometry Monogr.* No. 37, p. 51 (1956).

16. E. Forsyth and L. Katz, A matrix approach to the analysis of sociometric data: preliminary report. *Sociometry*, 9, 340–347 (1946).

17. L. Festinger, *The analysis of sociograms using matrix algebra.* In the Sociometry Reader, ed. J. L. Moreno. Glencoe: The Free Press, 1960.

8

Architecture and Group Membership

LEON FESTINGER

The previous selection by Wells demonstrates the capacity of architecture to serve as a communications network and to generate simple forms of interaction among office workers. However, the concern of environmental designers and planners over the influence of spatial organization is usually addressed to more intensive and more enduring forms of group life. For example, much of the discussion of the consequences of spatial organization is concerned with its power to generate a sense of community, a feeling of shared values, attitudes, and beliefs; or at a still more complex level of interaction, its role in stimulating organized community action aimed at achieving a specific political goal. Furthermore, in such discussions the environments under consideration are also complex—housing projects, suburban developments, and urban neighborhoods—and the residents come from different social and cultural backgrounds and are not usually constrained to spend a good deal of time in close proximity to other people as is the usual fate of office workers.

Festinger's selection is addressed to the question of the effectiveness of architecture in determining such group structures and membership patterns in residential environments. In general he concludes that, when looked at from the perspective of complex forms of social life, the influence of spatial organization is uncertain and variable. In one of the housing developments that he and his colleagues studied, the Westgate project at M.I.T., friendship patterns were directly related to the distance between dwelling units. An active and vital group life began in the project almost as soon as the graduate student tenants moved in. The residents were enthusiastically favorable toward their environment, even in the face of its physical inconveniences and material defects. However, in another project, Regent Hill, with a similar layout and in which assignments to housing were also involuntary, social cohesion and user satisfaction were both absent. Rather than choosing to associate with each other, neighbors were hostile, and residents did not even have good relations with people in the surrounding community.

Festinger uses the experience of these two projects to discuss the factors that occasion the different responses of users to their environments. He con-

Reprinted from Leon Festinger, "Architecture and Group Membership," in *Journal of Social Issues* 7, nos. 1 and 2 (1951): 152–163. © The Society for the Psychological Study of Social Forces.

centrates on the phenomenon of homogeneity: the similarity or presumed similarity of residents in terms of their cultural values, family and child-rearing norms, and social interests. In Westgate the residents were all graduate students, already in or destined to become members of the technically educated professional upper-middle class. The tenants in Regent Hill were divided: 40 per cent were old-timers, the others had moved in after the war. The newcomers assumed that the established residents belonged to a lower social class. When the tenants of a housing community are socially heterogeneous, it is apparently not so easy to encourage social cohesion by means of spatial organization.

□

The architect and planner have traditionally concerned themselves with supplying physical convenience and satisfying physical needs. They have, for example, been able to specify minimum standards for things like the number of square feet of floor space necessary for a given size family. They have acquired a great deal of knowledge concerning arrangements of rooms for maximum convenience, arrangement of streets for easy accessibility and the like. They must now, or in the very near future, also concern themselves with supplying *social* convenience and satisfying social needs. This growing emphasis on the social consequences of architecture and city planning results from two parallel developments:

1. New housing is more and more being built in planned developments. That is, communities are being built rather than homes. The architect under these circumstances assumes the responsibility for planning much that is important for the social as well as the physical life of people.

2. Basic research on social processes, the behavior of persons in groups, and the effects of group membership has proceded far enough to show the great importance of these things in the lives of people. The problems have begun to be clearly formulated and facts have begun to emerge which can be used by the architect.

These two independent developments must be brought together. In the face of the new problems with which the architect must cope and the new responsibilities he has assumed, he cannot afford to ignore the facts, present and potential, which offer help in carrying out his task. Let us examine in detail some of the points at which the research of the social scientist on group processes has bearing on what the architect does.

121

The Importance of Group Membership

A significant aspect of our society is that persons desire membership in groups. It is extremely rare to find a person who does not seek such membership and is content to live with a minimum of social contact with other people. It is more common to find people with membership in a wide variety of different kinds of groups, both formal and informal.

The process of entering and leaving groups is a continuing one for most people. The small informal social groups to which they belong change their membership; some friends drift away and new ones are made; a person will leave a club and, perhaps, join a different one.

To understand the significance of acquiring group memberships and of belonging to groups, it is first necessary to understand why people seek membership in groups and how groups acquire power over their members.

SOURCES OF ATTRACTION TO GROUPS

Social life, interpersonal relationships, and membership in groups are important aspects of person's lives because so many goals and satisfactions are attainable most easily in groups, and in some cases, only through association with other people. The multitude of attractions which draw people into groups and into associations with others may be conveniently summarized under three general headings:

Groups frequently mediate the attainment of important individual goals. This source of attraction is recognized by groups and used to attract members. Along these lines, a club will offer different facilities for use only by recognized members. While the overt use of such attractions is generally available only to organized, formal groups, informal groups also frequently attract members because of the goals which they mediate. Thus a person who seeks to be regarded as "upper class," for example, will be strongly attracted to associations whose members are regarded as having such status. By establishing such associations he then may achieve the goal of being himself included in this category.

It is, of course, unlikely that any social group has the mediation of goals as its sole attraction. Yet the mediation of goals should be separated from the other attractions for a number of reasons. First, the attraction of group membership is not so much in sheer belonging, but rather in attaining something by means of this membership. With some types of goals the attraction to the group may cease once the goal is attained. Secondly, with respect to such sources of attraction, a specific

122

group is rarely indispensable. There will generally be other, perhaps more difficult, means of attaining these goals. Thus the group, on both these counts, holds its members on a rather tenuous basis to the extent that the mediation of personal goals is the source of attraction.

The activities in which the group engages are frequently attractive to the member. Many groups form simply on the basis of a common activity which the members like to engage in, and the attraction to this activity may remain one of the major sources of attraction to the group. Thus both formal and informal groups will form to play bridge, tennis, poker, to discuss books or political issues, to have parties and dances, and so on. Here again, it is rare to find a group where this would be the sole source of attraction. Other sources of attraction will also be present, but it seems worthwhile to distinguish this one from the others on a theoretical basis.

Generally, no single group to which a person may belong has relevance for every aspect of his life. A group such as the family has a relatively wide realm of relevance. At the other extreme, groups with exceptionally narrow realms of relevance depend primarily on the activities in which they engage to attract and hold their members. In general, the realms of relevance of such groups are identical with the activities which are the source of attraction to the group. To the extent that this is true, the group may have relatively little importance in the lives of its members.

Almost all groups are, at least in part, attractive because people have needs that can be satisfied only by personal relationships with other people. Some of these needs are friendship, approval and support from other persons, respect and prestige from those with whom one associates, and the like. We are undoubtedly not yet aware of all the personal needs that fall into this general category, nor are we aware of why such needs exist and why they are as powerful as they seem to be. There is no question, however, that they are powerful motivators of human behavior. Since satisfaction of these needs can only occur in the course of personal associations with others, belonging to groups which offer the possibility of satisfying them is virtually a necessity for most humans. Indeed, the state of loneliness, of not knowing other people and having no close personal relationships, is a state of extreme psychological hardship.

THE PROCESS OF ENTERING AND LEAVING GROUPS

Having examined the attractions to groups, we may now look at the process by which people enter and leave groups and the circumstances under which such movement takes place. It is obvious that a person will attempt to move into groups which offer the possibility of satisfying his particular needs. It is also clear that persons will attempt to move out of groups which no longer satisfy their needs or whose negative aspects outweigh the positive satisfactions of belonging to the group. Disapproval by other members, low status in the group, and other such states of affairs can produce pressure to leave the group.

Moving out of one group and into some other one is, however, not an entirely unrestricted matter. While there are some groups out of which one may move at will and some groups into which one may move with relatively little difficulty, most groups exert some restraints against their members leaving and many groups exert even greater restraints against new members entering. Formal, organized groups frequently have rules governing the admission of new members. Informal groups also have such rules which, although not formalized, are frequently even more restrictive. An additional difficulty in entering some informal groups is the lack of an easy way of making contact with the group.

We have then the simultaneous existence of forces tending to move people in and out of groups and forces restraining such movement. Groups differ in their attraction for members, and members differ in how satisfying the group membership is for them.

Groups can influence the attitudes, opinions, and behavior patterns of their members. The manner in which these influences are exerted is most often informal and subtle. The expression of some opinion receives approval or disapproval; a certain manner of behaving gains acceptance; a certain way of looking at things becomes the normal and "correct" way. When pressures for uniformity arise among the members, the group may bring about such uniformity. Since we shall elaborate some of these powers of the group in the specific context of housing, we content ourselves here with summarizing some of the conditions under which they are effective.

The extent to which the group can produce lasting change in opinions, attitudes, and behavior in its members depends on the strength of the attraction to the group, that is, on the extent to which the group satisfies the needs of its members. The force on a member to remain in the group is the force which, in a sense, he applies upon himself to accept the opinions, and behaviors of others in the group as correct.

The areas where the group most easily exerts influence correspond to those areas relevant to the functioning of the group and to those needs which the group can and does satisfy in its members. If the exertion of influence becomes an overt, formalized process, the group can extend its influence to a broader area, but as long as the influence process remains subtle, informal, and unrecognized, influence will only be exerted within the group's realm of relevance.

Groups which are difficult for the member to leave, either because the group itself erects restraints against leaving or because outsiders do not easily permit members to leave the group, can exert power over members by threats of punishment. Such power is exercised in overt and recognized manner and is effective in producing overt change in members; it may not necessarily be effective in producing changes in opinions or attitudes which are not open to public examination.

The Social Importance of Architecture

In our discussion of entering and leaving groups we have omitted one major aspect, namely, involuntary membership in groups. Many group memberships are involuntary. One is born into a certain family and ethnic group, and, be it satisfactory or not, one remains a member.

Living in a house also means involuntary membership in a group. The decisions of the architect in designing the house, in laying out the site plan for a group of houses, and in deciding who will live in the houses determine to a large extent the nature of the group memberships which will be imposed upon the residents of the houses. When a person moves into a house, his social life and the group membership that will be attributed to him by outsiders will already have been determined to some extent by these decisions.

Even within the general community in which he lives and with which he is identified by other people, the specific site plan of the group of houses in which his own is located further affects the amount and nature of his social contacts. To illustrate these effects, let us refer to a number of empirical studies.

A study of group formation (3) was conducted in a housing project built by the Massachusetts Institute of Technology for occupancy by married veteran students. The development consisted of 100 single or semi-attached small houses arranged in courts consisting of from eight to thirteen houses. Each court was a U-shaped affair with the houses facing into a grassy area; the open end of each U faced onto a street which bisected the housing project. The project was rather unusual in that a great degree of homogeneity existed among the residents, who were all married veteran students at M.I.T. There was no freedom of choice of dwelling unit within the project, since all were assigned to houses in the order in which their names appeared on the waiting list. The study in question began soon after the project was fully occupied and, consequently, was able to trace the development of friendships and informal social groups quite thoroughly.

It is a fair summary to say that two major factors affecting the friendships which developed were (a) sheer distance between houses and (b) the direction in which a house faced. Friendships developed more frequently between next-door neighbors, less frequently between people whose houses were separated by another house, and so on. As the distance between houses increased, the number of friendships fell off so rapidly that it was rare to find a friendship between persons who lived in houses that were separated by more than four or five other houses. People also tended to make friends with those whose houses faced their own. Because of the arrangement of the courts in the housing project, these two factors combined to make it easy for social groups to develop within the court and difficult for social groups to develop on any other basis. Each court in the project became a more or less cohesive group with a social life of its own. The relatively little social contact that did exist between one court and another, was almost entirely limited to contact between adjacent courts. Because of the design of the project the social groups which developed were determined by the order in which the names happened to appear on the waiting list.

There were instances in which the site plan of the project had more profound effects than merely to determine with whom one associated. Indeed, on occasion the arrangement of the houses severely limited the social life of their occupants. It will be recalled that the open end of the U of each court faced a street which bisected the project. In order to have the street appear "lived on," ten of the houses near the street had been turned so that they faced the street rather than the court area like the other houses. This apparently small change in the direction in which a house faced had a considerable effect on the lives of the people who, by accident, happened to occupy these end houses. They had less than half as many friends in the project as did those whose houses faced the court area. The consistency of this finding left no doubt that the turning of these houses toward the street had made involuntary social isolates out of the persons who lived in them.

The same study investigated the development of social groups in an adjoining project that was also maintained for married veteran students of the same school. This project consisted of thirteen apartment buildings with ten apartments in each building. Each building had two floors with five apartments in a row on each floor. The same types of effects of architecture on friendship formation were found here. Once more, sheer physical distance between apartments within the same building was a major factor determining which friendships developed. Needless to say, there were relatively few friendships between residents of different floors of the same building and even fewer between residents of different buildings. Even along the same floor of the same building, the number of friendships decreased rapidly as one went from adjoining apartments to apartments separated by one, two, or three others.

Again, slight architectural features had important effects on the social life of the apartment residents. The positions of the stairways leading to the second floor enabled the residents of some apartments to make more friends, while leaving other apartments in relative social isolation. The position of the mailboxes in each building added to the social life of the residents of the apartment near which they were located. The social activity of some residents and the relative social isolation of others could largely be traced to such minor architectural features.

Results like these have been confirmed in other kinds of communities (4, 1). Living in a certain house in a certain neighborhood determines many of a person's group memberships, not only as others see them, but also as they are actually lived. Since such group memberships have much to do with how people behave toward each other, and since these group memberships are potential sources of satisfaction for many important needs, it is important that groups formed on a relatively involuntary basis be satisfying ones. If a group which one can easily leave is unsatisfying, one may find another group which provides more satisfaction, if such a group is easily accessible. But one can not easily avoid the group memberships that come with residence in a specific location unless one is prepared to suffer relative social isolation. Social isolation or continued group membership of an unsatisfying sort can seriously affect the total context within which the person lives. We shall discuss below two studies of general housing satisfaction and social functioning as examples of the wider effects of satisfactory and unsatisfactory involuntary group memberships occasioned by living in particular housing projects.

Effects of Involuntary Group Membership in a Housing Project

AN EXAMPLE OF SATISFYING GROUP MEMBERSHIP

The previously mentioned study by Festinger, Schachter and Back, in addition to investigating the determinants of group formation, concerned itself with the social life of the residents. It was clear that the group memberships provided in the housing community were satisfying ones for the residents. This may have been because of the homogeneity and common interests of the residents; it may have been affected by the temporary nature of residence in the project and perhaps by other factors. Whatever the basis for this satisfactory group life, we have here an example of involuntary group membership which does provide the satisfactions generally desired of group membership. Let us examine the results of this state of affairs.

Social and Emotional Aspects of Living in the Project. One of the most prominent aspects of life in Westgate was the ease with which friendships formed. Most people remarked about it in the interviews, emphasizing that it was one of the most satisfactory aspects of living there. On the whole, they felt it was easy to make friends, that the friendships they had made would probably be lasting ones, and that the resulting social life was satisfactory. The following comments from Westgate residents are typical:

> *There are wonderful people in this court. We have a lot of social life and do almost everything together.*
> *We don't very often go out of Westgate for amusements. Almost all of our friends are here, and there is really so much to do here.*

About two-thirds of the residents reported that their social life was entirely or primarily within the Westgate community. More than 90 per cent of the residents felt that they had enough friends in Westgate and had as much social life as they wanted.

There were several general consequences of this. The most prominent was a general satisfaction with the homes and with living in the community. Only one or two residents expressed any desire to leave Westgate and live elsewhere. More than half of the residents were vigorous in their statements that they would not consider leaving Westgate at all.

This general satisfaction existed in spite of, and seemed to compensate for, many physical inadequacies of the houses. At the time of our study there were many physical nuisances in the houses. Some were incompletely equipped, the grounds were muddy and had not yet been landscaped, they were difficult to heat in the winter, and the like. One example of the reaction to such physical inadequacies will suffice, however, to illustrate the point. At the time of the investigation, many of the houses had trouble with the roofs. The houses were prefabricated, and many of the roofs had not been assembled properly. All the roofs have since been fixed, but in the interviews about one third of the residents reported that the roofs leaked. Any rain accompanied by a moderately strong wind would apparently raise the roof slightly, and water would pour down the walls. One family reported that in a particularly strong rain the roof had started to blow off; the husband had to go outside and hold the roof down until the wind subsided.

It is remarkable, however, that even such serious physical inconvenience did not create a strong impression on the residents. Typically the reaction was, "Oh yes, there are many things wrong with these houses, but we love it here and wouldn't want to move."

The adequate and satisfying social life was sufficient to override many inconveniences. The result was a rather happy social and psychological existence. The phenomenon may perhaps best be summed up by the expression which many of the people in Westgate used: "We're all in the same boat."

Group Action and Group Standards in the Community. There are grounds for believing that successful community action is possible only under conditions like those found in Westgate where there is considerable identification with the community, and where people find satisfying social life and want to continue to belong to the community.

One late afternoon an unoccupied building adjoining Westgate caught fire and burned down. Sparks fell on some of the closer Westgate houses, and there was much concern about the fire spreading to the project. That evening a group of tenants made plans for starting a tenant organization which would try to obtain more adequate fire protection. Once started, the tenant organization also dealt with many other aspects of life in the project, including social activities. A tenant council of representatives from each of the courts in Westgate was established, and this council continued to function fairly successfully. This spontaneous beginning of a community organization which received enough active support in the community to enable its continued successful functioning in a number of activities is rather unusual, considering the difficulty of starting such community activities in other situations.

The attitudes of the tenants toward the community organization and

129

its activities, and their active participation in the tenant organization were to a major extent determined by their small group memberships within the Westgate project. It will be recalled that the physical structure of the project was such that small social groups tended to form along court lines. Each court became a more or less cohesive social group, somewhat separated from the other groups in the project. Each of these small court groups within the project tended to react to the tenant organization as a unit. In one court all but two or three of the residents might be favorably inclined to the organization and active in its affairs. In another court all but two or three of the residents would be quite hostile to the tenant organization and would be entirely inactive with respect to its activities.

The reactions of individual residents to the tenant organization were so influenced by the small informal groups to which they belonged as to produce relative uniformity within each of these groups. Within each group the degree of uniformity depended on how attractive the group was for its members. Those groups which were very attractive to their members showed high uniformity of opinion and behavior with respect to the tenant organization. Those groups which were relatively less attractive to their members showed correspondingly less uniformity. In other words, the degree to which a group was able to influence the attitudes, opinions, and behavior of its members depended on how much the members wanted to remain in the group. These small social groups, whose specific composition derived from the architectural design of the project, were a major influence on the thinking and behavior of the residents and were important in determining the structure of the community as a whole.

With this close relationship between social life and opinions about community-wide affairs, one might also expect that persons whose opinions and behavior differed from those prevailing around them would feel the effects of this divergence in their social life within the project. This was found to be the case. Those persons within each court who could be called deviates—that is, whose attitudes toward the tenant organization or whose behavior with respect to it, differed substantially from the norm of their social group—were relatively rejected by the other members. The deviates were infrequently mentioned as close friends.

Let us summarize the results of this study. There was a good deal of social life and a resultant satisfaction with living in the project. The social groups which formed exerted influences on the relationships of members to the total community, and social relationships within the project were affected by the similarity or difference of attitudes among the residents. Some of these effects, namely, the satisfying emotional life and the power of the group to influence its members, are results that we would expect from the general considerations about group membership which were discussed earlier in this selection. Where group membership is satisfying, it tends to lose its character of involuntary membership. But whether or not group memberships in Westgate were satisfying, it would have been difficult or impossible for most residents to escape from the memberships thrust upon them as a result of living in Westgate. The fact that the memberships were satisfying was fortuitous.

A government housing project built for shipyard workers in 1942 was studied by Festinger and Kelley (2). It illustrates the effect of involuntary group membership that is not satisfying. The project consisted of 100 single and semi-attached permanent housing units. It was built in the middle of a residential area of a town about fifteen miles from a large city. At the time of the study, 1947, about 40 per cent of the population of Regent Hill were older residents who had once worked in the shipyards and had remained in the project after the end of the war. The others were persons who had moved in later during the period of acute housing shortages. The great majority of the residents keenly felt that they had been forced to live in the project by circumstances beyond their control. For those who had moved in during the war, it was the shipyards and war exigencies that had forced them to live there. For the others, it was the acute housing shortage and impossibility of finding other places to live that had made them come to Regent Hill.

The group memberships forced upon them by living in the project were resented, and attempts were made to avoid them. Many residents stated that they had not expected to like the type of person who lived in a government housing project. They expected to find the other residents rather low-class people and did not want to be forced to associate with them. Thus, irrespective of the actual potentialities which these group memberships may have had, they were unsatisfying because the residents never encouraged the development of any group life and indeed tried to dissociate themselves from the community in which they were forced to live. Let us examine the consequences of this state of affairs.

The Social and Emotional Aspects of Membership in the Regent Hill Project. The residents of the project had on the whole an inadequate social life. Indeed, for many residents the state of affairs might be described as self-imposed social isolation. Most residents reported only one or two friends in the community, and about one-fourth did not have any friends there.

There was, in addition, a surprisingly great amount of hostility expressed toward neighbors in the project. In one interview survey more than 60 per cent of those interviewed expressed belief that their neighbors were low-class people with whom it was undesirable to associate. In other words, the residents had come to the project expecting to find undesirable neighbors in "a government housing project." They feared the group memberships forced upon them; choosing between such undesirable and unsatisfying group membership and no membership at all, they tended to choose the latter.

One might expect from such a state of affairs that the residents of the project would have tended to make friends and belong to groups in the surrounding community. This, however, was not the case. While they may have desired such group membership in the surrounding community, there were a number of factors which prevented their achieving it. Since they looked down on the project and its residents, they imagined that outsiders would also have the same attitudes toward people from the project. Thus, in any contact which they had with the people in the surrounding community they strove to detach themselves from the project. This, of course, placed severe limitations on the kinds of contacts they could have with the surrounding community and severely limited the number of channels available to them for making such contacts. The result was that the project residents were also rather isolated from the surrounding town. Only about 20 per cent of the project residents were members of any town clubs or organizations. There were relatively few friendships between project residents and townspeople. Compared to residents of the surrounding community who had been living there the same length of time, the project residents were clearly in a state of relative social isolation.

We thus have practically the opposite state of affairs from that of Westgate. Instead of a full and satisfying social life there was here a very unsatisfactory state of little social life and great difficulty in achieving group memberships which had the possibility of being satisfying. As one might expect, this state of affairs generalized into attitudes toward their homes and toward the community. Most residents were dissatisfied with living in the Regent Hill project. Many wanted to leave and expressed the intention of doing so as soon as they could find a suitable place elsewhere. The physical inconveniences which did exist in the project became very important and were major sources of irritation to the residents.

Group Standards and Group Action. The investigators in this study, after assessing and attempting to diagnose the state of affairs in the Regent Hill project, tried experimentally to change the pattern of social life within the project and to change the seemingly dominant pattern of hostility among neighbors. The experiment tried to stimulate contacts among the residents by getting them to cooperate on a program of community activities. In contrast to the spontaneity and ease with which a community organization and community activities had arisen in Westgate, such a program in Regent Hill, even with the help of skilled community workers, was by no means an easy affair. Feelings of noncooperation, hostility, threatened status and prestige, and reluctance to enter into contact with other project residents all made such a program difficult to start and carry on. We do not need to dwell here on the success of the program and the changes of various kinds that were created. The point we wish to make is that, in the absence of real need-satisfaction from the group memberships, the whole context of social and personal life was adversely affected.

In the preceding pages we have done little more than indicate in general the contribution which present and potential knowledge in the area of group membership and group life can make to the field of housing. It is clear that group membership has a very important place in the lives of people. It is also clear that the decisions of the architect, planner, or housing administrator will affect group memberships and, directly or indirectly, the total context of the lives of the people. We have described an instance in which the design of the houses and the physical and spatial relations among houses had an important influence on the formation of social groups. We have also described instances in which these involuntary group memberships were satisfying and others in which they were not satisfying. This difference in satisfaction affected the social life within the community and the satisfaction with living in the houses.

With the aid of a vigorous program of research we can learn much more about these phenomena. Before the social psychologist can materially affect the decisions of the architect and the planner, it is necessary to accumulate this additional knowledge. How do architectural design and site planning variations affect social intercourse among people? What kinds of social interactions exist among neighbors in a community? How does the nature of the group memberships affect family living patterns and other aspects of the functioning of individuals? How do the characteristics of the residents—their interests, backgrounds, anticipations of permanency, and the like—affect the formation and functioning of community groups? And how do community facilities interact with these other factors?

Many more questions like these can be asked, and they can be phrased specifically enough so that answers can be obtained. The more of these questions we answer, the more we will be able to build houses and communities which provide for people the satisfactory social and private lives we would like to see.

REFERENCES

1. Caplow, Theodore, and Forman, R. "Neighborhood interaction in a homogeneous community," *American Sociological Review,* 1950 **15**, 357–366.

2. Festinger, Leon, and Kelley, Harold H. *Changing Attitudes through Social Contact: An Experimental Study of a Housing Project.* Ann Arbor, Research Center for Group Dynamics, Institute for Social Research, University of Michigan, 1951.

3. Festinger, Leon, Schachter, Stanley, and Back, Kurt. *Social Pressures in Informal Groups.* New York: Harper & Brothers, 1950.

4. Merton, Robert K. "The social psychology of housing," in Dennis, W., ed., *Current Trends in Social Psychology.* Pittsburgh: University of Pittsburgh Press, 1948.

9

Silent Assumptions in Social Communication

EDWARD T. HALL

Any consideration of the influence of spatial organization on social interaction inevitably recalls developments in the field of "proxemics." Hall, who is the major inventor and exponent of this field, defines proxemics in the following selection as "the study of ways in which man gains knowledge of the content of other men's minds through judgments of behavior patterns associated with varying degrees of proximity to him."

Proxemics is usually of interest to architects and designers because it emphasizes the concept that spatial distance is a "silent language" through which men unwittingly convey attitudes, feelings, and judgments about their fellows. This emphasis fits naturally with the wish of architects to find in the behavioral sciences evidence that design variables are objectively meaningful.

In the context of the issues discussed in this section, proxemics has other significance. First, it provides a useful typology of distances, defined in terms of the kind of information or sentiment being communicated. Hall identifies four classes of distance, or as he calls them distance-sets: intimate, casual-personal, social-consultative, and public. Second, and this is really the obverse of the previous point, proxemics suggests that in order for certain sentiments to be communicated successfully, people must be located in particular degrees of proximity to each other. For example, the communication of the sentiment of love demands closer proximity than the expression of respect. Third, a model is developed for locating the mechanisms available for the exchange of particular kinds of messages at specific distance sets. These mechanisms are sensory and involve tactile-kinesthetic, visual, olfactory, heat-radiation, and oral-aural sensory systems. Finally, the proxemics approach indicates that the reliance on these mechanisms at any particular distance is culturally determined. Thus, according to Hall, Americans rely on eye contact to define a particular distance as an intimate distance, but presumably depend less than other people on olfactory and heat-radiation systems for this purpose.

Although the insights of proxemics suggest a relationship between its concerns and our understanding of how spatial organization influences social interaction, the ideas available in this field have unfortunately not really

Reprinted from Edward T. Hall, "Silent Assumptions in Social Communication," in *Disorders of Communication*, Research Publications, Association for Research in Nervous and Mental Disease 42 (1964): 41–55.

been applied in site planning, office design, or any of the other fields in which spatial organization is an important design factor. It would be interesting to know, for example, whether user response to high or low density housing and the capability of people in different societies to form viable communities in these settings bear any relation to cultural definitions of the kind of communication and interaction appropriate to different distances.

□

The investigations reported briefly in this selection deal with *proxemics,* the study of ways in which man gains knowledge of the content of other men's minds through judgments of behavior patterns associated with varying degrees of proximity to him. These behavior patterns are learned, and thus they are not genetically determined. But because they are learned (and taught) largely outside awareness, they are often treated as though they were innate. I have found this type of behavior to be highly stereotyped, less subject to distortion than consciously controlled behavior and important to individuals in the judgments they form as to what is taking place around them at any given moment in time.

Thoreau wrote *Walden* (1) over 100 years ago. Yet in a section entitled "Visitors" he describes how conversational distance and subject matter are functions of each other and, what is even more remarkable, he names some of the variables by means of which people unconsciously set distances.

One inconvenience I sometimes experienced in so small a house, is the difficulty of getting to a sufficient distance from my guest when we began to utter the big thoughts in big words. You want room for your thoughts to get into sailing trim and run a course or two before they make their port. The bullet of your thought must have overcome its lateral and ricochet motion and fallen into its last and steady course before it reaches the ear of the hearer, else it may plough out again through the side of his head. Also our sentences wanted room to unfold and form their columns in the interval. Individuals, like nations, must have suitable broad and natural boundaries, even a considerable neutral ground, between them. I have found it a singular luxury to talk across the pond to a companion on the opposite side. In my house we were so near that we could not begin to hear—we could not speak low enough to be heard; as when you throw two stones into calm water so near that they break each other's undulations. If we are merely loquacious and loud talkers, then we can afford to stand very near together, cheek by jowl, and feel each other's breath; but if we speak reservedly and thoughtfully we want to be farther apart, that all animal heat and moisture may have a chance to evaporate. If we would enjoy the most intimate society with that in each of us which is without, or above, being spoken to, we must not only be silent, but commonly so far apart bodily that we cannot possibly hear each other's voice in any case. Referred to this standard, speech is for the convenience of those who are hard of hearing; but there are many fine things which we cannot say if we have to shout. As the conversation began to assume a loftier and grander tone, we gradually shoved our chairs farther apart till they touched the wall in opposite corners, and then commonly there was not room enough.

The insights and sensitive observations of Thoreau are helpful in pointing up certain consistencies in behavior in heretofore unsuspected areas, such as perceptions of body heat. They strengthened my original premise that man's behavior in space is neither meaningless nor haphazard. Yet there are paradoxes associated with proxemic behavior that need explaining.

Some Paradoxes

A casual observer confronted with American reactions to being touched or approached too closely by foreigners is likely to dismiss such reactions as minor annoyances that will disappear as people get to know each other better. More careful investigation reveals, however, several puzzling questions, or anomalies, which suggest that there is more to behavior patterns based on interpersonal distance than meets the eye.

An anthropologist becomes accustomed to resistance to and denial of the idea that there are regularities in human behavior over which the individual has little or no control. But why do so many people, when faced with other people's behavior, take "interference" with space patterns so personally? And why is there apparently so little that they can do to relieve their feelings?

One of my interview subjects, a colleague, quite typically explained that, after 12 years of working with French culture, he still could not accustom himself to the French conversational distance. He found it "uncomfortably" close, and he found himself annoyed with Frenchmen, possibly because he felt they were getting too familiar. Like other Americans who have been brought up to resent being crowded, he used the device of barricading himself behind his desk.

Another anomaly is associated with architecture. Why is it that, even with a history of building dating back to predynastic Egypt, with surveying developed somewhere around 2500 B.C. and with the magnificence of the Parthenon achieved by the fifth century before Christ, architects have failed to develop a way of describing the experience of space? Recently Philip Thiel (2) published a notation system for describing open spaces.

By what means do people make spatial distinctions? How do people judge distance from each other and teach it to their young with such uniformity and still apparently not know that they are teaching it at all? Technically the work of transactional psychologists answered some questions and raised others (3), while Gibson's approach (4) is the most comprehensive treatment of how man perceives space visually. Asking subjects how they differentiate between distances or why they feel so strongly about matters of space, doesn't help—even the most cooperative subjects can give you only bits of information. Most people have only the vaguest notion of the rules governing the use of their immediate and distant receptors.

In approaching any new problem, the anthropologist must constantly remind himself that, even though he is faced with complexity on all sides, the components that go to make up the complexity must of necessity not be overly complex. Cultural systems are organized in such a way that the basic components (structure points) can be controlled by all *normal* members of the group. For example, varied and rich as languages are, all normal members of a group learn to speak and understand them.

In essence, one looks for simple distinctions that can be made by any normal person and that go beyond individual differences.

This is a report of a study in progress. Additional data will undoubtedly result in revisions. If the data seem obvious, I can only say that to me they seemed obvious *after* I had identified the principal structure points of the system. Then I wondered why it had taken so long to reach this particular point. Recently Bruner (5) stressed something the linguistic scientist has known for a long time: that people do not necessarily have to know the structure of a system of behavior in order to control it.

Research Strategy

A combination of research strategies was employed during this study. Techniques included observation, participant's observations, interviews—structured and unstructured—and biweekly sessions with four blind subjects.[1] Normal subjects were drawn predominantly from the Washington area from the educated-professional group. Fifteen Americans and 18 foreign subjects were interviewed in depth. Interviews lasted from 3 to 15 hours in units of 2 to 3 hours. Data were gathered from 100 additional subjects in unstructured, natural situations. Foreign subjects included English, French, German, Swiss, Dutch, Spanish, Arab, Armenian, Greek and West Africans studying in the United States. These subjects were used in much the same way as subjects are used by the linguist, *i.e.*, as examples of their own particular systems. A few hours with one subject does little more than provide some of the basic and most obvious structure points as well as contrasting examples of proxemic behavior.

Since people apparently cannot describe the patterns that enable them to discriminate between one distance and another, it is next to useless to question them directly about how they go about perceiving spatial relations. It has been necessary to resort to various projective-type devices as a means of getting subjects started thinking about their own spatial experiences. Some of the most valuable leads were gathered as a result of casual conversations when a subject would "warm up" and begin talking about an experience he had had with a particular person.

"Boy, you ought to see a guy we have in our office; everybody talks about it. They even kid him a lot. He comes right up to you, breathes in your face. I sure don't like seeing his face so close, with pop eyes and nose distorted all over the place. He feels you a lot, too. Sometimes we wonder if there isn't something wrong with him."

"He breathes down my neck; why can't he keep his hands off you?"

"Did you ever notice how close he stands to you—it gives me the willies."

"She's one of those who's always pawing you; did you ever notice how some people stand much too close?"

Many of these utterances are virtually stream-of-consciousness. They are valuable because they provide clues to what specific events in other people's behavior stand out as significant.

The Arabs and the English complain (for different reasons) because Americans do not listen. Greeks experience a great flatness in our interaction with them—like eating unsalted rice, they say. In each complaint there lie valuable data concerning the nature of the feedback mechanisms used by *both* parties.

In research of this sort one is faced with a paradox, namely, it is the commonplace that makes the difference when confronted with someone else's "commonplace." Another paradox is that, in writing and talking about one's reactions to being touched and breathed upon by a stranger, the description loses much of the immediate effect. The reactions are so obscure, so small and so seemingly inconsequential that at times it is difficult to realize they may add up to something.

The distinction that Hediger (6) makes between "contact" and "non-contact" species can also be made for man or groups of men. Indeed, it seems to be the first and possibly the most basic distinction between groups.

As the term implies, the "contact" group is characterized by considerable touching, both in private and public. The "non-contact" group perceives the contact group as overly familiar and sometimes "pushy," while the contact group refers to the non-contact as "standoffish," "high-hat," "cold," or "aloof."

In addition to the contact, non-contact category, man seems to share a number of features of the generalized mammalian pattern described by Hediger (6). Personal distance and social distance are certainly present though—inasmuch as a certain amount of confusion exists because of misunderstanding of Hediger's terminology—it may eventually become necessary to define operationally what is meant by these terms. The observations which follow refer to the non-contact group.

Distance Sets

For the American non-contact group, and possibly for others as well, four distance sets seem to encompass most, if not all, behavior in which more than one person is involved. These are referred to as intimate, casual-personal, social-consultative and public. Each distance set is characterized by a close and a far phase.

The perception of distance and closeness apparently is the result of an interplay of the distant and immediate receptor systems (visual, auditory, olfactory), the systems in the skin that record touch and heat flow and those in the muscles that feed back information concerning where a part of the body is at any given moment in time. *The transition from one group of receptors to another is the boundary point between distance sets,* as will be shown subsequently.

For Americans, space judgments seem to depend principally on the tactile-kinesthetic and visual senses, although the olfactory, heat-radiation and oral-aural systems are also involved.

The two most commonly observed sets are *casual-personal distance* and *social-consultative distance.*[2] The descriptions which follow are idealized stereotypes for subjects in non-excited or non-depressed states with 20–20 vision, without excessive background noise, and at average comfortable temperature (55° to 85° F.).

SOCIAL-CONSULTATIVE DISTANCE

The distinguishing features of this distance (close phase: 4 to 7 feet plus or minus 6 inches at each end; far phase: 7 to 12 feet plus or minus 6 inches at each end) are that intimate visual detail in the face is not perceived and that nobody touches or expects to touch unless there is some special effort. Voice level is normal for Americans. There is little change between the far and the close phases, and conversations can be overheard at a distance of up to 20 feet. (There is no loudness scale for the voice that is adaptable to descriptions such as these.)

I have observed that in over-all loudness, the American voice at these distances is under that of the Arab, the Spaniard, the South Asian Indian and the Russian; and it is somewhat above that of the English upper class, the Southeast Asian and the Japanese.

Close Phase: Social-Consultative Distance. The boundary between social-consultative and casual-personal distance lies at a point just beyond where the extended arms can no longer touch (4 to 7 feet).

Foveal vision (area of sharpest focus of the eye) at 4 feet covers an area of just a little larger than one eye (Table 9–1); at 7 feet the area of sharp focus extends to nose and parts of eyes, or mouth; eye and nose are sharply seen. In many Americans, this sharp vision shifts back and forth, or around the face. Details of skin texture and hair are clearly perceived. At 60° visual angle, head, shoulders, and upper trunk are seen at 4 feet distance; the same sweep includes the whole figure at 7 feet. Feet are seen peripherally, even if standing. Head size is perceived as normal. As one moves away from the subject, the foveal area can take in an ever-increasing amount.

A good deal of impersonal business takes place at this distance. In the close phase there is much greater implication of involvement than in the distant phase. People who work together a good deal tend to use close social-consultative distance. It is also a very common distance for people who are attending a casual social gathering.

Looking down at a person at this distance is to dominate him almost completely, as when a man talks to his secretary or receptionist on leaving or entering the office.

Distant Phase: Social-Consultative Distance. Business and social discourse conducted at this distance (7 to 12 feet) has a more formal character than in the close phase. Desks in offices of "important" people are large enough to hold anyone at this distance. In most instances, even with more or less standard desks, the chair opposite the desk is at about 8 or 9 feet from the man behind the desk.

141

TABLE 9-1

Areas Covered at Eight Distances by Four Visual Angles

Distances		Visual Angles			
		1°*	15° X 3°†	60° Sweep‡	180°
Intimate					
	6"	0.1"	2.5" X 0.3" eye, mouth	6" the face	head and shoulders
	18"	0.3" central iris	3.75 X 1" upper or lower face	18" head	upper body and arms
Casual- Personal					
Close	30"	0.5" tip of nose	6.25" X 1.5" upper or lower face	30" head, shoulders	whole figure
Far	48"	0.8" one eye	10" X 2.5" upper or lower face	48" waist up	
Social Con- sultative					
Close	7'	1.7" mouth, eye plus nose; nose plus parts of eye	20" X 5" the face	7' whole figure	
Far	12'	2.5" two eyes	31" X 7.5" faces of two people	12' figure w/ space around it	
Public					
	30'	6.3" the face	6'3" torso of 4 or 5 people	30'	
	340'	6'			
	500'	9'			
	1500'	26'			

*Computed to nearest 0.1 inch.
†Computed to nearest 0.25 inch.
‡Varies with culture.

At social-consultative distance, the finest details of the face, such as the capillaries in the eyes, are lost. Otherwise skin texture, hair, condition of teeth and condition of clothes are all readily visible. Neither heat nor odor from another person's body is apparently detectable at this distance. At least, none of my subjects mentioned either factor.

The full figure—with a good deal of space around it—is encompassed in a 60° angle. This is the distance which people move to when someone says "Stand away so I can look at you." Also, at around 12 feet, accommodation convergence ceases (4, 8); the eyes and the mouth are contained in the area of sharp vision so that it is not necessary to

142

shift the eyes to take in the face. During conversations of any significant length, visual contact has to be maintained and subjects will peer
around intervening objects.

If one person is standing and another seated, the seated person may
push his or her chair back to about 12 feet in order to reduce the tilt
of the head. Several subjects mentioned that "looking up" accentuated
the higher status of the other person. In the days of servants it was
taken for granted that none would approach a seated employer so close
as to make him look up. Today it may be that motorcycle policemen
use the device of resting one foot on a running board and looking
down on an offender as a way of increasing their psychological lever-
age. Judges' benches often accentuate differences in elevation.

The voice level is noticeably louder than for the close phase and can
usually be heard easily in an adjoining room if the door is open. As the
term implies, social-consultative distance is employed for professional
and social transactions as long as there is an emotionally neutral effect.
Raising the voice or shouting can have the effect of reducing social-
consultative distance to personal distance.

I have observed some interviews start at the far end of this scale and
move in; in others this process is reversed.

One of the functions of this distance is to provide for flexibility of
involvement so that people can come and go without having to talk.[3]
A receptionist in an office can usually work quite comfortably if she is
10 or more feet from people waiting to see her boss; if she is any closer,
she will feel she should talk to those waiting.

A husband coming back from work often finds himself sitting and
relaxing reading the paper at 10 or more feet from his wife. He may
also discover that his wife has arranged the furniture back-to-back (a
favorite device of the cartoonist, Chick Young, creator of *Blondie*). The
back-to-back arrangement is an appropriate solution to minimum space,
or a shortage of reading lights.

The social-consultative distance has the advantage of permitting an
easy shifting back and forth between one's activity and whoever else is
in the room. Participation with others at this distance is spotty and
brief. Questions and answers and introductory or opening remarks are
what one hears most often. Likewise, it is easy for one of several participants to disengage himself without offending.

CASUAL-PERSONAL DISTANCE

"Personal distance" (close phase: 18 to 30 inches; far phase: 30 to 48
inches) is the term originally used by Hediger to designate the distance

consistently separating the members of non-contact species. It might be thought of as a small protective sphere that an organism maintains between itself and others (6).

Far Phase: Casual-Personal Distance. Keeping someone "at arm's length" is one way of expressing this distance (2½ to 4 feet). It begins at a point that is just outside easy touching distance on the part of one person to a point where two can touch easily if they extend both arms.

Details of subject's features are clearly visible. Fine detail of skin, gray hair, "sleep" in eye and cleanliness of teeth are easily seen. Head size is perceived as normal.

Foveal vision covers only an area the size of the tip of the nose or one eye, so that the gaze must wander around the face; 15° clear vision covers the upper *or* lower face. Details of clothing—frayed spots, small wrinkles or dirt on cuffs—can be seen easily; 180° peripheral vision takes in the hands and the whole body of a seated person. Movement of the hands is detected, but fingers cannot be counted.

The voice is moderately low to soft.

No body heat is perceptible. The olfactory factor is not normally present for Americans. Breath odor can sometimes be detected at this distance, but Americans are trained to direct it away from others.

The boundary line between the far phase of the casual-personal distance and the close phase of social-consultative distance marks, in the words of one subject, "the limit of domination."

This is the limit of physical domination in the very real sense, for beyond it, a person cannot easily get his hands on someone else. Subjects of personal interest and involvement are talked about at this distance.

For a woman to permit a man inside the close personal zone when they are by themselves makes her body available to touch. Failure to withdraw signifies willingness to submit to touching.[4]

Close Phase: Casual-Personal Distance. There appears to be a distinct shift from the far phase to the close phase of casual-personal distance (1½ to 2½ feet). The distance roughly is only half that of the former. Olfaction begins to enter in, as well as heat gain and loss from the other person. The kinesthetic sense of closeness derives from the possibilities that are opening up in regard to what each participant can do to or with the other's body. At this distance one can hold or grasp the extremities.

A visual angle of 15° (clear vision) takes in the upper or lower face which is seen with exceptional clarity. The planes of the face and its

144

roundness are accentuated; the nose projects and the ears recede; fine hair of the face and back of neck, eyelashes and hair in nose, ears and pores are clearly visible.

This is as close as one can get without real distortions of the features. In fact, it is the distortion and the enlargement of the features that one encounters in the next closer zone—the intimate—that make it intimate.

INTIMATE DISTANCE

At intimate distance (full contact to 18 inches), two subjects are deeply involved with each other. The presence of the other person is unmistakable and may at times be overwhelming because of the greatly stepped-up sensory inputs. Olfaction, heat from the other person's body, touch or the possibility of touch, not only by the hands but also by the lips and the breath, all combine to signal in unmistakable ways the close presence of another body.

Far Phase: Intimate Distance. Hands can reach and grasp extremities but, because of the space between the bodies (6 to 18 inches), there is some awkwardness in caressing. The head is seen as enlarged in size and its features are distorted.

Ability to focus the eye easily is an important feature of this distance for Americans.[5]

In foveal vision the iris of the eye is enlarged over life size. Small blood vessels in the sclera are seen. Pores are enlarged. This is the distance at which personal services, such as removal of splinters, are provided. In apes it is the "grooming distance."

Fifteen-degree clear vision includes the upper or lower portion of the face which is perceived as enlarged. When looking at the eye, the nose is overlarge, distorted and exaggerated. So are other features, such as lips, teeth and tongue. During conversations, the hands tend to come in and move up toward the face so they will be included in the peripheral field.

Peripheral vision, 180°, includes the outline of head and shoulders and very often, hands.

The voice is normally held at a low level, and Joos' "intimate style" (9) prevails.[6]

Heat as well as odor of breath may be detected, even though it is directed away from the subject's face. Heat loss or gain from the other person's body begins to be noticed by some subjects if their attention is directed to heat.

145

Sensory input from all previously used sources has been stepped up considerably. New channels (such as the olfactory) are just beginning to come into play.

Close Phase: Intimate Distance. This is the distance (full contact to 6 plus or minus 2 inches) of lovemaking and wrestling, comforting and protecting. Physical contact is featured. Use of the distance receptors is greatly reduced except for olfaction and sensitivity to radiant heat, both of which are stepped up.

Vocalization at intimate distances plays a very minor part in the communications process, which is carried mainly by other channels. A whisper has the effect of expanding the distance. The moans, groans and grunts that escape involuntarily during fighting or sex are produced by the action. The two parties act as one as it were.

In the most close (maximum contact) phase, the muscles communicate. Pelvis, thighs and head can be brought into play, arms can encircle. Except at the outer limits, sharp vision is blurred at this distance, although this is not true of the highly plastic eye of the very young or or the extraordinarily nearsighted.

Much of the physical discomfort that Americans experience when others are inappropriately inside the intimate sphere is expressed as distortions of the visual system. One subject said in regard to people that got "too close"—"these people get so close, you're crosseyed! It really makes me nervous they put their face so close it feels like they're *inside you.*"

The expressions, "get your face out of mine," and "he shook his fist in my face" apparently express how many Americans perceive their body boundaries. That is, there is a transition between inside and the outside. At that point where sharp focus is lost, one feels the uncomfortable muscular sensation of being crosseyed from looking at something too close.

When close vision is possible within the intimate range—as with the young—the image is greatly enlarged and stimulates a significant portion (if not the total) of the retina. The detail that one sees at this distance is extraordinary. This, plus the felt pull of the eye muscles, structures the visual experience in such a way that it cannot be confused with the less intense personal, social-consultative and public distances.

Intimate distance is not favored in public among the American middle class. However, it is possible to observe the young in automobiles and on beaches using intimate distances. Crowded subways and buses may bring strangers into what would ordinarily be coded as intimate spatial relations, if it were not for several characteristically isolating compensatory devices. The correct behavior is to be as immobile as possible and, when part of the trunk or extremities contact another, to withdraw if possible. If this is not possible, the muscles in the affected area are kept tense. For members of the non-contact group it is taboo to relax and enjoy the contact. In crowded elevators the hands are kept at the side or used to steady the body by grasping railings and overhead straps. The eyes are fixed at infinity and should not be brought to bear on anyone for more than a passing glance. Men who take advantage of the crowded situation in order to feel or pinch women violate an important cultural norm dealing with the privacy of the body and the right of a person to grant or withhold from others access to it. Middle Eastern subjects do not express the outraged reactions to palpation in public places that one encounters among the non-contact American group.

PUBLIC DISTANCE: OUTSIDE THE CIRCLE OF INVOLVEMENT

Several important shifts occur in the transition from the personal, consultative and social distances to public distances (close phase: 12 feet to 25 feet plus or minus 5 feet; far phase: 30 feet to maximum carrying distance of voice).

Close Phase: Public Distance. In this phase of public distance (12 to 25 feet) participants cannot touch or pass objects to each other. Possibly some form of flight reaction may be present subliminally. At 12 feet an alert subject can take evasive or defensive action if a threatening move is made.

The voice is loud but not full volume. Rice (10) suggests that choice of words and phrasing of sentences is much more careful and there may be grammatical (or syntactic) shifts that differentiate speech at this distance from that at closer, less formal distances. Joos' choice of the term "formal style" (9) is appropriately descriptive: "formal texts . . . demand advance planning . . . the speaker is correctly said to think on his feet."

Because angular accommodation of the eyes is no longer necessary, there is an absence of feedback from the ocular muscles. The angle of sharpest vision (1°) covers the whole face. Fine details of the skin and eyes are no longer visible. The color of the eyes begins to be imperceivable (at 16 feet only the whites of the eyes are visible). Also at 16 feet the body begins to lose its roundness and to look flat.

Head size is perceived as considerably under life size. The 15° cone of clear vision includes the faces of two people (at 12 feet), 60° the

147

whole body with a little space around it. Peripheral vision includes other persons if they are present.

Far Phase: Public Distance. The far phase of public distance begins somewhere around 30 feet. It is the distance that is automatically set around important public figures. White's description of the spatial treatment accorded John F. Kennedy when his nomination became certain is an excellent example:

> *Kennedy loped into the cottage with his light, dancing step, as young and lithe as springtime, and called a greeting to those who stood in his way. Then he seemed to slip from them as he descended the steps of the split-level cottage to a corner where his brother Bobby and brother-in-law Sargent Shriver were chatting, waiting for him. The others in the room surged forward on impulse to join him. Then they halted. A distance of perhaps 30' separated them from him, but it was impassable. They stood apart, these older men of long-established power, and watched him. He turned after a few minutes, saw them watching him, and whispered to his brother-in-law. Shriver now crossed the separating space to invite them over. First Averell Harriman; then Dick Daley; then Mike DiSalle; then, one by one, let them all congratulate him. Yet no one could pass the little open distance between him and them uninvited, because there was this thin separation about him, and the knowledge they were there not as his patrons but as his clients. They could come by invitation only, for this might be a President of the United States (11).*

At this distance body stance and gestures are featured; facial expression becomes exaggerated as does the loudness of the voice. The tempo of the voice drops; words are enunciated more clearly. Joos' *frozen style* (9) is characteristic: "Frozen style is for people who are to remain strangers." The whole man may be perceived as *quite small* and he is *in a setting.* Foveal vision takes in more and more of the man until he is entirely within the small cone of sharpest vision. At this point, contact with him as a human being begins to diminish.

The 60° cone of vision takes in the setting. Peripheral vision seems to have as its principal function the alerting of the individual to movement at the side, which may represent danger.

Meaning and Distance

What significance do people attach to different distances? The very term "closeness" conjures up different images than "distance." "Getting *next to*" someone implies a number of things about your relationship. The expression, "I can't get together with him on that," has a literal, in addition to a figurative, meaning. In the world of actions from which words take their meaning, a wife who sees another woman standing too close to her husband gets the message loud and clear.

For that matter, anyone confronted with a person whose space pattern varies from his own, finds himself asking the following questions: Who does this man think he is? What is he trying to say? Is he trying to push me around, or why does he have to be so familiar?

Yet one of the first things one discovers in this research is that very similar spatial relationships can have entirely different meanings. What one makes of how others treat him in space is determined by one's ethnic past. This is *not* a matter, however, of generalizing about Latinos' standing closer than North Americans, of moving each space zone up a notch as it were. Rather it is a matter of entirely different systems, in which some items are shared but many others are not, including the order and selection of transactions that occur in the different distance sets (12). Thus, it does not necessarily imply any existing or intended relationship if an Arab walks up and places himself inside one's personal sphere in a public place. It may only mean that he wants the spot you are standing on for himself. Since there is no relationship or chance of one, he does not care what you think. The point, however, is so basic and so subtle that it is apt to be lost.

Summary

This selection has dealt with some rather specific aspects of how we gain knowledge as to the content of the minds of other men by means which function almost totally outside awareness. Proxemics represents one of several such out-of-awareness systems which fall within the general rubric of paracommunication.[7]

Communication of this sort, operating outside awareness as it does, appears to be an extraordinarily persistent form of culturally specific behavior which is responded to with considerable effect whenever people encounter patterns which are at variance with their own. It is also apparently a rather basic form of communication, many features of which are shared with other vertebrates.

How man codes distance is a function of which combinations of receptors he uses. These do not always seem to be the same from culture to culture and vary even within subcultures. Visual and kinesthetic cues are prominent in non-contact Americans. Olfactory and tactile cues are emphasized in Eastern Mediterranean urban Arab culture.

Recording of cues used to distinguish one distance from another is possible. It should be noted however, that proxemic research is in its infancy and suffers from many obvious flaws. This report represents a summary of some of what has been accomplished to date rather than a definitive statement of the field.

NOTES

1. These sessions were conducted in cooperation with Dr. Warren Brodey of the Washington School of Psychiatry in the winter of 1961 to 1962.
2. Not to be confused with "social distance," a term used by both Hediger (6) and Bogardus (7). "Social-consultative distance" as used here is not at all like Bogardus' "social distance," which is the distance separating two members of a group in a social hierarchy. It is much closer in meaning to Hediger's term "social distance."
3. In other countries the circle of involvement cannot be counted on to be the same as in the United States.
4. One female subject from a Mediterranean country repeatedly miscued American men who misinterpreted her failure to respond quickly (virtually with reflex speed) to a reduction in distance from *personal* to *close-personal*.
5. American Optical Company Phoroptor Test Card no. 1985-IA (20–20 vision at 0.37 M.) was used to test subjects in a variety of situations including subjects chosen from audiences during lectures. The distance at which the smallest type (0.37 M.) could be read was in all cases the same distance at which the investigator was told that he was now "too close." Twenty diopter lenses fitted to the eye reduced this distance from 15 inches to 19 inches to as little as 7 inches. Subjects were chosen in the 35- to 45-year age bracket. Two subjects with presbyopia failed to respond in this way. With them sharp vision ceased to be featured in the intimate zone.
6. ". . . an intimate utterance pointedly avoids giving the addressee information from outside of the speaker's skin. The point . . . is simply to remind (hardly 'inform') the addressee of some feeling . . . inside the speaker's skin."
7. "Paracommunication" is the term suggested as an appropriate designation by Joos (9) and George Trager (13) to refer to communicative behavior which does not have its base in language but is often synchronized with linguistic and paralinguistic phenomena.

REFERENCES

1. Thoreau, H. D.: Walden. The Macmillan Company, New York, 1929.
2. Thiel, P.: A sequence-experience notation for architectural and urban space. Town Planning Review, April 1961.
3. Kilpatrick, F. P., ed.: Explorations in Transactional Psychology. New York University Press, New York, 1961.
4. Gibson, J. J.: The Perception of the Visual World. The Riverside Press, Cambridge, 1950.
5. Bruner, J.: The Process of Education. Harvard University Press, Cambridge, Mass., 1959.
6. Hediger, H.: Studies of the Psychology and Behavior of Captive Animals in Zoos and Circuses. Butterworth Scientific Series, London, 1955.
7. Bogardus, E. S.: Social Distance. Antioch Press, Yellow Springs, Ohio, 1959.
8. Whitcomb, M.: Vision Committee, National Academy of Sciences, personal communication.

9. Joos. M.: The five clocks. Internat. J. Am. Linguistics, April, 1962.

10. Rice, F.: Institute for Applied Linguistic Research, personal communication.

11. White, T. H.: The Making of the President 1960. Atheneum Publishers, New York, 1961. (Reprinted by permission of the publisher.)

12. Hall, E. T.: Sensitivity and Empathy at Home and Abroad. Three Leather-bee Lectures, given at Harvard University Graduate School of Business Administration, Boston, Spring, 1962.

13. Trager, G. L.: Paralanguage: a first approximation. Stud. Linguistics, 13: 1–12, 1958.

10

The Social Psychology
of Privacy

BARRY SCHWARTZ

The concern for the impact of architecture on group cohesion, community development, and worker morale first emerged in the late nineteenth century in response to growing public anxiety over the violence and disorder of urbanized society. Higher population densities, the destruction of peasant and farm life, and the separation of home and work were seen as forces that were breaking up the basic social relationships that held cities together. Garden city planners, utopian architects, industrial technocrats—all made proposals for the organization of the physical environment that they hoped would restore the social bond.

In recent decades a new emphasis has emerged in urban design theory, namely a concern with preserving individuality and protecting people from the conformist pressures of group life. This emphasis is a response to the later stages of industrial society, which, with its mass culture and electronic media and surveillance systems, has an unprecedented technological power to invade privacy and destroy political liberty. In terms of design this concern takes the form of plans that promise to achieve a proper balance between community *and* privacy. Whereas garden city theorists aimed to provide village greens and open spaces to be used and maintained by all the residents of a neighborhood unit, the fashion now is to pay equal attention to private space. In the most sophisticated designs, a gradient of spaces is often proposed, starting with private spaces contiguous to the dwelling unit, going on to semiprivate spaces, under the control of immediate neighbors, and ending with public spaces, available to the surrounding community. (Alexander's selection in Part Five discusses an example of such a design scheme.)

Schwartz's essay shows that designing in terms of both community and privacy is based on sound sociological theory. He makes the point that privacy has important positive functions in personality development and that the chance to withdraw from the group also makes the individual more effective when he returns to active participation in group life. His selection discusses numerous examples from the research literature to indicate that when privacy disappears the maintenance of harmonious social relations

Reprinted from Barry Schwartz, "The Social Psychology of Privacy," *American Journal of Sociology* 73 (May 1968): 741–752. Reprinted by permission of the University of Chicago Press.

among peers is threatened, and that it is also essential for the preservation of authority and efficiency in social structures that are organized on hierarchical principles. However, the special relevance of Schwartz's discussion to this volume lies in his conviction that the physical environment plays an important mediating role in satisfying the dual and sometimes opposing demands of individuals and groups for both community and privacy. Schwartz describes the different kinds of environmental barriers that are developed in social situations, the functions of particular types of doors and windows as screening or transmission devices, and the elaborate ways in which institutions formulate social rules and conventions to govern the use of walls and barriers in private and public situations.

☐

Patterns of coming and staying together imply counterpatterns of withdrawal and disaffiliation which, as modalities of action, are worthy of analysis in their own right.[1] Simmel makes the identical point in his essay, "Brücke und Tür":

Usually we only perceive as bound that which we have first isolated in some way. If things are to be joined they must first be separated. Practically as well as logically it would be nonsense to speak of binding that which is not separate in its own sense. . . . Directly as well as symbolically, bodily as well as spiritually, we are continually separating our bonds and binding our separations.[2]

Simmel, however, ignores the question of how separation subserves integration—of how men are bound by taking leave of one another as well as by their coming together. One sociologically relevant approach to this problem is through the analysis of privacy, which is a highly institutionalized mode of withdrawal.

The Group-Preserving Functions of Privacy

Withdrawal into privacy is often a means of making life with an unbearable (or sporadically unbearable) person possible. If the distraction and relief of privacy were not available in such a case, the relationship would have to be terminated if conflict were to be avoided. Excessive contact is the condition under which Freud's principle of ambivalence most clearly exercises itself, when intimacy is most likely to produce open hostility as well as affection.[3] Issue must therefore be taken with Homans' proposition, "Persons who interact frequently with one another tend to like one another" (providing the relationship is not obligatory).[4] The statement holds generally, but misses the essential point that there is a threshold beyond which interaction is unendurable for both parties. It is because people frequently take leave of one another that the interaction-liking proposition maintains itself.

Guarantees of privacy, that is, rules as to who may and who may not observe or reveal information about whom, must be established in any stable social system. If these assurances do not prevail—if there is normlessness with respect to privacy—every withdrawal from visibility may be accompanied by a measure of espionage, for without rules to the contrary persons are naturally given to intrude upon invisibility. "Secrecy sets barriers between men," writes Simmel, "but at the same time offers the seductive temptations to break through the barriers." [5] Such an inclination is embodied in the spy, the Peeping Tom, the eavesdropper, and the like, who have become its symbols.

"Surveillance" is the term which is generally applied to institutionalized intrusions into privacy. And social systems are characterizable in terms of the tension that exists between surveillant and anti-surveillant modes. Much of our literature on the anti-utopia, for example, George Orwell's *1984*, which depicts the dis-eases of excessive surveillance, is directed against the former mode. But dangers of internal disorder reside in unconditional guarantees of invisibility against which many administrative arms of justice have aligned themselves. On the other hand, surveillance may itself create the disorder which it seeks to prevent. Where there are few structural provisions for privacy, social withdrawal is equivalent to "hiding." For Simmel, "This is the crudest and, externally, most radical manner of concealment." [6] Where privacy is prohibited, man can only imagine separateness as an act of stealth.[7]

Since some provisions for taking leave of one another and for removing oneself from social observation are built into every establishment, an individual withdrawal into privacy and the allowance of such a withdrawal by other parties reflects and maintains the code that both sides adhere to. Leave taking, then, contains as many ritualistic demands as the act of coming together. Durkheim, like Homans, is not altogether correct in his insistence that the periodic gatherings of the group are its main sources of unity.[8] After a certain point the presence of others becomes irritating and leave taking, which is a mutual agreement to part company, is no less a binding agent than the ritual of meeting. In both cases individual needs (for gregariousness and isolation) are expressed and fulfilled in collectively endorsed manners. The dissociation ritual presupposes (and sustains) the social relation. Rules governing privacy, then, if accepted by all parties, constitute a common bond providing for periodic suspensions of interaction.

If privacy presupposes the existence of established social relations its employment may be considered as an index of solidarity. Weak social relationships, or relationships in the formative stage, cannot endure the strain of dissociation. By contrast, members of a stable social structure feel that it is not endangered by the maintenance of interpersonal boundaries. This point is of course well reflected in the Frostian dictum, "Good fences make good neighbors."

Privacy Helps Maintain Status Divisions

It is also well known that privacy both reflects and helps to maintain the status divisions of a group. In the armed forces, for example, the non-commissioned officer may reside in the same building as the dormitoried enlisted man but he will maintain a separate room. The officer of higher rank will live apart from the non-commissioned, but on the same base, often in an apartment building; but officers of highest status are more likely to have private quarters away from the military establishment.

In organizational life the privacy of the upper rank is insured structurally; it is necessary to proceed through the lieutenant stratum if the top level is to be reached. In contrast, the lower ranks, enjoying less control over those who may have access to them, find their privacy more easily invaded. Even in domestic life persons of the lower stratum lack "the butler" by means of whom the rich exercise tight control over their accessibility to others.

Privacy is an object of exchange. It is bought and sold in hospitals, transportation facilities, hotels, theaters, and, most conspicuously, in public restrooms where a dime will purchase a toilet, and a quarter, a toilet, sink and mirror. In some public lavatories a free toilet is provided—without a door.

Privacy has always been a luxury. Essayist Phyllis McGinley writes:

> The poor might have to huddle together in cities for need's sake, and the frontiersman cling to his neighbor for the sake of protection. But in each civilization, as it advanced, those who could afford it chose the luxury of a withdrawing place. Egyptians planned vine-hung gardens, the Greeks had their porticos and seaside villas, the Romans put enclosures around their patios. . . . Privacy was considered as worth striving for as hallmarked silver or linen sheets for one's bed.[9]

In this same respect Goffman comments upon the lack of front and back region differentiation in contemporary lower-class residences.[10]

The ability to invade privacy is also reflective of status. The physician's high social rank, for instance, derives perhaps not only from his technical skill but also from his authority to ignore barriers of privacy.

However, this prerogative is not limited to those of high status. We must not forget the "non-person" who lacks the ability to challenge the selfhood of his superiors. Goffman cites Mrs. Frances Trollope:

> I had indeed frequent opportunities of observing this habitual indifference to the presence of their slaves. They talk to them, of their condition, of their faculties, of their conduct exactly as if they were incapable of hearing. . . . A young lady displaying modesty before white gentlemen was found lacing her stays with the most perfect composure before a Negro footman.[11]

In general society the assumption of the social invisibility of another is looked upon as indecency, that is, as a failure to erect a barrier of privacy between self and other, under prescribed conditions.

The general rule that is deducible from all of this is that outside of the kinship group an extreme rank is conferred upon those for whom privacy shields are voluntarily removed. The prestige afforded the physician is exaggerated in order to protect the self from the shame which ordinarily accompanies a revelation of the body to a stranger, particularly if he is of the opposite sex. Likewise, the de-statusing of the servant is necessary if he is to be utilized for purposes of bathing, dressing, etc.

Persons of either high or low rank who have access to the private concerns of their clients are subject to definite obligations regarding both the manner in which secret knowledge is to be obtained and, most importantly, the way in which it is treated once it has been obtained. Explicit or implicit guarantees of confidentiality neutralize the transfer of power which would otherwise accompany the bestowal of private information. Both the possession of an extreme rank and the assurance of confidentiality thus legitimize the "need to know" and the intrusions which it makes possible.

Privacy and Deviation

Up to this point we have tried to indicate privacy's stabilizing effect upon two dimensions of social order. Withdrawal subserves horizontal order by providing a release from social relations when they have become sufficiently intense as to be irritating. Privacy is also a scarce social commodity; as such, its possession reflects and clarifies status divisions, thus dramatizing (and thereby stabilizing) the vertical order. But we must recognize that privacy also opens up opportunities for such forms of deviance as might undermine its stabilizing effects. However, privacy admits of *invisible* transgression and therefore serves to maintain intact those rules which would be subverted by the public disobedience that might occur in its absence.

Moore and Tumin, in their discussion of the function of ignorance, stated: "All social groups . . . require some quotient of ignorance to preserve esprit de corps." [12] And Goffman has made it clear that every establishment provides "involvement shields" for its members wherein "role releases" may take place, particularly deviant ones.[13] As Merton puts it:

> Resistance to full visibility of one's behavior appears, rather, to result from structural properties of group life. Some measure of leeway in conforming to role expectations is presupposed in all groups. To have to meet the strict requirements of a role at all times, without some degree of deviation, is to experience insufficient allowances for individual differences in capacity and training and for situational exigencies which make strict conformity extremely difficult. This is one of the sources of what has been elsewhere noted in this book as socially patterned, or even institutionalized, evasions of institutional rules.[14]

Thus, each group has its own "band of institutionalized evasion" which expands and contracts as conditions change. Rose L. Coser, in this connection, has considered observability in terms of the social status of the observer. She indicates that persons of high rank tend to voluntarily deprive themselves of visibility by signaling their intrusion with a prior announcement.[15] The deviation band, then, is normally condoned by both the upper and lower strata.

Moore and Tumin stress the importance of preventing deviation from being known to the group as a whole.[16] No doubt, a publication of all of the sins, crimes, and errors that take place in a social unit would jeopardize its stability. The preoccupation of the press with sensational deviations from norms might be considered from this point of view. Similarly, the more one person involves himself with another on an emotional basis the more both will need private facilities to conceal nasty habits and self-defaming information from each other. If the child, for instance, became suddenly aware of all the non-public performances of his father, and if the latter were aware of all the perversions that are privately enacted by his offspring, a father-son relationship characterized by mutual admiration would be impossible. This same point is illustrated in well-adjusted marriages which depend not only upon mutually acceptable role playing but also upon the ability of both parties to conceal "indecent" performances. This presupposes a modicum of physical distance between husband and wife. Simmel, in addition, adds that a complete abandon of one's self-information to another "paralyzes the vitality of relations and lets their continuation really appear pointless." [17]

Privacy enables secret consumption. We observe, for example, the adolescent practices of smoking or drinking in their locked rooms. Similarly, "women may leave *Saturday Evening Post* on their living room table but keep a copy of *True Romance* ('something the cleaning woman must have left around') concealed in their bedroom." [18] However, some modes of secret consumption have come into the public light. The erotic "girlie magazines," for example, no longer need be employed privately by the middle-class male since the advent of the *Playboy* magazine. As some activities emerge from secrecy others go underground. Thus, the person who nowadays finds pleasure in the Bible will most likely partake of it in private rather than in a public place or conveyance. These new proprieties are perhaps specific instances of a general rule set down by Simmel, that

> *what is originally open becomes secret, and what was originally concealed throws off its mystery. Thus we might arrive at the paradoxical idea that, under otherwise like circumstances, human associations require a definite ratio of secrecy which merely changes its objects; letting go of one it seizes another, and in the course of this exchange it keeps its quantum unvaried.*[19]

Incidentally, just as the person must employ proper language for the public situations in which he finds himself, he is required to maintain an appropriate body language as well. Differing postures must be assumed in his public encounters. But public postures do not exhaust the many positions of which the human body is capable. Anyone who has maintained a single position over a long period of time knows that the body demands consistent postural variation if it is to remain comfortable and capable of good role performance. Privacy enables the person to enact a variety of non-public postures and thus prepares him physically for public life.

It should be stressed that the absence of visibility does not guarantee privacy. The hypertrophied super-ego certainly makes impossible the use of solitude for deviant objectives. The person who is constantly in view of an internalized father, mother, or God leads a different kind of private life than those possessed by a less demanding conscience. This reveals an interesting paradox. Privacy surely provides for some measure of autonomy, of freedom from public expectation; but as Durkheim so persistently reminded us, the consequences of leaving the general normative order are moral instability and social rootlessness. (It is for this reason that secret societies compensate for the moral anarchy inherent in pure autonomy by means of ritual.[20]) Is it then possible that through privacy the ego escapes the dominion of the public order only to subordinate itself to a new authority: the super-ego? In some measure this is certainly the case, but one may also venture the suggestion that the super-ego, like the social structure whose demands it incorporates, has its own "band of institutionalized evasion." The suger-ego cannot be totally unyielding, for if every deviation of the ego called into play its punitive reaction the consequences for the self would be most severe.

Privacy and Establishments

It was earlier noted that rules or guarantees of privacy subserve horizontal and vertical order. Such rules are embodied in the physical structure of social establishments. Lindesmith and Strauss, for instance, have noted that proprieties concerning interpersonal contact and withdrawal are institutionalized in the architecture of buildings by means of a series of concentric circles. Specific regulations permit or forbid entry into the various parts of this structure, with a particular view to protecting the sacred "inner circle." [21] A more specific instance of the physical institutionalization of norms is found in the case of the bathroom, whose variation in size and design is limited by the requirement that body cleansing and elimination be performed privately.[22] This norm is reinforced by the architectural arrangements in which it is incorporated. The fact that the bathroom is only built for one literally guarantees that the performances which it accommodates will be solos. However, this normative-physical restriction admits of more complicated, secondary proprieties. Bossard and Boll write:

> The fact that the middle-class family rises almost together, and has few bathrooms, has resulted in a problem for it, which has been resolved by a very narrowly prescribed ritual for many of them—a bathroom ritual. They have developed set rules and regulations which define who goes first (according to who must leave the house first), how long one may stay in, what are the penalties for overtime, and under what conditions there may be a certain overlapping of personnel.[23]

The very physical arrangement of social establishments thus opens and shuts off certain possibilities for interaction and withdrawal and creates a background of sometimes complex ritual in support of a foreground of necessary proprieties. Needless to say, the form taken by such ritual is always subject to modification by architectural means.

Charles Madge also urges the architect to take explicit account in his designs of the ambivalences of social life. Men, for example, are given to both withdrawal and self-display. This duality, notes Madge, requires an "intermediate area" in housing projects, such as a backyard or garden which separates the home or inner circle from the "common green." [24] But it is one thing to so divide our physical living space as to insure ourselves of interactional options; it is another to regulate the interactional patterns that the division of space imposes upon us. The latter task is most efficiently met by the door.

Doors. McGinley has referred to the door as a human event of significance equal to the discovery of fire.[25] The door must surely have had its origin among those whose sense of selfhood had already developed to the extent that they could feel the oppression of others and experience the need for protection against their presence. Continued use of the door very probably heightened that feeling of separateness to which it owed its creation. Doors, therefore, not only stimulate one's sense of self-integrity, they are required precisely because one has such a sense.

The very act of placing a barrier between oneself and others is self-defining, for withdrawal entails a separation from a role and, tacitly, from an identity imposed upon oneself by others via that role. Therefore, to waive the protection of the door is to forsake that sense of individuality which it guarantees. As Simmel points out, some measure of de-selfing is characteristic of everything social.[26]

I would like now to discuss various kinds of doors, including horizontal sliding doors (drawers) and transparent doors (windows). I shall also treat of walls, as relatively impermeable interpersonal barriers, in contrast to doors, which are selectively permeable.

Doors provide boundaries between ourselves (i.e., our property, behavior, and appearance) and others. Violations of such boundaries imply a violation of selfhood. Trespassing or housebreaking, for example, is unbearable for some not only because of the property damage that might result but also because they represent proof that the self has lost control of its audience; it can no longer regulate who may and who may not have access to the property and information that index its depths.[27] The victim of a Peeping Tom is thus outraged not only at having been observed naked but also for having lost control of the number and type of people who may possess information about her body. To prove this we note that no nakedness need be observed to make Peeping Tomism intolerable.

"Alone, the visual feeling of the window," writes Simmel, "goes almost exclusively from inward to outward: it is there for looking out, not for seeing in." [28] This interdiction insures that the inhabitants of an establishment may have the outside world at their visual disposal, and at the same time it provides for control over their accessibility to this world. But, whereas the shade or curtain may be employed to regulate accessibility between the private and public spheres of action, situational proprieties are depended upon for protection in public. One such norm is that of "civil inattention" which has been elaborated by Goffman.[29]

Unlike the window, "the door with an in and out announces an entire distinction of intention."[30] There must be very clear rules as to who may open what doors at what times and under what conditions. The front and back doors are normally the only doors that any member of a family may enter at any time and under any circumstances. A parent may enter a child's room at any time and may inspect and replenish drawers, but visiting friends may not. But the parent must learn that some private doors (drawers) may not be opened (although they may be to friends); if they are, new receptacles for ego-indexes will be found, for example, the area between mattress and spring. The child, however, must never inspect the contents of the drawers of his parents nor enter their room at night. Thus the right of intrusion is seen to be an essential element of authority, whose legitimacy is affected by the degree to which it is exercised. Correspondingly, authority is dependent upon immunity against intrusion. Cooley notes that "authority, especially if it covers intrinsic personal weakness, has always a tendency to surround itself with forms and artificial mystery, whose object is to prevent familiar contact and so give the imagination a chance to idealize . . . self-concealment serves, among other purposes, that of preserving a sort of ascendancy over the unsophisticated."[31] In this same connection, Riesman writes:

> As compared with the one room house of the peasant or the "long house" of many primitive tribes, he (the inner directed child) grows up within walls that are physical symbols of the privacy of parental dominance. Walls separate parents from children, offices from home, and make it hard if not impossible for the child to criticize the parents' injunctions by an "undress" view of the parents or of other parents. What the parents say becomes more real in many cases than what they do. . . .[32]

Moreover, it is possible to map personal relations in terms of mutual expectations regarding intrusion. The invasion of various degrees of privacy may be a duty, a privilege, or a transgression, depending upon the nature of the interpersonal bond. And, clearly, expectations regarding such impositions may not be mutually agreed to.

Parental obligations concerning the care of a child override the child's rights to seclusion and place him in a position of social nakedness wherein he has no control over his appearance to others. However, to be subject to limitless intrusion is to exist in a state of dishonor, as implied in the rule against "coming too close." This point is made in Simmel's discussion of "discretion" as a quality which the person-in-private has a right to demand of another who is in a position to invade his seclusion.[33] Compromises between child and parent are therefore necessary and generally employed by the manipulation of the door. For example, the bedroom door may be kept half open while the child sleeps, its position symbolic of the parents' respect for the youngster's selfhood. Furthermore, a general temporal pattern might emerge if a large number of cases were examined. During infancy the door to self is generally fully open;[34] it closes perhaps halfway as a recognition of self development during childhood, it shuts but is left ajar at pre-puberty, and closes entirely—and perhaps even locks—at the pubertal and adolescent stages when meditation, grooming, and body examination become imperative. Parents at this time are often fully denied the spectatorship to which they may feel entitled and are kept at a distance by means of the privacy that a locked door insures.

There are also certain situations wherein husband and wife must remain separate from one another. A spouse, for example, must generally knock before entering a bathroom if the other is occupying it. This is a token of deference not to nudity but to the right of the other party to determine the way he or she wishes to present the self to the other. This rule insures that the self and its appearance will remain a controllable factor, independent of the whims of others, and it contributes to self-consciousness as well. This is seen most clearly in total institutions like the armed forces where open rows of toilets are used first with some measure of mortification and later with a complete absence of consciousness of self. In such doorless worlds we find a blurring of the distinction between "front and back regions," between those quarters where the self is put on and taken off and those in which it is presented.[35] In conventional society those who confuse these two areas are charged with vulgarity.

In contrast to the door, the wall symbolizes "separation" rather than "separateness" and denies the possibility of the encounter and withdrawal of social exchange. It strips away that element of freedom which is so clearly embodied in the door. "It is essential," notes Simmel, "that a person be able to set boundaries for himself, but freely, so that he can raise the boundaries again and remove himself from them."[36] In privacy, continues Simmel, "A piece of space is bound with himself and he is separated from the entire world." [37] But in enforced isolation man is bound *to* space. While the door separates outside from inside, the wall annihilates the outside. The door closes out: the wall encloses. Yet doors are converted into walls routinely, as is seen in the popular practice of "sending a child to his room" for misdeeds and the like. In this sense, many homes contain private dungeons or, rather, provisions for transforming the child's room into a cell—which forces upon us the distinction between formal and informal imprisonment.

Privacy is not dependent upon the availability of lockable doors. Goffman, for example, discusses "free places" in the institution where inmates may, free of surveillance, "be one's own man . . . in marked contrast to the sense of uneasiness prevailing on some wards." [38] In addition there is "personal territory" established by each inmate: for one a particular corner; for another a place near a window, etc. "In some wards, a few patients would carry their blankets around with them during the day and, in an act thought to be highly regressive, each would curl up on the floor with his blanket completely covering him; within the covered space each had some margin of control." [39] Thus do men withdraw from others to be at one with themselves and to create a world over which they reign with more complete authority, recalling Simmel's observation that "the person who erects a refuge demonstrates, like the first pathfinder, the typically human hegemony over nature, as he cuts a particle of space from continuity and eternity." [40]

In summary, islands of privacy exist in all establishments and throughout even the most intimate household. These islands are protected by an intricate set of rules. When these rules are violated secret places are sought after, discovered, and employed as facilities for secret action. These places and their permeability constitute one type of map, as it were, of interpersonal relationships and reveal the nature of the selves participating in them.

Privacy, Property and Self. Implied in any reference to a private place is its contents, personal property. One perhaps more often than not withdraws into privacy in order to observe and manipulate his property in some way, property which includes, of course, body and non-body objects.

There are two types of objects: those which may be observed by the public (and which may be termed personal objects) and those which are not available to public view (private property). Private property, as we are using the term, may be further delineated in terms of those intimate others who may have access to it in terms of visibility or use. Some private objectifications of self may be observed by family members, but some may be observed by *no one except the self*. There is no doubt that these latter objects have a very special meaning for identity; some of these are sacred and must not be contaminated by exposing them to observation by others; some are profane, and exposure will produce shame, but both are special and represent an essential aspect of self and, from the possessor's point of view, must not be tampered with.

It is because persons invest so much of their selves in private and personal things that total institutions require separation of self and material objects. When individualism must be minimized private ownership is always a vice worthy of constant surveillance. In such situations the acquisition and storage of personal things persist in the form of the "stash," which might be anything from a long sock to the cuff of one's pants.[41]

It follows that those who have direct or indirect access to the belongings of others or to articles which have been employed by them in private ways enjoy a certain amount of power which, if judiciously employed, may serve their interests well. Hughes observes:

> *It is by the garbage that the janitor judges, and, as it were, gets power over the tenants who high-hat him. Janitors know about hidden love affairs by bits of torn-up letter paper; of impending financial disaster or of financial four-flushing by the presence of many unopened letters in the waste. Or they may stall off demands for immediate service by an unreasonable woman of whom they know from the garbage that she, as the janitors put it, "has the rag on." The garbage gives the janitor the makings of a kind of magical power over that pretentious villain, the tenant. I say a kind of magical power, for there appears to be no thought of betraying any individual and thus turning his knowledge into overt power.*[42]

But, certainly, power need not be exercised to be effective. The mere knowledge that another "knows" invokes in the treatment of that other a certain amount of humility and deference.

Deprivatization

We have attempted to show that the possibility of withdrawal into well-equipped worlds which are inaccessible to others is that which makes intense group affiliations bearable. But we have also seen that men are not always successful in protecting their invisibility. Accidental leakages of information as well as the diverse modes of espionage threaten the information control that privacy is intended to maintain. But information control also consists of purposeful information leakage and even of the renunciation of secrecy. Just as men demand respite from public encounter they need periodically to escape themselves, for a privacy which lacks frequent remissions is maddening. The over-privatized man is he who is relieved of public demand only to become a burden to himself: He becomes his own audience to performances which are bound for tedium. Self-entertainment is thus a most exhausting business, requiring the simultaneous performance of two roles: actor and spectator. Both tire quickly of one another. When privacy thereby exhausts itself new and public audiences (and audienceships) are sought.

Moreover, we are led to relinquish our private information and activities by the expediencies and reciprocities routinely called for in daily life. We all know, for example, that in order to employ others as resources it is necessary to reveal to them something of ourselves, at least that part of ourselves which for some reason needs reinforcement. When this occurs (providing support is forthcoming), two things happen. First, we achieve some degree of gratification; second, and most important, our alter (or resource) reveals to us information which was heretofore withheld, for self-revelation is imbued with reciprocal power: It calls out in others something similar to that which we give of ourselves. There is both mutual revelation and mutual gratification. It is easy to see that when stress or need is prolonged this process may become institutionalized: Intimacy is then no longer an alternative; it is enforced, and private activity becomes clandestine and punishable. The deprivatization process approaches completion when we are not only penalized for our withdrawals but feel guilty about them. A housewife who had probably undergone the deprivatization process confided to Whyte: "I've promised myself to make it up to them. I was feeling bad that day and just plain didn't make the effort to ask them in for coffee. I don't blame them, really, for reacting the way they did. I'll make it up to them somehow." [43]

But loss of privacy among conventional folk is free of many of the pains of social nakedness which are suffered by inmates and by others undergoing total surveillance. The civilian voluntarily subjects himself to publicity and is relatively free of the contamination of unwanted contacts. His unmaskings are selective and subject to careful forethought. The intruder is chosen rather than suffered; indeed, his resourcefulness depends upon his ability to "know" his client-neighbor.

Therefore, in civil life, we find valid rationalization for our self-revelations. The demand that we "be sociable" is too compelling and too rewarding to be ignored by any of us.

But a substantial self-sacrifice is made by those who actually believe themselves to be what they present to public view. An awareness of the masquerades and deceptions that are part of good role performance is necessary to recall ourselves to our *own* selfhood and to our opposition to that of others. We must indeed deceive others to be true to ourselves. In this particular sense privacy prevents the ego from identifying itself too closely with or losing itself in (public) roles. Daily life is therefore sparked by a constant tension between sincerity and guile, between self-release and self-containment, between the impulse to embrace that which is public and the drive to escape the discomfort of group demands. Accordingly, our identities are maintained by our ability to hold back as well as to affiliate. Thus Goffman writes:

> *When we closely observe what goes on in a social role, a spate of sociable interaction, a social establishment—or in any other unit of social organization—embracement of the unit is not all that we see. We always find the individual employing methods to keep some distance, some elbow room, between himself and that with which others assume he should be identified.*
>
> *Our sense of being a person can come from being drawn into a wider social unit; our sense of selfhood can arise through the little ways in which we resist the pull. Our status is backed by the solid buildings of the world, while our sense of personal identity often resides in the cracks.*[44]

For Goffman, privacy is one of "the little ways in which we resist the pull" of group commitments and reinforce our selfhood.

NOTES

1. The initiation of a social contact generally entails a withdrawal from a preceding one. Therefore, men may withdraw into new social circles as well as into seclusion. In this particular sense it would be most exact to employ the term "contact-withdrawal," as opposed to a single term for engagement and another for disengagement. However, this distinction does not apply to movements into privacy.
2. Georg Simmel, "Brücke und Tür," in *Brücke und Tür* (Stuttgart: K. F. Koehler, 1957), p. 1.
3. Sigmund Freud, *Group Psychology and the Analysis of the Ego* (New York: Bantam Books, Inc., 1960), pp. 41–42.
4. George C. Homans, *The Human Group* (New York: Harcourt, Brace & Co., 1950), p. 111.
5. Georg Simmel, "The Secret and the Secret Society," in Kurt Wolff, ed., *The Sociology of Georg Simmel* (New York: The Free Press, 1964), p. 334.
6. *Ibid.*, p. 364.
7. *Ibid.*
8. Émile Durkheim, *The Elementary Forms of the Religious Life* (Glencoe, Ill.: The Free Press, 1947), pp. 214–219.

9. Phyllis McGinley, "A Lost Privilege," in *Province of the Heart* (New York: Viking Press, 1959), p. 56.

10. Erving Goffman, *The Presentation of Self in Everyday Life* (Edinburgh: University of Edinburgh, 1958), p. 123.

11. *Ibid.*, p. 95.

12. Wilbur E. Moore and Melvin M. Tumin, "Some Social Functions of Ignorance," *American Sociological Review*, XIV (December, 1949), 792. See also Barney Glaser and Anselm Strauss, "Awareness Contexts and Social Interaction," *American Sociological Review*, XXIX (October, 1964), 669–679, in which social interaction is discussed in terms of "what each interactant in a situation knows about the identity of the other and his own identity in the eyes of the other" (p. 670). A change in "awareness context" accompanies acquisitions of knowledge, provisions of false knowledge, concealment of information, etc.

13. The "involvement shield" and Everett C. Hughes' concept of "role release" are elaborated in Erving Goffman's *Behavior in Public Places* (New York: The Free Press, 1963), pp. 38–39.

14. Robert K. Merton, *Social Theory and Social Structure* (New York: The Free Press, 1964), p. 343.

15. Rose L. Coser, "Insulation from Observability and Types of Social Conformity," *American Sociological Review*, XXVI (February, 1961), 28–39.

16. Moore and Tumin, *op. cit.*, p. 793.

17. Simmel, "The Secret and the Secret Society," *op. cit.*, p. 329.

18. Goffman, *The Presentation of Self in Everyday Life, op. cit.*, p. 26. Needless to say, many instances of the employment of privacy for "secret production" could be given.

19. Simmel, "The Secret and the Secret Society," *op. cit.*, pp. 335–336.

20. *Ibid.*, pp. 360–361.

21. Alfred R. Lindesmith and Anselm L. Strauss, *Social Psychology* (New York: Henry Holt & Co., 1956), p. 435. However, in an interesting statement, McGinley announces the death of the very idea of the "inner circle": "It isn't considered sporting to object to being a goldfish. On the same public plan we build our dwelling places. Where, in many a modern house, can one hide? (And every being, cat, dog, parakeet, or man, wants a hermitage now and then.) We discard partitions and put up dividers. Utility rooms take the place of parlors. Picture windows look not onto seas or mountains or even shrubberies but into the picture windows of the neighbors. Hedges come down, gardens go unwalled; and we have nearly forgotten that the inventor of that door which first shut against intrusion was as much mankind's benefactor as he who discovered fire. I suspect that, in a majority of the bungalows sprouting across the country like toadstools after a rain, the only apartment left for a citadel is the bathroom" (*op. cit.*, pp. 55–56).

In contrast, Edward T. Hall observes: "Public and private buildings in Germany often have double doors for soundproofing, as do many hotel rooms. In addition, the door is taken very seriously by Germans. Those Germans who come to America feel that our doors are flimsy and light. The meanings of the open door and the closed door are quite different in the two countries. In offices, Americans keep doors open; Germans keep doors closed. In Germany, the closed door does not mean that the man behind it wants to be alone or undisturbed, or that he is doing something he doesn't want someone else to see. It's simply that Germans think that open doors are sloppy and disorderly. To close the door preserves the integrity of the room and provides a protective boundary between people. Otherwise, they get too involved with each other. One of my German subjects commented, 'If our family hadn't had doors, we would have had to change our way of life. Without doors we would have had many, many more fights. . . . When you can't talk, you retreat behind a door. . . . If there hadn't been doors, I would always have been within reach of my mother'" (*The Hidden Dimension* [Garden City: Doubleday & Co., 1966], p. 127.) For a discussion of the norms regulating privacy among the English, French, Arab, and Japanese, see pp. 129–153.

22. Alexander Kira, *The Bathroom* (New York: Bantam Books, Inc., 1967),

pp. 178–184. The requirement of complete privacy for personal hygiene is only a recent phenomenon (see pp. 1–8).

23. J. H. S. Bossard and E. S. Boll, *Ritual in Family Living* (Philadelphia: University of Pennsylvania Press, 1950), pp. 113–114 (cited by Kira, *op. cit.*, pp. 177–178).

24. Charles Madge, "Private and Public Places," *Human Relations,* III (1950), 187–199. F. S. Chapin (in "Some Housing Factors Related to Mental Hygiene," *Journal of Social Issues,* VII [1951], 165) emphasizes that the need for relief from irritating public contact must be consciously and carefully met by the architect. On the other hand, Kira writes: "There are problems which cannot be resolved by architects and industrial designers alone, however; they also pose a challenge to the social scientists and to the medical and public health professions. This is an area in which the stakes are enormous and in which little or no direct work has been done." (*Op. cit.*, p. 192.)

25. See n. 21.

26. Simmel, "The Secret and the Secret Society," *op. cit.*, p. 373.

27. The law recognizes the psychological effect of such criminal acts and provides additional penal sanction for them. Wolfgang and Sellin report that "the chain store is more outraged by theft from a warehouse, where the offender has no business, than from the store where his presence is legal during store hours." Moreover, "the victim of a house burglary is usually very disturbed by the fact that the offender had the effrontery to enter the house illegally. . . . For these and similar reasons, breaking and entering as well as burglary carry more severe sanctions in the law" (Marvin E. Wolfgang and Thorsten Sellin, *The Measurement of Delinquency* [New York: John Wiley & Sons, 1964], pp. 219–220).

28. Simmel, "Brücke und Tür," *op. cit.*, p. 5.

29. Goffman, *Behavior in Public Places, op. cit.*, pp. 83–88.

30. Simmel, "Brücke und Tür," *op. cit.*, p. 4.

31. Charles Horton Cooley, *Human Nature and the Social Order* (New York: Schocken Books, Inc., 1964), p. 351.

32. David Riesman, *The Lonely Crowd* (Garden City: Doubleday & Co., 1953), p. 61. Another characteriologist, William H. Whyte, suggests that "doors inside houses . . . marked the birth of the middle class" (*The Organization Man* [Garden City, N.Y.: Doubleday & Co., 1956], p. 389).

33. Simmel, "The Secret and the Secret Society," *op. cit.*, pp. 320–324. Similarly, Erving Goffman writes: "There is an inescapable opposition between showing a desire to include an individual and showing respect for his privacy. As an implication of this dilemma, we must see that social intercourse involves a constant dialectic between presentational rituals and avoidance rituals. A peculiar tension must be maintained, for these opposing requirements of conduct must somehow be held apart from one another and yet realized together in the same interaction; the gestures which carry an actor to a recipient must also signify that things will not be carried too far" ("The Nature of Deference and Demeanor," *American Anthropologist,* LVIII [June, 1956], 488).

34. The absence of ability among infants and children to regulate the appearance and disappearance of their audience does not mean that privacy or separateness is not an important feature of their development; the privacy need is simply expressed differently. The infant, for example, can sometimes remove himself from the field of stimulation by going to sleep or wriggling away from the adult who holds him. This is probably why pathology resulting from overcontact is less likely than that due to undercontact, for the former is far more easily regulated by the infant than the latter. At a later stage of development, the infant learns that he can hold back and let go in reference not only to sphincters but to facial expressions and general dispositions as well. He comes to view himself as a causal agent as he inherits the power of voluntary reserve. When the child is locomoting he first confronts privacy imposed against him by others and begins to define himself in terms of where he may and may not go. On the other hand, his ambulatory ability gives him enormous control over his audience, a power in which he delights by "hiding." Espionage is practiced as well and suspected in others—whereby the condition of

shame begins to acquire meaning for the child. These incomplete comments suffice to illustrate the point that the privacy impulse is not at all inactive in infancy and childhood. They further suggest that each stage of development has its own mode of privacy, which may be defined in terms of the ego's relationship to those from whom privacy is sought and the manner in which withdrawal is accomplished.

35. Goffman, *The Presentation of Self in Everyday Life, op. cit.*, pp. 66–86.

36. Simmel, "Brücke und Tür," *op. cit.*, p. 4.

37. *Ibid.*, p. 3.

38. Erving Goffman, "The Underlife of a Public Institution," in *Asylums* (Garden City, N.Y.: Doubleday & Co., 1961), p. 231.

39. *Ibid.*, p. 246. For more on norms regulating territorial conduct in face-to-face encounters, see Nancy Felipe and Robert Sommer, "Invasions of Personal Space," *Social Problems*, XIV (May, 1966), 206–214; and Robert Sommer, "Sociofugal Space," *American Journal of Sociology*, LXXII (May, 1967), 654–660.

40. Simmel, "Brücke und Tür," *op. cit.*, p. 3.

41. Goffman, *Asylums, op. cit.*, pp. 248–254.

42. Everett C. Hughes, *Men and Their Work* (Glencoe, Ill.: The Free Press, 1958), p. 51.

43. Whyte, *op. cit.*, p. 390.

44. Goffman, *Asylums, op. cit.*, pp. 319–320.

11

Social Theory in Architectural Design

MAURICE BROADY

Despite the findings of behavioral science research, which indicate that design factors do not by themselves determine patterns of social interaction or produce social cohesion, many architects and planners continue to ignore the complexity of the relationship between spatial organization and group life. They believe instead in the doctrine of architectural determinism, or, to put it crudely, that the architect's decisions about the placement of buildings determine the social relationships of the occupants. Why does this doctrine persist? What alternative theory or conceptual orientation more in accord with behavioral science research should be substituted for it? What can architects do to increase the chances that the social consequences they have in mind will in fact be realized?

These are some of the questions that Broady discusses in his selection. He believes that the continued advocacy of the doctrine of architectural determinism is indicative of the intellectual blindness that leads members of every profession, whether law, architecture, or medicine, to believe that their function is socially critical. Because architects *hope* that certain social outcomes will result from their designs, they tend to expect that these outcomes will happen. They also tend to assume that the lay public will be as discriminating in judging the visual elements of a building as trained architects are and will give to purely architectural features the same weight they give to utilitarian qualities.

To the doctrine of architectural determinism, Broady opposes the theoretical distinction originally promulgated by Herbert Gans between the potential and the effective environment. The physical form is only a potential environment that provides clues for social behavior. The effective environment, the totality of the significant variables influencing behavior, includes not only the physical environment but also the social structure and cultural attributes of the people who use it.

Architects should find ways to apply this insight in their own work. If the use of the environment is heavily influenced by the people who will inhabit it, regardless of what the architect may intend, then it is incumbent on the designer to consult his prospective users before he develops a design.

Reprinted from Maurice Broady, "Social Theory in Architectural Design," *Arena*, The Architectural Association Journal, London, 81, no. 898 (January 1966): 149–154, by permission of the editor.

170

Broady also believes that every design scheme should be accompanied by a social and administrative program, which would help the implementation of the plans for the physical environment. To facilitate the future development of such collaborative undertakings, Broady calls for more rigorous instruction in the social sciences in schools of architecture and for the formation of joint architect-sociologist design and planning teams.

□

One does not have to talk with architects and town-planners for very long to discover that they are interested in social theory. There are, of course, the aesthetes pure and simple—the people I used to meet in the Liverpool School in the early fifties, whose fifth-year schemes were likely to be designs of swish villas for equally swish colleagues on the Riviera. But most of the designers I meet now are better described as "social consciences." They are idealists—even radicals. They share a sense of social purpose. They want to improve society and they believe that their work as architects or planners can help them to do so. They are, accordingly, interested in sociology. They have read their Geddes and their Mumford and now know all about the mums of Bethnal Green and the sidewalks in Greenwich Village. They talk a lot about "survey before plan"; they have even consorted (not perhaps very profitably) with the odd sociologist like myself.

For my part, I greatly enjoy these encounters with people who are convinced of the importance of their work and bubbling over with the desire to create new and better environments. It is a change from the atmosphere of a university where creativity may often be inhibited and vision narrowed by the demands of scholarship. I would not wish in any way to weaken this ardor and idealism. And yet, at times, one stands aghast at the naivety, the sheer lack of intellectual discipline which often marks the enthusiastic designer's confrontation with social theory. Perhaps one ought not to worry about all this hot air: for it may not be taken seriously even by its exponents. Indeed, it sometimes seems to be used not so much to guide design as to bolster morale and to add a patina of words to ideas intuitively conceived. In the end, however, one *must* be concerned. For phoney social theory is likely to produce phoney expectations and spurious designs. It may equally hinder effective collaboration between social scientists and designers and inhibit the development of more valid ideas about the relationship between architectural design and social structure. That is why a largely critical article (which this will be) is not as negative as might at first be supposed. For one of the best ways to begin to elaborate new ideas is to criticize the inadequacies of current theory.

At least three types of architectural theorizing can be found. There is, first of all, straight waffle:

> The vertical segregation of traffic as an urban system (meaning?) offers us potentially one effective component (why effective if only potentially offered?) in such a shaping-strategy (what?) not simply because in organisational terms (meaning again?), for example, cars can get to the right place without even having to cross pedestrian lines on the same plane, but because the very independence of each layer offers a potential for generating a new urban syntax (coo!) in as much as it allows for independent development of each level, etc.[1]

I suppose this simply means that the vertical segregation of traffic and pedestrians enables cars to move without bumping into people and allows traffic and pedestrian areas to be developed independently of each other: which is a good deal less significant a point than the original form of expression would lead one to imagine.

The second type of theorizing involves grafting a spurious social theory onto a useful and sensible technical solution. This is evident in a review of Denys Lasdun's cluster-blocks in Bethnal Green which states:

> The cluster concept offers a viable alternative on the visual side by creating tower accents without visually destroying the existing grain; on the human side it shows promise in possessing domestic scale in the component parts of those towers and maintaining something like the pre-existing sociological grouping of the street that gave the original urban grain to the district.

To which Edmund Cooney has tartly commented that

> the sociological thinking has been grafted onto an aesthetic dogma, and it has been assumed, without observation, that the graft has taken successfully and is bearing fruit. It might have been less confusing simply to explain that if housing policy required 64 households to be accommodated on such a small site then they would have to live in some form of high tower or slab, in which case a cluster block would look better than anything else.[2]

I myself first came across this unnecessary grafting of social ideas a number of years ago when a well-known architect was explaining the principle of vertical segregation of pedestrians and traffic. He had made an extremely good technical case for this idea; and he concluded —in no flippant manner—by arguing, on completely redundant social grounds, that this design would be entirely consonant with the *Zeitgeist* of the second half of the century (or something) since it would enable pedestrians to enjoy the sight of myriads of brightly colored cars flashing along below them and thus to be more fully part of the exciting flux of an automobile era. The *exact* detail of expression may well have escaped me in this example: but no one who has heard enthusiastic architects in their romantic vein will doubt its plausibility. Nor can one doubt that the function of these various kinds of utterance is not to clarify social understanding so much as to cheer their authors up and to show what remarkable chaps they really are. This kind of thinking may be necessary for the designer's morale and thus have *something* useful to contribute to his profession. But it is much more likely to confuse understanding and jeopardize clear thinking.

Architectural Determinism

Architects, however, are apt to subscribe to a much more fundamental and pervasive kind of theorizing which may be labelled "architectural determinism." It is more often found implicit in architects' thinking than in any clearly argued form: and it is probably the more dangerous for that. How influential it is, is difficult to say. But the fact that it has been vigorously defended in at least four architectural schools in which I have recently had occasion to criticize it and that it has also been the subject of critical comment by other sociologists on both sides of the Atlantic supports the view that it is fairly widely held among architects and town-planners.[3] Indeed, earlier this year, Gabriel Epstein made the point in a discussion on university design that plans ought not to be produced "in the sense in which architects were trained to think . . . not in the *determined* way of architects."[4] Nor is it difficult to catch examples. There was, for instance, the group-architect at Cumbernauld who asked my advice on whether it would be socially more desirable to place three point-blocks in triangle rather than in line. Then there was the planner at Basingstoke who assured me that the most satisfied and well-settled residents in the four estates which we were studying in the town would be found in the one that was outstanding in lay-out and design. Quite the reverse was in fact the case—24 per cent of the residents of that estate expressed themselves dissatisfied as compared with only 11 per cent in the three other estates.[5] And the Cumbernauld architect was rather taken aback when I said that I doubted whether it would make any real difference socially which way he placed his point-blocks!

That these expectations were both wrong is less interesting than the fact that they were held. For they indicate very clearly the assumptions which derive from an implicitly held theory of architectural deter-

173

minism. The theory has been expressed as follows: "The architect who builds a house or designs a site plan, who decides where the roads will and will not go, and who decides which directions the houses will face and how close together they will be, also is, to a large extent, deciding the pattern of social life among the people who will live in these houses." [6] It asserts that architectural design has a direct and determinate effect on the way people behave. It implies a one-way process in which the physical environment is the independent, and human behavior the dependent variable. It suggests that those human beings for whom architects and planners create their designs are simply moulded by the environment which is provided for them. It is of a kind with the other varieties of popular determinism—such as the view that national character is determined by climate—which save the layman the trouble and worry of observing accurately and thinking clearly.

The Neighborhood Unit Theory

The classic case of architectural determinism is the neighborhood unit theory. Here again, a dubious social theory was grafted onto a reasonable technical solution. The idea, as it was first elaborated by Clarence Perry in the 1920s, was essentially a means of relating physical amenities systematically to population, with particular regard to the safety and convenience of pedestrians and especially children. As Peter Mann has pointed out, Perry's *social* claims for the neighborhood unit were "very careful and extremely modest." [7] Much the same could be said of the Dudley Report [8] in which the idea received semi-official endorsement when it was published in 1944; while the report prepared in 1943 by the National Council of Social Service on *The Size and Social Structure of a Town* similarly argued that "Though physical planning and administrative measures *cannot by themselves change social relationships*, they can, if wisely and positively conceived, encourage and facilitate the growth of that spirit of fellowship without which true community life is impossible." [9] As so often happens, however, the qualifications embodied in this statement were in practice largely ignored. To the theory of how to allocate amenities in housing areas, which the neighborhood unit idea originally was, there was added after the war a crude social theory which asserted that the neighborhood plan, and the way in which amenities were allocated within it, *would* foster a sense of belonging and community spirit among the residents of each neighborhood.

One of the major puzzles in the history of recent planning theory is why this idea should have been so enthusiastically received in the years immediately after the war.[10] (Why, indeed, despite all the criticism to which it has been subjected, does it still find such ardent defenders not only in this country but in the States and on the Continent, too?) I think the answer is that it was really ideological: that it was accepted not because it could be shown to be valid, but because it was *hoped* that it would be so. You have only to think of the circumstances in which it was accepted to appreciate why this should have been the case. The new town idea had been buttressed by the criticisms which had been levelled at the inter-war housing estates. These estates had been criticized not only because they were ugly, badly designed and lacking even the basic social amenities, but also because the people who lived in them were said to miss the friendliness, neighborliness and the sense of belonging to a definite community which, despite bad housing and a poor physical environment, they had enjoyed in the slum districts from which they had been moved. How then, could the good housing of the new estates be combined with the friendliness of the slums? That was the sort of problem with which socially conscious, idealistic planners, architects, social workers and administrators were concerned in the 1930s.

In the answer which they found, the assumptions of architectural determinism stand out clearly. What was it about the slum street that made it so friendly? Obviously, they said, its amenities: its pubs and church halls and, above all, the dear little corner shops where Ma could get "tick" to bide her over till wage night and meet her friends for a chat. The answer for the new towns, then, was to provide the same kind of amenities (especially the little corner shops) and, *eureka!* people would be as friendly and neighborly in their new surroundings as they had been in the old. Of course, people do meet each other and chat in pubs and corner shops. But not all pubs and corner shops engender the neighborliness of the slum street. For what is much more important in explaining that neighborliness are the *social* facts, first, that the people who lived in the slums had often lived in the same street for several generations and thus had long-standing contacts with their neighbors and kin; and second, that people who suffer economic hardship are prone to band together for mutual help and protection. It is true that neighborliness is induced by environmental factors. Of these, however, the most relevant are social and economic rather than physical. But it can be readily understood why planners (and others who wished to do something to make life better for their fellow-men) should have been so ready to suppose that the prime factor in the growth of "community spirit" was the design of the *physical* environment which it was uniquely in their power to modify.

Inadequacies of Current Theory

There is no reason to expect that idealistic young architects graduating in the 1960s will think any differently. The disposition which I am criticizing has its roots deep in the intellectual bias of the architectural profession. We are all inclined to see the whole world through our own professional spectacles, and thus to see it distortedly. The lawyer, dealing daily as he is with divorces and separations, often seems to suppose that the family is held together only by the constraint of the law. Once admit a modification of the divorce laws, he seems to be saying, and fornication will be rampant and we shall all be running off with our neighbors' wives. The physicist is apt to suppose that the world could be run much better if only scientists were in charge; the psychologist, that the assumptions about rat behavior that are helpful in the lab are equally valid as general principles of human conduct. By the same token, the designer may easily come to believe that his work will achieve the social objectives which not only his client, but he himself, wishes to promote.

Nor does the architect's training help him to understand, except in a very superficial way, the approach of the social scientist to the kind of problems he is interested in. Sociologists, it is true, are invited to give short courses of lectures in many architectural schools. But they are usually expected to contribute on such a narrow, vocationally oriented tack that it is difficult for them to communicate so that it sinks in what social theory is all about, how it is established and by what criteria it should be evaluated. Architectural students, therefore, tend to get a general notion of how social surveys are conducted but —even if they are told—they usually fail to appreciate that a survey forms only part of a sociological *argument* and that it is in order to provide particular kinds of evidence for such arguments that surveys are undertaken. In my opinion, it is this imbalance between a rigorous training in visual and a superficial training in social scientific thinking that makes it possible for our students to accept a deterministic answer to the complex problem of how social organization and architectural design interact, and which thus contributes to that extreme, at times even obsessive anxiety about the effects that their work is likely to have on other people's lives which one so often notices in them. A further result of this imbalance is that students tend to collect lots of factual information only to be at a loss what to do with it all once they have got it and frequently fail to control their intuitive designer's approach with coherent and systematic thinking.[11]

The superficiality of architects' social theory can be shown quite as clearly in the detail of planning practice. In one planning scheme in which I was recently involved, the problem was being considered how shops should be allocated in residential areas. Two divergent views were advanced. On the one hand, it was proposed that, in order to maximize convenience, suites of shops should be located so that no resident was more than a quarter of a mile from one of them. This would have meant building one suite of 6,000 square feet for every 3,000 people. The alternative view held that the over-riding criterion in allocating shops was "to establish focal points that will foster a sense of community within the area served"; and this, it was argued, would be more effectively achieved by building one suite of 9,000 square feet for every 5,000 people.

This second view is a typical expression of the neighborhood unit idea that amenities should be sited so as to foster a sense of community. But the idea that such a minor difference of size as that between 3,000 and 5,000 people would have any material influence upon something so nebulous as a sense of community is sheer speculation masquerading as sociological truth. Neither figure can be said to be more valid than the other in this connection. If it is argued that the experience of Hemel Hempstead, for instance, indicates that a unit of 5,000 people is best, then similarly impressionistic evidence, of no more but no less validity, can be adduced from Crawley to show that there, in even larger neighborhoods which range in size from 5,500 to 7,000 residents, the sense of community is so strong that it has inhibited the development of identity with the town as a whole. Furthermore, even if differences could be shown in the degree of community feeling in neighborhoods of different sizes, it would still remain open to doubt whether such differences were caused, or even directly influenced by the size of the neighborhood or the way in which amenities were disposed within them. Accordingly, this kind of "sociological" argument seems designed to support a proposition which if it were valid, would be so for reasons quite different from this.

At first glance, the convenience argument seems much more plausible. It does not depend upon the singularly narrow definition of social welfare that is involved in regarding the development of community feeling as the primary criterion in allocating shops, and it at least seeks to achieve some tangible benefit for the consumer. Yet it is curious how narrow and conventional was the designer's view of what benefits the consumer might wish to have maximized. Convenience, after all, is only one aspect of economy: it is a measure of the economy of time and distance. But there is also economy of the purse. The housewife surely wants shops that are both convenient and cheap; and if the convenience of having shops within one quarter of a mile of everybody meant that only one grocer could make a living in each suite of shops, this might encourage, even if it did not oblige him to charge monopoly prices which could probably be avoided if convenience were marginally reduced, by increasing the radius served by the shops, in order to have two grocer's shops in competition with each other. Thus, the fact that the planner was thinking primarily in terms of *physical* distance prevented him from thinking realistically about shopping provision by taking into account all the social requirements which shops need to meet. In such simple but significant ways does inadequate social theory hinder sound thinking about design problems.

The Counter-Argument

But to return to the basic issue of the effect of architectural design on social organization. Surely, it will be argued, buildings and lay-outs *do* influence social behavior? There is certainly some evidence to support this view. In the end, one is likely to develop social contacts with people one meets and whom one meets within a residential area *is* affected by its lay-out. A number of studies of planned communities both here and in America have certainly shown the significance of proximity in the formation of social relationships.[12] Their conclusions are summed up by Irving Rosow in the phrase: "People select their friends primarily from those who live nearby and those whom their house faces." [13] Even the location of a kitchen door can matter! If it is at the side of the house, contacts are more likely to be made with the side-neighbor; if at the back of the house, with the party-neighbor.[14]

These data, however, valid though they are, have been used to support the belief that "the tenants' entire social life may hang on the smallest whim of the greenest draftsman. . . ." [15] But this kind of conclusion is hardly justified. In the first place, the relationship between proximity and friendship is obviously not absolute, for friendships *are* made with people who live down the street as well as in adjacent houses and in districts far away as well as near at hand. Even though Kuper's study of a Coventry estate showed that more intensive interaction between neighbors takes place in cul-de-sacs than in long ter-races of houses, there is also evidence that, in older areas of terraced-housing, street groups may be even more cohesive and active.[16] The second point is that, while design features may facilitate neighborly intercourse, they cannot be said to influence its quality. Those who subscribe to architectural determinism always seem to suppose that the influence of design will be beneficial. But people may be ran-corous as well as friendly, and, as several studies of neighboring fami-lies have shown, they may equally well wish to defend themselves against their neighbors as to welcome every opportunity to meet them.[17] How they will react to their physical environment depends on so much more than physical design; and if propinquity provides the occasion for contact between neighbors, how that contact develops depends chiefly upon social factors.

The Basingstoke example which was quoted earlier illustrates the point very clearly. The reason why the residents of the best-designed estate were the least satisfied was that their satisfaction depended only marginally upon architectural design. Broadly speaking, the working-class residents of the other estates had moved in order to get better housing. They, therefore, were well satisfied to have a house of their own, away from nagging in-laws and rapacious London landlords. The middle-class residents of the well-designed estate, on the other hand, had mostly had a decent enough house before moving to Basingstoke, and had moved chiefly to get a better job. For them, the fact that they were living in a reasonably well-designed house in the best laid-out estate in the town was inadequate compensation for their general disappointment with the social life of Basingstoke itself.

Two other examples will suffice to clinch the point. In one university a few years ago, the attempt was made to encourage staff and students to meet together informally by installing a coffee-lounge between the senior and junior common rooms, especially furnished with comfortable chairs and thick carpets. This has not worked. Nor, without supporting social and possibly administrative arrangements, could it possibly have done so. For it is quite unrealistic to suppose that the provision of a coffee-lounge could change a pattern of social segregation which rests upon substantial differences of function and responsibility, not to mention of age and status, and which the whole pattern of academic organization tends to emphasize.

Conversely, social intercourse, if deeply enough rooted, may con-tinue in the teeth of architectural disincentives. The Institute of Com-munity Studies, for instance, in a study of tenant reaction to four contrasting types of housing in the East End of London found that the people who felt most cut off from their neighbors and who considered that the layout of the building made it particularly difficult to keep in touch with other tenants were the residents of Denys Lasdun's cluster-block, but that these same tenants were nevertheless much more sociable than the residents of the other types of building. The reason had to do with their social background. For most of them had previously lived in one of the most gregarious tenements in the district and they simply carried on these social activities, such as baby-sitting for one another, visiting and going shopping together, which over time had become part of their way of life.[18]

In the light of such evidence, therefore, even if it be admitted that architectural design may influence, it cannot be said to determine social behavior. Indeed, there is much to be said for the view that it has, at most, only a marginal effect on social activity. Among other evidence, it is particularly interesting to note that whenever architects are discussing their own domestic affairs this is the view which they invariably appear to adopt. In the discussions that have been going on about the future of the AA School, it is, I suggest, significant that the discussion has been much less concerned with the present fabric and its many inadequacies than with the constitution of the School in these new circumstances—with how it is to be organized as a *social* institution. By the same token, the RIBA report on *The Architect and his Office* was equally unconcerned with the physical aspects of architectural offices but focussed again upon the way in which those offices were organized. If architects pay so little attention to architecture when their own professional activities are at issue, it is surely odd that they should be so excessively concerned with it when *other* people's affairs are concerned and so persuaded that architectural design can have the great effect upon them which they are inclined to ignore for themselves!

Towards a More Viable Social Theory

Clearly, then, as social theory, architectural determinism will not do. So where do we go from here? The answer is that we must now begin to develop a more realistic understanding of the relations between architectural design and human behavior: one, that is to say, which reflects what actually happens rather than what we hope might happen. I say "begin" advisedly, because in this country, at least, we have barely started to consider the problem systematically. All I can do here, therefore, is to make some very general remarks about some of the considerations that need to be taken into account.

These days, architects and planners are concerned not simply with buildings but with environments. As Hugh Wilson put it in his recent inaugural address: "If it (planning) is concerned *with the total environment,* with the creation of towns of quality and character *and with the well-being of people,* then I claim to be a planner." [19] The assumption which I have been criticizing is that environment is created uniquely by buildings and physical design. The first step in correcting this theory is to introduce the useful distinction, put forward by Herbert Gans, between a potential and an effective environment.[20] The point of this distinction is clear enough. The physical form is only a potential environment since it simply provides possibilities or clues for social behavior. The effective—or total—environment is the product of those physical patterns plus the behavior of the people who use them, and that will vary according to their social background and their way of life: to what sociologists, in their technical language, call social structure and culture.

This distinction entails two simple but important points which now need to be made clear. Designers often fail to realize how much difference it makes to their view of the world that they respond to buildings and townscapes with eyes more discriminating and intellects more sensitive to design than those of the average layman. Their failure to appreciate the point leads them to make the fallacious assumption that the users of buildings will react to them as they do themselves. There is substantial evidence to justify our being very skeptical of this belief. Vere Hole, for example, found that tenants in a Scottish housing estate which she was studying noticed and complained about practical things, such as the lack of made-up footpaths, but failed to remark upon the unsightly colliery slag-heaps or the monotonous appearance of their houses. Indeed, in another estate, they even failed to distinguish consciously between an older and a more modern style of housing.[21] A similar conclusion came out of a study of a Glasgow redevelopment scheme in which the authors were surprised to find how comparatively insensitive the tenants were to questions of design.[22] Nearer home, reactions to the Smithsons' "Economist" building ranged from the sophisticated comments of architects to the negative responses of members of "The Economist" staff, of whom Tom Houston reports that he "asked several of our people but failed to get an answer to the question: Does this place stimulate or not?" [23]

A similar disparity must also be noted between commonsense assumptions about the way human beings react to environmental stimuli and how they actually do react. The psychology of design is singularly ill-developed; but what we *do* know about it suggests that we should be equally cautious about commonsense, layman's psychology. For example, it has always been assumed that people can judge accurately how much daylight there actually is in a room. An investigation by Brian Wells of the Department of Building Science at Liverpool University, however, has shown that "the strength of beliefs about daylighting and view were *independent of physical context* . . . and that people tended to overestimate the proportion of daylight that they had to work by at increasing distances from the windows." [24] Any theory of the relationship between design and human behavior, therefore, needs to take full account of the empirical evidence adduced by social scientists which calls commonsense ideas so clearly in question.

The second point which we must go on to make is that human beings are a good deal more autonomous and adaptable than a deterministic theory would lead one to suppose. Architects, indeed, especially those who use prefabricated and standardized dwellings, for example, have been criticized for "stamping people to a common mould." The answer to this sort of criticism is simply to go and look at the interiors of those standardized rooms—better still, at the interior designs on the even more standardized cupboards in army barrack-rooms—to appreciate how little individuality is inhibited by standardization.

Furthermore, people may well be more adjustable than is often supposed. Cullingworth, for instance, found that, although 54 per cent of the residents of the Worsley overspill estate had not wished to leave Salford, by the time they had lived in Worsley for a few years, only 17 per cent of them wished to return to the city.[25] Similarly, while any movement of population inevitably causes some personal disturbance which people dislike, all the evidence shows that, for most people, this is a temporary phase and that they settle equally well in the new area as in the old.[26]

A further demonstration of the point came from an inquiry into the tenants' reaction to moving into the first precinct of the Hutchesontown-Gorbals redevelopment scheme in Glasgow. The scheme comprised flats and maisonettes. Allocation to the houses was made by ballot, so that it was a matter of chance which kind of dwelling each tenant got. When the tenants were asked about their preferences, it was discovered that the flat-dwellers preferred the flats and the maisonette-dwellers the maisonettes and that each group of tenants justified its preference by criticizing aspects of the other type of dwelling which did not trouble the people who actually lived in them.[27]

Conclusions

Two main conclusions follow from all this. First, architectural design, like music to a film, is complementary to human activity; it does not shape it. Architecture, therefore, has no kind of magic by which men can be redeemed or society transformed. Its prime social function is to facilitate people's doing what they wish, or are obliged to do. The architect achieves this by designing a physical structure that is able to meet known and predictable activities as conveniently and economically as possible. However, human behavior is like runny jelly—not formless, but wobbly and changeable; and since he cannot predict its changes, the designer also has to allow as best he can for such new demands as may come to be made of his buildings. More positively, perhaps, it is open to him to provide cues in the potential environment which he is creating which might serve as foci for these new activities or suggest them. He may even be able, as Mackintosh did for the modern movement, to set forth in design ideas and suggestions which may then directly influence a society's aesthetic and, through that, its whole *Weltanschauung*. But even this is far from architectural determinism: and the first conclusion, I believe, is that architects should be more modest and realistic about their ability to change the world through design.

The second conclusion is that architecture should be considered more carefully in relation to other factors that contribute to the total environment. This point applies particularly to town-planning. It seems to me that this is the *leitmotiv* of Jane Jacobs' critique of American planning practice.[28] For the main point of her book is that, instead of razing great areas of American cities to the ground and injecting "cataclysmic money" into massive and deadening rebuilding projects, planners should think about what might be done to encourage the process of rehabilitation which is undertaken, in places like Boston's North End, by the people of the district in the teeth of unsympathetic planning departments and credit-houses. It is similarly expressed in the report which I recently prepared for the Basingstoke development committee on the social aspects of town development, which began by proposing social unity and social vitality as the main social objectives of such a scheme and went on to suggest ways in which the pattern of social administration and the people themselves who would be moving into the town, *as well as* physical design, could jointly contribute to the achievement of those objectives.[29]

The adoption of this view-point leads, I believe, to a reappraisal of the sociologists' role in the design process. At present, I suspect, sociology is regarded simply as a method of inquiry, as tantamount to "doing a survey." The sociologist, then, is thought of *à la* Geddes, as the specialist fact-finder who provides some of the specifications of a "mass" demand to which large municipal building projects must be tailored. That this is too limited a view comes out very clearly when different groups of consumers take different views about the design of the same kind of building. Brian Wells, for instance, discovered that office-managers preferred large, open office spaces while supervisors and clerks preferred smaller spaces; and that both groups could produce good organizational reasons to support their preferences. If a social survey were all that were required, then the sociologist's task would end there. But, as Wells points out, he must go on to examine what consequences large and small office-areas have for social attitudes and behavior and to relate this analysis to the functions for which the office, as a social organization, is set up. In this sense, Wells concludes, "organizational and management problems will become part of the architectural and design problem."[30] Social theory is concerned precisely with these questions of social organization; and sociologists and social psychologists have at their disposal an increasingly sophisticated theory as well as the methods for analyzing organizational structures. They may thus be able to contribute more fully to the elucidation of design briefs.[31] Their contribution, however, would be the more valuable if it were based upon a clearer understanding of how physical design, people and patterns of administration interact to produce whatever we might mean by "total" or "effective" environments. If it is agreed that determinism is a most inadequate make-shift for such an understanding, then the somewhat critical tenor of this paper may perhaps be accepted as a positive step towards the development of a more fruitful and creative partnership than presently obtains between architecture and the social sciences.

NOTES

1. From an article in *Architectural Design*, 1963: my emphases and comments.
2. E. Cooney, *New Homes and Social Patterns*, Institute of Community Studies (mimeoed draft), p. 80.

3. See H. J. Gans, "Planning and Social Life"; I. Rosow, "The Social Effects of the Physical Environment," both in *Journal of the American Institute of Planners*, May 1961; M. Abrams, "Planning and Environment," *Journal of the Town Planning Institute*, May 1962; P. Willmott and E. Cooney, "Community Planning and Sociological Research: A Problem of Collaboration," *Journal of the American Institute of Planners*, May 1963 (also published in *Architectural Association Journal*, February, 1962).

4. *Architectural Association Journal*, January 1965, p. 167; my italics.

5. "The Social Implications of a Town Development Scheme," Southampton, 1962 (mimeo), p. 7.

6. L. Festinger, S. Schachter and K. Back, *Social Pressures in Informal Groups*, New York, 1950, p. 160.

7. P. H. Mann, *An Approach to Urban Sociology*, London, 1965, p. 172.

8. "Site Planning and Layout in Relation to Housing," in *Design of Dwellings*, London, 1944.

9. *The Size and Social Structure of a Town*, London, 1943.

10. For an alternative view, see N. Dennis, "The Popularity of the Neighbourhood Community Idea," *The Sociological Review*, December, 1958.

11. As Hugh Wilson commented in his inaugural address earlier in the year: "We all know those extensive publications of useless facts." *Architectural Association Journal*, February, 1965, p. 198.

12. For a useful bibliography and review of these studies, consult the articles already cited by H. J. Gans and I. Rosow, in *Journal of the American Institute of Planners*, May 1961.

13. I. Rosow, *op. cit.*, p. 131.

14. L. Kuper, "Blueprint for Living Together," in *Living in Towns*, London, 1953 and V. Hole, "Social Effects of Planned Rehousing," *The Town Planning Review*, July 1959, p. 168.

15. C. Bauer, quoted in I. Rosow, *op. cit.*

16. See, for example, M. Broady, "The Organization of Coronation Street Parties," *The Sociological Review*, December, 1956.

17. *Neighbourhood and Community*, Liverpool, 1954; J. M. Mogey, *Family and Neighbourhood*, Oxford, 1956.

18. P. Willmott and E. Cooney, *op. cit.*, pp. 125–126.

19. H. Wilson, *op. cit.*, p. 197: my italics.

20. H. J. Gans, "Some Notes on Physical Environment, Human Behaviour and their Relationships," quoted in M. Abrams, *op. cit.*, p. 122.

21. V. Hole, *op. cit.*, p. 169.

22. "The Design and Use of Central Area Dwellings," *Housing Review*, January–February, 1961.

23. *Architectural Association Journal*, February, 1965, p. 207.

24. "Subjective Responses to the Lighting Installation in a Modern Office Building and their Design Implications," *Building Science*, 1965, p. 66: my italics.

25. J. B. Cullingworth, "Social Implications of Overspill: the Worsley Social Survey," *The Sociological Review*, July 1960, pp. 80, 93.

26. M. Broady, "Social Adjustment in New Communities," *Royal Society of Health Congress*, 1962.

27. *Housing Review*, *op. cit.*

28. J. Jacobs, *The Death and Life of Great American Cities*, London, 1964.

29. M. Broady, "The Sociological Aspects of a Town Development Scheme," Basingstoke Town Development Joint Committee, 1964 (mimeo).

30. B. Wells, "A Psychological Study with Office Design Implications," *The Architects Journal Information Library*, 1964, p. 881.

31. Cf. Boris Ford's statement "I think we would genuinely have to go on to say that you architects are as ill-equipped to think sociologically as we academics have proved ourselves to be"; and Nicholas Malleson's plea for the social scientist as the "third party in the transaction between the brief-making academic and the architect holding the brief": in "University Planning," *Architectural Association Journal*, January 1965, pp. 160, 168.

185

PART THREE
Environmental Influences on Health and Well-Being

12

The Housing Environment
and Family Life

DANIEL M. WILNER, ROSABELLE PRICE WALKLEY,
THOMAS C. PINKERTON, AND MATTHEW TAYBACK

The oldest tradition of scientific investigation of the social effects of architecture and the planned environment deals with their effect upon health. As we stated earlier, Vitruvius was aware of this aspect of building, but empirical studies of the influence of housing and of work environments on disease and mortality first became widespread in the early nineteenth century. The stimuli for these studies were the increases in epidemic diseases and death rates that accompanied the rapid urbanization of European and American cities. These investigations provided the intellectual underpinnings for housing reform movements and for legislation to improve factory conditions on both sides of the Atlantic. Scientific work has continued unabated now for well over a century and a half, extending beyond physical health to include consideration of mental health and symptoms of social pathology, such as delinquency, crime, family disorganization, and divorce.

Several issues have emerged from this work around which current research tends to focus. One is the degree to which the negative or positive influence of housing on health is the result of the impact of the physical environment per se and the degree to which it can be attributed to the social characteristics of the people who live in good or bad housing. A second is the delineation in precise terms of those aspects of architecture and the environment that are principally responsible for the influence that the physical environment can exert on illness and social pathology. A third is the clarification of the kinds of behavior or illness that are most likely to be affected by the quality of the environment.

Information pertaining to all of these issues was collected for the study reported in the following selection. The selection itself is the summary and concluding chapter of a monograph written by Wilner and his associates describing a study they conducted in Baltimore during the 1950s. In their research the authors examined the effect that rehousing of a low-income Negro population from a slum area to a new, nearby public housing project had on the health of the individuals involved. The health of this test group

Reprinted from Daniel M. Wilner, Rosabelle Price Walkley,
Thomas C. Pinkerton, and Matthew Tayback, "Summary and
Conclusions," in *The Housing Environment and Family Life*
(Baltimore: The Johns Hopkins Press, 1962), pp. 241–252.

of about 300 families was compared with the health of a control group of about the same size who remained in the slum area. Data were collected and interviews conducted over a 6-year period.

Wilner and his colleagues discovered that the health of the test group improved in many respects. This result has been interpreted to mean that when housing conditions are highly inadequate, the physical environment itself can have a deleterious effect upon health, and that when a group that formerly lived in such conditions moves to better housing its illness rates will diminish. Because this study dealt with a group living in an unusually poor environment, its implications for the influence of more favorable environmental conditions is not clear. However, most epidemiologists and other specialists working in the field of environmental health have concluded that except in such cases of extreme environmental inadequacy, social factors have at least as much influence as physical factors upon the health of the population.

Wilner and his colleagues measured a vast array of housing characteristics for both the test and control populations. They examined housing structure; the type and condition of available facilities, including bathrooms, kitchens, water supply, and heating; and the quality of maintenance of the dwelling unit; they also made various measures of density, including number of people per floor area, persons per room, and persons per sleeping room. In general, they found that density was the most powerful factor for explaining variations in the health of the two groups.

For the most part, housing studies have shown that the environment has a greater impact on behavior within the dwelling unit and on attitudes toward the home environment itself than it does on behavior outside the home or on attitudes relating to problems and situations outside the home, such as attitudes toward work or school. The Baltimore study confirms this generalization, except for the interesting finding that the school performance of the children in the test group was superior to the performance of the children who remained behind in the slum.

□

This selection provides the summary and conclusions for three principal components of a study of the effects of housing on physical and mental health. The study was carried out at The Johns Hopkins University in the years 1954–1960 and involved measurement of approximately 1000 families (5000 persons) over a 3-year period of time (1955–1958).

The instigation to undertake the research arose from three principal considerations. First, is the scholarly general interest in the effects of man's physical environment on behavior, an environment which in our epoch is, of course, largely of man's own devising. Secondly, in a more pragmatic vein, is the belief and conviction among social planners and officials in public agencies that improved housing leads to an improve-

ment in health and the amelioration of social ills. A third consideration to some extent bridges the first two. This is the need to gain experience in the conduct of the sort of systematic research on complex
social variables that may lead to relatively unequivocal assessment of
effects.

A review of representative research revealed some demonstration of
the relationship between housing and health, the direction of the relationship in most cases being: the better the housing, the better the
health, and the fewer the social maladjustments. However, in many instances, an equally plausible relationship could very likely be demonstrated between health and many correlates of housing quality, such as
education, income, or general cultural level. In other words, because of
the research design principally employed—the cross-sectional study—
it has been difficult to rule out the effects of non-housing factors.

In an effort to provide more conclusive findings, a nearly classical
study design was adopted in the present research. It involved two
samples, each surveyed 11 times during the study: a test group originally living in the slum but subsequently moving to a new public
housing project; a control sample matched to the test families on many
characteristics and slated to *remain* in the slum. The housing development to which the test families moved consisted architecturally of
both high-rise and low-rise buildings.

Both groups were surveyed initially *before* the test sample moved to
good housing. Subsequently, a total of 10 "after" surveys were conducted with each family in the home. Detailed assessment was made of
housing quality, physical morbidity, and social psychological adjustment. In addition, the performance of every child attending public
school was assessed from school records.

Originally, the test group consisted of approximately 400 families
(2000 persons); the control group of 600 families (3000 persons). Two
problems arose which made necessary some adjustment of the two
samples before the final analysis of the data began. The first problem
was attrition in the samples over time. Such losses were not unexpected,
and, in fact, unusually time-consuming measures were used to keep
them to a minimum. In the course of the ten waves of morbidity and
adjustment surveys in the "after" period of the study, the sample loss
was approximately 1.3 per cent per wave, or about 13 per cent of the
originally constituted matched groups.

The second problem was totally unexpected. It was found that control families were, in the passage of time, not only moving about in the
city at the rate of approximately 10 per cent per wave, but also that

191

much of the movement was to improved housing—both public and private. This development undoubtedly was due to the increasing availability of adequate housing in the period 1955–1958, while the study was being conducted.

In order to adhere to the experimental conditions required by the study design, the original samples were adjusted to take losses and moves into account. There resulted two reduced effective samples, well-matched on a number of demographic, initial health and initial adjustment characteristics: a test group of 300 families (1341 persons), all in good housing after the initial move, and 300 control families (1349 persons), who, despite some improvement in housing during the study, were in poorer housing on the average, than the test families. Both samples consisted of low-income Negro families. All subsequent findings were based on these adjusted samples.

Physical Health

At the outset of the study, consideration of the ways in which the housing quality of test and control groups would differ led to a number of hypotheses and expectations regarding the role of housing in disease. Among important housing items considered were density and crowding, hot water and facilities for cleanliness, toilet, sharing of facilities, screening, rodent infestation, food storage and refrigeration. It was anticipated, for example, that variation in the quality of these factors would affect introduction of infective organisms into the dwelling unit and their subsequent transmission among family members either by airborne or contact means.

Beginning with initial over-all comparability on morbidity matters, it was expected that, as a consequence of subsequent differences in housing quality, test rates of the incidence of illness would be lower than control rates. The prediction of lower test incidence included both serious and less severe episodes of illness. There was, in addition, the expectation that rates of disability would be lower in the test group than among controls. Finally, it was expected that certain categories of disease might be particularly affected by the housing differences: acute respiratory infections, the communicable diseases of childhood, tuberculosis and syphilis, digestive complaints, and inflammatory and noninflammatory diseases of the skin. The incidence of accidents in and about the home was expected to be influenced by housing dimensions such as space, maintenance and repair. It was thought, also, that the generally "harder" living in the slum might contribute to a higher rate of exacerbation of chronic conditions in the control than in the test population.

MORBIDITY

The morbidity data provided findings which, in general, confirmed the hypotheses for persons under 35 years of age, and especially for children, but there was little confirmation of the hypotheses for persons of age 35–59.

Persons under 35 Years of Age: Episodes of Illness and Disability. For persons under 35 years of age, general confirmation of the hypotheses was observed in the last 2 years of the study for serious episodes, for less severe episodes, and for total days of disability.[1] Several subgroups, distinguished by age and sex, varied in degree of confirmation of the general directional trend.

Males under 20 years of age as a group appeared to show the greatest effects, the magnitude of the test-control differences appearing larger for them than for girls, both in rates of episodes and days of disability. While all of the more refined age groups contributed to the general findings for persons under 20, the 5–9 year-old group, for both sexes, showed most consistently lower test than control rates of illness and of disability.

Among young adults ages 20–34, females showed far greater and more consistent effects than did males. Test rates among the females in this age group were lower than control rates in episodes of any severity as well as in days of disability.

Persons under 35 Years of Age: Types of Illness. Expectations regarding the categories of disease that would be most affected by housing quality were only partially borne out. Among *children* (under 20 years of age), the findings indicated that in the final 2 years of the study, test rates were regularly lower than control rates in three illness categories: infective and parasitic conditions (mainly the communicable diseases of childhood), digestive conditions, and accidents.[2] The findings with respect to accidents are especially important and clear. Accidents were one-third lower in the housing project as contrasted with the slum. The data showed general confirmation of this fact among all age and sex groups under 20. In at least 1 of the 2 years, test rates were also lower than control rates in respiratory conditions, and allergic and metabolic episodes.

Among *adults* (20–34 years of age), hypotheses regarding communicable diseases, such as respiratory and digestive conditions, were in general not borne out. However, slightly lower test than control

193

rates of episodes were distributed over a wide range of conditions, including some that were predominantly chronic in nature, such as allergic, endocrine and metabolic diseases, mental disorders, and circulatory conditions.

Persons under 20 Years of Age: Morbidity in the "Interim" Period. The data for children during the "interim" period, approximately 5 months following the resettlement of test families into their new quarters, was of considerable epidemiologic interest. The findings showed during this period that test rates of illness and disability were *higher* than control rates for almost every age-sex category in the group under 20 years of age. Further examination of "interim" period data by classification of disease revealed that the higher test rates were entirely accounted for by three categories of conditions: infective and parasitic, respiratory, and digestive, all of which have communicability as a principal feature. The most likely explanation was that the test children, newly assembled into the housing project, were strangers to one another in more than just a social sense, and lacked group immunity to common communicable diseases. A similar phenomenon has been observed in the rise of infectious disease in other newly assembled groups, for example, new recruits in the armed services.

Persons 35–59 Years of Age. In contrast to the morbidity data for persons under 35, the findings for persons 35–59 years of age showed general nonconfirmation of the study hypotheses in the "after" period. In the final 2 years, test rates were higher than control rates, among males, for serious episodes of illness and days of disability; among females, for both serious and less severe episodes and for days of disability. The test-control differences, while not statistically significant, were of considerable magnitude. Investigation of the reasons for this unexpected direction of differences revealed the existence of a small but disproportionate number—more among tests than controls—of persons with a relatively large number of episodes in the "interim" period, and with a history of chronic illness at Wave 1. Adjusting the data to take this inequality into account resulted, for males, in lower test than control disability rates in the final year of the study, and for females, resulted in lower test than control episode and disability rates in the last two years.

MORTALITY

It was found, unexpectedly, that 10 control deaths in contrast to 2 test deaths occurred in the "after" period of the study. The 2 test deaths

194

were among children under 6 years of age. Of the control deaths, 5 were likewise very young children, and 5 were among persons 60 years of age and older.

Among the older persons, the finding of 5 control deaths compared to no test deaths was of interest in itself, although the numbers were too small to be anything but suggestive of the relationship of housing to mortality. One consequence of the control deaths among the older persons in the study was the necessity for removing the cohort of persons 60 years of age and older from the morbidity analysis. The 20 test and 20 control persons who originally constituted this age group had the highest rates of episodes of illness and disability of any of the age categories in the study. To analyze the morbidity of this cohort would therefore have involved estimating the illness rates of the controls who had died, and it was felt that this could not be done properly.

FREEDOM FROM ILLNESS

Wave-by-wave data as a per cent of all persons in the test and control samples showed only small differences between the two groups in the proportions of individuals who experienced *no* illness. At most, there was a modest directional trend in which tests were more likely than controls to be free of illness in nine out of the ten "after" waves. Test persons of all ages tended to be freer of illness than control persons, more so for males than for females.

CHILDBEARING EXPERIENCE

The general childbearing experience of females in the study was described in terms of the outcomes of pregnancy and the morbidity of the mother. The data reported were for Waves 3–11, this time period being designated in order to insure that pregnancies of the test women began after the move into the project, and, therefore, that the prenatal experience took place under good housing circumstances.

The findings revealed little to suggest that differential housing affected, in any significant way, the outcomes of pregnancies. There was similarity between the test and control mothers as to the number of pregnancies that occurred and the ages of the women at outcome. There appeared to be a slight excess of perinatal mortality among the test outcomes, but there was evidence of somewhat greater incidence of prematurity among the control live births. Little difference occurred between the two groups in the incidence of either minor or more serious complaints during the pregnancies. A slightly smaller proportion of

195

the test than of the control pregnancies were *free* of episodes of illness related to childbearing, the test-control difference being equally distributed among major and minor complaints.

Social Psychological Adjustment

Test-control differences in the quality of housing were expected to play a role not only in physical health but also in matters of social psychological adjustment. Of the specific elements that distinguished test from control housing, it was expected that a few factors, such as space in the dwelling unit, would influence both morbidity and social adjustment. However, several elements of housing quality that were thought to affect social attitudes and behavior differed from those believed to influence morbidity. Among these were aspects of the larger housing environment such as architecture and community facilities, as well as the esthetic qualities of the dwelling unit.

It was also apparent that there was a difference between social-psychological adjustment and physical health or illness, in connection with their dimensional aspects. Whereas morbidity may be considered as consisting primarily of a unitary dimension, measured by episodes of illness and days of disability, attitudes and behavior in social settings, on the other hand, were thought of as multidimensional, consisting of a number of relatively discrete components. Six major social psychological content areas were therefore delineated, and measures were devised for each area which were felt to be suitable for testing the relationship to housing quality.

For each major area, hypotheses were formulated regarding the differences that would be likely to emerge between the test and control groups over time, following the move of the test families to good housing. Various housing elements, individually or in combination, were singled out as likely to be related to the subject matter of the particular adjustment area. Since some of the content areas more clearly involved interchange with the physical environment while others were more deeply rooted in the self, the degree to which confirmation of the hypotheses was expected varied according to the area. Thus, the areas, in their anticipated order of confirmation of housing connectedness, were: reactions to housing and space, relations with neighbors, personal and family relations, attitudes and behavior toward neighborhood and community, social self-concept and aspirations, and psychological state.

The basic social adjustment findings indicated that a majority of the items in each area showed at least a directional trend confirming the expectations specified for the area. However, in most of the areas, by no means all of the test-control differences confirming the hypotheses reached statistically acceptable levels of confidence. The anticipated order in which the areas would confirm the hypotheses was in general borne out, the one major exception being personal and family relations. The status of each area is indicated in the following brief review of the original expectations and the subsequent findings.

REACTIONS TO HOUSING AND SPACE

It was expected that, due to the alteration in numerous physical aspects of their housing, test women would be more likely than controls to express "positive" reactions to specific aspects of the housing environment, and would in other ways indicate awareness of the improvement in their living circumstances.

The data showed marked confirmation of the expectations. A larger proportion of test than control women liked their apartments, commented favorably on the safety of their children's play places, felt they were getting their money's worth for the amount of the rental, indicated an increased likelihood for personal privacy, and reported less friction and dissension directly related to space.

RELATIONS WITH NEIGHBORS

Closer and more amicable relations with neighbors were expected to occur among test than among control families as a consequence of differences in their physical environments. Some of the factors in the housing project that were considered conducive to the formation of these relationships by the test group were: a dwelling architecture providing many opportunities for daily contact, a dwelling unit possessing some esthetic qualities and sufficient room space, and the existence of facilities used in common and under non-competitive circumstances.

The hypotheses of this content area were in general confirmed. Notably, the rehoused families, in contrast to the controls, underwent a marked increase in neighborly interaction of a mutually supportive variety, such as helping out with household activities, with children, and in time of illness. This heightened interaction was not viewed as infringing on privacy. The test women were more likely than controls to report both pleasant *and* unpleasant experiences with nearby women, but they were also more apt to have formed new, close friendships in the immediate neighborhood.

PERSONAL AND FAMILY RELATIONS

Housing-related factors, such as greater space, and general practical and esthetic improvement of the dwelling unit were expected to be conducive to better personal relations within the test families, as manifested by an increase in mutually shared activities (in connection with both routine tasks and leisure-time pursuits), greater feelings of warmth and compatibility, and lessened friction among family members.

The data for this area showed directional trends confirming the hypotheses only in connection with common family activities and the mothers' reactions to, and discipline of, children. Other aspects of intra-familial activities, cooperation, and affect revealed findings that were mixed or counter to the hypotheses.

ATTITUDES AND BEHAVIOR TOWARD NEIGHBORHOOD AND COMMUNITY

The project and the slum neighborhoods were viewed as differing from one another with respect to general physical characteristics, availability and accessibility of community facilities, characteristics of the inhabitants, and quality of the individual dwelling unit. It was expected that these factors would give rise to differences between the test and control groups in feelings of allegiance to, and interest in, the neighborhood, extent of participation in community and neighborhood activities, and in other indicators of good citizenship.

The findings revealed that test-control differences in the expected direction emerged in a number of matters related to the immediate neighborhood. Test respondents showed more pride in their immediate neighborhoods than did control respondents, reported more activities devoted to keeping up the neighborhood, and gave far more favorable views regarding its adequacy as a place to live and to raise children. Other topics which pertained more to the "broader" neighborhood or community, such as satisfaction with proximity to various facilities, interest in "larger issues," and evaluation of Baltimore as a place to live, showed either no systematic test-control differences or only a slight advantage for the test group.

SOCIAL SELF-CONCEPT AND ASPIRATIONS

Although change in perceived social status is customarily associated with altered occupation and income, it was anticipated that an alteration in housing quality, alone, and without attendant increment in income, might give rise to upgrading of self-perceived class affiliation, particularly for members of a socially and economically deprived group like the test families. This in turn led to the supposition that having achieved as self-concept the image of persons "on the way up," the test families might also acquire heightened aspirations: for themselves, in connection with such matters as home ownership or better jobs; for their children, in connection with schooling, future jobs, and other benefits.

In general, the findings revealed partial confirmation of the hypotheses. Test respondents, more than controls, were likely to indicate felt improvement in their position in life, and to report themselves as rising in the world. However, the expectation that heightened aspirations would accompany this perceived betterment was, with a few exceptions, generally not borne out.

PSYCHOLOGICAL STATE

It was expected that the move from a generally depressed and deprived environment to good housing might result, for the test women, in some psychological alterations. These changes were viewed as probably involving intermediary processes rather than being directly relatable to the more tangible, physical elements of housing quality improvement.

Findings for the series of ten psychosocial scales consisting of variables pertaining to the *self*, revealed directional trends confirming expectations on all the scales. Those topics dealing with general morale (Optimism-Pessimism, Satisfaction with Personal State of Affairs, and Potency) were more likely than the scales involving stressful, inner feeling states (Mood, Control of Temper, and Nervousness) to show test-control differences confirming the hypotheses.

School Performance of Children

Consideration of several direct and indirect outcomes of differences in test-control housing quality suggested the possibility of differential scholastic achievement of the test and control children. The housing variable expected to be most directly related to school performance was that of dwelling unit density which, being lower for the test children, was expected to provide greater opportunity to study and to do homework unhampered by interruptions from other family members. In addition, there was the possible advantage accruing to test children related to some other expected effects of good housing: better morale, increased parental aspirations for the education of children, and activi-

199

ties related to their aspirations. Finally, it was anticipated that illness rates, expected to be lower among test than control children, might also play a role in school performance.

To test these hypotheses, a total of 486 test and 510 control school-age children were identified in September, 1956. Approximately 150 in each group were excluded in the interest of maintaining uniformity of school records and in view of the unavailability of data on intitial comparability. After follow-up losses, the records of 293 test and 287 control children attending Baltimore city public schools were examined for evidence relevant to school performance. Age, sex, and grade distributions showed a generally fair degree of comparability between the two groups of children, with test children tending to be slightly in excess in age 10 and under, and grade 5 and under.

Three types of tests were administered to Baltimore public school children: intelligence (Kuhlmann-Anderson and Otis), arithmetic achievement (Metropolitan and Stanford), and reading achievement (Iowa, Metropolitan, and Stanford). The data showed that these tests were administered fairly equally to test and control children, slight differences in pattern of administration being related to the age and grade differences.

Mean scores of the test and control children on the intelligence and achievement measurements were similar in the "before" period, thus indicating close initial comparability of the groups. *In the "after" period, mean test scores (adjusted for grade level of children tested) were also closely similar. Thus, the hypotheses regarding housing and one measure of school performance were not borne out.*

Examination of records of promotions showed that, in a 1-year "before" period, test and control children were comparable in the proportions experiencing normal promotions from grade to grade. *In a 2-year "after" period, test children were considerably more likely to be promoted at a normal pace, control children being held back more often for one or more semesters. In connection with record of promotions, then, study hypotheses were confirmed.*

Efforts to reconcile the findings regarding test performance and promotions suggest several possibilities. One is that promotion standards varied systematically in schools attended by test children in comparison with those attended by control children. There is no evidence in the data to indicate such differential standards. In fact, many test and control children attended the same schools. Where they attended different schools, it is worth noting that "test" and "control" schools were under the same general school administration.

200

Another possible reason for the test-control promotion difference is suggested by the data on daily attendance at school. Corresponding to morbidity differences already described, mean daily attendances of test children was considerably higher than that of control children.

Improved housing quality may thus play an indirect role in school performance of children in a way not completely anticipated by the original hypotheses, by lessening illness and in turn making possible more regular attendance at school. School promotion, while undoubtedly affected by intelligence and intellectual achievement as in more general school samples, is evidently also related in a significant way to regularity of school attendance. The data suggest a modest but specific illustration of the interweaving of environmental, physical, and social variables.

NOTES

1. Serious episodes were those that involved either medical attention or had one or more days of attendant disability; less severe episodes were without either medical attention or disability.

2. Disease classifications derived from the *Manual* of the *International Statistical Classification of Diseases, Injuries, and Causes of Death*, World Health Organization Geneva, 1949.

13

Medical Consequences of Environmental Home Noises

LEE E. FARR

The previous selection by Wilner and his colleagues illustrates the fact that when housing conditions are well below a society's standards, the negative influence on health can be substantial. It would be dangerous, however, to conclude that such findings imply that if housing conditions conformed to current standards, the occupants would necessarily be healthy. For the fact of the matter is that most of the environmental standards developed in our society and incorporated into building codes and design conventions have been oriented to too narrow a conception of the way in which the physical environment and health interact.

The validity of this observation seems to be confirmed in the following selection by Farr. Farr's subject is the effect on health of noise within the home, and more particularly, the process through which unwanted and intrusive sound works its deleterious effect on the psychological and physiological functioning of the human organism. He points out that most discussions of urban and domestic noise have been concerned with the negative consequences of very loud sounds, which can cause hearing impairment, and that building standards have been shaped in order to prevent noise levels that cause direct damage to hearing acuity. However, Farr notes that even noise levels that are acceptable in terms of these standards typically cause nervous tension, anxiety, psychosomatic illness, and, indeed, exacerbate the effects of specific infectious diseases. The reason that these effects have been ignored in setting standards is that epidemiologists and physicians have failed to note that the critical factor in noise is that it is unwanted sound, in other words, that there is an important subjective and social element in people's response to sound, which must be taken into account if the full range of its effects on health are to be understood. Thus quieter sounds made by a neighbor are more annoying than louder sounds made by oneself. With urban densities increasing in our society, the psychological and social processes in the response to noise are likely to become more important relative to the purely biological or somatic impacts. Farr concludes therefore that present American standards for permissible domestic noise are too lenient and recommends collaborative research among architects, physicians,

Reprinted from Lee E. Farr, "Medical Consequences of Environmental Home Noises," *Journal of the American Medical Association* 202, no. 3 (October 16, 1967): 171–174.

and behavioral scientists, as well as collaborative efforts to change building codes.

☐

Noise, or "unwanted and intrusive sound," as a pollutant of personal home environment is a matter of wide public interest. This concern has arisen from a combination of only a few factors. First is the increase in city populations indoctrinated with ideas of home automation. Second is the efficiency with which mechanical devices for household and individual use have been adapted from more costly commercial models. Third, there has been a period of extraordinary prosperity for the great majority of people in the United States which, in turn, has generated a financial capability previously undreamed of for each household and which now permits each abode to have several of the devices increasingly considered not as luxuries but as necessities of modern living. Fourth, the advertising and the general mood of the past few years has, in part, dictated a selection of devices based upon advertising impact rather than on personal need for these so-called laborsaving devices. The general mores of today's society have reinforced advertising appeals by making status symbols of these domestic units. On such a basis, possession is emphasized over performance. Fifth, and finally, an ever-increasing fraction of the ever-increasing number of city dwellers are living in the composite structures known as apartments.

Urbanization, population explosions, technology, and prosperity have thus set the stage for another phase of man's ever-broadening battle to control his surroundings sufficiently to prevent his environment from damaging him. In this instance, home sounds can threaten the health and well-being of one's emotional state.

Crowded conditions in cities have led to less space per home, with gradual abandonment of single dwellings for multiple, because of cost and convenience factors. In apartment dwellings a wall, frequently a very thin one, separates one from his fellows, and no sound-absorbent band of space, plants, earth, or trees serves to diminish sound transmittal from one household to the next.

Exposure to noise is upsetting emotionally and frequently may lead to outbursts of fury or threats, neither of which satisfies and each of which leaves frustration as a legacy. While sound can be generated at levels potentially hazardous to hearing by mechanical devices very frequently found in the home, exposure is not steady enough or sufficiently prolonged to cause hearing impairment—though Rosen's ob-

TABLE 13-1

Intensity of Sounds Common in the Home*

Appliances Being Operated	Apartment A (db)	Apartment B (db)
Living Room†		
Quiet	50	50
Vacuum Cleaner (nozzle engaged on carpet)	72	72
Vacuum Cleaner (nozzle free)	81	73‡
Hi-Fi (loud but not vibrant)	80	75
Television (average volume)	–	68
Kitchen §		
Quiet	56	56
Stove Vent Fan	84‖	68‡
Stove Vent Fan and Dishwasher	88	71‡
Stove Vent Fan, Dishwasher, and Garbage Disposal	91	84‡
Garbage Disposal Empty	–	72
Garbage Disposal with Ice Cubes	–	78
Dishwasher Only	–	69
Bedroom		
Quiet	53	50
Air Conditioner (central system)	–	55
Air Conditioner and Air Filter Fan Unit	–	57
Bathroom		
Quiet	–	53
Ventilating Fan	–	63
Ventilating Fan and Toilet	–	72

*Measurements were made with a sound level meter (C scale). The apartments were in different buildings with different floor plans.

†Measurements were made 6 feet from the vacuum cleaner, 16 feet from the hi-fi, and 8 feet from the television.

§Measurements were from the center of the kitchen.

‡Newer models.

‖Lower and steady sound productions. When hard materials such as bones were introduced into the disposal unit, the sound level rose to above 100 db.

servations on the African tribe living in a quiet environment whose members retain youthful hearing acuity into the older ages gives one pause.[1,2] Measurement of the intensity of some of these sounds reveals intensities sufficient to impair hearing if the exposure were for eight hours per day for the usual working week (Table 13-1). However, when one examines the impact of homemade sounds on man, it is his emotional status rather than his hearing acuity that is in the greater danger.

Both aspects of sound problems must be mentioned—presence and absence. Absence of certain components of sound in a heterogeneous environment may also be pointed to as capable of causing a type of trauma that should be mentioned. Absence of sound perception may follow absence of a given sound and be absolute, or it may appear to exist as a result of a loss of hearing acuity. This is well-documented for the older-age groups. The real or apparent absence of certain sound elements commonly perceived in the background spectra may result in a sense of uneasiness readily interpreted as annoyance. Through inability to effect proper selection and discrimination within certain sound spectra because of hearing acuity loss, a similar annoyance can develop. The effect can be of the same type and degree as that which ensues from sound intrusion. Gaps in sound spectra may have much the same psychological attributes as does noise.

During the last 30 years, much attention has been given to effects of various sound intensities upon the hearing acuity of workers. Maximum permissible levels of sound intensity for factories and offices have been established by regulation. In relation to home environment, until very recently there has been no evidence that design and operational criteria for any single unit in the home need be examined other than for performance or for salability. No attention whatever was given to its operational sound intensity.

In this same 30 years, only one paper on the subject is recorded in the literature, and it touches only obliquely on the necessity and desirability for control of sound in the home. It was written in 1938 by McCord et al., who stated:

It follows as a natural consequence that occupants of buildings, living in artificial atmosphere and thus not dependent on open windows and doors, will in some measure be protected against extraneous noise arising from traffic, nearby buildings, or low flying aircraft.

The multiple and insidious ill effects of noise constitute an inadequately recognized, baneful influence on lives of millions of persons throughout the country, especially those who live in urban areas. Noise deafness constitutes the most serious and tangible of the ill noise effects (echoseoses), but there is in addition a host of scarcely measurable injuries made evident by neurosis, loss of sleep, excessive fatigue, emotional disturbances and the like that jeopardise the complete well-being of most persons, and in which noise may well play a part.[3]

In December 1963, Farr read a paper at the Scientific Assembly of the American Medical Association calling attention to the mechanical devices in the home as sources of noise which could be of significance in health impairment.[4] In the last three years, industry has been extremely progressive in changing design to provide increased performance at less intense sound levels for many devices used in the home (Table 13-1). Industry now uses quietness as a selling quality—a market-tested attribute which shows the need for such attention.

It must be reaffirmed that we are not concerned with noise as an agent in the home which induces hearing loss but rather with the attitudes of household members toward the inescapable sounds of household operation today and with the effects of those attitudes upon the person's health.

Sound as Noise

Noise was defined earlier in this paper as unwanted sound, and it must be emphasized that high sound intensity *is not* a requisite component. Noise thus defined, becomes a highly personal subjective reaction to, and interpretation of, sound perceived. While noise as a quality must not be confused with loudness, in general, a loud, sharp sound will have all of the attributes of noise, since it is usually, particularly if unexpected, intrusive by virtue of its intensity and has a high annoyance value. It seems reasonable that under most circumstances sounds of high intensity are less easily ignored, day or night, than are sounds of low intensity.

We are thus dealing largely with what Kryter called the annoyance value of sound.[5] This he characterized under five qualities: (1) unexpectedness, (2) interference, (3) inappropriateness, (4) intermittency, and (5) reverberation. To Kryter's listing one additional and very important quality should be added—the origin of sound. Self-generated sound commands a very high tolerance in the individual generating it, yet it may have two or more of Kryter's annoyance values of sound. But sound generated by another person or an impersonal sound, such as a sonic boom, has a very high annoyance value, for external sound generally seems to amplify each of the qualities responsible for annoyance.

Age is another factor which may result in sound becoming annoying and irritating, for at advanced ages most people have a loss in hearing acuity. The gradual loss of hearing with advancing age increases the likelihood of extraneous sounds causing interference in communication with greater frequency and at lower intensities of the extraneous sound. Inability to discriminate effectively between some sounds of approximately equal intensities may lead to social embarrassment, which in turn leads to changes in patterns of behavior in efforts to mitigate the degree of interference. These behavioral changes are assumed to temper the source of embarrassment to the person who suffers from the loss of hearing acuity.

In some instances, such a changed pattern appears also to have been

206

incorporated into "status symbols of success." During the era when the older patterns of executive privileges were established, it was undoubtedly true that the executive was an older person. The older executive may compensate, in part, for his loss of hearing acuity by reducing background noise. For example, the pattern of office privileges and amenities by which the executive has a quiet noise-controlled office may reflect the very simple fact that the executive, usually being older, may have lost some of his hearing acuity. If this be so, his ability to select and discriminate among a variety of sounds may have been reduced. This fact is then noted in establishment of a new criterion for executive behavior. This same type of behavior and status pattern is carried over into the executive's home where certain noise control mechanisms are effected, usually by distance rather than specific noise suppression or sound absorbing measures.

The ability to discriminate among sounds and select at will the desired sounds from a complex of heterogeneous sounds as a background or to reject the undesired sounds is in part a function of hearing acuity. When heterogeneous background noise becomes significant, as at a cocktail party in full progress, the problem of discrimination and selection of conversational sound from an adjacent person speaking may require a major effort in an older person. The inability to clearly distinguish what is said then can result in a rejection of participation in such gatherings by this individual, despite the fact that invitations to such affairs within some circles are a measure of success. The high and complex noise level in the background in the instance cited may be traumatic to an individual, because it transcends his speech interference level.

This suggestive pattern of executive behavior has been interfered with by the explosive advance of technology which has catapulted young men into executive positions, and now we are increasingly seeing executives sitting at open desks or at least in glass-walled cubicles.

The converse picture of this loss of discriminating ability is epitomized by a teen-ager studying in front of the television or radio set at or near full volume. This same teen-ager, if a telephone call be anticipated, will hear with astonishing perception the ring of a distant telephone and immediately sort this sound pattern out of a varied mixture of high-intensity environmental sounds. Perhaps this high level of discriminatory ability explains, in part, the tolerance of teen-agers to a background of complex sounds of high intensity.

The differences noted above in ability to discriminate among various

207

sounds in a complex background of sound may help to explain why certain sound backgrounds may be annoying to some and a matter of indifference to others. However, sounds of such intensity as are made by many household devices in present-day living quarters are well capable of generating sounds in excess of that necessary to transcend the speech interference level and of interfering with other types of sound communications as well.

Sound in the Home

While acoustical engineers and architects of this country have been aware of the deterioration of sound environment in the home, their major concern and effort have been directed toward control of noise in places of employment to protect the health of employees. Factories, offices, and many public gathering places have been engineered acoustically at but a small cost increment, with a readily observed return in increased industrial efficiency and improvement in industrial health. Home designers, meanwhile, seem to have concentrated upon appearance, with little thought of quality control of sound, and upon style, which could be merchandised as a status symbol.[6] The ultimate result has been inadvertently to turn kitchens into miniature transient simulators of old-fashioned boiler factories by introducing a variety of sound-producing mechanical devices useful in the performance of kitchen tasks. The ventilating fan over the stove, the dishwasher, the garbage disposal unit, the blender, all make significant contributions to sound, which the steel cabinets or hard plastic covered surfaces reflect, augment, and cause to reverberate. From a basic sound intensity level of 56 db, these may produce an increment to over 100 db in an ordinary kitchen (Table 13-1). A tired, taut person will certainly not leave a kitchen pleasantly relaxed; nor do the roars, squeaks, whirrs, and whines issuing from it lead to quiet contemplation of pleasant meals by those who are waiting.

Further, the sound intensity is of such loudness that for many apartment dwellers conversation in the living room is virtually impossible while some of these devices are in operation. In a large living room tested, a standard vacuum cleaner raised the sound level from 50 to 73 db when the nozzle was fully engaged on the rug, but when this was lifted, the intensity rose to 81 db. The occupants of this household consider their hi-fi record player to be very loud at 80 db. In each case, the instruments were placed in a position simulating that of the user's ear and about 6 feet from the sound source.[4]

Neither have the bedrooms or bathrooms escaped this blight of noise. Bedroom air conditioners, bathroom ventilating fans, and poorly designed plumbing all make their contribution to this melee of sound.

Effects on Illness

The effects of noise in exacerbating disease may be seen in a specific infectious disease, such as tetanus. In other disease states such as anxieties, duodenal ulcer, and other kindred so-called tension ills, the additive deleterious effect of noise is real and immediate. Any disease which may be associated with an emotional charge requires as part of the therapy a calm, relaxed, quiet environment. This is particularly true of disturbed emotional states. The frequency of the latter has brought the attention of psychiatrists to this problem, but it has usually been noted only in passing, although its significance was appreciated as the following quote from Denzel attests:

> We know that noise interferes with rest and relaxation and especially with sleep. While sleep, the complete withdrawal from the world around us, is an obvious necessity for physical and emotional health, less complete withdrawal into the quiet of our homes may also be necessary if we want to retain individual integrity . . . It appears rational and feasible to take positive steps to reduce the sound level of our modern environment if enough people feel the need to do so.[7]

It has already been noted that loudness is not a necessary quality of noise. The cacophony resulting from several radios and televisions tuned to low intensities, but to a variety of programs, can lead to a most annoying experience for the involuntary listener and may be just as destructive of sleep as a loud shot. Increasingly, thought has been given to temperature and humidity control within the home, as well as light, color, and ventilation. It is time that man realizes that his home can be designed to acoustic criteria, resulting in a pleasant environment for him and medically conducive to a state of well-being—permitting him to daily relax, refresh, restore, and reinvigorate himself for the tasks, chores, and strains of life.

Studies on Sound Control

While physicians and psychologists have not been unmindful of the desirability of maintaining sound control in homes, they have done little experimental work on the problem. This stems directly from the complexity inherent in making objective measurements of effects resulting from subjective interpretation. Sound must jar the mood to become noise, and if it does so, then noise results whether the sound be a classical rendition of Bach or a soft off-key hum of a contented individual doing personal chores.

The trauma of noise may bring to the surface a scarcely submerged tension and result in an emotional outburst, or it may provoke symptomatology manifesting itself as a well-recognized medical syndrome. The control of pathways which lead to these diverse expressions is not known. Perhaps with telemetry now becoming a practical means of study, it may be possible to design adequate, meaningful experiments dealing with this problem.

Because of a lack of medical clarity in estimating the significance of noise as an agent of disease, some have sought to control the bane of noise by advocating legislative enactments setting forth specific criteria of construction materials and designs to provide acoustic control in buildings to be used as homes.[8] It is true that often government is looked to as a source of authority which, if properly exercised, can banish many problems involving numbers of people, but there is also some disillusionment with this source as an efficacious agent for control of one's immediate environment. It is clear that the definitive control of a person's immediate environment must be exercised by that individual both to promote health and well-being and to avoid or mitigate illness. Further, it is seen that especially in setting the standards of acoustic criteria for personal needs, no wide area exists for specific exercise of community police powers or extension of community health services. The questions to be resolved are essentially personal, though some broad limits may be set for guidance.

With a basic design which takes into account existing ambient sound patterns, it is possible to construct private quarters in which acoustical properties can be emphasized by choice of furnishings to augment or minimize sound effects just as these are used to accentuate light or color. The physician must join with the acoustical engineer, the architect, and the decorator to establish general acoustical standards of personal environment. Once these standards are agreed upon they can be readily attained by selecting construction materials for their special qualities of absorbance and reflectance. If necessary, these can be created to meet the need, for with the new plastic materials, surface qualities and hardness can be varied at will.

NOTES

1. Rosen, S., et al: Presbycusis Study of a Relatively Noise Free Population in the Sudan, *Ann Otol* 71:727–744 (Sept) 1962.

2. Rosen, S.: Hearing Studies in Selected and Rural Populations: Series 2, *Trans NY Acad Sci* 29:9 (Nov) 1966.

3. McCord, C. P.; Teal, E. E.; and Witheridge, W. N.: Noise and Its Effect on Human Beings: Noise Control as By-Product of Air Conditioning, *JAMA* 110:1553–1560 (May 7) 1938.

4. Farr, L. E.: The Trauma of Everyday Noise, read before the Scientific Assembly of the American Medical Association, Portland, Ore, Dec 3, 1963; abstracted, *JAMA* 187: 36–37 (Jan. 25) 1964.

5. Kryter, K. D.: The Effects of Noise on Man, *J. Speech Hearing Dis* [*Monogr*] 1:17 (Sept) 1950.

6. Farr, L. E.: "The Increasing Medical Significance of Environmental Domestic Noise," in *Texas Conference on Our Environmental Crisis*, Austin, Tex: University of Texas Press, 1966, pp. 210–219.

7. Denzel, H. A.: Noise and Health, *Science* 143:992 (March 6) 1964.

8. Kupferman, T.: H. R. Bill 14602, *Congressional Record* April 21, 1966, pp 8339–8361.

14

Effects of Esthetic Surroundings:
I. Initial Short-Term Effects of
Three Esthetic Conditions upon Perceiving
"Energy" and "Well-Being" in Faces[1]

ABRAHAM H. MASLOW AND NORBETT L. MINTZ

Architects have long been interested in studies that investigated the effects on behavior of such relatively simple properties of the perceived environment as color, light levels, the presence or absence of daylight, and the like, because of their obvious implications for design. However, the design tradition is also concerned with the effects stemming from the esthetic properties of buildings. The esthetic environment differs from the perceived environment in being more complex. Perceptions of beauty and ugliness, of course, also depend upon the senses, but they involve to a greater degree the cognitive capacities of the organism and are heavily influenced by cultural experience.

Despite the considerable discussion among designers, design critics, and philosophers of esthetics about the effects of "beautiful" environments on people, there has been very little empirical research into the question. One of the few examples of such research is reported in the following selection by Maslow and Mintz. The authors asked three groups of college undergraduates to evaluate the degree of energy and well-being displayed in photographs of human faces. One group sat in a "beautiful" room, the second group in an "ugly" room, and the third in an "average" room. The three rooms were decorated and furnished by the authors and Mrs. Maslow.

The group in the beautiful room consistently rated the photographs higher in energy and well-being than did the groups in the average or ugly rooms. To make sure that the differences in the ratings associated with each setting could really be attributed to the esthetic properties of the rooms and not to the attitudes of the examiners, and to find out if the differences endured or were simply an initial adaptive response, the examiners themselves were treated as subjects, although they did not know it. According to Mintz the response patterns of the examiners, who worked in the rooms over a 3-week period, were similar to those of the subjects they tested. Observations of the

Reprinted from Abraham H. Maslow and Norbett L. Mintz, "Effects of Esthetic Surroundings: I. Initial Short-Term Effects of Three Esthetic Conditions upon Perceiving 'Energy' and 'Well-Being' in Faces," *Journal of Psychology* 41 (1956): 247–254.

examiners' behavior indicated that in the ugly room they reacted with boredom, fatigue, and hostility; in the beautiful room they reacted with pleasure, felt comfortable, and had a desire to continue their activity. Indeed, the response to the different esthetic surroundings became more pronounced with time.

This selection also implies that judgments of beauty and ugliness are not totally idiosyncratic, but rather are shared among groups of people. Furthermore, the selection demonstrates that these shared judgments of esthetic quality do affect the way people react psychologically to activities going on around them. However, there is a danger that the architect may over-interpret these findings when he comes to utilize them in dealing with practical design issues. For example, it is not clear from the Maslow and Mintz study how widely standards of esthetic judgment are shared in the population as a whole. Their respondents were all college undergraduates. Would low-income groups have responded to the three rooms in the same way? Would a trained architect have agreed with the authors, Mrs. Maslow, and the undergraduates as to what constitutes a beautiful room? One rather suspects that a hidden cultural dimension was affecting both the standards that defined beauty and ugliness and the reactions to the different settings.

☐

The Problem

Esthetically sensitive individuals together with city planners, art educators, and related workers have long been intuitively aware of the effects of esthetic surroundings. Yet as far as we know there have been no experimental studies published on the effects of beautiful and ugly environments upon people. Surveys of the experimental esthetics (1,3), color (12), and art (5) literature show research to be centered on "formal" properties of rhythm, style, color, line, etc., color preference and personality studies, color-concept matching experiments, and projective technique and art therapy work. We have found research on the effects of music (9,16,17) and color (2,4,6,7,10,11,13,14,15,18) to be focused on the behavioral consequences of different melodic styles or hues *per se*, but not on music or color as part of the complex esthetic environment. The present experiment was undertaken as an initial step in studying the effects of beauty and ugliness upon people. It tested the short-term effects of three visual-esthetic conditions: "beautiful," "average," and "ugly" rooms.

Method

Three rooms were used. The "beautiful" room (BR) impressed people as "attractive," "pretty," "comfortable," "pleasant." It was 11' × 14' × 10' and had two large windows, beige-colored walls, an indirect overhead light, and furnishings to give the impression of an attractive, comfortable study. Furnishings included a soft armchair, a mahogany desk and chair combination, two straight-backed chairs, a small table, a wooden bookcase, a large Navajo rug, drapes for the windows, paintings on the walls, and some sculpture and art objects on the desk and table. These were all chosen to harmonize as pleasantly as possible with the beige walls.[2] The "ugly" room (UR) evoked comments of "horrible," "disgusting," "ugly," "repulsive." It was 7' × 12' × 10' and had two half-windows, battleship-gray walls, an overhead bulb with a dirty, torn, ill-fitting lampshade, and "furnishings" to give the impression of a janitor's storeroom in disheveled condition. There were two straight-backed chairs, a small table, tin cans for ashtrays, and dirty, torn window shades. Near the bare walls on three sides were such things as pails, brooms, mops, cardboard boxes, dirty-looking trash cans, a bedspring and uncovered mattress, and assorted refuse. The room was neither swept nor dusted and the ashtrays were not emptied. The "average" room (AR) was a professor's office 15' × 17' × 10', with three windows, battleship-gray walls, and an indirect overhead light. Furnishings included two mahogany desk and chair combinations, two straight-backed chairs, a metal bookcase, window shades, a metal filing cabinet, and a cot with a pleasant-looking green bedspread. It gave the appearance of a clean, neat, "worked-in" office in no way outstanding enough to elicit any comments. To help restrict room differences to the visual mode, the experiment was done in the evening when the building was quiet; the S's chair in the three rooms was of the same type; the rooms were well-lit (though UR had direct, harsh light); and the windows were always open, preventing the dust and dirt in UR from developing a musty odor.

A six-point, two dimension rating scale was used to test the effects of the conditions upon an S's judgment of ten negative-print photographs of faces. The dimensions to be rated were "energy" and "well-being" for each photograph. The rating scale thus had ten judgments per dimension, each judgment with a weight of from 1–6. Summing the dimensions separately would give two total scores, each having a possible range of from 10–60. These totals were averaged, giving an average "energy" and "well-being" score for each S. This average score could likewise range between 10 and 60. The ten photographs were arranged alternately male and female, with two dummy extras[3] preceding and following this series. Duplicate series were used for the three rooms.

As each S was met by the interviewer (NLM), he was told approximately the following: "We are conducting an experiment on facial stereotypy. You are familiar with Shakespeare's Cassius who had a lean and hungry look; this is an example of facial stereotypy. There cannot be any right or wrong answers as we are interested in the *impressions* faces give you." At this point Kohler's expressive-line figures (8, p. 225) were demonstrated. "In just the same way as these lines appeared to have particular concept characteristics, we think faces will have certain trait characteristics. You are going to see negative prints like this sample. By negative printing, and dressing the people in this unusual fashion, we minimized hairline, clothing, and expression and emphasized bone structure and shape. We want you to give your impressions of these faces, similar to the way you gave impressions of the lines previously." The BR and UR Ss were sent to their respective rooms to be tested by a naive examiner who also thought the experiment was on facial stereotypy. The interviewer brought the AR Ss to their room and tested them. This elaborate prelude served two purposes. It insured the naivete of the Ss and examiners (just one S guessed the purpose, and then only when thinking about the test a few days later), and it helped to reduce tension.

A test of visual-esthetic environment should emphasize spontaneity and informality or else task orientation or test anxiety may reduce the effects. This was demonstrated in a pilot study of similar design to this one, which failed to show significant differences between conditions in part due to the Ss anxiety and task orientation; they hardly looked away from the test material.[4] Therefore, as each S entered the room the examiner was called out on some pretext. The S was left in the room for two minutes, allowing him to "soak" in the visual field. When the examiner returned he engaged the S in a rambling discussion of "fatigue/energy" and "displeasure/well-being" with the intention of getting the S to name the moods just discussed. By allowing the S to choose his own concepts instead of being given our concepts for the dimensions, we felt there was greater likelihood of achieving a common semantic process among the Ss. Assuming the S chose "weary/zestful" and "irritable/content," the examiner then continued: "Now I would like you to tell me if this first face looks slightly, rather, or very weary, or slightly, rather, or very zestful. Then do the same for irritable/content." This was done for each of the ten faces plus the four dummy extras. The S was encouraged to give any other impressions, and task-interrupting, idle conversation initiated by the examiner kept the atmosphere informal. The scores were marked on a score-sheet by the examiner. The S was in the room with the examiner at least 10 minutes additional to the time spent in the room alone.

Twenty-six male and sixteen female undergraduate Brandeis University students volunteered for this experiment. They were recruited at large and simply told that we wanted them for "a study in faces and traits." Sixteen were for the BR group, sixteen for the UR group, and ten for the AR group. There were an even number of males and females in BR and UR, only males in AR. A naive male and a naive female were hired to examine the BR and UR Ss; one of the authors (NLM) examined the AR group.

The following controls were used with the BR and UR groups. Each experimenter tested eight Ss in the BR group and eight in the UR group, four of which were of one sex and four of the other. Half of the Ss in each group were asked to rate "energy" first and half to rate "well-being" first. After these groups were tested, the AR group was added to give additional information. Analysis of the BR and UR groups indicated these controls would be unnecessary, so all AR Ss were males, tested by a male examiner, and asked to rate "energy" first.[5]

Our hypotheses were that scores obtained in the "beautiful" room would be higher (more "energy" and "well-being") than those in either the "average" or "ugly" rooms, and that scores in the "ugly" room would be lower (less "energy" and "well-being") than those in either the "average" or "beautiful" rooms.

Results

Table 14–1 gives the results of an analysis of variance on the differences in scores obtained in the three rooms. The scores for the three rooms were significantly different, as shown by the F ratio. Since the variances were not significantly heterogenous, the F indicates a significant difference in the means. Table 14–2 shows these differences. The average ratings for "energy" and "well-being" in BR were significantly higher (beyond the .001 level) than ratings in UR, and significantly higher (beyond the .05 level) than ratings in AR. The average ratings in AR were higher, but not significantly so, than ratings in UR.

TABLE 14-1

Differences in Scores Obtained for Three Room Conditions
Based on an Average Score for Each of 42 Ss

Source of Variation	df	Variance Estimate	F	p
Between Rooms	2	153.25	6.49	.01
Within Rooms	39	23.63		
Total	41			

Since an average score below 35 would indicate the S generally rated the ten faces as "fatigued" and "displeased," while one above 35 would indicate the S rated the faces as having "energy" and "well-being," Table 14–2 indicates a second result.[6] It can be seen that the mean for the UR group is within the "fatigued" and "displeased" range; the mean for AR at the upper limit of the "fatigued" and "displeased" range; and the mean for the BR group within the "energy" and "well-being" range.

Discussion

We may summarize the results as follows. The Ss in our "beautiful" room gave significantly higher ratings (more "energy" and "well-being") than Ss in either the "average" or "ugly" rooms. Also, while the mean for the scores in the "beautiful" room fell in the "energy" and "well-being" range, the means for the other two groups fell in the "fatigued" and "displeased" range, indicating a qualitative difference in the group scores. We can be rather confident that the difference between the

TABLE 14-2

Differences between the Means of Scores in Three Room Conditions

Room	Mean	Compared to Room	Mean Difference	t*	p†
UR	31.81	AR	2.19	1.12	.30
AR	34.00	BR	3.99	2.04	.05
BR	37.99	UR	6.18	3.54	.001

*The within rooms variance estimate of Table 14-1 was used as the estimate of the standard error of the difference.

†Since the standard error was based on 39 df, the *t* was entered as a *CR* in the normal probability table.

scores obtained in BR and UR is reliable. While the scores in AR are significantly lower than those in BR and somewhat higher than those in UR (results which are in the expected order), we cannot be as confident of where, between BR and UR, the AR group is placed. Recognizing the situational nature of our definitions of beauty, average and ugly, there still are interesting implications if our research would continue to find the effects of "average" surroundings to lie closer to those of "ugly" than to those of "beauty," rather than finding that effects of "average" lie midway between the two, or closer to "beauty." This, of course, would have immediate relevance for professors and their offices.

While many questions remain to be answered by research now in progress, certain points may be noted at the present time. We may begin by excluding the possibility that differences between groups resulted from suggestion or a "role-playing" attitude assumed by the examiners or the Ss. Indirect interviewing of the examiners after each day's testing, and each S after being tested, assured us that the examiners and Ss continued to be unaware of the experimental purpose. The controls for noise, odor, time of day, type of seating, examiners, etc., make us rather confident that the potent factor lay in the visual-esthetic qualities of the three rooms.

Regarding the effects obtained, a number of problems come to mind, some of which will be treated in the second section of this selection. Were these merely short-term effects; would the Ss adapt to the rooms with time and negate the initial differences obtained? How many individuals in each group were affected by the conditions? Were the Ss affected by the rooms *per se*? The possibility also exists that the results could have been obtained via the effect of conditions upon the examiners. This, of course, would not change the major implication of the findings; it would shift the emphasis from the rooms having a short-term effect directly upon the Ss to their having a long-term effect upon the examiners, which sufficiently affected the interpersonal relations between examiner and S so as to cause differences in group scores irrespective of which examiner was present.

In considering what may be the "potent" visual-esthetic aspects of the rooms, we may tentatively exclude as crucial in themselves the differences between room sizes, and neatness, orderliness, or cleanliness. Although UR was the smallest, AR was the largest; although UR was dirty and messy, AR was clean and neat. Both UR and AR had gray walls and cold colors in contrast to beige walls and warm colors in BR. While this may be important for understanding the difference between BR and AR scores, by itself it would not explain the possibly genuine difference between AR and UR scores. At present the most reasonable conclusion appears to be that all of these aspects were operating to produce three esthetically different-appearing rooms, which in the case of "beautiful" and "ugly" resulted in clear differences between Ss ratings of the "energy" and "well-being" of faces.

Summary of Section One

An experiment was conducted as an initial step in studying the effects of esthetic surroundings upon people. Three visual-esthetic conditions were used: "beautiful," "average," and "ugly" rooms. In each room, subjects unaware of the experimental purpose were asked to rate the "fatigue/energy" and "displeasure/well-being" of ten negative-print photographs of faces. The results were: (1) the group in the "beautiful" room gave significantly higher ratings (more "energy" and "well-being") than groups in either the "average" or "ugly" rooms; (2) the "average" room group had somewhat higher ratings than the "ugly" room group; (3) the mean score for ratings in the "beautiful" room fell in the "energy" and "well-being" range, while the mean for the ratings in the other two rooms fell within the "fatigued" and "displeased" range. Discussion pointed out that: (1) suggestion, "role-playing," or variables other than visual-esthetic ones did not account for the differences obtained; (2) there seems at present to be no single visual-esthetic quality that can account for the differences among all three groups; (3) the effects may possibly have been obtained by the rooms' affecting the subject-examiner relationship.

Effects of Esthetic Surroundings:
II. Prolonged and Repeated Experience in
a "Beautiful" and an "Ugly" Room [7]

NORBETT L. MINTZ

The Problem

The first section of this selection reported that when Ss spent 10–15 minutes rating a series of face-photographs, Ss tested in a "beautiful" room rated the faces as having significantly more "energy" and "well-being" than Ss tested in either an "average" or an "ugly" room. In discussing these results, one question was, "Were these merely short-term effects; would the Ss adapt to the rooms with time and negate the initial differences obtained?" The differences might simply reflect either activity appropriate to a "laboratory" situation, or initial adjustments to the room conditions. If this were so, then Ss having prolonged or repeated experience in less "experimental" circumstances either would show no effects at all, or effects that would rapidly diminish with time. This section utilizes material obtained from the examiners of the previous section that pertains to this problem.

Method

The Brandeis undergraduates who were the male and female examiners referred to in the previous section were also the "subjects" of this study. They were told that they were to be examiners in an experiment "on facial stereotypy." The examiners thus did not know that they were testing the effects of esthetic surroundings, and were *unaware that*

Reprinted from Norbett L. Mintz, "Effects of Esthetic
Surroundings: II. Prolonged and Repeated Experience in a
'Beautiful' and an 'Ugly' Room," *Journal of Psychology* 41(1956):
459–466.

they were to be "subjects" themselves. Therefore, the examiners' behavior can show what happens when people are not acting as Ss in an "experiment."

The examiners each spent six sessions (two per week) testing a total of thirty-two Ss. They tested Ss concurrently; while one examiner tested someone in the "B" room, the other examiner was testing another S in the "U" room. (In the previous section these were referred to as BR and UR respectively.) The first week had two sessions, on successive days, and each was an hour long; the second week had two sessions, separated by one day, and each was two hours long; the third week had two sessions, on successive days, and each was an hour long. The examiners spent the whole of one session in the same room; they would switch rooms on alternate sessions. Each examiner thus spent three sessions in the "B" room and three sessions in the "U" room.

Two measures plus observational notes form the basis of this report. The first measure was the same six-point, two-dimension rating scale used to test the effects of conditions upon Ss of the first section. The dimensions rated were "energy/fatigue" and "displeasure/well-being" for a series of ten negative print face-photographs. Each face was rated as being very, rather, or slightly "fatigued," or slightly, rather, or very "energetic"; likewise for the dimension "displeasure/well-being." Each judgment had a weight of from 1–6; a total score was computed by summing the 10 rating-weights for each dimension and averaging the two sums. This average, which could range from 10–60, then represented a score of "energy" *and* "well-being." Before the formal part of the experiment began, the writer tested each examiner (as if they were Ss) for 15 minutes in one of the two rooms followed by a 15-minute retest with duplicate photographs in the other room. This "practice" period served both to show the examiners the procedure, and to obtain data from these examiners that would be comparable to data obtained from the 32 Ss they would test. The examiners also administered the rating scale to themselves at the end of each session. Each examiner thus had three self-tests in the "B" room and three in the "U" room. This procedure enabled weekly checks on any effects. The purpose given for these retests was, "to establish the reliability of the tests."

The effects of conditions upon the examiners' general interest in and enjoyment of the testing situation might be inferred from a comparison of testing-times for the thirty-two pairs of test situations. Since the

TABLE 14-3

Rating Scale Total Scores for the "B" Room and the "U" Room

| Rooms* | Examiners as *Ss* "Practice" Periods | | Prolonged Sessions, Examiners Testing *Ss* | | | | | |
| | | | First Week | | Second Week | | Third Week | |
	"B"	"U"	"B"	"U"	"B"	"U"	"B"	"U"
"Sheila"	39.0	36.5	35.0	33.5	37.0	33.0	36.0	33.5
"Sid"	38.5	35.0	36.0	34.0	38.0	32.0	36.0	32.5
Means	38.75	35.75	35.50	33.75	37.50	32.50	36.00	33.00
Differences	3.00		1.75		5.00		3.00	

*"Sheila" was in the "B" room for the first "practice" period and the "U" room for the second; "Sid" was in the "U" room for the first "practice" period and the "B" room for the second. "Sheila" was in the "U" room for the first session of each week and the "B" room for the second; "Sid" was in the "B" room for the first session and the "U" room for the second.

examiners tested *Ss* concurrently and since the test procedure and the time each pair of *Ss* entered the rooms was identical for both examiners, the number of times an examiner in the "U" room finished before an examiner in the "B" room can provide a second measure of the effects. Besides recording testing-times, the writer took observational notes whenever possible.

The data will be examined as follows: In these more natural circumstances, will any effects be found? Will any effects that are found *rapidly decrease* after initial adjustments (*i.e.* after the first week)?

Results of Rating Scale

Table 14–3 shows that there were differences between scores for both the 15-minute "practice" periods and the prolonged sessions. The two examiners had higher scores (more "energy" and "well-being") in the "B" room. An analysis of variance for two subjects with repeated mea-

TABLE 14-4

Analysis of Variance for Scores in Prolonged "B" and "U" Room Sessions

Source	df	Mean Square	F	p
Sessions	5	7.5	18.75	<.01
Examiners	1	.1	—	
E × S	5	.4		
Total	11			

TABLE 14-5
Mean Difference between "B" and "U" Sessions of the Same Week

First Week			Second Week			Third Week		
$\bar{X}_\Delta$	t^*	p	$\bar{X}_\Delta$	t^*	p	$\bar{X}_\Delta$	t^*	p
1.75	2.74	<.05	5.00	7.81	<.001	3.00	4.76	<.01

*Based upon the E X S mean square, with 5 df, of Table 14-4.

sures was computed to test these differences between prolonged sessions. The results are presented in Table 14–4. The overall F test for the difference between sessions was significant well beyond the .01 level of confidence. The difference between examiners was negligible. Table 14–5 presents the analysis of the mean difference in scores obtained between a "B" room and "U" room session of the same week. Scores were significantly higher in the "B" room for *each* of the three weeks of prolonged sessions. Table 14–5 also shows that the mean difference in scores for the first week was the *smallest* obtained during the 3 weeks, while that for the *second* week was the largest. Thus, the effects did *not* decrease after the first week.

Results of Testing-Time Comparisons

Table 14–6 tabulates which examiner finished testing first for each of the thirty-two pairs of test situations. When "Sheila" was in the "U" room and "Sid" was in the "B" room, "Sheila" finished before "Sid" a total of thirteen times, compared with twice when she was in the "B" room and "Sid" was in the "U" room. When "Sid" was in the "U" room and "Sheila" was in the "B" room, "Sid" finished before "Sheila" a total of fourteen times, compared with three times when he was in the "B" room and "Sheila" was in the "U" room. The total combined sum shows that the examiner in the "U" room finished testing before the examiner in the "B" room twenty-seven times out of the thirty-two situations; this difference was significant beyond the .001 level of confidence. The combined sums in Table 14–6 show that the examiner in the "U" room finished before the examiner in the "B" room seven out of eight times the first week, thirteen out of sixteen times the second week, and again seven out of eight times the third week. Thus, once again the effects did *not* decrease after the first week.

TABLE 14-6

Number of Times an Examiner Ends
First in the "B" Room and in the "U" Room

Weeks	One		Two		Three		Totals		
Testing Rooms	"B"	"U"	"B"	"U"	"B"	"U"	"B"	"U"	p
"Sheila" First	0	3	2	7	0	3	2	13	.02
"Sid" First	1	4	1	6	1	4	3	14	.01
Combined Sums	1	7	3	13	1	7	5	27	.001

Observational Notes

The following are the notes taken by the writer. It must be emphasized that they are *selective* notes; that is, the writer recorded only those comments and behavior that appeared relevant.

"Sheila"—During the 15-minute "practice" period in the "B" room, she handled and admired an ashtray and remarked enthusiastically upon a piece of sculpture. She commented, "The rug on the floor doesn't quite match the rest of the decor." When taken to the "U" room for the second 15-minute period, she remarked, while rating a picture, "They all look more *blah* (fatigued) in here." As she was led to the "U" room for the first testing session, she exclaimed, "I have to start in here? After testing two *Ss* she asked the writer, "Can't we change rooms, now, or something to break up the monotony? I'm falling asleep in there." On the second session of the first week "Sheila" tested four *Ss* in the "B" room; when told she is through for that day she said, "Only four subjects? I was just getting warmed up."

"Sheila" spent the first 2-hour session of the second week in the "U" room. After the first hour, while the examiners had a 5-minute break, she smiled, stretched, and said (to "Sid"), "The dungeon is all yours." She assumed that they were to switch after 1 hour. When she was told this was not the case, she asked, "You mean I've got to spend the next hour in there too?" She was told that she must test four more *Ss* in the "U" room. When the next *S* arrived, "Sheila" led him down the corridor in the direction of the "U" room. The corridor is a dead end, at the end of which, on the left wall, is the door opening into the "U" room. However, instead of opening this left-wall door, she turned to the *right* wall and opened the only other door at the end of that corridor, mistakingly leading her *S* into the women's toilet! Has the rat in his T maze ever performed a more classical avoidance response?

After testing this S in the correct room, "Sheila" approached the writer and told him she was tired and was developing a headache. "Could we quit early?" She was told that this "would ruin the experimental design." She unhappily returned to the "U" room. The writer found that while waiting for this next S, "Sheila" had fallen asleep.

The second 2-hour session "Sheila" knew she was to spend in the "B" room. As she met the writer, she remarked, "A 2-hour session today? Good; I really feel like working tonight." This mood was sustained throughout that session. The first session of the third week she again was in the "U" room. Throughout this session she waited in the corridor for her Ss; previously she had waited for her next S in whichever room she was testing. At the end of this session she asked, "Tomorrow is the last day (of the experiment)? How nice; I'll end testing upstairs (the "B" room)."

"Sid"—During the 15-minute "practice" period in the "U" room "Sid" remarked, as he entered the room, "Ugh, what the hell did they do, empty the whole building's junk in here?" When taken to the "B" room for the second 15-minute period, he asked, "Is this M's office? Pretty nice. He really makes things comfortable for himself." At the end of the first session, which he spent in the "B" room, he said, "I was really beginning to feel like a wheel in here, sitting in a swivel chair and making like a psychologist. It's a lot of fun." When he was told, at the start of the second session, that he was to test in the downstairs ("U") room, (the rooms were simply called the "upstairs" and the "downstairs" room throughout the experiment) "Sid" remarked, "I knew I couldn't be in 'heaven' forever." After testing one S he approached the writer and said, "I think it's pretty stupid to use this room for an experiment." He was reminded that we were replicating a previous experiment and "must do it exactly the same." At the end of the second session he said, in a question-assertion manner, "Next week I return upstairs, eh?"

The first 2-hour session of the second week "Sid" was in the "B" room. He gave a pleased smile when the writer told "Sheila" that they would not switch rooms after the break. The second 2-hour session he spent in the "U" room. At the break he was generally aggressive in his conversation. He complained about having to add up the scoresheets (a procedure initiated the *first* session of the second week), and in a half-jocular, half-aggressive manner told the writer, "I think I'll just let you add them up from now on." When "Sheila" asked for a match, "Sid" looked in his shirt pockets, found a pack of cigarettes, but no matches. After the break, as he led his next S toward the "U" room, he took a cigarette from his shirt pocket and lit it from matches he suddenly found in his pants pocket. At the end of that session, he asked, "Next week I go back upstairs?" The last session of the third week, "Sid" commented as he entered the "U" room, "Well, this is the last time I'll have to see this hole." [8]

Discussion

The results of the rating scale, the testing-time comparisons, and the observational notes all demonstrated the significant effects of esthetic surroundings. Furthermore, these effects were not limited to initial adjustments. In fact, there were indications on the rating scale and in the observational notes that the 2-hour sessions of the second week *exaggerated* the effects.

May we infer that if the groups previously reported had prolonged experience in these conditions, they too would have continued to show differences in effects? It may be remembered that the 15-minute "practice" periods obtained data from the examiners comparable to data of the previous report. Therefore, the scores of the *initial* 15-minute "practice" period that "Sheila" spent in the "B" room and that "Sid" spent in the "U" room may be compared to the means reported previously for the "B" room and "U" room groups. The means for the groups were 37.99 and 31.81 respectively, with a standard deviation of 4.8. "Sheila" had an initial "B" score of 39.0 and "Sid" had an initial "U" score of 35.0 (see Table 14–3). Although their scores were slightly higher, they were well within one standard deviation for the respective group means; in other words, their scores were not significantly different from scores obtained in similar conditions from unselected college students.

Since the examiners did not have atypical results, it might be expected that the "B" room group would have continued to show higher scores. If bias was introduced by the choice of examiners, it possibly was reflected in the observational notes. That is, other examiners might not have had such gross behavioral changes, or might not have been as free in expressing their feelings.

In the first section, Maslow and Mintz also asked, "Were the Ss affected by the rooms *per se*? . . . the results could have been obtained via the effect of conditions upon the examiners." In like manner it may be asked, "Were the effects upon the examiners brought about by the rooms *per se*?" It is conceivable, for example, that the examiner in the "U" room finished testing first simply because his S "hurried" the procedure along. However, there is ample evidence from the behavioral notes to indicate that the results were not solely determined by the Ss being tested. There probably was a complex relationship whereby the esthetic conditions affected the Ss and the examiners, and the Ss and examiners in turn affected each other.

Summary and Conclusions of Section Two

The present section investigated whether the effects of esthetic surroundings reported in the first section simply reflect either "laboratory" activity or initial adjustments to the room conditions. During a period of 3 weeks, two examiners, *unaware* that they were "subjects" for this study, each spent prolonged sessions testing Ss in a "beautiful" room and in an "ugly" room. On a rating scale, the examiners had short-term effects similar to those reported previously; furthermore, during the entire 3 weeks of prolonged sessions the ratings continued to be significantly higher in the "B" room. The testing-time comparisons showed that an examiner in the "U" room usually finished testing more quickly than an examiner in the "B" room. Observational notes showed that in the "U" room the examiners had such reactions as monotony, fatigue, headache, sleep, discontent, irritability, hostility, and avoidance of the room; while in the "B" room they had feelings of comfort, pleasure, enjoyment, importance, energy, and a desire to continue their activity. It is concluded that visual-esthetic surroundings (as represented by the "B" room and "U" room) can have significant effects upon persons exposed to them. These effects are not limited either to "laboratory" situations or to initial adjustments, but can be found under naturalistic circumstances of considerable duration.

NOTES

1. This research was supported by Brandeis University. We wish to express our thanks to R. Held and R. B. Morant for their helpful discussion and assistance, and J. Glick for his photography work. The second section of this selection will present the more complex data obtained from Ss moving into a second esthetic condition.

2. We wish to thank B. Maslow for her assistance in this.

3. Used for purposes to be discussed in the second section of this selection.

4. The pilot study was conducted by B. Maslow and A. H. Maslow.

5. A four-way classification analysis of variance was done on BR and UR for rooms, experimenters, sexes, and rating order. The scores for rooms were significantly different, but those for experimenters, sexes, and rating order were not, nor did the four variables interact significantly.

6. A *rho* based on the 42 *Ss* for the separate dimension totals ("fatigue/energy" and "displeasure/well-being") showed the dimensions to have a positive correlation of .79, significant beyond the .001 level.

7. The writer extends his appreciation to the Maslows for inspiring this research, to R. M. Held, J. B. Klee, and R. B. Morant for helpful discussion, and especially to "Sheila" and "Sid" for their cooperation. A Brandeis University research fellowship provided the necessary leisure time.

8. On completing this study, the writer told the examiners the real purpose of the experiment. They evidenced surprise at the whole procedure. Especially impressive was their reaction to the notes; *they were not aware that their activities were in such close relationship to the room conditions,* though they both realized that they did not prefer to test in the downstairs ("U") room.

REFERENCES

1. Chandler, A. R. & Barnhart, E. N. *A bibliography of psychological and experimental esthetics, 1864–1937.* Berkeley: U. of California Press, 1938.

2. Deutsch, F. Psycho-physical reactions of the vascular system to influences of light and to impressions gained through light. *Folia Clinica Orientalia,* 1937, Vol. I, Facs. 3 & 4.

3. Drought, R. A. A survey of studies in experimental esthetics. *J. of Educa. Research,* 1929, *20,* 97–102.

4. Ehrenwald, N. Referred to by Ellinger, F. *The biologic fundamentals of radiation therapy.* New York: Elsevier Pub. Co., 1941.

5. Faulkner, R. A survey of recent research in art and art education. In G. M. Whipple, ed., *Art in American life and education, fortieth yearbook, NSSE.* Chicago: U. of Chicago Press, 1941, pp. 369–377.

6. Goldstein, K. Some experimental observations concerning the influence of colors on the function of the organism. *Occup. Ther.,* 1942, *21,* 147–151.

7. Goldstein, K. & Rosenthal, O. Zum Problem der Wirkung der Farben auf den Organismus. *Schweiz. Arch. Neurol. Psychiat.,* 1930, *26,* 3–26.

8. Kohler, W. *Gestalt psychology.* New York: Liveright, 1929.

9. Mitchell, S. D. & Zanker, A. The use of music in group therapy. *J. of Mental Sci.,* 1948, *94,* 737–738.

10. Mitra, S. C. & Datta, A. The influence of color on the estimation of area. *Indian J. Psychol.,* 1939, *14,* 91–94.

11. Mogensen, M. F. & English, H. B. The apparent warmth of colors. *Amer. J. Psychol.,* 1926, *37,* 427–428.

12. Norman, R. D. & Scott, W. A. Color and affect: a review and semantic evaluation. *J. Gen. Psychol.,* 1952, *46,* 185–223.

13. Pierce, D. H. & Weinland, J. D. The effect of color on workmen. *Person. J.,* 1934, *13,* 34–38.

14. Prescott, D. B. Psychological analysis of light and color. *Occup. Ther.,* 1942, *21,* 135–146.

15. Pressey, S. L. The influence of color upon mental and motor efficiency. *Amer. J. Psychol.,* 1921, *32,* 326–356.

16. Rubin, H. E. & Katz, E. Aurotone films for the treatment of psychotic depressions in an army general hospital. *J. Clin. Psychol.,* 1946, 333–340.

17. Schullien, D. M. & Schoen, M. *Music and medicine.* New York: H. Schuman, 1948.

18. Wallis, W. A. The influence of color on apparent size. *J. Gen. Psychol.,* 1935, *13,* 193–199.

15

Grieving for a Lost Home

MARC FRIED

The importance of paying attention to the cultural background of users when trying to understand the effects of the environment on health and well-being cannot be stressed often enough. Farr's selection on home noises points out that even environments that meet established building codes can have deleterious effects because of the way in which the response to noise is mediated through psychological processes and cultural values. Oddly enough, the reverse of this point also seems to be true: environments that are officially regarded as unhealthful and injurious to well-being sometimes have a salutary influence on users, again because of the associations and social experiences the inhabitants have built up over time with the supposedly dangerous or unpleasant environment.

The latter theme is the fundamental concern of the following selection by Fried. Fried interviewed families displaced from the West End of Boston who were forced to find housing in other parts of the city or in the surrounding metropolitan region when the buildings in which they had lived for many years were torn down. The buildings were demolished because, according to the official physical criteria of the urban renewal agency, they were slums in a blighted area: there were too few bathrooms, they did not allow sufficient daylight into the interior, and many of them were poorly maintained. Although the housing undoubtedly was "blighted" in the technical sense defined by these standards, it was part of a social environment that was highly satisfactory to the residents and possessed many characteristics, such as social cohesion, established friendship networks, and a sense of community, that the residents were unable to reproduce in the settings to which they moved. The loss of familiar associations turned out to have a serious negative effect on many of the former West End population, which showed up in the form of poorer mental health. Fried discusses these effects in terms of the "grief reaction," a feeling of depression comparable to the loss one feels after the death of a loved one.

Fried's selection is particularly apposite to the concerns of this volume, because, in addition to demonstrating the importance of the cultural context for plotting the effect of the environment on health, he explains the grief reaction by referring to the sense of spatial identity, or sense of place, a favorite concept of architects and designers when they discuss the signifi-

Reprinted from Marc Fried, "Grieving for a Lost Home," in
The Urban Condition, Leonard J. Duhl, ed. (New York: Basic
Books, 1963), pp. 151–171. © 1963 by Basic Books, Inc., Publishers.

cance of the built environment for behavior and attitudes. He asserts that the sense of spatial identity is fundamental to human functioning, describes its social and psychological components, discusses the way in which the loss of this sense was revealed in many of his interviews, and makes several practical suggestions about how to conduct urban renewal programs so that the sense of place is not totally destroyed in the process of relocation.

☐

Introduction

For some time we have known that the forced dislocation from an urban slum is a highly disruptive and disturbing experience. This is implicit in the strong, positive attachments to the former slum residential area—in the case of this study the West End of Boston—and in the continued attachment to the area among those who left before any imminent danger of eviction. Since we were observing people in the midst of a crisis, we were all too ready to modify our impressions and to conclude that these were likely to be transitory reactions. But the post-relocation experiences of a great many people have borne out their most pessimistic pre-relocation expectations. There are wide variations in the success of post-relocation adjustment and considerable variability in the depth and quality of the loss experience. But for the majority it seems quite precise to speak of their reactions as expressions of *grief*. These are manifest in the feelings of painful loss, the continued longing, the general depressive tone, frequent symptoms of psychological or social or somatic distress, the active work required in adapting to the altered situation, the sense of helplessness, the occasional expressions of both direct and displaced anger, and tendencies to idealize the lost place. (1)

At their most extreme, these reactions of grief are intense, deeply felt, and, at times, overwhelming. In response to a series of questions concerning the feelings of sadness and depression which people experienced *after* moving, many replies were unambiguous: "I felt as though I had lost everything," "I felt like my heart was taken out of me," "I felt like taking the gaspipe," "I lost all the friends I knew," "I always felt I had to go home to the West End and even now I feel like crying when I pass by," "Something of me went with the West End," "I felt cheated," "What's the use of thinking about it," "I threw up a lot," "I had a nervous breakdown." Certainly, some people were overjoyed with the change and many felt no sense of loss. Among 250 women, however,

230

26 per cent report that they still feel sad or depressed two years later, and another 20 per cent report a long period (six months to two years) of sadness or depression. Altogether, therefore, at least 46 per cent give evidence of a fairly severe grief reaction or worse. And among 316 men, the data show only a slightly smaller percentage (38 per cent) with long-term grief reactions. The true proportion of depressive reactions is undoubtedly higher since many women and men who report no feelings of sadness or depression indicate clearly depressive responses to other questions.

In answer to another question, "How did you feel when you saw or heard that the building you had lived in was torn down?" a similar finding emerges. As in the previous instance, the responses are often quite extreme and most frequently quite pathetic. They range from those who replied: "I was glad because the building had rats," to moderate responses such as "the building was bad but I felt sorry," and "I didn't want to see it go," to the most frequent group comprising such reactions as "it was like a piece being taken from me," "I felt terrible," "I used to stare at the spot where the building stood," "I was sick to my stomach." This question in particular, by its evocative quality, seemed to stir up sad memories even among many people who denied any feeling of sadness or depression. The difference from the previous result is indicated by the fact that 54 per cent of the women and 46 per cent of the men report severely depressed or disturbed reactions; 19 per cent of the women and about 31 per cent of the men report satisfaction or indifference; and 27 per cent of the women and 23 per cent of the men report moderately depressed or ambivalent feelings. Thus it is clear that, for the majority of those who were displaced from the West End, leaving their residential area involved a moderate or extreme sense of loss and an accompanying affective reaction of grief.

While these figures go beyond any expectation which we had or which is clearly implied in other studies, the realization that relocation was a crisis with potential danger to mental health for many people was one of the motivating factors for this investigation.[1] In studying the impact of relocation on the lives of a working-class population through a comparison of pre-relocation and post-relocation interview data, a number of issues arise concerning the psychology of urban living which have received little systematic attention. Yet, if we are to understand the effects of relocation and the significance of the loss of a residential environment, it is essential that we have a deeper appreciation of the psychological implications of both physical and social

231

aspects of residential experience. Thus we are led to formulations which deal with the functions and meanings of the residential area in the lives of working class people.

The Nature of the Loss in Relocation: The Spatial Factor

Any severe loss may represent a disruption in one's relationship to the past, to the present, and to the future. Losses generally bring about fragmentation of routines, of relationships, and of expectations, and frequently imply an alteration in the world of physically available objects and spatially oriented action. It is a disruption in that sense of continuity which is ordinarily a taken-for-granted framework for functioning in a universe which has temporal, social, and spatial dimensions. From this point of view, the loss of an important place represents a change in a potentially significant component of the experience of continuity.

But why should the loss of a place, even a very important place, be so critical for the individual's sense of continuity; and why should grief at such loss be so widespread a phenomenon? In order to clarify this, it is necessary to consider the meaning which this area, the West End of Boston, had for the lives of its inhabitants. In an earlier paper we tried to assess this, and came to conclusions which corroborate, although they go further, the results from the few related studies.

In studying the reasons for satisfaction that the majority of slum residents experience, two major components have emerged. On the one hand, the residential area is the region in which a vast and interlocking set of social networks is localized. And, on the other, the physical area has considerable meaning as an extension of home, in which various parts are delineated and structured on the basis of a sense of belonging. These two components provide the context in which the residential area may so easily be invested with considerable, multiply-determined meaning. . . . The greatest proportion of this working-class group . . . shows a fairly common experience and usage of the residential area . . . dominated by a conception of the local area beyond the dwelling unit as an integral part of home. This view of an area as home and the significance of local people and local places are so profoundly at variance with typical middle-class orientations that it is difficult to appreciate the intensity of meaning, the basic sense of identity involved in living in the particular area (2).

Nor is the intense investment of a residential area, both as an important physical space and as the locus for meaningful interpersonal ties, limited to the West End (3). What is common to a host of studies is the evidence for the integrity of the urban, working-class, slum community as a social and spatial unit. It is the sense of belonging someplace, in a particular place which is quite familiar and easily delineated, in a

232

wide area in which one feels "at home." This is the core of meaning of the local area. And this applies for many people who have few close relationships within the area. Even familiar and expectable streets and houses, faces at the window and people walking by, personal greetings and impersonal sounds may serve to designate the concrete foci of a sense of belonging somewhere and may provide special kinds of interpersonal and social meaning to a region one defines as "home."

It would be impossible to understand the reactions both to dislocation and to relocation and, particularly, the depth and frequency of grief responses without taking account of working-class orientations to residential areas. One of our primary theses is that the strength of the grief reaction to the loss of the West End is largely a function of prior orientations to the area. Thus, we certainly expect to find that the greater a person's pre-relocation commitment to the area, the more likely he is to react with marked grief. This prediction is confirmed again and again by the data.[2,3] For the women, among those who had said they liked living in the West End *very much* during the prelocation interviews, 73 per cent evidence a severe post-relocation grief reaction; among those who had less extreme but positive feelings about living in the West End, 53 per cent show a similar order of grief; and among those who were ambivalent or negative about the West End, only 34 per cent show a severe grief reaction. Or, considering a more specific feature of our formulation, the pre-relocation view of the West End as "home" shows an even stronger relationship to the depth of post-relocation grief. Among those women who said they had no real home, only 20 per cent give evidence of severe grief; among those who claimed some other area as their real home, 34 per cent fall into the severe grief category; but among the women for whom the *West End* was the real home, 68 per cent report severe grief reactions. Although the data for the men are less complete, the results are substantially similar. It is also quite understandable that the length of West End residence should bear a strong relationship to the loss reaction, although it is less powerful than some of the other findings and almost certainly it is not the critical component.

More directly relevant to our emphasis on the importance of places, it is quite striking that the greater the area of the West End which was known, the more likely there is to be a severe grief response. Among the women who said they knew only their own block during the prerelocation interview, only 13 percent report marked grief; at the other extreme, among those who knew most of the West End, 64 per cent have a marked grief reaction. This relationship is maintained when a

233

wide range of interrelated variables is held constant. Only in one instance, when there is a generally negative orientation to the West End, does more extensive knowledge of the area lead to a somewhat smaller proportion of severe grief responses. Thus, the wider an individual's familiarity with the local area, the greater his commitment to the locality. This wider familiarity evidently signifies a greater sense of the wholeness and integrity of the entire West End and, we would suggest, a more expanded sense of being "at home" throughout the entire local region. It is striking, too, that while familiarity with, use of, and comfort in the spatial regions of the residential area are closely related to extensiveness of personal contact, the spatial patterns have independent significance and represent an additional basis for a feeling of commitment to that larger, local region which is "home."

The Sense of Spatial Identity

In stressing the importance of places and access to local facilities, we wish only to redress the almost total neglect of spatial dimensions in dealing with human behavior. We certainly do not mean thereby to give too little emphasis to the fundamental importance of interpersonal relationships and social organization in defining the meaning of the area. Nor do we wish to underestimate the significance of cultural orientations and social organization in defining the character and importance of spatial dimensions. However, the crisis of loss of a residential area brings to the fore the importance of the local spatial region and alerts us to the greater generality of spatial conceptions as determinants of behavior. In fact, we might say that a *sense of spatial identity* is fundamental to human functioning. It represents a phenomenal or ideational integration of important experiences concerning environmental arrangements and contacts in relation to the individual's conception of his own body in space.[4] It is based on spatial memories, spatial imagery, the spatial framework of current activity, and the implicit spatial components of ideals and aspirations.

It appears to us also that these feelings of being at home and of belonging are, in the working class, integrally tied to a *specific* place. We would not expect similar effects or, at least, effects of similar proportion in a middle-class area. Generally speaking, an integrated sense of spatial identity in the middle class is not as contingent on the external stability of place or as dependent on the localization of social patterns, interpersonal relationships, and daily routines. In these data, in fact, there is a marked relationship between class status and depth of grief; the higher

234

the status, by any of several indices, the smaller the proportions of severe grief. It is primarily in the working class, and largely because of the importance of external stability, that dislocation from a familiar residential area has so great an effect on fragmenting the sense of spatial identity.

External stability is also extremely important in interpersonal patterns within the working class. And dislocation and relocation involve a fragmentation of the external bases for interpersonal relationships and group networks. Thus, relocation undermines the established interpersonal relationships and group ties of the people involved and, in effect, destroys the sense of group identity of a great many individuals. "Group identity," a concept originally formulated by Erik Erikson, refers to the individual's sense of belonging, of being a part of larger human and social entities. It may include belonging to organizations or interpersonal networks with which a person is directly involved; and it may refer to "membership" in social groups with whom an individual has little overt contact, whether it be a family, a social class, an ethnic collectivity, a profession, or a group of people sharing a common ideology. What is common to these various patterns of group identity is that they represent an integrated sense of shared human qualities, of some sense of communality with other people which is essential for meaningful social functioning. Since, most notably in the working class, effective relationships with others are dependent upon a continuing sense of common group identity, the experience of loss and disruption of these affiliations is intense and frequently irrevocable. On the grounds, therefore, of both spatial and interpersonal orientations and commitments, dislocation from the residential area represents a particularly marked disruption in the sense of continuity for the majority of this group.

The Nature of the Loss in Relocation: Social and Personal Factors

Previously we said that by emphasizing the spatial dimension of the orientation to the West End, we did not mean to diminish the importance of social patterns in the experience of the local area and their effects on post-relocation loss reactions. Nor do we wish to neglect personality factors involved in the widespread grief reactions. It is quite clear that pre-relocation social relationships and intrapsychic dispositions *do* affect the depth of grief in response to leaving the West End. The strongest of these patterns is based on the association between depth of grief and pre-relocation feelings about neighbors. Among those women who had very positive feelings about their neighbors, 76 per cent show severe grief reactions; among those who were positive but less extreme, 56 per cent show severe grief; and among those who were relatively negative, 38 per cent have marked grief responses. Similarly, among the women whose five closest friends lived in the West End, 67 per cent show marked grief; among those whose friends were mostly in the West End or equally distributed inside and outside the area, 55 per cent have severe grief reactions; and among those whose friends were mostly or all outside, 44 per cent show severe grief.

The fact that these differences, although great, are not as consistently powerful as the differences relating to spatial use patterns does not necessarily imply the *greater* importance of spatial factors. If we hold the effect of spatial variables constant and examine the relationship between depth of grief and the interpersonal variables, it becomes apparent that the effect of interpersonal contacts on depth of grief is consistent regardless of differences in spatial orientation; and, likewise, the effect of spatial orientations on depth of grief is consistent regardless of differences in interpersonal relationships. Thus, each set of factors contributes independently to the depth of grief in spite of some degree of internal relationship. In short, we suggest that *either* spatial identity or group identity may be a critical focus of loss of continuity and thereby lead to severe grief; but if *both* bases for the sense of continuity are localized *within the residential area* the disruption of continuity is greater, and the proportions of marked grief correspondingly higher.

It is noteworthy that, apart from local interpersonal and social relationships and local spatial orientations and use (and variables which are closely related to these), there are few other social or personal factors in the pre-relocation situation which are related to depth of grief. These negative findings are of particular importance in emphasizing that not all the variables which influence the grief reaction to dislocation are of equal importance. It should be added that a predisposition to depression markedly accentuates the depth of grief in response to the loss of one's residential area. But it is also clear that prior depressive orientations do not account for the entire relationship. The effects of the general depressive orientation and of the social, interpersonal, and spatial relationships within the West End are essentially additive; both sets of factors contribute markedly to the final result. Thus, among the women with a severe depressive orientation, an extremely large proportion (81 per cent) of those who regarded the West End as their real home show marked grief. But among the women without a depressive orientation, only a moderate proportion (58 per cent) of those who similarly viewed the West End as home show severe grief. On the other hand, when the West End is not seen as the person's real home, an increasing severity of general depressive orientation does *not* lead to an increased proportion of severe grief reactions.

The Nature of the Loss in Relocation: Case Analyses

The dependence of the sense of continuity on external resources in the working class, particularly on the availability and local presence of familiar places which have the character of "home," and of familiar people whose patterns of behavior and response are relatively predictable, does not account for all of the reaction of grief to dislocation. In addition to these factors, which may be accentuated by depressive predispositions, it is quite evident that the realities of *post*-relocation experience are bound to affect the perpetuation, quality, and depth of grief. And, in fact, our data show that there is a strong association between positive or negative experiences in the post-relocation situation and the proportions who show severe grief. But this issue is complicated by two factors: (1) the extent to which potentially meaningful post-relocation circumstances can be a satisfying experience is *affected* by the degree and tenaciousness of previous commitments to the West End, and (2) the post-relocation "reality" is, in part, *selected* by the people who move and thus is a function of many personality factors, including the ability to anticipate needs, demands, and environmental opportunities.

In trying to understand the effects of pre-relocation orientations and post-relocation experiences of grief, we must bear in mind that the grief reactions we have described and analyzed are based on responses given approximately two years after relocation. Most people manage to achieve some adaptation to their experiences of loss and grief, and learn to deal with new situations and new experiences on their own terms. A wide variety of adaptive methods can be employed to salvage fragments of the sense of continuity, or to try to re-establish it on new grounds. Nonetheless, it is the tenaciousness of the imagery and affect of grief, despite these efforts at dealing with the altered reality, which is so strikingly similar to mourning for a lost person.

In coping with the sense of loss, some families tried to remain physically close to the area they knew, even though most of their close interpersonal relationships remain disrupted; and by this method, they appear often to have modified their feelings of grief. Other families try to move among relatives and maintain a sense of continuity through some degree of constancy in the external bases for their group identity. Yet others respond to the loss of place and people by accentuating the importance of those role relationships which remain. Thus, a number of women report increased closeness to their husbands, which they often explicitly relate to the decrease in the availability of other social relationships for both partners and which, in turn, modifies the severity of grief. In order to clarify some of the complexities of pre-relocation orientations and of post-relocation adjustments most concretely, a review of several cases may prove to be instructive.

It is evident that a very strong positive pre-relocation orientation to the West End is relatively infrequently associated with a complete absence of grief; and that, likewise, a negative pre-relocation orientation to the area is infrequently associated with a strong grief response. The two types which are numerically dominant are, in terms of rational expectations, consistent: those with strong positive feelings about the West End and severe grief; and those with negative feelings about the West End and minimal or moderate grief. The two "deviant" types, by the same token, are both numerically smaller and inconsistent: those with strong positive pre-relocation orientations and little grief; and those with negative pre-relocation orientations and severe grief. A closer examination of those "deviant" cases with strong pre-relocation commitment to the West End and minimal post-relocation grief often reveals either important reservations in their prior involvement with the West End or, more frequently, the denial or rejection of feelings of grief rather than their total absence. And the association of minimal pre-location commitment to the West End with a severe grief response often proves on closer examination to be a function of a deep involvement in the West End which is modified by markedly ambivalent statements; or, more generally, the grief reaction itself is quite modest and tenuous or is even a pseudo-grief which masks the primacy of dissatisfaction with the current area.

Grief Patterns: Case Examples

In turning to case analysis, we shall concentrate on the specific factors which operate in families of all four types, those representing the two dominant and those representing the two deviant patterns.

1. The Figella family exemplifies the association of strong positive pre-relocation attachments to the West End and a severe grief reaction. This is the most frequent of all the patterns and, although the

Figella family is only one "type" among those who show this pattern, they are prototypical of a familiar West End constellation.

Both Mr. and Mrs. Figella are second-generation Americans who were born and brought up in the West End. In her pre-location interview, Mrs. Figella described her feelings about living in the West End unambiguously: "It's a wonderful place, the people are friendly." She "loves everything about it" and anticipates missing her relatives above all. She is satisfied with her dwelling: "It's comfortable, clean and warm." And the marriage appears to be deeply satisfying for both husband and wife. They share many household activities and have a warm family life with their three children.

Both Mr. and Mrs. Figella feel that their lives have changed a great deal since relocation. They are clearly referring, however, to the pattern and conditions of their relationships with other people. Their home life has changed little except that Mr. Figella is home more. He continues to work at the same job as a manual laborer with a modest but sufficient income. While they have many economic insecurities, the relocation has not produced any serious financial difficulty for them.

In relocating, the Figella family bought a house. Both husband and wife are quite satisfied with the physical arrangements but, all in all, they are dissatisfied with the move. When asked what she dislikes about her present dwelling, Mrs. Figella replied simply and pathetically: "It's in Arlington and I want to be in the West End." Both Mr. and Mrs. Figella are outgoing, friendly people with a very wide circle of social contacts. Although they still see their relatives often, they both feel isolated from them and they regret the loss of their friends. As Mr. Figella puts it: "I come home from work and that's it. I just plant myself in the house."

The Figella family is, in many respects, typical of a well-adjusted working-class family. They have relatively few ambitions for themselves or for their children. They continue in close contact with many people; but they no longer have the same extensiveness of mutual cooperation in household activities, they cannot "drop in" as casually as before, they do not have the sense of being surrounded by a familiar area and familiar people. Thus, while their objective situation is not dramatically altered, the changes do involve important elements of stability and continuity in their lives. They manifest the importance of externally available resources for an integral sense of spatial and group identity. However, they have always maintained a very close marital relationship, and their family provides a substantial basis for a sense of continuity. They can evidently cope with difficulties on the strength of their many internal and external resources. Nonetheless, they have suffered from the move, and find it extremely difficult to reorganize their lives completely in adapting to a new geographical situation and new patterns of social affiliation. Their grief for a lost home seems to be one form of maintaining continuity on the basis of memories. While it prevents a more wholehearted adjustment to their altered lives, such adjustments would imply forsaking the remaining fragments of a continuity which was central to their conceptions of themselves and of the world.

2. There are many similarities between the Figella family and the Giuliano family. But Mrs. Giuliano shows relatively little pre-relocation commitment to the West End and little post-relocation grief. Mr. Giuliano was somewhat more deeply involved in the West End and, although satisfied with the change, feels that relocation was "like having the rug pulled out from under you." Mr. and Mrs. Giuliano are also second-generation Americans, of similar background to the Figellas'. But Mrs. Giuliano only moved to the West End at her marriage. Mrs. Giuliano had many objections to the area: "For me it is too congested. I never did care for it . . . too many barrooms, on every corner, too many families in one building. . . . The sidewalks are too narrow and the kids can't play outside." But she does expect to miss the stores and many favorite places. Her housing ambitions go beyond West End standards and she wants more space inside and outside. She had no blood relatives in the West End but was close to her husband's family and had friends nearby.

Mr. Giuliano was born in the West End and he had many relatives in the area. He has a relatively high status manual job but only a modest income. His wife does not complain about this although she is only moderately satisfied with the marriage. In part she objected to the fact that they went out so little and that he spent too much time on the corner with his friends. His social networks in the West End were more extensive and involved than were Mrs. Giuliano's. And he missed the West End more than she did after the relocation. But even Mr. Giuliano says that, all in all, he is satisfied with the change.

Mrs. Giuliano feels the change is "wonderful." She missed her friends but got over it. And a few of Mr. Giuliano's hanging group live close by so they can continue to hang together. Both are satisfied

240

with the house they bought although Mrs. Giuliano's ambitions have now gone beyond this. The post-relocation situation has led to an improved marital relationship: Mr. Giuliano is home more and they go out more together.

Mr. and Mrs. Giuliano exemplify a pattern which seems most likely to be associated with a beneficial experience from relocation. Unlike Mr. and Mrs. Figella, who completely accept their working-class status and are embedded in the social and cultural patterns of the working class, Mr. and Mrs. Giuliano show many evidences of social mobility. Mr. Giuliano's present job is, properly speaking, outside the working-class category because of its relatively high status and he himself does not "work with his hands." And Mrs. Giuliano's housing ambitions, preferences in social relationships, orientation to the class structure, and attitudes toward a variety of matters from shopping to child rearing are indications of a readiness to achieve middle-class status. Mr. Giuliano is prepared for and Mrs. Giuliano clearly desires "discontinuity" with some of the central bases for their former identity. Their present situation is, in fact, a transitional one which allows them to reintegrate their lives at a new and higher status level without too precipitate a change. And their marital relationship seems sufficiently meaningful to provide a significant core of continuity in the process of change in their patterns of social and cultural experience. The lack of grief in this case is quite understandable and appropriate to their patterns of social orientation and expectation.

3. Yet another pattern is introduced by the Borowski family, who had an intense pre-location commitment to the West End and relatively little post-relocation grief. The Borowskis are both second-generation and have four children.

Mrs. Borowski was brought up in the West End but her husband has lived there only since the marriage (fifteen years before). Her feelings about living in the West End were clear: "I love it—it's the only home I've ever known." She had reservations about the dirt in the area but loved the people, the places, and the convenience and maintained an extremely wide circle of friends. They had some relatives nearby but were primarily oriented towards friends, both within and outside the West End. Mr. Borowski, a highly skilled manual worker with a moderately high income, was as deeply attached to the West End as his wife.

Mr. Borowski missed the West End very much but was quite satisfied with their new situation and could anticipate feeling thoroughly at home in the new neighborhood. Mrs. Borowski proclaims that "home is where you hang your hat; it's up to you to make the adjustments." But she also says, "If I knew the people were coming back to the West End, I would pick up this little house and put it back on my corner." She claims she was not sad after relocation but, when asked how she felt when the building she lived in was torn down, a strangely morbid association is aroused: "It's just like a plant . . . when you tear up its roots, it dies! I didn't die but I felt kind of bad. It was home. . . . Don't look back, try to go ahead."

Despite evidences of underlying grief, both Mr. and Mrs. Borowski have already adjusted to the change with remarkable alacrity. They bought a one-family house and have many friends in the new area. They do not feel as close to their new neighbors as they did to their West End friends, and they still maintain extensive contact with the latter. They are comfortable and happy in their new surroundings and maintain the close, warm, and mutually appreciative marital relationship they formerly had.

Mr. and Mrs. Borowski, and particularly Mrs. Borowski, reveal a sense of loss which is largely submerged beneath active efforts to deal with the present. It was possible for them to do this both because of personality factors (that is, the ability to deny the intense affective meaning of the change and to detach themselves from highly "cathected" objects with relative ease) and because of prior social patterns and orientations. Not only is Mr. Borowski, by occupation, among the highest group of working-class status, but this family has been "transitional" for some time. Remaining in the West End was clearly a matter of preference for them. They could have moved out quite easily on the basis of income and many of their friends were scattered throughout metropolitan Boston. But while they are less self-consciously mobile than the Giulianos, they had already shifted to many patterns more typical of the middle class before leaving the West End. These ranged from their joint weekly shopping expeditions to their recreational patterns, which included such sports as boating and such regular plans as yearly vacations. They experienced a disruption in continuity by virtue of their former spatial and group identity. But the bases for maintaining this identity had undergone many changes over the years; and they had already established a feeling for places and people, for a potential redefinition of "home" which was less contingent on the immediate and local availability of familiar spaces and familiar friends. Despite their preparedness for the move by virtue of cultural orientation, social experience, and personal disposition, the change

242

was a considerable wrench for them. But, to the extent that they can be categorized as "over-adjusters," the residue of their lives in the West End is primarily a matter of painful memories which are only occasionally reawakened.

4. The alternate deviant pattern, minimal pre-relocation commitment associated with severe post-relocation grief, is manifested by Mr. and Mrs. Pagliuca. As in the previous case, this classification applies more fully to Mrs. Pagliuca, since Mr. Pagliuca appears to have had stronger ties to the West End. Mr. Pagliuca is a second-generation American but Mrs. Pagliuca is first-generation from an urban European background. For both of them, however, there is some evidence that the sadness and regret about the loss of the West End should perhaps be designated as pseudo-grief.

Mrs. Pagliuca had a difficult time in the West End. But she also had a difficult time before that. She moved into the West End when she got married. And she complains bitterly about her marriage, her husband's relatives, West Enders in general. She says of the West End: "I don't like it. The people . . . the buildings are full of rats. There are no places to play for the children." She liked the apartment but complained about the lady downstairs, the dirt, the repairs required, and the coldness during the winter. She also complains a great deal about lack of money. Her husband's wages are not too low but he seems to have periods of unemployment and often drinks his money away.

Mr. Pagliuca was attached to some of his friends and the bars in the West End. But he didn't like his housing situation there. And his reaction tends to be one of bitterness ("a rotten deal") rather than of sadness. Both Mr. and Mrs. Pagliuca are quite satisfied with their post-relocation apartment but are thoroughly dissatisfied with the area. They have had considerable difficulty with neighbors: ". . . I don't like this; people are mean here; my children get blamed for anything and everything; and there's no transportation near here." She now idealizes the West End and claims that she misses everything about it.

Mr. Pagliuca is an unskilled manual laborer. Financial problems create a constant focus for difficulty and arguments. But both Mr. and Mrs. Pagliuca appear more satisfied with one another than before relocation. They have four children, some of whom are in legal difficulty. There is also some evidence of past cruelty toward the children, at least on Mrs. Pagliuca's part.

It is evident from this summary that the Pagliuca family is deviant in a social as well as in a statistical sense. They show few signs of adjusting to the move or, for that matter, of any basic potential for successful adjustment to further moves (which they are now planning). It may be that families with such initial difficulties, with such a tenuous basis for maintaining a sense of continuity under any circumstances, suffer most acutely from disruption of these minimal ties. The Pagliuca family has few inner resources and, having lost the minimal external resources signified by a gross sense of belonging, of being tolerated if not accepted, they appear to be hopelessly at sea. Although we refer to their grief as "pseudo-grief" on the basis of the shift from pre-relocation to post-relocation statements, there is a sense in which it is quite real. Within the post-relocation interviews their responses are quite consistent; and a review of all the data suggests that, although their ties were quite modest, their current difficulties have revealed the importance of these meager involvements and the problems of re-establishing anew an equivalent basis for identity formation. Thus, even for Mr. and Mrs. Pagliuca, we can speak of the disruption in the sense of continuity, although this continuity was based on a very fragile experience of minimal comfort, with familiar places and relatively tolerant people. Their grief reaction, pseudo or real, may further influence (and be influenced by) dissatisfactions with any new residential situation. The fact that it is based on an idealized past accentuates rather than minimizes its effect on current expectations and behavior.

Conclusions

Grieving for a lost home is evidently a widespread and serious social phenomenon following in the wake of urban dislocation. It is likely to increase social and psychological "pathology" in a limited number of instances; and it is also likely to create new opportunities for some, and to increase the rate of social mobility for others. For the greatest number, dislocation is unlikely to have either effect but does lead to intense personal suffering despite moderately successful adaptation to the total situation of relocation. Under these circumstances, it becomes most critical that we face the realities of the effects of relocation on working-class residents of slums and, on the basis of knowledge and understanding, that we learn to deal more effectively with the problems engendered.

In evaluating these data on the effect of pre-location experiences on

244

post-relocation reactions of grief, we have arrived at a number of conclusions:

1. The affective reaction to the loss of the West End can be quite precisely described as a grief response showing most of the characteristics of grief and mourning for a lost person.

2. One of the important components of the grief reaction is the fragmentation of the sense of spatial identity. This is manifest, not only in the pre-location experience of the spatial area as an expanded "home," but in the varying degrees of grief following relocation, arising from variations in the pre-relocation orientation to and use of local spatial regions.

3. Another component, of equal importance, is the dependence of the sense of group identity on stable, social networks. Dislocation necessarily led to the fragmentation of this group identity which was based, to such a large extent, on the external availability and overt contact with familiar groups of people.

4. Associated with these "cognitive" components, described as the sense of spatial identity and the sense of group identity, are strong affective qualities. We have not tried to delineate them but they appear to fall into the realm of a feeling of security in and commitment to the external spatial and group patterns which are the tangible, visible aspects of these identity components. However, a predisposition to depressive reactions also markedly affects the depth of grief reaction.

5. Theoretically, we can speak of spatial and group identity as critical foci of the sense of continuity. This sense of continuity is not *necessarily* contingent on the external stability of place, people, and security or support. But for the working class these concrete, external resources and the experience of stability, availability, and familiarity which they provide are essential for a meaningful sense of continuity. Thus, dislocation and the loss of the residential area represent a fragmentation of some of the essential components of the sense of continuity in the working class.

It is in the light of these observations and conclusions that we must consider problems of social planning which are associated with the changes induced by physical planning for relocation. Urban planning cannot be limited to "bricks and mortar." While these data tell us little about the importance of housing or the aspects of housing which are important, they indicate that considerations of a non-housing nature are critical. There is evidence, for example, that the frequency of the grief response is not affected by such housing factors as increase or decrease in apartment size or home ownership. But physical factors may be of great importance when related to the subjective significance of different spatial and physical arrangements, or to their capacity for gratifying different socio-cultural groups. For the present, we can only stress the importance of local areas as *spatial and social* arrangements which are central to the lives of working-class people. And, in view of the enormous importance of such local areas, we are led to consider the convergence of familiar people and familiar places as a focal consideration in formulating planning decisions.

We can learn to deal with these problems only through research, through exploratory and imaginative service programs, and through a more careful consideration of the place of residential stability in salvaging the precarious thread of continuity. The outcomes of crises are always manifold and, just as there is an increase in strain and difficulty, so also there is an increase in opportunities for adapting at a more satisfying level of functioning. The judicious use of minimal resources of counseling and assistance may permit many working-class people to reorganize and integrate a meaningful sense of spatial and group identity under the challenge of social change. Only a relatively small group of those whose functioning has always been marginal and who cannot cope with the added strain of adjusting to wholly new problems are likely to require major forms of intervention.

In general, our results would imply the necessity for providing increased opportunities for maintaining a sense of continuity for those people, mainly from the working class, whose residential areas are being renewed. This may involve several factors: (1) diminishing the amount of drastic redevelopment and the consequent mass demolition of property and mass dislocation from homes; (2) providing more frequently for people to move within their former residential areas during and after the renewal; and (3) when dislocation and relocation are unavoidable, planning the relocation possibilities in order to provide new areas which can be assimilated to old objectives. A closer examination of slum areas may even provide some concrete information regarding specific physical variables, the physical and spatial arrangements typical of slum areas and slum housing, which offer considerable gratification to the residents. These may often be translated into effective modern architectural and areal design. And, in conjunction with planning decisions which take more careful account of the human consequences of urban physical change, it is possible to utilize social, psychological, and psychiatric services. The use of highly skilled resources, including opportunities for the education of professional and even lay personnel in largely unfamiliar problems and methods, can minimize some of the more destructive and widespread effects of relocation; and, for some families, can offer constructive experiences in dealing with new adaptational possibilities. The problem is large. But only by assuring the integrity of some of the external bases for the sense of continuity in the working class, and by maximizing the opportunities for meaningful adaptation, can we accomplish planned urban change without serious hazard to human welfare.

NOTES

1. This is implicit in the prior work on "crisis" and situational predicaments by Dr. Erich Lindemann under whose initiative the current work was undertaken and carried out.

2. The analysis involves a comparison of information from interviews administered *before* relocation with a depth of grief index derived from follow-up interviews approximately two years *after* relocation. The pre-relocation interviews were administered to a randomly selected sample of 473 women from households in this area at the time the land was taken by the city. The post-relocation interviews were completed with 92 per cent of the women who had given pre-relocation interviews and with 87 per cent of the men from those households in which there was a husband in the household. Primary emphasis will be given to the results with the women since we do not have as full a range of pre-relocation information for the men. However, since a split schedule was used for the post-relocation interviews, the depth of grief index is available for only 259 women.

3. Dr. Jason Aronson was largely responsible for developing the series of questions on grief. The opening question of the series was: Many people have told us that just after they moved they felt sad or depressed. Did you feel this way? This was followed by the three specific questions on which the index was based: (1) Would you describe how you felt? (2) How long did these feelings last? (3) How did you feel when you saw or heard that the building you had lived in was torn down? Each person was given a score from 1 to 4 on the basis of the coded responses to these questions and the scores were summated. For purposes of analysis, we divided the final scores into three groups: minimal grief, moderate grief, and severe or marked grief. The phrasing of these questions appears to dispose the respondent to give a "grief" response. In fact, however, there is a tendency to reject the idea of "sadness" among many people who show other evidence of a grief response. In cross-tabulating the "grief" scores with a series of questions in which there is no suggestion of sadness, unhappiness, or dissatisfaction, it is clear that the grief index is the more severe criterion. Those who are classified in the severe grief category almost invariably show severe grief reactions by any of the other criteria; but many who are categorized as "minimal grief" on the index fall into the extremes of unhappiness or dissatisfaction on the other items.

4. Erik Erikson includes spatial components in discussing the sense of ego identity and his work has influenced the discussion of spatial variables (4). In distinguishing the sense of spatial identity from the sense of ego identity, I am suggesting that variations in spatial identity do not correspond exactly to variations in ego identity. By separating these concepts, it becomes possible to study their interrelationships empirically.

REFERENCES

1. Abraham, K., "Notes on the Psycho-analytical Investigation and Treatment of Manic-Depressive Insanity and Allied Conditions" (1911), and "A Short Study of the Development of the Libido, Viewed in the Light of Mental Disorders" (1924), in *Selected Papers of Karl Abraham*, Vol. I, New York: Basic Books, 1953; Bibring, E., "The Mechanisms of Depression," in *Affective Disorders*, P. Greenacre, ed., New York: International Univ. Press, 1953; Bowlby, J., "Processes of Mourning," *Int. J. Psychoanal.*, 42:317–340, 1961; Freud, S., "Mourning and Melancholia" (1917), in *Collected Papers*, Vol. III, New York: Basic Books, 1959; Hoggart, R., *The Uses of Literacy: Changing Patterns in English Mass Culture*, New York: Oxford Univ. Press, 1957; Klein, M., "Mourning and Its Relations to Manic-Depressive States," *Int. J. Psychoanal.*, 21:125–153, 1940; Lindemann, E., "Symptomatology and Management of Acute Grief," *Am. J. Psychiat.*, 101:141–148, 1944; Marris, P., *Widows and Their Families*, London: Routledge and Kegan Paul, 1958; Rochlin, G., "The Dread of Abandonment," in *The Psychoanalytic Study of the Child*, Vol. XVI, New York: International Univ. Press, 1961; Volkart, E. H., with S. T. Michael, "Bereavement and Mental Health," in *Explorations in Social Psychiatry*, A. H. Leighton, J. A. Clausen, and R. N. Wilson, eds., New York: Basic Books, 1957.

2. Fried, M., and Gleicher, P., "Some Sources of Residential Satisfaction in an Urban Slum," *J. Amer. Inst. Planners*, 27:305–315, 1961.

3. Gans, H., *The Urban Villagers*, New York: The Free Press, 1963; Gans, H., "The Human Implications of Current Redevelopment and Relocation Planning," *J. Amer. Inst. Planners*, 25:15–25, 1959; Hoggart, R., *op. cit.*; Hole, V., "Social Effects of Planned Rehousing," *Town Planning Rev.*, 30:161–173, 1959; Marris, P., *Family and Social Change in an African City*, Evanston, Ill.: Northwestern Univ. Press, 1962; Mogey, J. M., *Family and Neighbourhood*, New York: Oxford Univ. Press, 1956; Seeley, J., "The Slum: Its Nature, Use, and Users," *J. Amer. Inst. Planners*, 25:7–14, 1959; Vereker, C., and Mays, J. B., *Urban Redevelopment and Social Change*, New York: Lounz, 1960; Young, M., and Willmott, P., *Family and Kinship in East London*, Glencoe, Ill.: The Free Press, 1957.

4. Erikson, E., "Ego Development and Historical Change," in *The Psychoanalytic Study of the Child*, Vol. II, New York: International Univ. Press, 1946; "The Problem of Ego Identity," *J. Amer. Psychoanal. Assoc.*, 4:56–121, 1956.

16

Health Consequences of
Population Density and Crowding

JOHN CASSEL

No discussion of the effects of the environment on health can be considered complete without paying some attention to the phenomenon of overcrowding. The assumption that overcrowding produces negative effects underlies many proposals in favor of lower density settlement patterns, population control, and designing buildings to ensure privacy. The subject of overcrowding is also important because of all the many environmental variables whose association with health have been repeatedly studied over the last century, it has been the fact of high urban density that has been most often shown to be related to poor health and social pathology.

Cassel's selection is especially important because it argues that the relationship between overcrowding and illness and social pathology is not nearly as simple or unidirectional as the current excitement over the phenomenon of the "behavioral sink" among rats and mice has led people to believe. He summarizes the major bodies of evidence that have offered support to the view that overcrowding is bad for health and indicates that the evidence is not substantial. In many studies the more densely settled urbanized populations evidenced superior health to the lower density rural populations. Furthermore, Cassel points out that it is often isolated population groups that show a greater susceptibility to chronic and epidemic diseases. There is even some evidence that suggests that overcrowding can not only be neutral, but actually beneficial to health.

On the basis of the present evidence, Cassel proposes a model for identifying the critical factors other than population density that determine the response of the human organism and of human groups to overcrowding. His fundamental thesis is that to the degree that population density is associated with poor health, the negative association comes about because density

Reprinted from John Cassel, "Health Consequences of Population Density and Crowding," in *The Consequences of Population Change and Their Implications for National and International Policies*. Forthcoming from The Johns Hopkins Press.

increases the salience of the social environment as a determinant of the organism's reaction to potentially infectious stimuli. The effects of the physical environment on health, therefore, cannot be predicted without knowledge of the social experiences and characteristics of people living at different density levels. Two social factors are singled out and given special weight in Cassel's scheme: the hierarchical status structure of the urban community and social group and the individual's location within the hierarchy; and the degree of social integration and social cohesion within the group or community. Cassel argues that individuals higher up in the status hierarchy, regardless of the density levels under which they live, are less likely to suffer from bad health. He also believes that people who live in more cohesive communities are healthier. By applying this model, Cassel is led toward the conclusion that many of the negative effects on health associated with urban densities are not caused by the densities but rather by the rapidity of urban growth and the relatively limited experience of many recent urban migrants in learning how to adapt to the stresses imposed by city life.

☐

The view that crowding and increased population density are deleterious as far as health is concerned, is so widespread and generally accepted as to have become almost a medical axiom. Furthermore, it is currently believed that the harmful effects of crowding are not merely confined to increasing the spread of infectious diseases but also increase the risk of non-infectious disease. These views can perhaps be best illustrated by two quotations from a standard text on epidemiology, which with minor variations can be found in all textbooks dealing with the subject.

It has long been recognized that crowded communities provide a more fertile ground for the spread of infection than more scattered communities. (1) *. . . The deleterious effects of crowding are not, however, confined to matters concerned with the spread of infection, but are also seen in increased mortality from all causes, both infectious and non-infectious.* (2)

The evidence supporting this point of view is derived largely from four sources:

A. The higher death and morbidity rates that traditionally have been reported from the more densely populated urban centers.

B. The dramatic increase in death rates, primarily due to infectious diseases that have followed industrialization and urbanism.

C. The higher rates of various diseases reported under crowded conditions such as military training camps, nurseries, etc.

250

D. Animal studies, which have shown that as the number of animals housed together increases, with other factors such as diet, temperature and sanitation kept constant, maternal and infant mortality rates rise, the incidence of atherosclerosis increases, and the resistance to insults such as drugs, micro-organisms, and x-rays is reduced.

A careful review of recent data, however, indicates some important inconsistencies in the relationship between crowding and health status which throw some doubt on this generally accepted formulation, particularly on the processes through which crowding may influence health. It would appear from these data that the relationship between crowding and health status is a far more complex phenomenon than was originally envisaged, and that while under certain circumstances crowding is clearly associated with poor health states, under other circumstances it may be neutral or even beneficial. The data casting some doubt on this relationship will be briefly reviewed under the same categories that have provided the evidence used to support the notion that crowding inevitably leads to deleterious health consequences.

URBAN-RURAL DEATH AND MORBIDITY RATES

As is shown in Figure 16–1, death rates for all causes in the United States were indeed higher in urban areas than in rural prior to 1950. By 1960, however, the ratio had become reversed, rural rates being higher than urban, and since 1960 the ratio of rural to urban deaths has been steadily increasing. Thus, paradoxically, even though cities have been increasing in size since 1940, death rates have fallen more rapidly in these crowded circumstances than in the more sparsely populated rural areas. Part of this phenomenon may be due to the improved medical care and sanitation in the cities and part to the migration of younger people to the cities leaving an older, more susceptible population behind in the rural areas. These processes, it could be argued, might overwhelm or obscure the effects of crowding. That these can only be partial explanations for this reversal in the rural-urban health ratios is evident from the data shown in Table 16–1. While the rural excess in both incidence and mortality rates from typhoid fever, for example, may well be due to differences in sanitation, and the more effective immunization programs in cities account for the lower urban rates of diphtheria and pertussis, the rural excess in the incidence of scarlet fever can hardly be due to either of these processes as we do not as yet possess any means to

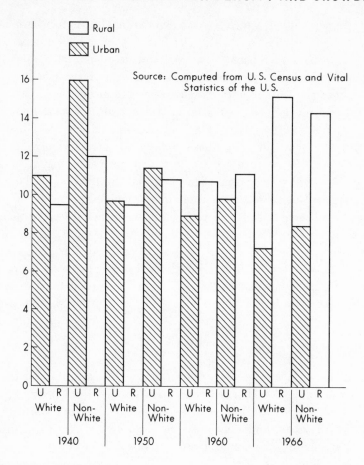

Figure 16–1 Death Rates—All Causes, U.S. (by Place of Residence 1940, 1950, 1960, and 1966). Computed From U.S. Census and Vital Statistics of the U.S.

prevent the occurrence of streptococcal infections. Similarly, as far as the migration hypothesis is concerned, this could not explain the excess mortality rates in rural children both black and white, male and female.

Data from other parts of the world tend to confirm this seeming paradox. Dubos (3), for example, reports that despite the fact that Hong Kong and Holland are among the most crowded areas in the world, they enjoy one of the highest levels of physical and mental health in the world. The data from Britain in 1961 on the age standardized mortality ratios for all causes of death is even more convincing (4). (See the table on p. 254.)

TABLE 16-1
Selected Urban-Rural Differences in Health Status, U.S. 1959-1961

		Incidence		Mortality	
		Metropolitan Counties	Non-Metropolitan Counties	Metropolitan Counties	Non-Metropolitan Counties
Childhood Mortality Rates Per 100,000 Population—All Causes (Ages 5-14 years)[1]	White Male			48.6	59.7
	White Female			32.3	37.6
	Non-White Male			67.5	82.3
	Non-White Female			45.5	60.9
Typhoid Fever[2]		3.3	7.0	0.1	0.1
Diphtheria[2]		3.2	7.1	0.2	0.6
Pertussis[2]		111.1	141.1	0.4	1.6
Scarlet Fever and Streptococcal Sore Throat[2]		1579	2374	0.5	1.1
Influenza[2]				13.5	41.9

[1]SOURCE: Shapiro, Sam et al., *Infant, Perinatal, Maternal, and Childhood Mortality in the United States*, Vital and Statistical Monographs APHA, Harvard University Press, 1968.
[2]SOURCE: Dauer, Carl C. et al., *Infectious Diseases*, Vital and Statistical Monographs APHA, Harvard University Press, 1968.

	Males	Females
Urban areas population 100,000 +	101	98
Urban areas population 50,000-99,999	91	90
Urban areas population under 50,000	104	105
Rural areas	91	98

THE RISE IN DEATH RATES THAT FOLLOWED INDUSTRIALIZATION AND URBANISM

Tuberculosis has been used as an example par excellence of a disease which following industrialization, and the accompanying crowding, showed a marked increase in rates. What is not so well recognized, however, is that in all countries for which data is available, tuberculosis rates having risen for 75–100 years following industrialization, started to fall spontaneously, and have continued to fall in the face of ever increasing population density. Improvements in medical care and anti-tuberculosis programs cannot account for this reversal in trends, at least initially. The fall in Britain and the U.S., for example, started in 1850 and 1900 respectively (5); that is, 50 to 100 years before any useful anti-tuberculosis drugs were discovered and several decades before any organized anti-tuberculosis programs were initiated.

Furthermore, in some relatively recent studies it has been found that, contrary to prevailing theory, tuberculosis does not necessarily occur under crowded conditions but under some circumstances at least occurs more frequently in people who are socially isolated. In a careful study conducted in Britain, for example, all the families living in a city were x-rayed to determine the prevalence of tuberculosis in relationship to an index of crowding derived from dividing the number of people in a household by the number of rooms in that house (6). While a strong social class gradient in the prevalence of tuberculosis was discovered within each social class, no relationship between the crowding index and tuberculosis prevalence was found. In fact, those lodgers who were living alone in the houses had a tuberculosis rate some three to four times higher than family members even though the lodgers were, by definition, living in uncrowded conditions. Similar results were found in a study in the U.S.A. (7) in which it was found that tuberculosis was occurring most frequently in people living alone in a single room and not in those living under the most crowded conditions.

254

THE HIGHER RATES OF DISEASE (PARTICULARLY INFECTIOUS
DISEASE) REPORTED UNDER CROWDED CONDITIONS
SUCH AS MILITARY TRAINING CAMPS, ETC.

While there can be little doubt that outbreaks of disease, particularly acute upper respiratory disease, are more common under the crowded conditions of military training camps, for example, than under less crowded conditions, there is considerable doubt that such outbreaks can be ascribed solely to the physical fact of increased crowding.

In recent years, for example, intensive study of outbreaks of upper respiratory infection in recruits in military training camps have indicated that the agent responsible is usually the adenovirus IV. The orthodox explanation for such outbreaks holds that they result from the herding together of large numbers of susceptible young men with a few infected individuals and that the crowded conditions facilitate the spread of the agent. Such an explanation, however, fails to account for some of the known facts. For example, the same agent, the adenovirus IV, is widespread in civilian populations, but even under conditions of crowding such as occur in colleges and schools has never been implicated in an outbreak of upper respiratory infection. Furthermore, the permanent staff of the military installations, even though living under the same crowded conditions as the recruits, are not involved in such outbreaks. Finally, when immunization experiments against adenovirus IV have been conducted under appropriate double blind conditions, the immunized companies, while displaying a reduction in the number of cases ascribed to adenovirus IV, have experienced just as much upper respiratory illness as have the control companies, but now due to a different agent—adenovirus VII. Studies conducted by my colleagues on Marine recruits in Parris Island, South Carolina (8), on the patterning of such outbreaks, provide further evidence against the orthodox explanation. The basic training program lasts for 8 weeks. As can be seen from Figure 16-2, the number of upper respiratory infections increases from the first through the fourth week, decreases in the fifth and sixth weeks, and begins to increase again in the seventh and eighth weeks. As far as can be determined, there are no differences in crowding during these 8 weeks, and furthermore, as shown in Figure 16-3, sick calls from all causes including musculo-skeletal, skin infections, trauma, and all other causes display an identical pattern. Not only is this regularity observed for all platoons, but there are systematic differences in the rate of infection

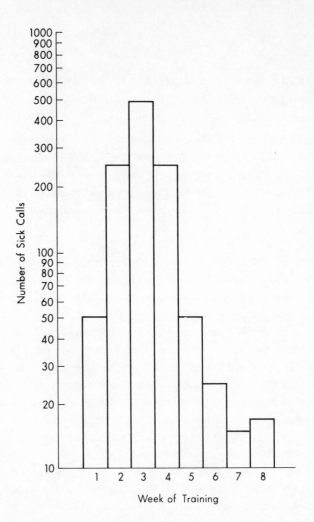

Figure 16–2 Recruit Sick Calls—Respiratory or Gastro–Intestinal Infection
(by Week of Training: Parris Island, April–August 1967).

between platoons (living under identical conditions), some exhibiting a markedly higher rate for their entire 8 weeks than others.

As indicated later in this selection, such data do not necessarily refute the role of crowding in changing susceptibility to disease, but they do provide clues which may necessitate a change in our thinking concerning the processes through which crowding can influence health and the circumstances under which this occurs.

ANIMAL STUDIES

Even the animal data which at first sight appear so convincing need to be re-examined both in terms of their consistency and in terms of

256

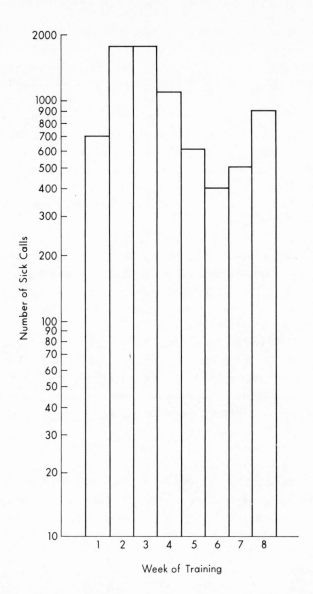

Figure 16-3 Recruit Sick Calls—All Causes (by Week of Training: Parris Island, April–August 1967).

the extrapolation that can be made to human populations. Alexander Kessler at the Rockefeller University, for example, has indicated that under extreme conditions of crowding in mice no increase in pathology was noted once the population had achieved its maximum density and no further population growth was occurring. Under these circumstances asocial behavior was common but physical pathology no more frequent than in the control group living under uncrowded conditions.

257

During the phase of rapid population growth, however, which preceded this plateau, disease was much more frequent than in the control group (9).

It is apparent, therefore, even from these fragmentary illustrative data that population density and/or crowding does not inevitably lead to poorer health status. For the remainder of this selection I intend to examine some of the reasons that may account for these conflicting data and to suggest the need to reformulate some of our conceptual models if the effects of such phenomena are to be better understood in the future.

Part of the reason for the discrepancies in the data presented above lies in the well recognized fact that many studies have used different and often inadequate indicators of crowding. The indicators used have frequently been unable to distinguish between a high population density in some arbitrary delineated areas of land and increased social interaction. Secondly, crowding under certain circumstances may be associated with certain factors which themselves can influence health (poverty, poor nutrition, poor housing, etc.) but under other circumstances may be associated with different factors. The relationship of crowding to disease states, therefore, may be a reflection of these other factors rather than the crowding per se.

Perhaps of greater importance than the inadequacy of the indicators or the presence of "contaminating" factors has been the failure of most investigators to identify explicitly the processes through which increased social interaction can lead to disease. The orthodox model which, implicitly at least, is espoused by the majority of authorities holds that crowding increases the risk for disease mainly through an increased opportunity for the spread of infection. Newer data and re-examination of older data is making this view increasingly untenable. It obviously cannot account for the increase in non-infectious disease, which occurs under conditions of crowding, but even for infectious diseases there is a growing body of opinion which indicates that such a view is at best only a partial explanation for any effects crowding may have. Dubos, the pioneer micro-biologist, has perhaps stated this view most clearly:

The sciences concerned with microbial diseases have developed almost exclusively from the study of acute or semi-acute infections caused by virulent micro-organisms acquired through exposure to an exogenous source of infection. In contrast, the microbial diseases most common in our communities today arise from the activities of micro-organisms that are ubiquitous in the environment, exist in the body without causing obvious harm under ordinary circumstances, and exert pathological stress. In such a type of microbial disease the event of infection is of less importance than the hidden manifestation of the smoldering infectious process and than the physiological disturbances that convert latent infection into overt symptoms and pathology. (10)

According to Dubos, then, microbial disease is not necessarily acquired through exposure to a new micro-organism. In a large number of cases disease occurs through factors which disturb the balance between the ubiquitous organisms and the host that is harboring them. It may well be that under conditions of crowding this balance may be disturbed, but this disturbance is then not a function of the physical crowding but of other processes. The studies reported above on upper respiratory infections in Marine recruits woud tend to support this point of view, suggesting that a large proportion of the recruits are harboring viruses when entering into their military training, and that something about the military environment, particularly something about the environment of their own platoon or company, leads to the type of physiological stress to which Dubos refers that converts latent infection into overt symptoms and pathology. As is discussed below, it would appear that these factors that produce the physiological stress are unlikely to occur in the absence of crowding but are not themselves due necessarily to the physical presence of many infected individuals.

In addition to being guided by what now may be considered an inappropriate set of hypotheses, most research into the health consequences of crowding has failed to take into account the adaptability of living organisms. The current views are, to a large extent, based upon data which has examined health conditions under varying degrees of crowding at one point in time. It is less common to find studies in which the reactions of individuals to crowded conditions have been studied with the passage of time. Those few studies that have been conducted would indicate that organisms have the power to adapt to a wide range of conditions, including crowding, provided that the changes which they called upon to adapt to occur reasonably slowly, and would suggest then that many of the deleterious effects of crowding will occur only, or maximally, in those individuals who are newcomers to the crowded scene. Such a formulation may explain Kessler's findings in his long-term studies of crowding among mice, which, as has been indicated, are in contradiction to other animal studies which have examined the effects of crowding on first generation animals only.

Toward a Reformulation of the Conceptual Model

As is evidenced in the preceding section of this selection, it is our opinion that a considerable amount of the confusion concerning the health consequences of crowding resides in the lack of utility of the network of hypotheses that have been utilized to determine research strategy and interpret research results. Stated in its most simplistic form the hypothesis implicit in most of existing research holds that crowding is "bad" simply because it increases the opportunity for interpersonal contact and thus facilitates the inter-change of external disease agents. That this model does not explain many of the known phenomena and is generally an inadequate guide for the development of research strategy is illustrated in some of the data presented previously. If, then, the relationships between crowding and human health are to be elucidated in a more satisfactory manner a more appropriate set of hypotheses needs to be elaborated.

As has been indicated, animal experiments have quite convincingly demonstrated some of the short-term health consequences of increased population density. While these findings cannot necessarily be extrapolated directly to man, and will, we believe, have to be modified by taking into account the adaptability of biological organisms before drawing long-term conclusions, some of the underlying concepts that have been discovered in such studies may have extreme utility in developing new sets of hypotheses for studies in man. Welch (11), for example, in studying the effects of increased population size on mice, noted that as the size of the population increases, physiological changes occur in the animal such as enhancement of the adrenocortical and adrenal medullary secretions. He has postulated that increased population size leads to increased social interaction, and among gregarious animals such increased social interaction enhances emotional involvement and elicits central activation necessary for sensory fixation and recognition even in emotionally neutral encounters. Thus, he postulates that *every such stimulus* contributes to the level of activation of brainstem reticular formation and major endocrine systems. Thus, Welch's studies seem to indicate that one of the effects of increased population size and density is *to increase the importance of the social environment as a determinant of physiological response to various stimuli*, including disease-producing agents to which the population is subjected. This seems to me to be an extraordinarily important possibility. It would suggest that the effect of any disease-producing agent, be this a micro-organism, a toxin, or some other physico-chemical element, cannot be assessed in the absence of knowledge concerning the size and nature of the group within which the exposed population interacts, and that the larger the interacting group the more important will these group phenomena be in modifying the responses to such factors. Such a formulation receives at least circumstantial support from the studies on the level of blood pressure that have been conducted over the last 30 years in every continent in the world (12–37). These studies have indicated that, with few exceptions, populations living in small, cohesive societies tend to have low blood pressures which do not differ in the young and the aged. In a number of these studies, groups who have left such societies and who have had contact with Western urban culture, were also studied and found to have higher levels of blood pressure and to exhibit the familiar relationships between age and blood pressure found in studies of Western populations.

This formulation, useful as it may be as a general proposition, requires further specification and modification if it is to determine future research strategy. Specifically, it seems important to recognize that the influences of increases in population size are going to vary for different categories of individuals. The first such category is constituted by hierarchical position within the group. Welch (11) and Mason (38) have shown, in animal experiments, that those animals occupying subordinate positions within any group tend to respond in a far more extreme fashion to standardized stimuli than do those in dominant positions. These responses include changes in endocrine secretions as well as manifestations of disease and pathology. To the best of my knowledge, no human studies have been conducted to test whether this particular phenomenon applies in humans, but there seems no a priori reason to suspect that it does not. The second category that needs to be taken into consideration, and one in which there is both human as well as animal evidence, revolves around the degree to which the exposed populations have or have not been prepared by previous experience for the demands and expectations of the new situations. In other words, the general formulation needs to be modified by invoking the concept of the adaptability of the biological organisms. As has already been indicated, Kessler's work indicated that those cohorts of mice born and reared in a situation of extreme population density, did not display the same reactions as did their progenitors to whom this was a newer and less familiar set of experiences. As applied to humans, the extraordinary regularity with which various diseases have waxed and then waned as populations have become exposed and presumably adapted to urban living and the accompanying industrialization could well be taken as evidence supporting this point of view. The rise and fall of tuberculosis following industrialization, for example, has already been mentioned. As tuberculosis began to decline, it was replaced as a central health problem, in both Britain and the United States, by major malnutrition syndromes. In Britain, rickets was the scourge; in the United States, pellagra. These disorders, in turn, reached a peak and declined for reasons that are only partly understood and were themselves replaced by some of the diseases of early childhood. These, too, waxed and then waned largely, but not entirely, under the influence of the improvements in the sanitary environment and through the introduction of immunization programs, to be replaced between the World Wars by an extraordinary increase in the rate of duodenal ulcer, particularly in young men. This phenomenon, while more marked in Britain, occurred in the United States as well, and in both countries, for totally unknown reasons, the rates have declined in a dramatic fashion. Duodenal ulcer has now been replaced by our modern epidemics of coronary heart disease, hypertension, cancer, arthritis, diabetes, mental disorders, and the like. There is some evidence now that some of these disorders have reached a peak and at least in some segments of the population are declining. Death rates for hypertensive heart disease, for example, apparently have been declining in the United States since about 1940 to 1950, that is, before the introduction of anti-hypertensive drugs (39). Furthermore, there is some evidence in both Britain and the United States that the social class distribution of many of the "modern" diseases is changing. While 30 years ago coronary heart disease, for example, was more prevalent in Britain among the upper social classes, today there is almost no class difference. This change has occurred coincidentally with the increased length of exposure of the upper social classes to urban twentieth-century ways of living and with the more recent involvement in these ways of living of many of the lower social classes who have been the migrants from rural to urban situations.

Some more direct evidence for this formulation also exists. Hinkle and his co-workers (40) found marked differences in disease prevalence in a group of managers who had completed college as opposed to those doing the same job for the same pay in the same company but who had not completed college prior to coming to the industry. Those who had completed college were, with few exceptions, fourth generation Americans; sons of managers, proprietors, and white-collar workers and had grown up in families in middle to high income groups in good neighborhoods. In contrast, the group who had not completed college were hired as skilled craftsmen and later advanced to managerial status. They were sons and grandsons of immigrants, their fathers were skilled or unskilled laborers with an average of grammar school education or less, and they had grown up in families of low income in modest to sub-standard neighborhoods. This latter group (presumably the less well prepared group for the demands and expectations of managerial status) shared a significantly greater number of illnesses of all sorts than did the former group. The findings of a study by Cassel and Tyroler (41) lead to similar conclusions. They studied two groups of rural mountaineers; one of which was composed of individuals who were the first of their family ever to engage in industrial work, while the second comprised workers in the same factory, drawn from the same mountain coves, of the same age, and doing the same work for the same wages as the first group, but differing from the first group in that they were children of previous workers in this factory. This study was undertaken to test the hypothesis that the second group, that is the sons of previous factory workers, by virtue of their prior familial experience, would be better prepared for the expectations and demands of industrial living than would the first group, and would thus exhibit fewer signs of ill health. Health status was measured by responses to the Cornell Medical Index and by various indices of sick absenteeism. As predicted, the sons of previous factory workers had lower Cornell Medical Index scores (fewer symptoms) and lower rates of sick absenteeism after the initial few years of service, at each age than had the "first generation" workers. Perhaps even more convincing was the study conducted by Haenszel and his associates (42) on death rates from lung cancer in the U.S. These investigators discovered that death rates from lung cancer, when controlled for degree of cigarette smoking, were considerably higher in the farm-born who had migrated to cities than they were in lifetime urban dwellers. The study initially had been designed in an attempt to quantify the importance of length of exposure to atmospheric pollution of the cities, but despite the lifetime of exposure, urban livers had apparently "adapted" better to the effects of such atmospheric pollution than had the migrants.

A further concept that has to be taken into account in developing a useful formulation is the strong possibility that, under certain circumstances, group membership can exert a protective influence on the individual. Holmes (7) in his studies on tuberculosis in Seattle, for example, has shown that the disease occurs most frequently in "marginal" people; that is, in those individuals deprived of meaningful social contact. He found higher rates of tuberculosis in those ethnic groups who were distinct minorities in the neighborhoods in which they lived, in people living alone in one room, in those who had had·multiple occupational and residential moves, and who were more often single or divorced than was true of the general population. Similar findings have been found in respect to schizophrenia, accidents, suicide, and other respiratory diseases (43–47). One of the concomitants of increasing population density, particularly when associated with increasing urbanization, is the atomization of those groups which in rural folk societies provide emotional support and thus presumably some degree of protection for the individual. While, in the course of time, new types of groups develop to fulfill some of the functions originally played by the family and kin group, it is often difficult, particularly for the newcomer to such scenes, to become effectively integrated into such groups.

Finally, given the importance of the social environment under conditions of increasing population density and crowding, the question of specificity has to be raised. Is it to be anticipated that the social processes (both positive and negative) inherent in group membership and position within the group, particularly under conditions of populations newly experiencing growth and crowding, are likely to result in specific disease syndromes or merely to increase general susceptibility to illness? This question is the subject of considerable controversy at the moment, and both points of view have been hotly argued. In a penetrating review on the subject, Thurlow (48) indicates that the argument centers around the question of whether certain stimuli, particularly those of a social and psychological nature, operate in a non-specific fashion increasing general susceptibility to all illnesses, or whether such stimuli merely increase the predilection for illness reporting and illness behavior. A further point of view holds that the non-specific effect of social processes is but a reflection of our ignorance and that with further study more specific "agents" will be discovered for which these social processes can be visualized as "vehicles." These agents, it is held, will be related to some specific disease entity. Most of these arguments are based upon the supposition that social and emotional processes are the direct initiators of disease conditions through the activation of inappropriate neuro-endocrine arousal mechanisms. While this may undoubtedly be a useful formulation, the animal work quoted above would seem to indicate that a more likely role of the social factors is to increase the susceptibility of the organism to other disease-producing agents, that is, to act in an indirect fashion in the etiology of any disease syndrome or pattern. This formulation then would clearly indicate that the health consequences of such social processes are likely to be non-specific. The manifestations of specific disease syndromes thus will be dependent not upon the nature of the social processes but upon the presence or absence of other disease-producing agents of a biological or a physico-chemical nature, as well as the constitution, both genetic and experiential of the individuals exposed to such situations. Thus it would not seem unreasonable to postulate that individuals deprived of meaningful group membership, exposed to ambiguous and conflicting demands for which they have had no previous experience, and frustrated insofar as their goals and aspirations are concerned, who are exposed to the tubercle bacillus, may well be victims of tuberculosis. Similar individuals, not so exposed to the tubercle bacillus but who from childhood have lived on a high saturated fatty acid diet, who tend to be sedentary and heavy cigarette smokers, may well be victims of myocardial infarction. The point being made is that if the circumstances under which population density and crowding are deleterious to health are to be elucidated, it would seem important that we recognize the limitations of the existing classificatory schemes used to identify disease entities. These schemes, to a large extent, have been developed because of their usefulness for therapeutic purposes, and the possibility needs to be raised that they may not be the best methods for classifying disease outcome for purposes of identifying the factors responsible for genesis.

Conclusions

On the basis of these findings and the theories that emerge from them a number of predictions or "working hypotheses" concerning the health consequences of future population growth and crowding can tentatively be advanced.

It can be anticipated that in most developing countries rapid population growth, particularly if associated with a deterioration in housing and nutritional status will, in all likelihood, be accompanied initially by increased death and disease rates. This increased health burden will be greatest on those segments of the population who have had least previous experience with living in crowded conditions. Over a period of some decades the diseases responsible for these high death and morbidity rates will probably decline, and while this will result in an improvement in the overall disease rates, "new" diseases will replace the old, requiring a major change in the nature and format of the health services. While the diseases responsible for the initial rise in rates are likely to be acute infectious diseases and diseases associated with under and malnutrition, the later diseases are more likely to be chronic long-term disorders. Even though the rate for these disorders will be lower than for the acute diseases, the disability resulting from them will pose as great a strain on the national economy as did the high rates of the earlier diseases.

The more rapid the rate of population growth and the more it is accompanied by disruption of important social groups, the more dramatic will these effects be. The rate of population growth and the ensuing crowding will largely determine the ability of the population to adapt successfully to the new situation, and the degree to which new types of social groups can develop to fulfill the function originally played by the family and kin group will in large part determine how deleterious such changes are.

While the changing disease patterns described above are likely to occur in all developing countries undergoing rapid population growth, the *specific* diseases constituting this pattern are likely to vary. The particular diseases which will be most prevalent will depend not so much on the degree and rate of crowding as on the constitution (both genetic and experiential) of the population and the nature of physical and biological agents to which the population is, or has been, exposed.

Finally, if the harmful effects on health of crowding are to be prevented and an orderly and healthful rate of population growth to be planned, the processes through which crowding is related to health need to be understood better than they are today. As indicated in this selection the relatively simplistic notion that crowding exerts its deleterious effects solely through facilitating the inter-personal spread of disease agents is no longer adequate to explain the known phenomena. A more appropriate formulation would seem feasible if we recognize that increased population density increases the importance of the social environment as a determinant of physiological response to various stimuli, including potentially disease-producing agents; that within this social environment the quality of social interactions and position within the group seem to be important factors; and that adaptation to these social changes can and does occur given time, but that the newcomers to the situation will always be the segment of the population at highest risk.

REFERENCES

1. Taylor, Ian and John Knowleden, *Principles of Epidemiology*, Little, Brown, and Co., Boston, 1957, p. 199.
2. *Ibid.*, p. 199.

3. Dubos, René, "The Human Environment in Technological Societies." *The Rockefeller Review*, July–August, 1968.

4. From The Registrar General's Decennial Supplement England and Wales 1961, Area Mortality Tables, H. M. S. O., London, 1967.

5. Grigg, E. R. N., "The Arcana of Tuberculosis." *Am. Rev. TB.*, 78, 1958, 151–172, 426–453, 583–603.

6. Brett, G. Z. and B. Benjamin, "Housing and Tuberculosis in a Mass Radiography Survey." *British Journal of Preventive and Social Medicine*, Vol. 11, No. 1, January, 1957, p. 7.

7. Holmes, Thomas H., "Multidiscipline Studies of Tuberculosis." In *Personality Stress and Tuberculosis*, Phineas J. Sparer ed., International Univ. Press, N.Y., 1956.

8. Stewart, G. T. and A. W. Voors, "Determinants of Sickness in Marine Recruits." *American Journal of Epidemiology*, Vol. 89, No. 3, May 14, 1968, pp. 254–263.

9. Kessler, Alexander, Doctoral Dissertation, "Interplay between Social Ecology and Physiology, Genetics, and Population Dynamics."

10. Dubos, René, *Man Adapting*. Yale University Press, New Haven, 1965, pp. 164–165.

11. Welch, Bruce L., "Psychophysiological Response to the Mean Level of Environmental Stimulation: A Theory of Environmental Integration." In *Symposium on Medical Aspects of Stress in the Military Climate*, Walter Reed Army Institute of Research, April, 1964.

12. Scotch, Norman A. and H. Jack Geiger, "The Epidemiology of Essential Hypertension II. Psychologic and Sociocultural Factors in Etiology." *J. Chron. Dis.*, 16, 1963, 1183–1213.

13. Kilborn, L. G., "A Note on the Blood Pressure of Primitive Races with Special Reference to the Maio of Kiweichaw." *Chinese J. Physiol.*, 11, 1937, 135.

14. Krakower, A., "Blood Pressure of Chinese Living in Eastern Canada." *Am. Heart J.*, 9, 1933, 376.

15. Kean, B. H., "Blood Pressure Studies on West Indians and Panamanians Living on Isthmus of Panama." *Arch. Int. Med.*, 68, 1941, 466.

16. Saunders, G. M., "Blood Pressure in Yucatans." *Am. J. Med. Sci.*, 185, 1933, 843.

17. Kean, B. H., "Blood Pressure of the Cuna Indians." *Am. J. Trop. Med.*, 24, 1944 (Suppl), 341.

18. Levine, V. E., "The Blood Pressure of Eskimos." *Fed. Proc.*, 1, 1942, 121.

19. Alexander, F., "A Medical Survey of the Aleutian Islands." *New England J. Med.*, 240, 1949, 1035.

20. Fulmer, H. S. and R. W. Roberts, "Coronary Heart Disease Among the Navajo Indians." *Ann. Int. Med.*, 59, 1963, 740–764.

21. Fleming, H. C., "Medical Observations on the Zuni Indians." *Contribution to Museum of American Indians*, Heye Foundation, 7, No. 2, New York, 1924.

22. Kaminer, B. and W. P. Lutz, "Blood Pressure in Bushmen of the Kalahari Desert." *Circulation*, 22, 1960, 289.

23. Donninson, C. P., "Blood Pressure in the African Native." *Lancet*, 1, 1929, 56.

24. Mann, G. V., *et al.*, "Cardiovascular Disease in the Masai." *J. Atherosclerosis Res.*, 4, 1964, 289.

25. Abrahams, D. G., C. A. Able, and G. Bernart, "Systemic Blood Pressure in a Rural West African Community." *W. Afr. Med. J.*, 9, 1960, 45.

26. Scotch, N. A., "A Preliminary Report on the Relation of Sociocultural Factors to Hypertension Among the Zulu." *Ann. New York Acad. Sci.*, 86, 1960, 1000.

27. Scotch, N. A., "Sociocultural Factors in the Epidemiology of Zulu Hypertension." *Am. J. Pub. Health*, 52, 1963, 1205–1213.

28. Bibile, S. W., *et al.*, "Variation with Age and Sex of Blood Pressure and Pulse Rate for Ceylonese Subjects." *Ceylon J. Med. Sci.*, 6, 1949, 80.

29. Padmayati, S. and S. Gupta, "Blood Pressure Studies in Rural and Urban Groups in Delhi." *Circulation*, 19, 1959, 395.

267

30. Lowell, R. R. H., I. Maddocks, and G. W. Rogerson, "The Casual Arterial Pressure of Fejians and Indians in Fiji." *Australasian Annals of Med.*, 9, 1960, 4.

31. Murphy, W., "Some Observations on Blood Pressures in the Humid Tropics." *N. Zealand Med. J.*, 54, 1955, 64.

32. Murril, R. I., "A Blood Pressure Study of the Natives of Ponape Island." *Human Biology*, 21, 1949, 47.

33. Maddocks, I., "Possible Absence of Hypertension in Two Complete Pacific Island Populations." *Lancet*, 2, 1961, 396.

34. Whyte, W. M., "Body Fat and Blood Pressure of Natives of New Guinea: Reflections on Essential Hypertension." *Australasian Annals Med.*, 7, 1958, 36.

35. Cruz-Coke, R., R. Etcheverry, and R. Nagel, "Influence of Migration on Blood Pressure of Easter Islanders." *Lancet*, 1, 1964, 697–699.

36. Hoobler, S. W., G. Tejada, M. Guzman, *et al.*, "Influence of Nutrition and 'Acculturation' on the Blood Pressure Levels and Changes with Age in the Highland Guatamalan Indian." *Circulation*, 32, 1965, 4.

37. Lowenstein, F. W., "Blood Pressure in Relation to Age and Sex in the Tropics and Subtropics: A Review of the Literature and an Investigation in Two Tribes of Brazil Indians." *Lancet*, 1, 1961, 389.

38. Mason, John W., "Psychoendocrine Approaches in Stress Research." *Medical Aspects of Stress in the Military Climate*, U.S. Government Printing Office, Washington, 1965.

39. Paffenberger, Ralph S., Jr., Robert N. Milling, Norman D. Poe, *et al.*, "Trends in Death Rates from Hypertensive Disease in Memphis, Tennessee 1920–1960." *J. Chron. Dis.*, 19, 1966, 847–856.

40. Christenson, William N. and Lawrence E. Hinkle, Jr., "Differences in Illness and Prognostic Signs in Two Groups of Young Men." *J.A.M.A.*, 177, 1961, 247–253.

41. Cassel, John and H. A. Tyroler, "Epidemiological Studies of Culture Change I. Health Status and Recency of Industrialization." *Arch. Envir. Health*, 3, 1961, 25.

42. Haenszel, William, Donald B. Loveland, and Monroe G. Sirken, "Lung-Cancer Mortality as Related to Residence and Smoking Histories." *J. Nat. Cancer Inst.*, 28, 1962, 947–1001.

43. Dunham, H. Warren, "Social Structures and Mental Disorders: Competing Hypotheses of Explanation." *Milbank Mem. Fund Quart.*, 39, 1961, 259–310.

44. Mishler, Elliot G. and Norman A. Scotch, "Sociocultural Factors in the Epidemiology of Schizophrenia: A Review." *Psychiatry*, 26, 1963, 315–351.

45. Tillman, W. A. and G. E. Hobbs, "Social Background of Accident Free and Accident Repeaters." *Am. J. Psychiat.*, 106, 1949, 321.

46. Durkheim, Emile, *Suicide*. The Free Press, Glencoe, Ill., 1957.

47. Holmes, Thomas H., Personal Communication.

48. Thurlow, H. John, "General Susceptibility to Illness: A Selective Review." *Canadian Med. Ass. J.*, 97, 1967, 1–8.

PART FOUR
The Social Meaning of Architecture

17

Images of Urban Areas: Their Structure and Psychological Foundations

DERK DE JONGE

It is evident from the intensity with which people react to architecture that an examination of the utilitarian features of architecture and the influence of these features on social interaction or health does not by any means exhaust the range of architectural properties relevant to man and society. The kind of joy, agony, frustration, pleasure, and ideological commitment that so often characterizes the human reaction to the environment would hardly develop if a building were only a bundle of heat, light, and humidity conditions; a communications network; or an implied level of population density. A building is also a specific three-dimensional form, a set of decorative elements including color and materials, and an interior space possessing particular qualities of enclosure. Those who hold strong views about architecture, and the number who do is far greater than the number of architects and design professionals, usually are reacting to these features of a building as well as to its operational virtues or disadvantages.

The architectural tradition, of course, has long emphasized the formal, stylistic, esthetic, and architectonic dimensions of buildings, and most architectural criticism has explored the origins and significance of these design qualities. Until recently the discussion of the ontological status of the non-utilitarian features of architecture, their source in the nature of man, and the processes through which they work their effect on society has been conducted without much assistance from the social sciences. The selection by de Jonge, and the others in Part Four, are illustrative of the emerging sociological, anthropological, and psychological literature that attempts to relate behavioral studies to some of these classical interests of designers.

De Jonge's principal concern is with what one might call the "reality" of urban form and the relevance of urban form to behavior in space. Is there a procedure for describing an environment in such a way that independent observers will agree about its visual organization? Will urban settlements that are eligible or imageable be easier for city residents to navigate?

Reprinted from Derk de Jonge, "Images of Urban Areas: Their Structure and Psychological Foundations," *Journal of the American Institute of Planners* 28, no. 4 (November 1962): 266–276. Reprinted by permission of the Journal of the American Institute of Planners.

De Jonge is interested in the problem of form independent of judgments of its beauty; also, an important part of his goal was to test the usefulness of the conceptual model for describing the properties of urban form first developed by Kevin Lynch. This kind of research is important because it confronts the accusation often leveled against the design tradition that judgments about the formal coherence of the environment are highly subjective and do not correspond to a reality that can be understood by the public.

The study reported by de Jonge was conducted in Holland. He examined urban form in the central areas of Amsterdam, Rotterdam, and the Hague, as well as in two neighborhoods in Delft. Following Lynch, the degree of order and regularity in the form of each settlement was first analyzed in terms of five design features: paths, nodes, landmarks, districts, and edges. Two groups of people were then asked about their perceptions of the environment: about twenty urban design and planning professionals, who were selected to represent the judgments of trained experts on design matters, and a sample of about 100 lay people, mostly wives of skilled workers and white collar employees. Information about their perceptions was obtained by asking the respondents to draw a map of the area. They were also interviewed to determine their spatial orientation and to learn how easy they found it to move through the area.

According to de Jonge, there was a high degree of consensus in the perceptions and judgments of the design professionals and the public. In general the imageability of urban form, as represented by the map drawings, was stronger where the street plan had a regular pattern, and where, as in central Amsterdam, there was a single dominant path or route running through the settlement and outstanding landmarks. In areas in which, according to the method of analysis developed by Lynch, the basic form was not highly legible, more attention was given in the maps to isolated landmarks. De Jonge also suggests that spatial orientation was easier in the more imageable settlements and in the neighborhoods in which the environment was not visually monotonous.

$\square$

The ideal of city planning is the arrangement of human artifacts in urban space to ensure optimum conditions for the development of social life and human happiness. We can achieve this object only to a limited extent, as we do not have sufficient knowledge of the means to attain this goal. But we may assume that one of the conditions for an effective use of urban space is that residents and visitors should be able to find their way about with ease, or at least without a great effort.

A fascinating study of the images of a city that exist in people's minds, and which enable them to orient themselves in urban areas has been made by Kevin Lynch.[1] He has found that people consistently use and organize sensory clues from the environment, relying on a selection of impressions to simplify the over-all structure. One urban environment lends itself better to this process than another. A city is most likely to evoke a strong image in any given observer if it can be apprehended as a pattern of high continuity, with a number of distinctive parts clearly interconnected. Lynch has called this quality "imageability."

In order to test the idea of imageability, he made analyses of the central areas of Boston, Jersey City, and Los Angeles. A systematic field reconnaissance of each area, made by a trained observer, was compared with the images of a small sample of residents. In a lengthy interview, each informant was requested to give descriptions, indicate locations, and make sketches of the area in question. He was also asked to perform a number of imaginary trips. Lynch found there were distinct differences in the imageability of the three cities studied and that the images were generally composed of five kinds of elements: path, nodes, landmarks, districts, and edges. If a city is to have a satisfying form, these elements must be patterned together in a legible structure. Paths may form a network (a grid, for example) in which repetition makes relationships sufficiently regular and predictable. It is also necessary that the parts have "identity"—that is, those qualities by which one object can be distinguished from another and recognized as a separate entity.

The work of Lynch has rightly been called "one of the most important contributions to large-scale design theory." [2] It has further been pointed out that the sample of informants was too small and too specialized to allow generalization of the findings. This will be possible only after further systematic empirical study, for which the methods and concepts contributed by Lynch's pioneer research can serve as starting-points.

The Scope of This Inquiry

The following account describes an attempt to make a contribution in this field. The purpose of this piece of research was to find answers to the following questions:

a. Can the research methods and techniques developed by Lynch be used, in a simplified form, for studies that are less elaborate, but that can cover a wider variety of urban areas and of informants?

b. If this is so, are the conclusions formulated by Lynch about the formation and nature of city images confirmed by such studies, and can any further relations be established between "urban form" and "city image"?

c. At what level can the results be generalized?

This investigation was made at the Housing and City Planning Research Section in the Department of Architecture of the Technical University of Delft (Holland).

In the first phase of the inquiry some twenty staff members of the Department of Architecture in Delft were interviewed to see what their images were of the central areas of Amsterdam, Rotterdam, The Hague, Utrecht, Leyden, and Delft. The structures of these cities are entirely different from those of the American cities studied by Lynch; further, there are also considerable variations in pattern from one Dutch city to another. The character of these central areas has been determined largely by topographic and historic factors. In Rotterdam, however, there was extensive reconstruction on more modern lines after the large-scale destruction during the last war.

In the second phase the investigation was extended to about one hundred people, selected at random, living in a number of urban residential neighborhoods in South Holland. In each area twenty to forty people, predominantly wives of skilled workers and white-collar employees, were interviewed. For most of the areas studied, the images of a number of laymen were compared with those of the professional city planners working in Delft; in some cases, further comparisons were made with maps drawn by professionals in other fields. For the downtown areas, a systematic comparison of the cities was made both for each individual informant and for all the informants together.

The main questions asked were:

1. *To what extent are you familiar with this area?*

2. *Will you draw a rough map of the area such as you imagine it for yourself? Can you also indicate the boundaries of the area?*

3. *What are, in your opinion, the most striking elements and buildings in this area?*

4. *Are there any places, here or elsewhere, where you find orientation difficult?*

In recording the statements of the informants, attention was given to the order of the elements in the sketch maps, remarks as to ease or difficulty in orientation, and the relation of the imaged area to the surrounding parts of the city. Each interview took about a quarter of an hour to half an hour.

The planners were asked to approach the subject in a non-technical way—to think of the everyday use they make of the area, rather than of their professional views. Under these conditions, their reactions did not differ significantly from those of other people of the same educational level. Many housewives, however, found it difficult, if not impossible, to draw sketch maps of their neighborhood. In these cases, the interview was focused on routes and problems of orientation, without direct reference to maps.

In the registration and presentation of the map images a technique was adopted that is somewhat different from the one used by Lynch. In comparing the map images of his subjects and of trained observers, Lynch transferred elements from sketch maps to accurate base maps. Thus the objective structure of urban space (represented on his base maps) as well as the subjective perception of this structure entered into the picture. To a certain extent, subjective and objective data were mixed on every map.

As a social scientist, I have first of all aimed at studying the relations between objective data (rendered on accurate maps and recorded by means of aerial photos) and subjective images (appearing in the form of sketch maps). I have kept the two kinds of maps apart, so that they are given in "pure" form. Thus, any resemblance between an accurate map (or aerial photo) and the image map will be inherent in them, and not a result of the method of recording or presentation. The sketch maps chosen for illustration here are typical ones, showing features which appear on most of the sketches of a particular area.

Results

The reactions of the informants showed a high degree of uniformity and consistency so far as the main points of image formation and image structure were concerned. In general, the quality of the sketch maps produced paralleled orientation in the field. Where most people had difficulties in sketching a rough map of an area, orientation was also difficult, for casual visitors if not for residents. Where people generally found it easy to draw a sketch map that was both simple and adequate, orientation was also easy, provided that the identity of the separate elements of the area was clear enough.

On the whole the methods and techniques described by Lynch were found to be useful instruments for the investigation of people's images of urban areas. This is also true if they are simplified for use in extensive investigations, including the comparison of several urban areas and their respective images. So the question formulated under (a) can be answered in the affirmative. Additional data must be presented in order to answer the questions posed under (b) and (c). In doing this I shall focus on the most interesting areas: Amsterdam, Rotterdam, The Hague, and three residential neighborhoods.

Amsterdam

Objective Structure. Three key elements in the structure of the old town are closely related to the river: the Mint Square, the Dam, and the Central Station. The Mint Square, with its notable Mint Tower, is located where the river first enters the ancient city. Where the mouth of the Amstel used to be, the Central Station has been built on an artificial island in the estuary. Midway between the Mint Square and the Central Station is the Dam, a great square that marks the site of the original dam on the river, and is now the location of the Royal Palace. As a public meeting place for important occasions, the Dam has a national and civic importance comparable to that of Trafalgar Square in London. Two parallel streets connect the Mint Square to the Central Station, passing through the Dam at mid-point. One is a major traffic route, called Damrak on one side of the Dam, Rokin on the other. The other route is a narrow shopping street called Nieuwendijk north of the Dam and Kalverstraat to the south.

Around this old linear core, the city laid out a major extension in the seventeenth century. Its dominant element consists of three major concentric canals, which, together with a number of radial streets and canals, form a spider web pattern. The major canals are further distinguished by rows of impressive homes built by prosperous merchants in the seventeenth century. A large number of the one-time patricians' homes are now used as offices, but there are still many artists and bohemians whose ideal is to live in an old house along one of the fine old canals. The present-day central shopping area of Amsterdam is situated partly within the old linear city and partly along some of the radial streets intersecting the belt of canals.

General Characteristics of the Image. As Lynch had conjectured, the map structure of Amsterdam produces a very strong image. Every informant indicates as the central path the main route along the river bank from the Central Station via the Dam Square to the Mint. This route is visualized as an axis placed in the middle of a series of concentric semi-circles, representing the major canals. The shopping streets (Nieuwendijk and Kalverstraat) form a secondary element accompanying the main route, although in fact this narrow path, with its attractive shop windows, is the route that most people take when they walk. The Central Station Square, the Dam Square, and the Mint are seen as

Figure 17–1 Photograph and Sketch Maps of Amsterdam.

A. Amstel River   D. Central Station (just above edge)
B. Mint Square   E. Damrak
C. Dam   F. Rokin

(Air photo by K.L.M. Aerocarto N.V.—archief Topografische Dienst.)

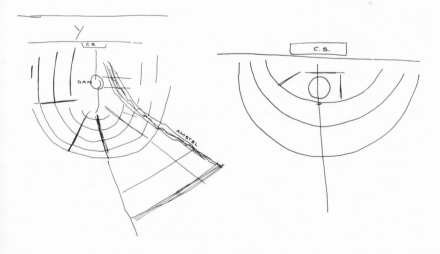

nodes marked by unique landmarks (the railroad station, the Royal Palace and the Mint Tower respectively).

Irregularities in the actual plan are smoothed out in the image. The central main route is seen as a straight line, although in reality there are some bends. The semi-circles of the image are more abstract than the spiderweb of the actual plan. This simplified pattern is accurate enough for general orientation. Since the main structure of the city is essentially regular, minor irregularities are not troublesome.

It should be noted that the bends in the major canals can be seen from any point along them. This feature gives a sense of direction, since the city center is on the inner side of the curve. The spiderweb structure also gives great prominence to the most central spaces: the Central Station and the Dam, either of which can be regarded as the center of the semi-circle. Further, the series of canals makes the whole central area of Amsterdam stand out clearly from the surrounding nineteenth-century neighborhoods.

The strong predominance of the main elements in the spatial structure should also be noted: informants give comparatively little attention to separate buildings. At the same time, many elements have a clear identity, so that there is no tedious repetition. The main difficulty for strangers seems to be in distinguishing the three major canals from one another. According to the police, people sometimes think their parked car has been stolen because they have returned to the wrong canal.

Rotterdam

Objective Structure. The ancient city took the form of a triangle, situated on a bend in the river Meuse (Maas). What is now the wide Coolsingel artery was once a canal at the western boundary of the old city. Gradually the central business and shopping district has been shifting westward—a process accelerated by the postwar reconstruction that was necessary after the devastation of much of the center by the bombardment of 1940.

Those elements of the city whose function is most central are now largely located near the Coolsingel, and the Central Station is even farther to the west. Thus the situation is quite different from that in Amsterdam. The triangle of the old city is intersected by an elevated railway. The Central Station is near a second traffic artery, the Weena, which runs at a right angle to the Coolsingel. The two arteries come together at the Hofplein traffic circle.

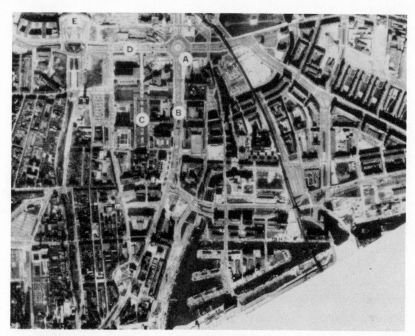

Figure 17–2 Photograph and Sketch Map of Central Rotterdam.

A. Hofplein Traffic Circle   D. Weena
B. Coolsingel   E. Central Station
C. Lijnbaan Shopping Mall

(Air photo by K.L.M. Aerocarto N.V.—archief Topografische Dienst.)

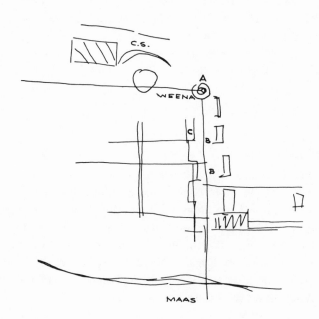

Hardly any old houses or other buildings that were worthwhile from an aesthetic or historic point of view have survived the blitz and the reconstruction. The Coolsingel is characterized by a great number of big, modern buildings (including Breuer's Bijenkorf Department Store) along this wide artery. A new shopping mall, the Lijnbaan, runs partly parallel and partly at right angles to the Coolsingel. Large scale building activities are constantly going on in the center of Rotterdam, such as the construction of new buildings and a tunnel works for the new subway.

The Image. Those informants who have the clearest image visualize this central area as an L-shaped configuration of the Weena and Coolsingel–plus–Lijnbaan. The link between these two parts of the L is the Hofplein node, with its characteristic form and its fountains. The Coolsingel is the major path mentioned by about 90 per cent of the informants. The Lijnbaan is indicated on the sketch maps by approximately the same number. Eighty per cent draw the Central Station, 70 per cent indicate the Weena as a major path, and 60 per cent show the Hofplein node.

Most informants have no clear picture of the boundaries between the central area and surrounding parts of the city. Thus in five sketches the elevated railway is indicated as the edge of the central area, while in five others it is there, but not as a boundary line. There is also a lack of clarity in the relation of the central area to other elements, such as the harbor and the district on the other side of the elevated railroad.

Individual buildings and other objects are mentioned to a greater extent than in Amsterdam. This may be due in part to the fact that buildings are more widely separated in Rotterdam, so that each of them is seen more clearly at some distance. But the fact that the over-all image of Rotterdam is weaker than that of Amsterdam may also explain why more attention is given to elements.

The Hague

Objective Structure. The plan of the central area developed largely in the Middle Ages. Here is the ancient Binnenhof (Earl's Court) in which the Parliament buildings and a number of ministries are located. Adjoining the Binnenhof are some squares and a large rectangular lake. West of the Binnenhof lies the main shopping area. Within this chessboard structure there are a number of irregularities, such as discontinuities in paths near the lake, and a curious bend in the Hofweg (Court Way) round the Binnenhof.

Figure 17–3   Photograph and Sketch Map of Earl's Court and Surroundings,
The Hague.

A. Earl's Court (Binnenhof)   D. Grote Marktstraat
B. Lake   E. Lange Voorhoot
C. Hofweg

(Air photo by K.L.M. Aerocarto N.V.—archief Topografische Dienst.)

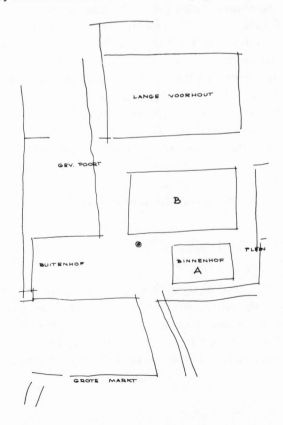

It should be noted that the general spatial structure of The Hague, a roughly rectangular grid parallel to the North Sea coast line, is different from that of most cities in the west of the Netherlands. The Hague traditionally lacked independent status, and the city has never been strongly fortified. In most other Dutch cities, fortifications have promoted a more concentric structure. According to an old saying, The Hague is "the finest village of Europe," and this phrase is still used jocularly to distinguish The Hague from Amsterdam and Rotterdam.

The Image. The method of composing most sketch maps of The Hague differs fundamentally from the methods used for the other two cities. In Amsterdam and Rotterdam, the paths and nodes that are important for transportation tend to be the primary elements of the pattern. In The Hague the dominant element is the Court with the adjoining lake. These two objects are taken as the starting-point for the majority of the sketch maps, and then other nearby elements are placed in relation to them. In doing this, many people move outward in a spiral; but on the whole they do not go very far.

The old canals (*singels*) round the eighteenth-century city do not play any part in the images recorded. They seem to disappear into the chessboard pattern of which they form part. It should also be noted that in the field these canals are not at all conspicuous elements. On the other hand, the bend in the Hofweg path is sketched by eighteen out of nineteen informants drawing this route. This can be explained by the fact that here is a striking departure from the general structure, clearly visible at a point just before the central open space.

In The Hague there is no wide, straight, and clearly dominant path as in Amsterdam or Rotterdam. Hardly any landmarks can be seen from a distance. Yet, the number of separate elements and buildings that are mentioned, in addition to the main ones, is quite large.

Most people are very vague as to the extent of the city's central area, and almost none have definite ideas of its boundaries.

Comparison of the Images of Amsterdam, Rotterdam, and The Hague

From a comparison of these three cities it is apparent that Amsterdam produces the strongest and clearest image. This is because here we have an urban area with a unique spatial structure standing out from its environs as the result of a deliberate aesthetic creation. In Rotterdam some clarity is achieved by wide major paths and big buildings placed in large spaces, but there is less unity of structure than in Amsterdam. (See Table 17–1.)

Although the center of Amsterdam has many fine and interesting buildings and places, more separate elements are mentioned for Rotterdam, and still more for The Hague. Apparently people tend to concentrate more on details when the total structure is less clear.

For both Rotterdam and The Hague, about one-third of the informants state that they find the pattern (if any) more difficult to comprehend than that of Amsterdam, in spite of the fact that the majority live farther from Amsterdam than from the other two cities. In general the map image of The Hague is vaguer and less unified than that of Rotterdam. Almost no one has been able to relate the central area of The Hague to the over-all grid of this city in his sketch.

Amsterdam is loved by many people, both residents and strangers. There are many reasons for this love, but one among them may be the beautiful structure of the central area, with both a clear over-all pattern and many identifiable parts.

Two Residential Neighborhoods in Delft

Objective Structure. A comparative study was made of two residential neighborhoods built in Delft in recent years. One of them, the Bomenbuurt, has a very simple structure. It numbers about 635 dwellings on an area of 300 × 350 meters. There is a mixed development of rowhouses and apartment buildings of two or three stories. Generally, rowhouses have been built on one side of a street and an apartment block on the other. All the dwellings have concrete outer walls, and all have been built according to a new, non-traditional method.

The street pattern is a rectangular grid, with one diagonal line leading from the edge of the neighborhood to a community building and a small square with a few shops. Near this square there are also a number of semi-detached houses. This is a comparatively small area with a regular street plan, showing irregularity only near the core.

The Voordijkhoornsepolder is about twice as large (about 850 × 325 meters), and numbers some 1200 dwellings: one-family houses, apartments, maisonettes, and seven high-rise blocks, three of which had been completed when the study was made.

The street pattern is roughly rectangular, with a number of small deviations from the right angle and the straight line. A broad road, the van Foreestweg, divides the neighborhood into two halves. On this road are

TABLE 17-1

City Elements Included on Sketch Maps	Number of Informants Identifying Each Element
Amsterdam: *Total Number of Informants, 25*	
PATHS:	
Main Path, Central Station to Mint	22
Drawn as a Straight Line	15
Semi-Circle of Canals	20
Other Paths, Secondary	17
NODES:	
Central Station Square	18
Dam Square	17
Mint Circut	9
Other Nodes	10
Rotterdam: *Total Number of Informants, 22*	
PATHS:	
Coolsingel	19
Coolsingel plus Lijnbaan	18
Weena	15
Other Paths	24
NODES:	
Station Square	17
Hofplein	13
BUILDINGS:	
Town Hall	10
Wholesale Trade Building	6
Bijenkorf Department Store	6
Exchange	6
OTHER ELEMENTS:	7
The Hague: *Total Number of Informants, 25*	
PATHS:	
Hofweg	19
Bend Indicated in Sketch	18
Grote Markstraat	15
Spui	12
Kneuterdijk	11
Poten	9
OTHER ELEMENTS:	
Lake near Earl's Court	21
Earl's Court	19
Outer Court	15
All Others, Combined	60

some twenty-five shops, a small canal, and a sizeable square. There are some supermarkets that are used also by people from the adjacent parts of Delft. One large, central, green area is situated on both sides of the square, and within the neighborhood there are four other green spaces, with apartment blocks and houses around them. Thus each street is situated in a characteristic way in relation to the edge of the neighborhood, the center of the neighborhood, or one of the squares.

The Image. The interviews showed that in the Bomenbuurt visitors, and even some absent-minded residents, often took the wrong street in consequence of the great uniformity in layout and architecture. This was especially true of the central streets when approached from the north. From the southern entrance—the diagonal line along the shops—it was much easier to find the right street. When coming from the North, some people even relied on minor details, such as the window curtains of the apartments or houses. A succession of more than three similar elements seems to impede spontaneous recognition and consequent choice of the right street.

Thus, in the most monotonous part of the Bomenbuurt there was regularity of structure, but lack of identity of the parts. Informants also had a number of complaints about the uniform appearance of the housing blocks and the "ugly" appearance of the concrete outer walls.

In the Voordijkhoornsepolder the situation was quite different. As each street and each housing block had its own distinctive orientation and architecture, identity was established more or less automatically by residents and visitors. Here there were many fewer complaints of monotonous blocks or streets. Variety among the elements was greatly increased by the different types of dwellings and by the presence of open spaces of various dimensions.

This comparison demonstrates that present-day planning can avoid monotony even in modern housing developments, and create a pattern that makes orientation easy.

The Leeuwendaal Neighborhood

As an example of a difficult area to be oriented properly in, several informants mentioned the Leeuwendaal neighborhood in Rijswijk (a suburb of The Hague). This area was rebuilt about the turn of the century, and the street plan reveals *Art Nouveau* influences. The streets run mostly in gentle curves, the interrelations of which (if any) cannot be comprehended in the field.

Interviews with some thirty residents showed that many casual visitors lose their way, and that even people who have lived here for decades find it difficult to draw an adequate sketch map. The one reproduced here shows an attempt that failed. The curves of the longest streets that are basic to the total pattern were not imaged adequately; thus it became impossible to link them up correctly with other streets.

Most inhabitants were able to find their way in the area not because they comprehended the total pattern (which was too complicated for them to remember), but because they knew each path separately. Those who only visited the area occasionally knew just a few isolated routes, which is what one tends to do in an area where orientation is difficult.

Conclusions

The following conclusions can be drawn: Formation of a map image is easiest where there is a street plan with a regular pattern, and a single dominant path, characteristic nodes, and unique landmarks. Where the general pattern is not clear, a greater amount of attention is given to isolated landmarks, individual paths, and visual details.

People tend to imagine patterns that are almost regular as perfectly regular. There is a stereotyping of the perception and recollection of spatial relations. Circles, semi-circles, and right angles are very easy to imagine, while quarter-circles and minor bends tend to create difficulties in orientation and map image formation.

Orientation is difficult in areas with an irregular street pattern, consisting of paths with curves that are not clearly connected with each other in a readable configuration. However, difficulties may also arise where the structure is quite clear but the elements are too uniform to be distinguished from each other. It seems that identity is especially difficult to establish where there are more than three elements of the same appearance.

We have seen that there is some dislike for neighborhoods that are too monotonous. At the same time, an area where visitors have trouble orienting themselves may be popular with residents on account of its quaint and exclusive character or because of other attractive qualities. This view is further supported by the fact that there are in Holland a number of expensive villa parks with complicated road patterns (Wassenaar, Bloemendaal, and Zeist) that have long been popular with people in upper-income brackets.

On the whole, Lynch's conclusions about image formation and image structure are further confirmed by this material; and it has been shown how these principles work in a number of different urban areas.

Figure 17–4   Leeuwendaal Neighborhood. (Sketch map appears below.)

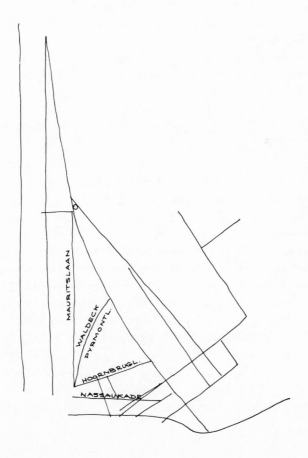

The fact that research in Holland has led to much the same conclusions as those of Lynch's is in itself an indication that his findings are not limited to the comparatively small sample he used. Further indications of the validity of the above conclusions on map image formation are to be found in two kinds of data: 1) orientation maps, and 2) the "laws" of Gestalt psychology.

1. Simple maps for rapid and easy orientation in given areas are issued by tourist offices, transit companies, and such institutions. In this connection, Lynch mentions the pocket map of subway lines of the London Transport Corporation. This map has also been commented upon by Arnheim, who says:

(It) gives the needed information with the utmost clarity and at the same time delights the eye through the harmony of its design. This is achieved by renouncing all geographic detail except for the pertinent topological properties—that is, sequence of stops and interconnections. All roads are reduced to straight lines; all angles to the two simplest: ninety degrees and forty-five degrees. The map leaves out and distorts a great deal, and just because of this it is the best possible picture of what it wants to show.[3]

Arnheim has also noted that more than three or four similar elements are "visually undistinguished."

The orientation maps show the same kind of selection of details and simplification of pattern as the sketch maps drawn by our informants. In addition, landmarks are often indicated on these maps in the form of small drawings showing the objects in perspective. Although most readers will remember such maps from their own experience, I add for purposes of illustration two maps of the island of Dordrecht. One is an ordinary topographical map; the other an orientation map issued by the municipal ferry service, which runs three ferries to the surrounding islands. This map shows the locations of the ferries, and of bridges, main roads, and railroads. The path structure has been simplified and landmarks are indicated in perspective.

2. A basic problem for Gestalt psychology has been to identify factors that organize the visual field into independent units. Many experiments have been made with figures composed of points and lines, in which subjects were asked to indicate what configurations they recognized. A number of conditions were thus found to play an important, if not exclusive, part in producing visual form: proximity, similarity, closed form, "good contour," common movement, and experience.[4] The perception of separate elements as one visual form is further promoted by such characteristics as regularity, symmetry, inclusiveness, harmony, maximal simplicity, and conciseness.

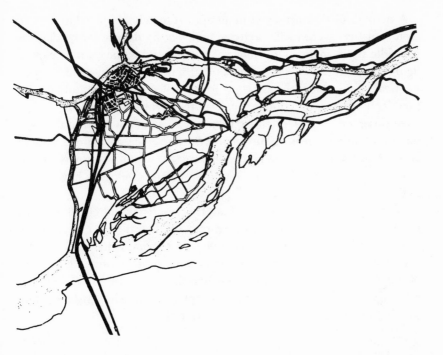

Figure 17–5 Maps of the Island of Dordrecht. (Orientation map, prepared by municipal ferry service, appears below.)

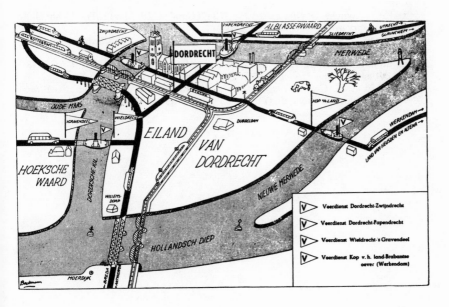

A number of dots arranged in an approximately circular fashion are seen as if they were really a circle, angles of 87 degrees or 93 degrees look like right angles. Drawings with gaps tend to be seen as closed, figures which are not quite symmetrical tend to be perceived as symmetrical. Thus, much the same process of selection, simplification, and predilection for "pure" forms (such as the right angle and the circle) were observed in the Gestalt experiments as were observed in the map images of urban areas studied here. So our research can be said to have shown that people's perceptions of the main pattern of urban space tend to follow the same "laws" Gestalt psychologists have found in their laboratory experiments.

We may therefore conclude that the results with regard to map images can be generalized, at any rate for literate man in Western society. Of course it still remains to be seen to what extent and in what way insight into image structure can be used to increase the liveability of cities and towns. This problem cannot be solved by social scientists alone; it calls for study by designers and social psychologists working jointly to investigate this important aspect of design.

NOTES

1. Kevin Lynch, *The Image of the City* (Cambridge, Mass.: The Technology Press and Harvard University Press, 1960).

2. David A. Crane, Review in *Journal of the American Institute of Planners*, 27 (May, 1961), 152.

3. Rudolph Arnheim, *Art and Visual Perception: A Psychology of the Creative Eye* (Berkeley: University of California Press, 1954), p. 123.

4. David Katz, *Gestalt Psychology, its Nature and Significance*, trans. Robert Tyson (London: Methuen, 1951), pp. 24–28 and 40–41.

18

Furniture Arrangement as a Symbol of Judicial Roles

JOHN N. HAZARD

In the previous selection, de Jonge discusses the degree of consensus in descriptions by the public of the form of urban areas and touches on the role of imageability in helping urban dwellers orient themselves while moving through urban space. The implication of this approach is that form acquires its social importance because of the way in which it is tied to the perceptual apparatus of the human organism. However, it is important to realize that form also acquires significance through its links to the cognitive faculties, which endow buildings with social meaning. Through its connection with the psychic structure of the organism, with the needs of the human personality for order and communication, and with the influence on personality of cultural experience, architecture is capable of serving as a symbol that can represent, reflect, and express values, group norms, and ideological beliefs. The passionate reactions to buildings of clients, designers, and users are apparently founded on this symbolic capacity of architecture rather than on its geometric or esthetic properties. It is not the building itself, therefore, but what the building seems to stand for that typically matters to people. Architects, of course, try to capitalize on architectural symbolism and claim proudly that their design constitutes a "statement"; designers like to say that architecture is a language, or that plans and forms can be "read" for their social meaning.

The symbolic content of architectural form is well illustrated in Hazard's discussion of what can be learned about the judicial systems of various nations simply by examining the furniture arrangements in their courtrooms. Among the formal properties he comments on are the respective locations of judges, juries, press, defendants, and prosecutors; the height of the chairs in which they are seated; and the spatial distance separating the actors in the courtroom. Hazard advises legal scholars that these architectural data offer an important clue to such questions in comparative law as the relative importance in a society of common and civil law traditions, the rights of the accused, and the nature of the hierarchical relationship between state authority and the populace.

Reprinted from John N. Hazard, "Furniture Arrangement as a Symbol of Judicial Roles," *ETC.: A Review of General Semantics* 19, no. 2 (July 1962): 181–188. Reprinted by permission of the International Society for General Semantics.

In view of the fact that Hazard is discussing those aspects of architectural form that were discussed in Part Two under the heading of Spatial Organization and Social Interaction, it should be emphasized that his selection does not deal with the actual behavioral effects of courtroom design or with the social or legal rationale for furniture arrangements. For example, each of the different arrangements presumably developed in an effort to dispense justice more equitably, but Hazard's selection does not attempt to evaluate the corresponding legal systems in terms of their fairness. Instead, he argues that the spatial organization of a courtroom is a sign system through which a society tries to communicate its ideal model of the relationship between judges, prosecutors, juries, and others involved in judicial proceedings. The aspect of form being considered here, in other words, is very similar to the concept so popular with architects of the building's "intention," the kind of social outcome it is supposed to achieve. However, just as in the case of the architect's intention, the determination of the quality of justice that is dispensed in a particular society with a particular form of courtroom remains an empirical question that must await further research.

☐

Walk into an empty courtroom and look around. The furniture arrangement will tell you at a glance who has what authority. In nearly every country, judges now look down on their courtrooms from a raised platform, and when the bench is collegial, the presiding judge has a chair whose back protrudes several inches above the rest. This is so even in the Soviet Union where the judge has been elevated above his 1917 role when he was wise friend and conciliator to his village. Today, he sits with his colleagues even in the lowest court upon a platform rather than around a table with the parties. His dignity is enhanced not only by his elevated chair but by the attendant's cry, "All stand," as he and the lay assessors file into the room to take their places. Only a robe is missing to command respect. And in the People's Republic of Poland, after the "October" of 1956, even the robe was redraped on judicial shoulders, with its purple piping in traditional designation of the majesty of the law. The portrait of power was further enhanced at that time by encircling his neck with a great gold seal and chain of office in traditional Polish fashion.

The judge's commanding seat catches first attention, but the eye soon wanders to the other furniture. In a British or American courtroom, the jury box stands out to the right of the enclosure behind the "bar." Between it and the judge's bench on a raised platform somewhat lower than that of the judge stands the chair waiting for the witness, facing outward into the room so that all can hear, including the press for whom a gallery or at least a bench is often reserved to give meaning to the concept of "publicity" characteristic of the common law concept of "due process."

Compare the assize court in the canton of Geneva, and you will find the jury, but in a different place. It is in no box separated from the judge, but arranged on two rows of chairs to the judge's left behind the great semi-circular bench that extends the width of the room. One scarcely needs to be told that the judge retires with the jury in this Swiss canton, and that he shares with the jurymen the decision on guilt and punishment. At the eastern end of Europe there is no jury box at all, for the Soviet legal procedure relies on two lay assessors in every type of case, both criminal and civil, to share with the judge the decision on matters both of fact and law. This is so in all of the Eastern European states that have adopted the Soviet legal system, and has been accepted even in Communist China.

Witness stands in continental Europe traditionally face in toward the judge rather than out toward the courtroom. The assembled public sees only the back of the witness's head when he testifies and hears little of what he says unless he raises his voice. In Geneva the press is aided because the press bench is placed along the right hand wall below the great semi-circular bench of judge and jury but forward of the public's seats. Reporters may hear and see everything and perform their critical democratic function of informing the wider public of what transpires. In the Eastern European courtrooms there are no special press galleries, unless the defendant happens to be an American U-2 pilot and the affair a cause célèbre. Soviet concepts of "due process" require no participation of a press independent of the state and prepared to sound the tocsin if injustice is done. If the press is present, it is because the court has a case with a public message which the judges believe the public should hear.

The prosecutor's seat is placed in a wide variety of positions in various legal systems. In the American courtroom the casual visitor will note no chair that can be quickly identified as one of special dignity. The district, state's or United States' attorney, as he is likely to be called, will sit in a chair placed on the other side of the center aisle from the chair of the defense counsel and inside the "bar." This chair has no ornate carved seal on its back, but is whatever standard model the janitor chooses to set at the table. Both prosecutor and defense counsels are placed on the same level, without benefit of elevation above the courtroom's floor, and the prosecutor is not farther forward or on the side to provide his voice with a more effective sounding board than that of his opponent.

This location of equality with that of the defense is suited to the prosecutor's standing in a legal system that reveres the adversary procedure under which the prosecutor is in theory as well as in fact a state's attorney charged with presenting the strongest possible case for the state and expecting to be countered with the strongest possible case for the defense so that there are created conditions like that of an ancient tournament. The judge becomes under this system the arbiter to assure conformity to the procedural rules that have evolved over centuries to constitute the rules of fair play, and the jurymen will decide the issues on the basis of those facts the judge permits them to hear. The humble location of the state's attorney's chair indicates to the jury that his word is no more weighty than that of counsel for the defense.

Consider the contrast offered by Geneva. The prosecutor in the assize court sits at the left end of the great semicircular bench at the middle of which sits the judge in frock coat, flanked by his jury at the other end. The prosecutor's seat places him well above the level of the chairs of the counsel for defense, the accused, and the witness stand, all of which are on the main floor. He carries by virtue of his location a certain majesty, not wholly distinguishable from the majesty of the judge. He is above the battle, and the procedural codes place a special responsibility upon him accordingly. He is required to be impartial, to be more than a state's attorney. In some countries, as in France, he is technically an arm of the magistracy.

The nonpartisan position of the prosecutor adheres even in the Soviet Union, where the procedural codes require the prosecutor to act in protection of legality even against a judgment in his favor by the court but too severe in its sentence. Look at the Cour Correctionelle in Paris' Palais de Justice, and you will find "Le Parquet" on a raised platform to the left of the judge's bench, less elevated and somewhat in front of the judges but quite unrelated to the position given the "avocat" who must plead for the defense. The continental prosecutor has such an unfamiliar position to the Anglo-American attorney, that it has often been suggested that he be called by his title in his own language to avoid confusion caused by a term that has other connotations for the common-law-trained mind.

While placing a special burden upon the prosecutor and treating him as more than an attorney for the state than is usual in Western Europe, the Soviet procedural codes espouse the adversary proceeding while retaining elements of the inquisitorial procedure of Western Europe as well. Thus, the Soviet prosecutor's chair is on the main floor at the same level as defense counsel, but it is usually placed at a desk on the left side of the room permitting the prosecutor to put his back to the wall and face the witness and the parties without rising. This seat puts him at an advantage over the defense counsel, and his dignity is further enhanced by a special uniform of office. This might create in the accused's mind an image of greater dignity than the judges, for they wear the clothes of the average Soviet man of the street.

The prosecutor's special position in continental Europe once created a struggle over furniture arrangement in the People's Republic of Poland that illustrates the problem with exceptional clarity. Before the Gomulka reforms of 1956, attempting to overcome some of the extreme Soviet influences upon communist Poland, the prosecutor sat at the left end of the same bench as the judges, and to the untutored defendant, he must have looked like a fourth judge, albeit seated around the corner from the other three. This made for too much dignity in the eyes of the reformers of 1956, and they hit upon a solution of some novelty. They brought in the carpenters to cut a narrow slit in the table at the prosecutor's end, so that today the Polish prosecutor sits at the same level as the judges above the rest of the room, but his table is physically distinct from that of the judges. He is almost but not quite as authoritative as the men and women charged with reaching the decision. His status is clearer than before, but he still has special dignity. He wears a black robe like a judge, except that his is piped with red in preservation of the traditional color of the medieval inquisitor for the Church, from whom his office is descended.

The Polish defense attorney, since the reform, also wears the black robe of his office, as does the barrister of the English court, but he has no specially designed wig as does his English counterpart to mark his position and difference from the judge and Crown's attorney each with his distinctive wig. The defense attorney's mark in Poland is the green piping that runs along the hem of his garment giving his robe a bit of color down the front.

Bitter conflict over the location of the prosecutor's chair has raged in Germany since the war. Perhaps under the impact of common law thinking, there has been a demand in some German states for a change in the prosecutor's place from the exalted traditional seat at the end of the bench with the judges to a position on the main floor no more prestigious than that of defense counsel. This movement has had its effect in one state as has the demand that the witness' chair face out toward the courtroom rather than in toward the judges' bench.

295

Next, there will be in many European criminal courts one more chair that would not appear in the American or English courtroom at all. This is the chair reserved for the attorney of the "civil plaintiff." Having no differing standards of proof for civil and criminal cases, the continental jurists have no difficulty in deciding the rights of the victim to damages at the same time as they determine the guilt of the accused. In consequence, the victim, or his survivor in the event of his death, is in the courtroom not solely as a witness, but as a party, and his attorney may rise to question witnesses or plead arguments if he believes that the prosecutor is failing in his duty.

Last, but not inconsequential among the participants in the trial, is the court secretary, for on him falls the task of preparing the record without which no appellate system can have validity, unless the appellate judges are authorized to recall witnesses and retry the case. The American courtroom is characterized by the early entrance of the court stenographer with his silent stenotype machine. He takes his place just under the judge's nose at a table placed where everything from the bench, the witness stand, and the tables for state's attorney and defense can be heard. He is expected to record every word spoken by any participant, and to reproduce it during the night in neatly typed pages made available to all concerned on payment of costs. His chair and his silent machine with endless strips of stenographic paper symbolize the determination of American courts to record everything.

Contrast Geneva or Cambridge, England. The court secretary will be sitting below the judge with a heavy desk typewriter. He will sit motionless while the testimony proceeds, but when the witness finishes, he cocks an ear to the bench without turning around and types swiftly and noisily what His Honor dictates as the substance of the testimony. Then he will strip his machine and place the page before the witness who has remained in place to affix his signature in verification. No English court wants to be burdened with a record of hundreds of pages of all that has been said, for this seems to the British to be cumbersome, wordy and confusing.

In the Soviet courtroom the secretary presents a sharp contrast. Usually a young woman, the secretary sits at the end of the bench in the People's Court with foolscap, ink pot, and pen to record what she can catch and thinks important without benefit of dictation by a judge, except in the unusual and complicated instance. It is no wonder that the U.S.S.R. Supreme Court has had to remand a case for retrial in some instances because of the inadequacy of the record for appellate purposes.

296

When considering the making of court records it is well to consider the bench to which the British assize judge mounts in majestic scarlet robe and wig following the blaring of trumpets from the courthouse steps as his carriage rumbles up from his temporary lodgings. That bench is completely clean of papers. There is no record of prior proceedings. The judge begins his hearing with a *tabula rasa*. Not so on the continent. Every judge who mounts the bench on the other side of the English Channel will have before him several volumes of "dossier" awaiting verification at the trial. In these volumes stands another symbol of a basic difference between the procedures of the common and civil law.

Civil law systems, including the Soviet, provide for preliminary review of the case, not as a grand jury would hear a United States attorney in New York, merely to determine whether there is likelihood of adequate evidence to proceed to trial, but to determine to the best of the preliminary investigator's opinion whether conviction can be expected to occur. The continental preliminary investigator is a magistrate charged with a special function like that of the judge's at the trial, to determine "objective truth," to create within his own mind a sense of "intimate conviction" of guilt. In consequence a continental trial in most countries, even in the words of some distinguished continental experts, is a verification of the work of the preliminary investigator, or the *juge d'instruction*, as he may be called.

By procedural codes the trial judges, where the "instruction" has occurred, must verify in open court by rehearing the witnesses and looking at the material evidence anew everything on which a finding of guilt is to be rested. In fact, there are times when to a common-law-trained mind, the judges violate "due process," for they permit reading of the testimony at the preliminary investigation when a witness who has testified before cannot return for reasons that seem like nothing more than inconvenience. In France, the trial judge will even read the preliminary record of testimony of a defendant who refuses to speak at the trial.

Perhaps in the light of the situation it is not facetious to suggest that while comparative law scholars are currently concerned with exhaustive examination of what is meant by the rule of law in various legal systems, a comparison of furniture arrangement in the courtroom merits a chapter in their study.[1]

NOTE

1. A first attempt to move in this direction has appeared in Sybille Bedford's *The Faces of Justice: A Traveller's Report* (New York, 1961).

19

Fear and the House-as-Haven in the Lower Class

LEE RAINWATER

The literature on architectural symbolism conventionally distinguishes three levels of symbolic meaning: syntactical meaning, or the meaning that an element of form or style acquires by virtue of its location in a chain of form or style elements; semantic meaning, or the meaning it acquires because of the norm, idea, or attitude that it represents or designates; and pragmatic meaning, or the meaning that is to be understood in relation to the architect, client, or social group that invents or interprets the building's form or style.

Rainwater's selection can be looked upon as an attempt to explore the semantic and pragmatic meanings of housing in American society. The research on which it is based consists of 2,500 depth interviews with working-class people living in many different communities. Those interviewed were asked how they felt about their present homes, what plans they had for changing their housing, and what the relation of these plans was to their personal and familial goals.

With regard to the semantic meaning of housing, Rainwater's major point is that symbolic attitudes toward the house are very different for slum dwellers, members of the traditional working class, and families in the modern working class who are on their way upward into the middle class. The primary aim of the slum dwellers is to find a house or apartment that will provide safe shelter, in other words, adequate room for sleeping, relaxing, and eating, and a haven from noise, odors, dirt, and interpersonal violence and abuse. Families from the traditional working class can apparently count on their house being relatively safe, and what they seek in housing is a reasonably comfortable dwelling unit and neighborhood, nicely maintained and stocked with conveniences that ease the burden of domestic work on the mother. Only in the advanced working class and in the middle class does one find a more elaborate conception of the house as a private domain that offers opportunities for recreation and expressive self-fulfillment and a stage for the display of affluence.

In terms of the pragmatic meaning of housing, two facts seem clear. First, the different meanings assigned to housing by slum dwellers, traditional

Reprinted from Lee Rainwater, "Fear and the House-as-Haven in the Lower Class," *Journal of the American Institute of Planners* 32, no. 1 (January 1966): 23–31. Reprinted by permission of the Journal of the American Institute of Planners.

working-class people, and members of the middle class reflect their previous experience with the environment. Slum dwellers, for example, are emphatic in their concern that the house serve as a haven because they inhabit a world in which homicide, burglary, and social pathology are commonplace. Members of the other social classes have correspondingly more favorable experiences that establish the context for the meanings that they assign to the house. Second, it seems that underlying the different meanings assigned to the house is a hierarchy of human needs that the dwelling unit is able to satisfy. At the bottom of the hierarchy are the basic biological needs for air, light, warmth, and protection against molestation. At the next level upward are the needs for greater efficiency and comfort, induced by the requirement that family members should be able to function at work or school. When the satisfaction of these needs is assured, then the house can begin to acquire its significance as a place for display and the attainment of pleasure.

The varying meanings of the house for different social groups have implications for design. At the very least, they suggest that architects, most of whom are drawn from the middle class, should not try to impose design features significant to themselves on lower- and working-class users without making certain they are also responding to the simpler meaning of housing to people whose first priority is the achievement of a safe and healthy environment.

☐

Men live in a world which presents them with many threats to their security as well as with opportunities for gratification of their needs. The cultures that men create represent ways of adapting to these threats to security as well as maximizing the opportunities for certain kinds of gratifications. Housing as an element of material culture has as its prime purpose the provision of shelter, which is protection from potentially damaging or unpleasant trauma or other stimuli. The most primitive level of evaluation of housing, therefore, has to do with the question of how adequately it shelters the individuals who abide in it from threats in their environment. Because the house is a refuge from noxious elements in the outside world, it serves people as a locale where they can regroup their energies for interaction with that outside world. There is in our culture a long history of the development of the house as a place of safety from both nonhuman and human threats, a history which culminates in guaranteeing the house, a man's castle, against unreasonable search and seizure. The house becomes the place of maximum exercise of individual autonomy, minimum conformity to the formal and complex rules of public demeanor. The house acquires a sacred character from its complex intertwining with the self and from the symbolic character it has as a representation of the family.[1]

These conceptions of the house are readily generalized to the area around it, to the neighborhood. The fact is most readily perceived in the romanticized views people have about suburban living.[2] The suburb, just as the village or the farm homestead, can be conceptualized as one large protecting and gratifying home. But the same can also be said of the city neighborhood, at least as a potentiality and as a wish, tenuously held in some situations, firmly established in others.[3] Indeed, the physical barriers between inside and outside are not maintained when people talk of their attitudes and desires with respect to housing. Rather, they talk of the outside as an inevitable extension of the inside and of the inside as deeply affected by what goes on immediately outside.

When, as in the middle class, the battle to make the home a safe place has long been won, the home then has more central to its definition other functions which have to do with self-expression and self-realization. There is an elaboration of both the material culture within the home and of interpersonal relationships in the form of more complex rituals of behavior and more variegated kinds of interaction. Studies of the relationship between social class status and both numbers of friends and acquaintances as well as kinds of entertaining in the home indicate that as social status increases the home becomes a locale for a wider range of interactions. Whether the ritualized behavior be the informality of the lower middle class family room, or the formality of the upper middle class cocktail party and buffet, the requisite housing standards of the middle class reflect a more complex and varied set of demands on the physical structure and its equipment.

The poverty and cultural milieu of the lower class make the prime concern that of the home as a place of security, and the accomplishment of this goal is generally a very tenuous and incomplete one. (I use the term "lower class" here to refer to the bottom 15 to 20 percent of the population in terms of social status. This is the group characterized by unskilled occupations, a high frequency of unstable work histories, slum dwellings, and the like. I refer to the group of more stable blue-collar workers which in status stands just above this lower class as the "working class" to avoid the awkwardness of terms like "lower-lower" and "upper-lower" class.) In the established working class there is generally a somewhat greater degree of confidence in the house as providing shelter and security, although the hangovers of concern with a threatening lower class environment often are still operating in the ways working class people think about housing.[4]

In Table 19–1, I have summarized the main differences in three

TABLE 19-1

Variations in Housing Standards within the Lower and Working Classes

		Most Pressing Needs in Housing	
Focus of Housing Standard	*Core Consumer Group*	*Inside the House*	*Outside Environs*
Shelter	Slum Dwellers	Enough Room; Absence of Noxious or Dangerous Elements	Absence of External Threats Availability of Minimum Community Services
Expressive Elaboration	Traditional Working Class	Creating a Pleasant, Cozy Home with Major Conveniences	Availability of a Satisfying Peer Group Society and a "Respectable Enough" Neighborhood
All-American Affluence	Modern Working Class	Elaboration of the Above along the Line of a More Complex Material Culture	Construction of the All-American Leisure Style in Terms of "Outdoor Living"; "Good" Community Services

orientations toward housing standards that are characteristic of three different consumer groups within the lower and working classes. I will elaborate below on the attitudes of the first group, the slum dwellers, whose primary focus in housing standards seems to be on the house as a shelter from both external and internal threat.

Attitudes toward Housing

As context for this, however, let us look briefly at some of the characteristics of two working class groups. These observations come from a series of studies of the working class carried out by Social Research, Inc. over the past ten years. The studies have involved some 2,000 open-ended conversational interviews with working class men and women dealing with various life style areas from child rearing to religion, food habits to furniture preferences. In all of this work, the importance of the home and its location has appeared as a constant theme. These studies, while not based on nationally representative samples, have been carried out in such a way as to represent the geographical range of the country, including such cities as Seattle, Camden, Louisville, Chicago, Atlanta, as well as a balanced distribution of central city and suburban dwellers, apartment renters, and home owners. In these studies, one central focus concerned the feelings working class people have about their present homes, their plans for changes in housing, their attitudes toward their neighborhoods, and the relation of these to personal and familial goals. In addition, because the interviews were open-ended and conversational, much information of relevance to housing appeared in the context of other discussions because of the importance of housing to so many other areas of living.[5] In our studies and in those of Herbert Gans and others of Boston's West End, we find one type of working class life style where families are content with much about their housing—even though it is "below standard" in the eyes of housing professionals—if the housing does provide security against the most blatant of threats.[6] This traditional working class is likely to want to economize on housing in order to have money available to pursue other interests and needs. There will be efforts at the maintenance of the house or apartment, but not much interest in improvement of housing level. Instead there is an effort to create a pleasant and cozy home, where housework can be carried out conveniently. Thus, families in this group tend to acquire a good many of the major appliances, to center their social life in the kitchen, to be relatively unconcerned with adding taste in furnishings to comfort. With respect to the immediate outside world the main emphasis is on a concern with the availability of a satisfying peer group life, with having neighbors who are similar, and with maintaining an easy access back and forth among people who are very well known. There is also a concern that the neighborhood be respectable enough—with respectability defined mainly in the negative, by the absence of "crumbs and bums." An emphasis on comfort and contentment ties together meanings having to do with both the inside and the outside.

Out of the increasing prosperity of the working class has grown a different orientation toward housing on the part of the second group which we can characterize as modern instead of traditional. Here there is a great emphasis on owning one's home rather than enriching a landlord. Along with the acquisition of a home and yard goes an elaboration of the inside of the house in such a way as not only to further develop the idea of a pleasant and cozy home, but also to add new elements with emphasis on having a nicely decorated living room or family room, a home which more closely approximates a standard of all-American affluence. Similarly there is a greater emphasis on maintenance of the yard outside and on the use of the yard as a place where both adults and children can relax and enjoy themselves. With this can come also the development of a more intense pattern of neighbor-hood socializing. In these suburbs the demand grows for good com-munity services as opposed to simply adequate ones, so that there tends to be greater involvement in the schools than is the case with traditional working class men and women. One of the dominant themes of the modern working class life style is that of having arrived in the mainstream of American life, of no longer being simply "poor-but-honest" workers. It is in the service of this goal that we find these elaborations in the meaning of the house and its environs.

In both working class groups, as the interior of the home more closely approximates notions of a decent standard, we find a decline in concerns expressed by inhabitants with sources of threat from within and a shift toward concerns about a threatening outside world—a desire to make the neighborhood secure against the incursions of lower class people who might rob or perpetrate violence of one kind or another.

As we shift our focus from the stable working class to the lower class, the currently popular poor, we find a very different picture. In addition to the large and growing literature, I will draw on data from three studies of this group with which I have been involved. Two studies deal with family attitudes and family planning behavior on the part of lower class, in contrast to working class couples. In these studies, based on some 450 intensive conversational interviews with men and women living in Chicago, Cincinnati, and Oklahoma City housing was not a subject of direct inquiry. Nevertheless we gained considerable insight into the ways lower class people think about their physical and social environment, and their anxieties, goals, and coping mechanisms that operate in connection with their housing arrangements.[7]

The third study, currently on-going, involves a five year investigation of social and community problems in the Pruitt-Igoe Project of St. Louis. This public housing project consists of 33 11-story buildings near downtown St. Louis. The project was opened in 1954, has 2,762 apartments, of which only some 2,000 are currently occupied, and has as tenants a very high proportion (over 50 percent) of female-headed households on one kind or another of public assistance. Though originally integrated, the project is now all Negro. The project com-munity is plagued by petty crimes, vandalism, much destruction of the physical plant, and a very bad reputation in both the Negro and white communities.[8] For the past two years a staff of ten research assistants has been carrying out participant observation and conversational interviewing among project residents. In order to obtain a comparative focus on problems of living in public housing, we have also interviewed in projects in Chicago (Stateway Gardens), New York (St. Nicholas), and San Francisco (Yerba Buena Plaza and Westside Courts). Many of the concrete examples which follow come from these interviews, since in the course of observation and interviewing with project tenants we have had the opportunity to learn a great deal about both their experiences in the projects and about the private slum housing in which they previously lived. While our interviews in St. Louis provide us with insight into what it is like to live in one of the most disorganized public housing communities in the United States, the interviews in the other cities provide the contrast of much more average public housing experiences.[9] Similarly, the retrospective accounts that respondents in different cities give of their previous private housing experience provides a wide sampling in the slum communities of four different cities.

In the lower class we find a great many very real threats to security, although these threats often do seem to be somewhat exaggerated by lower class women. The threatening world of the lower class comes to be absorbed into a world view which generalizes the belief that the environment is threatening more than it is rewarding—that rewards reflect the infrequent working of good luck and that danger is endemic.[10] Any close acquaintance with the ongoing life of lower class people impresses one with their anxious alienation from the larger world, from the middle class to be sure, but from the majority of their peers as well. Lower class people often seem isolated and to have but tenuous participation in a community of known and valued peers. They are ever aware of the presence of strangers who tend to be seen as potentially dangerous. While they do seek to create a gratifying peer group society, these groups tend to be unstable and readily fragmented. Even the heavy reliance on relatives as the core of a personal community does not do away with the dangers which others may bring. As Walter Miller has perceptively noted, "trouble" is one of the major focal concerns in the lower class world view.[11] A home to which one could retreat from such an insecure world would be of great value, but our data indicate that for lower class people such a home is not easy to come by. In part, this is due to the fact that one's own family members themselves often make trouble or bring it into the home, but even more important it is because it seems very difficult to create a home and an immediate environment that actually does shut out danger.[12]

Dangers in the Environment

From our data it is possible to abstract a great many dangers that have some relation to housing and its location. The location or the immediate environment is as important as the house itself, since lower class people are aware that life inside is much affected by the life just outside.

In Table 19–2, I have summarized the main kinds of danger which seem to be related to housing one way or another. It is apparent that these dangers have two immediate sources, human and nonhuman, and that the consequences that are feared from these sources usually represent a complex amalgam of physical, interpersonal, and mortal damage to the individual and his family. Let us look first at the various sources of danger and then at the overlapping consequences feared from these dangers.

There is nothing unfamiliar about the nonhuman sources of danger. They represent a sad catalogue of threats apparent in any journalist's account of slum living.[13] That we become used to the catalogue, however, should not obscure the fact that these dangers are very real to many lower class families. Rats and other vermin are ever present companions in most big city slums. From the sense of relief which residents in public housing often experience on this score, it is ap-

TABLE 19-2

A Taxonomy of Dangers in the Lower Class Home and Environs:
Each of These Can Involve Physical, Interpersonal, and Moral Consequences

Source of Danger	
Nonhuman	*Human*
Rats and Other Vermin	Violence to Self and Possessions
Poisons	Assault
Fire and Burning	Fighting and Beating
Freezing and Cold	Rape
Poor Plumbing	Objects Thrown or Dropped
Dangerous Electrical Wiring	Stealing
Trash (broken glass, cans, etc.)	Verbal Hostility, Shaming, Exploitation
Insufficiently Protected Heights	Own Family
Other Aspects of Poorly Designed	Neighbors
or Deteriorated Structures	Caretakers
(e.g. thin walls)	Outsiders
Cost of Dwelling	Attractive Alternatives that Wean
	Oneself or Valued Others Away
	from a Stable Life

parent that slum dwellers are not indifferent to the presence of rats in their homes. Poisons may be a danger, sometimes from lead-base paints used on surfaces which slum toddlers may chew. Fires in slum areas are not uncommon, and even in a supposedly well designed public housing project children may repeatedly burn themselves on uncovered steampipe risers. In slums where the tenant supplies his own heating there is always the possibility of a very cold apartment because of no money, or, indeed, of freezing to death (as we were told by one respondent whose friend fell into an alcoholic sleep without turning on the heater). Insufficiently protected heights, as in one public housing project, may lead to deaths when children fall out windows or adults fall down elevator shafts. Thin walls in the apartment may expose a family to more of its neighbor's goings-on than comfortable to hear. Finally, the very cost of the dwelling itself can represent a danger in that it leaves too little money for other things needed to keep body and soul together.

That lower class people grow up in a world like this and live in it does not mean that they are indifferent to it—nor that its toll is only that of possible physical damage in injury, illness, incapacity, or death. Because these potentialities and events are interpreted and take on symbolic significance, and because lower class people make some efforts to cope with them, inevitably there are also effects on their interpersonal relationships and on their moral conceptions of themselves and their worlds.

The most obvious human source of danger has to do with violence directed by others against oneself and one's possessions. Lower class people are concerned with being assaulted, being damaged, being drawn into fights, being beaten, being raped. In public housing projects in particular, it is always possible for juveniles to throw or drop things from windows which can hurt or kill, and if this pattern takes hold it is a constant source of potential danger. Similarly, people may rob anywhere—apartment, laundry room, corridor.

Aside from this kind of direct violence, there is the more pervasive ever-present potentiality for symbolic violence to the self and that which is identified with the self—by verbal hostility, the shaming and exploitation expressed by the others who make up one's world. A source of such violence, shaming, or exploitation may be within one's own family—from children, spouse, siblings, parents—and often is. It seems very likely that crowding tends to encourage such symbolic violence to the self but certainly crowding is not the only factor since we also find this kind of threat in uncrowded public housing quarters.[14] Most real and immediate to lower class people, however, seems to be the potentiality for symbolic destructiveness by their neighbors. Lower class people seem ever on guard toward their neighbors, even ones with whom they become well-acquainted and would count as their friends. This suspiciousness is directed often at juveniles and young adults whom older people tend to regard as almost uncontrollable. It is important to note that while one may and does engage in this kind of behavior oneself, this is no guarantee that the individual does not fear and condemn the behavior when engaged in by others. For example, one woman whose family was evicted from a public housing project because her children were troublemakers thought, before she knew that her family was included among the twenty families thus evicted, that the evictions were a good thing because there were too many people around who cause trouble.

Symbolic violence on the part of caretakers (all those whose occupations bring them into contact with lower class people as purveyors of some private or public service) seems also endemic in slum and public housing areas. Students of the interactions between caretakers and their lower class clients have suggested that there is a great deal of punitiveness and shaming commonly expressed by the caretakers in an effort to control and direct the activities of their clients.[15]

The defense of the client is generally one of avoidance, or sullenness and feigned stupidity, when contact cannot be avoided. As David Caplovitz has shown so well, lower class people are subjected to considerable exploitation by the commercial services with which they deal, and exploitation for money, sexual favors, and sadistic impulses is not unknown on the part of public servants either.[16]

Finally, outsiders present in two ways the dangers of symbolic violence as well as of physical violence. Using the anonymity of geographical mobility, outsiders may come into slum areas to con and exploit for their own ends and, by virtue of the attitudes they maintain toward slum dwellers or public housing residents, they may demean and derogate them. Here we would have to include also the mass media which can and do behave in irresponsibly punitive ways toward people who live in lower class areas, a fact most dramatically illustrated in the customary treatment of the Pruitt-Igoe Project in St. Louis. From the point of view of the residents, the unusual interest shown in their world by a research team can also fit into this pattern.

Finally, the lower class person's world contains many attractive alternatives to the pursuit of a stable life. He can fear for himself that he will be caught up in these attractive alternatives and thus damage his life chances, and he may fear even more that those whom he values, particularly in his family, will be seduced away from him. Thus, wives fear their husbands will be attracted to the life outside the family, husbands fear the same of their wives, and parents always fear that their children will somehow turn out badly. Again, the fact that you may yourself be involved in such seductive pursuits does not lessen the fear that these valued others will be won away while your back is turned. In short, both the push and the pull of the human world in which lower class people live can be seen as a source of danger.

Having looked at the sources of danger, let us look at the consequences which lower class people fear from these dangers. The physical consequences are fairly obvious in connection with the nonhuman threats and the threats of violence from others. They are real and they are ever present: One can become the victim of injury, incapacitation, illness, and death from both nonhuman and human sources. Even the physical consequences of the symbolic violence of hostility, shaming, and exploitation, to say nothing of seduction, can be great if they lead one to retaliate in a physical way and in turn be damaged. Similarly there are physical consequences to being caught up in alternatives such as participation in alcohol and drug subcultures.

There are three interrelated interpersonal consequences of living in a world characterized by these human and nonhuman sources of danger. The first relates to the need to form satisfying interpersonal relationships, the second to the need to exercise responsibility as a family member, and the third to the need to formulate an explanation for the unpleasant state of affairs in your world.

The consequences which endanger the need to maintain satisfying interpersonal relations flow primarily from the human sources of danger. That is, to the extent that the world seems made up of dangerous others, at a very basic level the choice of friends carries risks. There is always the possibility that a friend may turn out to be an enemy or that his friends will. The result is a generalized watchfulness and touchiness in interpersonal relationships. Because other individuals represent not only themselves but also their families, the matter is further complicated since interactions with, let us say, neighbors' children, can have repercussions on the relationship with the neighbor. Because there are human agents behind most of the nonhuman dangers, one's relationships with others—family members, neighbors, caretakers—are subject to potential disruptions because of those others' involvement in creating trash, throwing objects, causing fires, or carrying on within thin walls.

With respect to the exercise of responsibility, we find that parents feel they must bring their children safely through childhood in a world which both poses great physical and moral dangers, and which seeks constantly to seduce them into a way of life which the parent wishes them to avoid. Thus, childrearing becomes an anxious and uncertain process. Two of the most common results are a pervasive repressiveness in child discipline and training, and, when that seems to fail or is no longer possible, a fatalistic abdication of efforts to protect the children. From the child's point of view, because his parents are not able to protect him from many unpleasantnesses and even from himself, he loses faith in them and comes to regard them as persons of relatively little consequence.

The third area of effect on interpersonal relations has to do with the search for causes of the prevalence of threat and violence in their world. We have suggested that to lower class people the major causes stem from the nature of their own peers. Thus, a great deal of blaming others goes on and reinforces the process of isolation, suspiciousness, and touchiness about blame and shaming. Similarly, landlords and tenants tend to develop patterns of mutual recrimination and blaming, making it very difficult for them to cooperate with each other in doing something about either the human or nonhuman sources of difficulty.

Finally, the consequences for conceptions of the moral order of one's world, of one's self, and of others, are very great. Although lower class people may not adhere in action to many middle class values about neatness, cleanliness, order, and proper decorum, it is apparent that they are often aware of their deviance, wishing that their world could be a nicer place, physically and socially. The presence of nonhuman threats conveys in devastating terms a sense that they live in an immoral and uncontrolled world. The physical evidence of trash, poor plumbing and the stink that goes with it, rats and other vermin, deepens their feeling of being moral outcasts. Their physical world is telling them they are inferior and bad just as effectively perhaps as do their human interactions. Their inability to control the depredation of rats, hot steam pipes, balky stoves, and poorly fused electrical circuits tells them that they are failures as autonomous individuals. The physical and social disorder of their world presents a constant temptation to give up or retaliate in kind. And when lower class people try to do something about some of these dangers, they are generally exposed in their interactions with caretakers and outsiders to further moral punitiveness by being told that their troubles are their own fault.

Implications for Housing Design

It would be asking too much to insist that design per se can solve or even seriously mitigate these threats. On the other hand, it is obvious that almost all the nonhuman threats can be pretty well done away with where the resources are available to design decent housing for lower class people. No matter what criticisms are made of public housing projects, there is no doubt that the structures themselves are infinitely preferable to slum housing. In our interviews in public housing projects we have found very few people who complain about design aspects of the insides of their apartments. Though they may not see their apartments as perfect, there is a dramatic drop in anxiety about nonhuman threats within. Similarly, reasonable foresight in the design of other elements can eliminate the threat of falling from windows or into elevator shafts, and can provide adequate outside toilet facilities for children at play. Money and a reasonable exercise of architectural skill go a long way toward providing lower class families with the really safe place of retreat from the outside world that they desire.

There is no such straightforward design solution to the potentiality of human threat. However, to the extent that lower class people do have a place they can go that is not so dangerous as the typical slum dwelling, there is at least the gain of a haven. Thus, at the cost perhaps of increased isolation, lower class people in public housing sometimes place a great deal of value on privacy and on living a quiet life behind the locked doors of their apartments. When the apartment itself seems safe it allows the family to begin to elaborate a home to maximize coziness, comfortable enclosure, and lack of exposure. Where, as in St. Louis, the laundry rooms seem unsafe places, tenants tend to prefer to do their laundry in their homes, sacrificing the possibility of neighborly interactions to gain a greater sense of security of person and property.

Once the home can be seen as a relatively safe place, lower class men and women express a desire to push out the boundaries of safety further into the larger world. There is the constantly expressed desire for a little bit of outside space that is one's own or at least semiprivate. Buildings that have galleries are much preferred by their tenants to those that have no such immediate access to the outside. Where, as in the New York public housing project we studied, it was possible to lock the outside doors of the buildings at night, tenants felt more secure.

A measured degree of publicness within buildings can also contribute to a greater sense of security. In buildings where there are several families whose doors open onto a common hallway there is a greater sense of the availability of help should trouble come than there is in buildings where only two or three apartments open onto a small hallway in a stairwell. While tenants do not necessarily develop close neighborly relations when more neighbors are available, they can develop a sense of making common cause in dealing with common problems. And they feel less at the mercy of gangs or individuals intent on doing them harm.

As with the most immediate outside, lower class people express the desire to have their immediate neighborhood or the housing project grounds a more controlled and safe place. In public housing projects, for example, tenants want project police who function efficiently and quickly; they would like some play areas supervised so that children are not allowed to prey on each other; they want to be able to move about freely themselves and at the same time discourage outsiders who might come to exploit.

A real complication is that the very control which these desires imply can seem a threat to the lower class resident. To the extent that caretakers seem to demand and damn more than they help, this cure to the problem of human threat seems worse than the disease. The crux of the caretaking task in connection with lower class people is to provide and encourage security and order within the lower class world without at the same time extracting from it a heavy price in self-esteem, dignity, and autonomy.

NOTES

AUTHOR'S NOTE: This selection is based in part on research aided by a grant from the National Institute of Mental Health, Grant No: MH-09189 "Social and Community Problems in Public Housing Areas." Many of the ideas presented stem from discussions with the senior members of the Pruitt-Igoe Research Staff—Alvin W. Gouldner, David J. Pittman, and Jules Henry—and with the research associates and research assistants on the project.

1. Lord Raglan, *The Temple and the House* (London: Routledge & Kegan Paul Limited, 1964).

2. Bennett M. Berger, *Working-Class Suburb* (Berkeley: University of California Press, 1960) and Herbert Gans, "Effect of the Move From the City to Suburb," in Leonard J. Duhl, ed., *The Urban Condition* (New York: Basic Books, 1963).

3. Anselm L. Strauss, *Images of the American City* (New York: The Free Press, 1961).

4. In this paper I am pulling together observations from a number of different studies. What I have to say about working class attitudes toward housing comes primarily from studies of working class life style carried out in collaboration with Richard Coleman, Gerald Handel, W. Lloyd Warner, and Burleigh Gardner. What I have to say about lower class life comes from two more recent studies dealing with family life and family planning in the lower class and a study currently in progress of social life in a large public housing project in St. Louis (being conducted in collaboration with Alvin W. Gouldner and David J. Pittman).

5. These studies are reported in the following unpublished Social Research, Inc. reports: *Prosperity and Changing Working Class Life Style* (1960) and *Urban Working Class Identity and World View* (1965). The following publications are based on this series of studies: Lee Rainwater, Richard P. Coleman, and Gerald Handel, *Workingman's Wife: Her Personality, World and Life Style* (New York: Oceana Publications, 1959); Gerald Handel and Lee Rainwater, "Persistence and Change in Working Class Life Style," and Lee Rainwater and Gerald Handel, "Changing Family Roles in the Working Class," both in Arthur B. Shostak and William Gomberg, *Blue-Collar World* (New York: Prentice-Hall, 1964).

6. Marc Fried, "Grieving for a Lost Home," and Edward J. Ryan, "Personal Identity in an Urban Slum," in Leonard J. Duhl, ed., *The Urban Condition* (New York: Basic Books, 1963); and Herbert Gans, *Urban Villagers* (New York: The Free Press, 1962).

7. Lee Rainwater, *And the Poor Get Children* (Chicago: Quadrangle Books, 1960), and Lee Rainwater, *Family Design: Marital Sexuality, Family Size and Family Planning* (Chicago: Aldine Publishing Company, 1964).

8. Nicholas J. Demerath, "St. Louis Public Housing Study Sets Off Community Development to Meet Social Needs," *Journal of Housing*, XIX (October, 1962).

9. See, D. M. Wilner, *et al.*, *The Housing Environment and Family Life* (Baltimore: The Johns Hopkins Press, 1962).

10. Allison Davis, *Social Class Influences on Learning* (Cambridge: Harvard University Press, 1948).

11. Walter Miller, "Lower Class Culture as a Generating Milieu of Gang Delinquency," in Marvin E. Wolfgang, Leonard Savitz, and Norman Johnson, eds., *The Sociology of Crime and Delinquency* (New York: John Wiley & Sons, 1962).

12. Alvin W. Schorr, *Slums and Social Insecurity* (Washington, D.C.: Department of Health, Education and Welfare, 1963).

13. Michael Harrington, *The Other America* (New York: Macmillan Co., 1962).

14. Edward S. Deevey, "The Hare and the Haruspex: A Cautionary Tale," in Eric and Mary Josephson, *Man Alone* (New York: Dell Publishing Company, 1962).

15. A. B. Hollingshead and L. H. Rogler, "Attitudes Toward Slums and Private Housing in Puerto Rico," in Leonard J. Duhl, *The Urban Condition* (New York: Basic Books, 1963).

16. David Caplovitz, *The Poor Pay More* (New York: The Free Press, 1963).

20

Pecuniary Canons of Taste

THORSTEIN VEBLEN

If we accept the concept of a hierarchy of human needs to which architecture responds, then it is evident, as Rainwater argues in the previous selection, that the particular significance that a building assumes in the psychic life of its occupants is determined partly by whether the building does or does not satisfy the need for shelter. In the case of housing, for example, if the basic needs are not met, then the house is regarded simply as a haven; if the environment is safe, then the house can begin to assume a more complex significance in the lives of its users.

In the following selection, taken from his *The Theory of the Leisure Class,* Veblen offers a theory to explain the meaning of architecture and of objects in the more affluent sectors of society. At these upper reaches of the class system, it is obvious that an explanation cannot be deduced from information about the frustration of elementary biological needs, since the members of the leisure class are generally not deprived in this sense. When they do suffer from a lack of commodiousness, as sometimes happens to the wealthy who would rather sacrifice modern conveniences than forego the symbolic pleasures of their villas and rundown town houses, the choice is deliberate.

Veblen's method for explaining the symbolic content of architecture is to examine the properties or features of architectural style that seem to be most highly valued in the leisure class and that mold what he calls its "canon of taste." In the present selection this method is illustrated in a discussion of lawns, yards, and parks, which, as Veblen says, "appeal so unaffectedly to the taste of Western peoples." He argues that lawns and greenswards in public grounds have very little practical use for a society no longer dependent upon grazing. Indeed, Veblen argues, it is this very characteristic of "reputable futility" that is the clue to why lawns are valued: their care is so costly of time and money and their maintenance so often a frustrating task that the possession of a lawn testifies indubitably to the capacity of its owner to indulge in wasteful expenditure. Through the operation of the principle of "pecuniary emulation" even those classes in the population that cannot afford to waste energy and resources in the ownership and maintenance of a lawn, nevertheless strive to possess one. In this way standards of architectural

Reprinted from Thorstein Veblen, "Pecuniary Canons of Taste,"
The Theory of the Leisure Class (New York: Modern Library,
1934), pp. 130–139; 149–159. Reprinted by permission of the
Viking Press, Inc.

design, which are set at the top of the social order, percolate downward and become also the canons of taste of the middle and lower classes.

Although Veblen believed that the motivation that underlay the development of established taste was that the style chosen should evidence the capacity for waste, he apparently also believed it was possible to distinguish the intrinsic beauty of an object or building from the component of beauty attributed to it by virtue of its service as an object of "invidious comparison." In fact, he looked upon his book and its method as a means for liberating him and his readers from the esthetic misperceptions induced by the common human desire to engage in "pecuniary emulation." He was, for example, a rebel against Victorian ideas of beauty, and preferred styles of architecture and domestic art that were close to what later came to be known as the machine or industrial esthetic. Thus, in the following selection one finds Veblen declaiming against the "endless variety of fronts presented by the better class of tenements and apartment houses" and instead taking the position that "the dead walls and sides and back of these structures are commonly the best features of the buildings."

☐

Any valuable object in order to appeal to our sense of beauty must conform to the requirements of beauty and of expensiveness both. But this is not all. Beyond this the canon of expensiveness also affects our tastes in such a way as to inextricably blend the marks of expensiveness, in our appreciation, with the beautiful features of the object, and to subsume the resultant effect under the head of an appreciation of beauty simply. The marks of expensiveness come to be accepted as beautiful features of the expensive articles. They are pleasing as being marks of honorific costliness, and the pleasure which they afford on this score blends with that afforded by the beautiful form and color of the object; so that we often declare that an article of apparel, for instance, is "perfectly lovely," when pretty much all that an analysis of the aesthetic value of the article would leave ground for is the declaration that it is pecuniarily honorific.

This blending and confusion of the elements of expensiveness and of beauty is, perhaps, best exemplified in articles of dress and of household furniture. The code of reputability in matters of dress decides what shapes, colors, materials, and general effects in human apparel are for the time to be accepted as suitable; and departures from the code are offensive to our taste, supposedly as being departures from aesthetic truth. The approval with which we look upon fashionable attire is by no means to be accounted pure make-believe. We readily, and for the most part with utter sincerity, find those things pleasing that are in vogue. Shaggy dress stuffs and pronounced color effects, for instance, offend us at times when the vogue is goods of a high, glossy finish and neutral colors. A fancy bonnet of this year's model unquestionably appeals to our sensibilities to-day much more forcibly than an equally fancy bonnet of the model of last year; although when viewed in the perspective of a quarter of a century, it would, I apprehend, be a matter of the utmost difficulty to award the palm for intrinsic beauty to the one rather than to the other of these structures. So, again, it may be remarked that, considered simply in their physical juxtaposition with the human form, the high gloss of a gentleman's hat or of a patent-leather shoe has no more of intrinsic beauty than a similarly high gloss on a threadbare sleeve; and yet there is no question but that all well-bred people (in the Occidental civilized communities) instinctively and unaffectedly cleave to the one as a phenomenon of great beauty, and eschew the other as offensive to every sense to which it can appeal. It is extremely doubtful if any one could be induced to wear such a contrivance as the high hat of civilized society, except for some urgent reason based on other than aesthetic grounds.

By further habituation to an appreciative perception of the marks of expensiveness in goods, and by habitually identifying beauty with reputability, it comes about that a beautiful article which is not expensive is accounted not beautiful. In this way it has happened, for instance, that some beautiful flowers pass conventionally for offensive weeds; others that can be cultivated with relative ease are accepted and admired by the lower middle class, who can afford no more expensive luxuries of this kind; but these varieties are rejected as vulgar by those people who are better able to pay for expensive flowers and who are educated to a higher schedule of pecuniary beauty in the florist's products; while still other flowers, of no greater intrinsic beauty than these, are cultivated at great cost and call out much admiration from flower-lovers whose tastes have been matured under the critical guidance of a polite environment.

The same variation in matters of taste, from one class of society to another, is visible also as regards many other kinds of consumable goods, as, for example, is the case with furniture, houses, parks, and gardens. This diversity of views as to what is beautiful in these various classes of goods is not a diversity of the norm according to which the unsophisticated sense of the beautiful works. It is not a constitutional difference of endowments in the aesthetic respect, but rather a difference in the code of reputability which specifies what objects properly lie within the scope of honorific consumption for the

316

class to which the critic belongs. It is a difference in the traditions of propriety with respect to the kinds of things which may, without derogation to the consumer, be consumed under the head of objects of taste and art. With a certain allowance for variations to be accounted for on other grounds, these traditions are determined, more or less rigidly, by the pecuniary plane of life of the class.

Everyday life affords many curious illustrations of the way in which the code of pecuniary beauty in articles of use varies from class to class, as well as of the way in which the conventional sense of beauty departs in its deliverances from the sense untutored by the requirements of pecuniary repute. Such a fact is the lawn, or the close-cropped yard or park, which appeals so unaffectedly to the taste of the Western peoples. It appears especially to appeal to the tastes of the well-to-do classes in those communities in which the dolicho-blond element predominates in an appreciable degree. The lawn unquestionably has an element of sensuous beauty, simply as an object of apperception, and as such no doubt it appeals pretty directly to the eye of nearly all races and all classes; but it is, perhaps, more unquestionably beautiful to the eye of the dolicho-blond than to most other varieties of men. This higher appreciation of a stretch of greensward in this ethnic element than in the other elements of the population, goes along with certain other features of the dolicho-blond temperament that indicate that this racial element had once been for a long time a pastoral people inhabiting a region with a humid climate. The close-cropped lawn is beautiful in the eyes of a people whose inherited bent it is to readily find pleasure in contemplating a well-preserved pasture or grazing land.

For the aesthetic purpose the lawn is a cow pasture; and in some cases to-day—where the expensiveness of the attendant circumstances bars out any imputation of thrift—the idyl of the dolicho-blond is rehabilitated in the introduction of a cow into a lawn or private ground. In such cases the cow made use of is commonly of an expensive breed. The vulgar suggestion of thrift, which is nearly inseparable from the cow, is a standing objection to the decorative use of this animal. So that in all cases, except where luxurious surroundings negative this suggestion, the use of the cow as an object of taste must be avoided. Where the predilection for some grazing animal to fill out the suggestion of the pasture is too strong to be suppressed, the cow's place is often given to some more or less inadequate substitute, such as deer, antelopes, or some such exotic beast. These substitutes, though less beautiful to the pastoral eye of Western man than the cow, are in such cases preferred because of their superior expensiveness or futility, and their consequent repute. They are not vulgarly lucrative either in fact or in suggestion.

Public parks of course fall in the same category with the lawn; they too, at their best, are imitations of the pasture. Such a park is of course best kept by grazing, and the cattle on the grass are themselves no mean addition to the beauty of the thing, as need scarcely be insisted on with any one who has once seen a well-kept pasture. But it is worth noting, as an expression of the pecuniary element in popular taste, that such a method of keeping public grounds is seldom resorted to. The best that is done by skilled workmen under the supervision of a trained keeper is a more or less close imitation of a pasture, but the result invariably falls somewhat short of the artistic effect of grazing. But to the average popular apprehension a herd of cattle so pointedly suggests thrift and usefulness that their presence in the public pleasure ground would be intolerably cheap. This method of keeping grounds is comparatively inexpensive, therefore it is indecorous.

Of the same general bearing is another feature of public grounds. There is a studious exhibition of expensiveness coupled with a make-believe of simplicity and crude serviceability. Private grounds also show the same physiognomy wherever they are in the management or ownership of persons whose tastes have been formed under middle-class habits of life or under the upper-class traditions of no later a date than the childhood of the generation that is now passing. Grounds which conform to the instructed tastes of the latter-day upper class do not show these features in so marked a degree. The reason for this difference in tastes between the past and the incoming generation of the well-bred lies in the changing economic situation. A similar difference is perceptible in other respects, as well as in the accepted ideals of pleasure grounds. In this country as in most others, until the last half century but a very small proportion of the population were possessed of such wealth as would exempt them from thrift. Owing to imperfect means of communication, this small fraction were scattered and out of effective touch with one another. There was therefore no basis for a growth of taste in disregard of expensiveness. The revolt of the well-bred taste against vulgar thrift was unchecked. Wherever the unsophisticated sense of beauty might show itself sporadically in an approval of inexpensive or thrifty surroundings, it would lack the "social confirmation" which nothing but a considerable body of like-minded people can give. There was, therefore, no effective upper-class opinion that would overlook evidences of possible inexpensiveness in the man-

318

agement of grounds; and there was consequently no appreciable divergence between the leisure-class and the lower middle-class ideal in the physiognomy of pleasure grounds. Both classes equally constructed their ideals with the fear of pecuniary disrepute before their eyes.

To-day a divergence in ideals is beginning to be apparent. The portion of the leisure class that has been consistently exempt from work and from pecuniary cares for a generation or more is now large enough to form and sustain an opinion in matters of taste. Increased mobility of the members has also added to the facility with which a "social confirmation" can be attained within the class. Within this select class the exemption from thrift is a matter so commonplace as to have lost much of its utility as a basis of pecuniary decency. Therefore the latter-day upper-class canons of taste do not so consistently insist on an unremitting demonstration of expensiveness and a strict exclusion of the appearance of thrift. So, a predilection for the rustic and the "natural" in parks and grounds makes its appearance on these higher social and intellectual levels. This predilection is in large part an outcropping of the instinct of workmanship; and it works out its results with varying degrees of consistency. It is seldom altogether unaffected, and at times it shades off into something not widely different from that make-believe of rusticity which has been referred to above.

A weakness for crudely serviceable contrivances that pointedly suggest immediate and wasteless use is present even in the middle-class tastes; but it is there kept well in hand under the unbroken dominance of the canon of reputable futility. Consequently it works out in a variety of ways and means for shamming serviceability—in such contrivances as rustic fences, bridges, bowers, pavilions, and the like decorative features. An expression of this affectation of serviceability, at what is perhaps its widest divergence from the first promptings of the sense of economic beauty, is afforded by the cast-iron rustic fence and trellis or by a circuitous drive laid across level ground.

The select leisure class has outgrown the use of these pseudo-serviceable variants of pecuniary beauty, at least at some points. But the taste of the more recent accessions to the leisure class proper and of the middle and lower classes still requires a pecuniary beauty to supplement the aesthetic beauty, even in those objects which are primarily admired for the beauty that belongs to them as natural growths.

The popular taste in these matters is to be seen in the prevalent high appreciation of topiary work and of the conventional flower-beds of public grounds. Perhaps as happy an illustration as may be had of this dominance of pecuniary beauty over aesthetic beauty in middle-class tastes is seen in the reconstruction of the grounds lately occupied by the Columbian Exposition. The evidence goes to show that the requirement of reputable expensiveness is still present in good vigor even where all ostensibly lavish display is avoided. The artistic effects actually wrought in this work of reconstruction diverge somewhat widely from the effect to which the same ground would have lent itself in hands not guided by pecuniary canons of taste. And even the better class of the city's population view the progress of the work with an unreserved approval which suggests that there is in this case little if any discrepancy between the tastes of the upper and the lower or middle classes of the city. The sense of beauty in the population of this representative city of the advanced pecuniary culture is very chary of any departure from its great cultural principle of conspicuous waste.

The love of nature, perhaps itself borrowed from a higher-class code of taste, sometimes expresses itself in unexpected ways under the guidance of this canon of pecuniary beauty, and leads to results that may seem incongruous to an unreflecting beholder. The well-accepted practice of planting trees in the treeless areas of this country, for instance, has been carried over as an item of honorific expenditure into the heavily wooded areas; so that it is by no means unusual for a village or a farmer in the wooded country to clear the land of its native trees and immediately replant saplings of certain introduced varieties about the farmyard or along the streets. In this way a forest growth of oak, elm, beech, butternut, hemlock, basswood, and birch is cleared off to give room for saplings of soft maple, cottonwood, and brittle willow. It is felt that the inexpensiveness of leaving the forest trees standing would derogate from the dignity that should invest an article which is intended to serve a decorative and honorific end.

• • •

The connection here indicated between the aesthetic value and the invidious pecuniary value of things is of course not present in the consciousness of the valuer. So far as a person, in forming a judgment of taste, takes thought and reflects that the object of beauty under consideration is wasteful and reputable, and therefore may legitimately be accounted beautiful; so far the judgment is not a *bona fide* judgment of taste and does not come up for consideration in this connection. The connection which is here insisted on between the reputability and the apprehended beauty of objects lies through the effect which the fact of reputability has upon the valuer's habits of thought. He is in the habit of forming judgments of value of various kinds—economic, moral, aesthetic, or reputable—concerning the objects with which he has to do, and his attitude of commendation towards a given object on any other ground will affect the degree of his appreciation of the object when he comes to value it for the aesthetic purpose. This is more particularly true as regards valuation on grounds so closely related to the aesthetic ground as that of reputability. The valuation for the aesthetic purpose and for the purpose of repute are not held apart as distinctly as might be. Confusion is especially apt to arise between these two kinds of valuation, because the value of objects for repute is not habitually distinguished in speech by the use of a special descriptive term. The result is that the terms in familiar use to designate categories or elements of beauty are applied to cover this unnamed element of pecuniary merit, and the corresponding confusion of ideas follows by easy consequence. The demands of reputability in this way coalesce in the popular apprehension with the demands of the sense of beauty, and beauty which is not accompanied by the accredited marks of good repute is not accepted. But the requirements of pecuniary reputability and those of beauty in the naïve sense do not in any appreciable degree coincide. The elimination from our surroundings of the pecuniarily unfit, therefore, results in a more or less thorough elimination of that considerable range of elements of beauty which do not happen to conform to the pecuniary requirement.

The underlying norms of taste are of very ancient growth, probably far antedating the advent of the pecuniary institutions that are here under discussion. Consequently, by force of the past selective adaptation of men's habits of thought, it happens that the requirements of beauty, simply, are for the most part best satisfied by inexpensive contrivances and structures which in a straightforward manner suggest both the office which they are to perform and the method of serving their end.

It may be in place to recall the modern psychological position. Beauty of form seems to be a question of facility of apperception. The proposition could perhaps safely be made broader than this. If abstraction is made from association, suggestion, and "expression," classed as elements of beauty, then beauty in any perceived object means that the mind readily unfolds its apperceptive activity in the directions which the object in question affords. But the directions in which activity readily unfolds or expresses itself are the directions to which long and close habituation has made the mind prone. So far as concerns the essential elements of beauty, this habituation is an habituation so close and long as to have induced not only a proclivity to the apperceptive form in question, but an adaptation of physiological structure and function as well. So far as the economic interest enters into the constitution of beauty, it enters as a suggestion or expression of adequacy to a purpose, a manifest and readily inferable subservience to the life process. This expression of economic facility or economic serviceability in any object—what may be called the economic beauty of the object—is best served by neat and unambiguous suggestion of its office and its efficiency for the material ends of life.

On this ground, among objects of use the simple and unadorned article is aesthetically the best. But since the pecuniary canon of reputability rejects the inexpensive in articles appropriated to individual consumption, the satisfaction of our craving for beautiful things must be sought by way of compromise. The canons of beauty must be circumvented by some contrivance which will give evidence of a reputably wasteful expenditure, at the same time that it meets the demands of our critical sense of the useful and the beautiful, or at least meets the demand of some habit which has come to do duty in place of that sense. Such an auxiliary sense of taste is the sense of novelty; and this latter is helped out in its surrogateship by the curiosity with which men view ingenious and puzzling contrivances. Hence it comes that most objects alleged to be beautiful, and doing duty as such, show considerable ingenuity of design and are calculated to puzzle the beholder —to bewilder him with irrelevant suggestions and hints of the improbable—at the same time that they give evidence of an expenditure of labor in excess of what would give them their fullest efficiency for their ostensible economic end.

This may be shown by an illustration taken from outside the range of our everyday habits and everyday contact, and so outside the range of our bias. Such are the remarkable feather mantles of Hawaii, or the well-known carved handles of the ceremonial adzes of several Polynesian islands. These are undeniably beautiful, both in the sense that they offer a pleasing composition of form, lines, and color, and in the sense that they evince great skill and ingenuity in design and construction. At the same time the articles are manifestly ill fitted to serve any other economic purpose. But it is not always that the evolution of ingenious and puzzling contrivances under the guidance of the canon of wasted effort works out so happy a result. The result is quite as often a virtually complete suppression of all elements that would bear scrutiny as expressions of beauty, or of serviceability, and the substitution of evidences of misspent ingenuity and labor, backed by a conspicuous ineptitude; until many of the objects with which we surround ourselves in everyday life, and even many articles of everyday dress and ornament, are such as would not be tolerated except under the stress of prescriptive tradition. Illustrations of this substitution of ingenuity and expense in place of beauty and serviceability are to be seen, for instance, in domestic architecture, in domestic art or fancy work, in various articles of apparel, especially of feminine and priestly apparel.

The canon of beauty requires expression of the generic. The "novelty" due to the demands of conspicuous waste traverses this canon of beauty, in that it results in making the physiognomy of our objects of taste a congeries of idiosyncrasies; and the idiosyncrasies are, moreover, under the selective surveillance of the canon of expensiveness.

This process of selective adaptation of designs to the end of conspicuous waste, and the substitution of pecuniary beauty for aesthetic beauty, has been especially effective in the development of architecture. It would be extremely difficult to find a modern civilized residence or public building which can claim anything better than relative inoffensiveness in the eyes of any one who will dissociate the elements of beauty from those of honorific waste. The endless variety of fronts presented by the better class of tenements and apartment houses in our cities is an endless variety of architectural distress and of suggestions of expensive discomfort. Considered as objects of beauty, the dead walls of the sides and back of these structures, left untouched by the hands of the artist, are commonly the best feature of the building.

What has been said of the influence of the law of conspicuous waste upon the canons of taste will hold true, with but a slight change of terms, of its influence upon our notions of the serviceability of goods for other ends than the aesthetic one. Goods are produced and consumed as a means to the fuller unfolding of human life; and their utility consists, in the first instance, in their efficiency as means to this end. The end is, in the first instance, the fullness of life of the individual, taken in absolute terms. But the human proclivity to emulation has seized upon the consumption of goods as a means to an invidious comparison, and has thereby invested consumable goods with a secondary utility as evidence of relative ability to pay. This indirect or secondary use of consumable goods lends a honorific character to consumption, and presently also to the goods which best serve this emulative end of consumption. The consumption of expensive goods is meritorious, and the goods which contain an appreciable element of cost in excess of what goes to give them serviceability for their ostensible mechanical purpose are honorific. The marks of superfluous costliness in the goods are therefore marks of worth—of high efficiency for the indirect, invidious end to be served by their consumption; and conversely, goods are humilific, and therefore unattractive, if they show too thrifty an adaptation to the mechanical end sought and do not include a margin of expensiveness on which to rest a complacent invidious comparison. This indirect utility gives much of their value to the "better" grades of goods. In order to appeal to the cultivated sense of utility, an article must contain a modicum of this indirect utility.

While men may have set out with disapproving an inexpensive manner of living because it indicated inability to spend much, and so indicated a lack of pecuniary success, they end by falling into the habit of disapproving cheap things as being intrinsically dishonorable or unworthy because they are cheap. As time has gone on, each succeeding generation has received this tradition of meritorious expenditure from the generation before it, and has in its turn further elaborated and fortified the traditional canon of pecuniary reputability in goods consumed; until we have finally reached such a degree of conviction as to the unworthiness of all inexpensive things, that we have no longer any misgivings in formulating the maxim, "cheap and nasty." So thoroughly has this habit of approving the expensive and disapproving the inexpensive been ingrained into our thinking that we instinctively insist upon at least some measure of wasteful expensiveness in all our consumption, even in the case of goods which are consumed in strict privacy and without the slightest thought of display. We all feel, sincerely and without misgiving, that we are the more lifted up in spirit for having, even in the privacy of our own household, eaten our daily meal by the help of hand-wrought silver utensils, from hand-painted china (often of dubious artistic value) laid on high-priced table linen. Any retrogression from the standard of living which we are accustomed to regard as worthy in this respect is felt to be a grievous violation of our human dignity. So, also, for the last dozen years candles have been a more pleasing source of light at dinner than any other. Candle-light is now softer, less distressing to well-bred eyes, than oil, gas, or electric light. The same could not have been said thirty years ago, when candles were, or recently had been, the cheapest available light for domestic use. Nor are candles even now found to give an acceptable or effective light for any other than a ceremonial illumination.

A political sage still living has summed up the conclusion of this whole matter in the dictum: "A cheap coat makes a cheap man," and there is probably no one who does not feel the convincing force of the maxim.

The habit of looking for the marks of superfluous expensiveness in goods, and of requiring that all goods should afford some utility of the indirect or invidious sort, leads to a change in the standards by which the utility of goods is gauged. The honorific element and the element of brute efficiency are not held apart in the consumer's appreciation of commodities, and the two together go to make up the unanalyzed aggregate serviceability of the goods. Under the resulting standard of serviceability, no article will pass muster on the strength of material sufficiency alone. In order to [have] completeness and full acceptability to the consumer it must also show the honorific element. It results that the producers of articles of consumption direct their efforts to the production of goods that shall meet this demand for the honorific element. They will do this with all the more alacrity and effect, since they are themselves under the dominance of the same standard of worth in goods, and would be sincerely grieved at the sight of goods which lack the proper honorific finish. Hence it has come about that there are to-day no goods supplied in any trade which do not contain the honorific element in greater or less degree. Any consumer who might, Diogenes-like, insist on the elimination of all honorific or wasteful elements from his consumption, would be unable to supply his most trivial wants in the modern market. Indeed, even if he resorted to supplying his wants directly by his own efforts, he would find it difficult if not impossible to divest himself of the current habits of thought on this head; so that he could scarcely compass a supply of the necessaries of life for a day's consumption without instinctively and by oversight incorporating in his home-made product something of this honorific, quasi-decorative element of wasted labor.

It is notorious that in their selection of serviceable goods in the retail market, purchasers are guided more by the finish and workmanship of the goods than by any marks of substantial serviceability. Goods, in order to sell, must have some appreciable amount of labor spent in giving them the marks of decent expensiveness, in addition to what goes to give them efficiency for the material use which they are to serve. This habit of making obvious costliness a canon of serviceability of course acts to enhance the aggregate cost of articles of consumption. It puts us on our guard against cheapness by identifying merit in some degree with cost. There is ordinarily a consistent effort on the part of the consumer to obtain goods of the required serviceability at as advantageous a bargain as may be; but the conventional requirement of obvious costliness, as a voucher and a constituent of the serviceability of the goods, leads him to reject as under grade such goods as do not contain a large element of conspicuous waste.

It is to be added that a large share of those features of consumable goods which figure in popular apprehension as marks of serviceability, and to which reference is here had as elements of conspicuous waste, commend themselves to the consumer also on other grounds than that of expensiveness alone. They usually give evidence of skill and effective workmanship, even if they do not contribute to the substantial serviceability of the goods; and it is no doubt largely on some such ground that any particular mark of honorific serviceability first comes into vogue and afterward maintains its footing as a normal constituent element of the worth of an article. A display of efficient workmanship is pleasing simply as such, even where its remoter, for the time unconsidered outcome is futile. There is a gratification of the artistic sense in the contemplation of skilful work. But it is also to be added that no such evidence of skilful workmanship, or of ingenious and effective adaptation of means to end, will, in the long run, enjoy the approbation of the modern civilized consumer unless it has the sanction of the canon of conspicuous waste.

21

Place, Symbol, and Utilitarian Function in War Memorials

BERNARD BARBER

It should be clear from the selections presented in Part Four that an important dimension of the built environment is the weight of social meaning that architecture carries. Architecture as we know it is highly dependent upon the symbol-making and symbol-understanding capacities of man. But does this symbolic dimension of architecture perform any function in society that could not be performed equally well, or better, by other modes of communication, such as literature or music?

The following analysis by Barber of the underlying intellectual issues in the post–World War II disputes over the location and design of war memorials offers a basis for answering these questions. Barber's discussion is based on a content analysis of the popular literature dealing with war memorial design, which was apparently abundant in the mid and late 1940s. He argues that physical objects, and ceremonial architecture in particular, serve two special functions in the cultural life of man. In the first place, buildings concretize beliefs by providing a physical focus to which sentiments can be attached. Barber is referring here to the idea often advanced by sociologists of religion, namely that most people are unable to sustain a commitment to abstract concepts, ideologies, and beliefs unless such ideas and norms are embodied in an objective presence that can be seen and touched. Secondly, ceremonial architecture localizes sentiments by creating a place in which groups with shared feelings can gather to express and reaffirm them. This notion, too, is borrowed from the sociology of religion, which has pointed out the fragility of ideas of the sacred. Religious ideas, ideas of God, concepts of national loyalty, and sentiments of reverence for the dead are hard for people to sustain in isolation. Individuals who cherish such ideas need the emotional support of others, which they can find when they join together in the ceremonies that typically occur (or take "place") in churches, public plazas, or at the sites of war memorials.

Like many sociologists who think in the tradition of the sociology of religion and functional anthropology, Barber reifies the concept of "the social order." He is arguing not only that individuals who wish to memorialize the dead need the visual and emotional support that architecture provides;

Reprinted from Bernard Barber, "Place, Symbol, and Utilitarian Function in War Memorials," *Social Forces* 28 (October 1949): 64–68.

he is also saying that "society" needs ceremonial places and environments because, in order for the social order to be cohesive, integrative values must be continuously reaffirmed. As evidence in support of this position, Barber cites cases in which the design of war memorials that emphasized utilitarian or esthetic purposes were abandoned when these designs were revealed to be incompatible symbolically with the values of American society.

□

In the recent years just preceding and following the end of World War II, popular American journals have contained numerous reports of recommendations and plans for memorials to those who participated and died in that war. Practically all of the discussion has been cast in polemical, either-or terms. The main line of battle, often openly drawn, has been between the larger army of those who favor "living memorials," that is, memorials with some present utilitarian function, and the smaller or at least less articulate group of those who resent the intrusion of secular purposes into sacred spheres.[1] This literature and the social activities it represents afford a convenient opportunity for a re-examination and elaboration of the theory of social symbolism. Perhaps a sociological analysis of the relations among physical place, social symbol, and utilitarian function in war memorials will add to our knowledge as well as facilitate practical planning in this area.

The essential purpose of a war memorial, although not necessarily the only one, is to express the attitudes and values of a community toward those persons and deeds that are memorialized. These sentiments can be and have been expressed in a large number of different ways both in different periods of history and contemporaneously in any given society. Misunderstanding results from the failure to appreciate this fact, that it is the sentiments and values which give significance to the form chosen to embody them. The memorial is a symbol of the feelings of the social group.

Physical objects and places are almost always required for the localization of the memorial symbol.[2] Memorial places and objects are the locations at which the sentiments represented may be appropriately and publicly expressed by individuals, alone or in groups. The coming together of a group at the memorial place both confirms the legitimacy of the sentiments expressed and reinforces their strength in those who gather together to express them. Ceremonies, ritual, and attitudes of "high seriousness" are the vehicles of this expression and reinforcement.[3] It should be pointed out, parenthetically, that such ceremonies and attitudes occur at all physical places connected with the funda-

328

mental values of the society, for example, in such places as houses of parliament, important battlefields, and, of course, churches.[4]

Most war memorials implicitly recognize this social function of physical place, but many provide for it inadequately. A few ignore it altogether. Thus, certain war memorials, such as a college scholarship fund, which do not provide for the ceremonial coming together of those who feel the sentiments which inspire them to create this symbol, operate at a disadvantage. However, this is not necessarily a mortal disadvantage, because the sentiments involved may be neither originally strong nor persistent over a period of time. But where the sentiments are originally powerful and where they persist, some kind of spatial localization of the memorial symbol is necessary for their expression.

This is not to say that any and all physical places are appropriate for the expression of values which a community may wish to memorialize. There are conditions for the compatibility of place and sentiment.[5] Although it requires further empirical refinement and grounding, Durkheim's distinction between the "sacred" and the "profane" is still useful in this connection. The "sacred" is that toward which men feel respect; what is "profane" is properly carried on in a utilitarian context.[6] Some part of the physical place of all war memorials is required to be sacred in this sense.[7] These qualities, of sacredness and profaneness, are not, of course, given in the nature of physical space as such. They are projected upon space only by social values and their concomitant sentiments. For this reason, any physical space can be made sacred by the appropriate attitudes.

Just because they do take their meaning from the expression of sentiments, social symbols like war memorials are not endlessly rigid and stable. Their significance has to be continually defined and affirmed by manifestation of the relevant sentiments. When these are not forthcoming, symbols lose their meaning. There are a large number of memorials from previous wars which have lost their meaning for the present generation. Memorials lose their meaning more quickly still, perhaps, when inappropriate sentiments are expressed toward them. It has been pointed out very often that there is a delicate balance between the sacred and the profane, that there is a contagiousness about them by which they infect each other with their own significance. If some war memorials, expressing sacred sentiments, are contaminated by profane and secular sentiments by virtue of their very physical location, those war memorials are unsuited to their essential purpose. For example, there is some opposition to students' activities centers as war memorials in colleges for this reason. Older college graduates tend to feel that it is impossible, not merely difficult, to house sacred war memorials and profane daily activities in the same building.[8] The point can be seen most clearly if we consider certain activities which are irreducibly secular in our society and thus wholly inappropriate in collocation with the values embodied in war memorials. For example, despite their obvious public utility, public toilets have *never* been suggested as appropriate places for war memorials. The mere imaginative juxtaposition of such notions even in the present scientific context, let alone one of proposed action, causes embarrassed feelings and nervous laughter.

We can now state the several functions of memorials and their relations to one another and to physical place more inclusively and more systematically. Any physical place or object, and thus any war memorial, can have at least three different types of function. First, it may, as we have already said, have symbolic functions—to express certain social values and sentiments, and also to strengthen them. This function for the present generation, as against the past one which is memorialized, is too often not appreciated by those who have been planning war memorials. Second, it may have esthetic functions—to appeal to our socially-conditioned standards of taste and beauty. And, third, it may have utilitarian functions—to serve as an instrument for the achievement of certain proximate social purposes and limited ends. A war memorial will have, by definition, the symbolic functions. It will almost certainly have esthetic functions, since societies tend to endow all physical place of which they are at all aware with some esthetic significance. But it may or may not have utilitarian functions. A war memorial may be just a plaque or a monument, free-standing, for example like the Cenotaph in London or the Tomb of the Unknown Soldier in Arlington Cemetery.

Until the quite recent historical past in Western Society, in the construction of war memorials, emphasis was chiefly on their symbolic and esthetic functions. A trend of attention toward utilitarian functions began in the late nineteenth century. In the United States, this trend has culminated after this last war in a great cry for "living memorials." [9] Among the types of living war memorials already existing and proposed are the following: a community building, a civic center, a city hall, a museum, a library, an auditorium, a municipal theater, a park, a playground, a swimming pool, a bandstand, a community forest, a boulevard, a bridge, a "boulevard of light," and an arboretum.[10] Undoubtedly a complete explanation for this change of emphasis must be discovered in the larger transformation of social processes in our society.[11] But some partial sources may be suggested. First of all, the desire for useful memorials is an expression of the hostility to "waste" in our society, especially as this was supposed to have been exemplified in the more grandiose of past attentions wholly to the symbolic and esthetic functions of monuments. Secondly, there are those among the advocates of "living memorials" who have unwarrantedly inferred from the obsolescence of some *particular* monument the *general* unimportance of the symbolic functions of war memorials. And most important of all, this change of emphasis is the result of a culturally induced rationalistic blindness to the importance of the symbolic functions of war memorials, or, in any case, to the necessary limits of the utilitarian functions.[12]

We can now perhaps give a general answer to the question of whether any given community must choose either a "dead" monument or a living memorial. We can say that a war memorial may be a mixture of the symbolic, the utilitarian, and the esthetic, but only when the necessary conditions under which these three functions can be related to one another have been complied with. What are some of these necessary conditions?

In the matter of the relation between the symbolic and the esthetic, obviously the esthetic aspect of the memorial place or object must not offend those who want their sentiments symbolized. For example, a memorial which was built in a Japanese architectural style, however esthetically noble that style intrinsically, would not be appropriate as a memorial to those who died in a war against the Japanese. Nor should the esthetic emphasis in a war memorial ever be made primary, as in a building or monument which was beautiful for the sake of beauty itself. Under this canon, good taste in war memorials requires "dignity" rather than "beauty."

The relation between the symbolic and the utilitarian is of more immediate practical concern. As we have already pointed out, certain purposes are so irreducibly utilitarian in terms of the cultural definitions that they inevitably clash with the sacred sentiments of war memorials. Other utilitarian functions have a varying appropriateness for the deeds memorialized. Let us consider the basis of this variable suitability in connection with a war memorial for college undergraduates. Those utilitarian activities contributing to the most important values of undergraduate life are considered appropriate for a war memorial, e.g., college chapels, scholarships, and libraries. Into an intermediate range of appropriateness fall such other student memorials as extra-curricular activities centers and athletic facilities. These represent desirable but subordinate values in college life. Least suitable, perhaps not appropriate at all, indeed, would be war memorials built around a student "dance palace" or a student beer hall. Dancing and drinking beer are normal activities for most undergraduates, but they are peripheral to the values of college life and therefore least appropriate as vehicles for the expression of sacred sentiments. We may state the relation of symbolic and utilitarian functions in its most general form, thus: The compatibility of utilitarian activities and symbolic functions in a war memorial is determined by the degree to which the utilitarian activities are expressive of the same set of values as the activities which are being memorialized. As utilitarian activities diverge from such expression, they must be placed lower on the rough continuum of symbolic appropriateness.[13]

We may note other examples of this principle in non-war memorials. Thus, the Walter Reed Hospital is especially appropriate as a memorial to Dr. Walter Reed of the United States Army, who gave his life in the service of the values to which the hospital is devoted. Endowed chairs in universities are especially noble tributes to scholars who have spent their lives in university teaching and research. Famous athletes are fittingly remembered in athletic facilities, as in the Hobey Baker hockey rink at Princeton University. The book-collecting and cultural interests of Harry Elkins Widener are appropriately memorialized in the university library at Harvard. By contrast, a library would be a grotesque memorial for some chieftain of an urban political machine, however much his admirers might wish to have his deeds recalled.

When the symbolic and utilitarian functions of war memorials are compatible with reference to a common system of values, the memorial serves to strengthen these values and thereby contributes to the solidarity of the society. In the case of an incompatibility, however, the inconsistent values embodied in the war memorial are dysfunctional for the integration of the group. Thus, if the activities of "dance palaces" are as important as national patriotism, that is, if this is implied by some war memorial which places them together so that they seem to be merged, then the actual values of the society, which do not hold the former to be compatible with the latter, are being called into question. The consequence is a reduction in the integration of the group.

These, then, are some of the general relations between the different functions of war memorials. Obviously no single highly concrete statement can be made about their application in all societies or all subcommunities of a single society. Since the symbolic functions of war memorials take their significance from the cultural values of a society, and since, further, the compatibility of the symbolic, the esthetic, and the utilitarian functions also derives from these values, any particular war memorial can only be considered appropriate or not in terms of the values of a particular society or particular sub-community of that society. Keeping these general relations in view, each particular group must choose a suitable memorial for itself. Since values vary among societies, appropriate war memorials will always, as they have done in the past and still do, take different concrete forms. Owing to the difficulty of suitably combining the several possible component functions, excellent war memorials can only be constructed by the most careful consideration of these functions and their relations in the atmosphere of a particular set of social values.

NOTES

1. See, for example, the following typical materials: Various issues of the journal, *The American City*, especially all issues of 1945 and 1946. This magazine was the rallying center for those favoring the "living memorial." Joseph Hudnut, "The Monument Does Not Remember," *The Atlantic Monthly* (September 1945) is the most sophisticated and noblest attempt to justify the "living memorial." Lincoln Rothschild, "What 'Lives' in a War Memorial?" *The Saturday Review of Literature* (June 1, 1946) argues for the artistic and symbolic memorial. Margaret Cresson, "Memorials Symbolic of the Spirit of Man," *The New York Times Magazine Section* (July 22, 1945), is "a statement of the case for beauty" in war memorials.

2. For a study of the temporalized concentration of localized memorial activities, see W. Lloyd Warner's study of Memorial Day, "The American Town," in W. F. Ogburn, ed., *American Society in Wartime* (Chicago: The University of Chicago Press, 1943), esp. pp. 51–62.

3. The classic statement of the relation between social symbol, physical space, and the values of a society remains that of E. Durkheim, *The Elementary Forms of the Religious Life*, trans. by J. W. Swain (Glencoe, Illinois: The Free Press, 1948), pp. 230–231. An excellent empirical study of the way in which physical space becomes a symbol of the values of a society may be found in W. Firey, *Land Use in Central Boston* (Cambridge: Harvard University Press, 1947), esp. chaps. III and IV.

4. The tendency of visitors to these places to speak in whispers or in subdued voices can be taken as a crude operational index of these attitudes of respect.

5. There are also conditions of minimum accessibility of physical place to the society dedicating the war memorial. These conditions are neglected, for example, by those who propose memorial forests. In our urban society, a memorial forest is not likely to be accessible enough to any but a very small community. See *The American City* (February 1946).

6. Durkheim, *op. cit.*, pp. 37–38, 206ff. See also, Talcott Parsons, *The Structure of Social Action* (New York: McGraw-Hill Book Co., 1937), esp. pp. 411ff.

Cresson, *op. cit.*, quotes Mumford: "A memorial is a religious act of dedication. . . ."; and also Fletcher Steele: "A monument to commemorate an ideal . . . should be set apart from the humdrum affairs of life lest its chief function be forgotten."

7. "Within the structure there should be . . . a hallowed chamber of dignity and beauty wherein the pilgrim or the passer-by may pause for meditation and

333

dedication to the end that 'from these honored dead we take increased devotion to that cause for which they gave the last full measure of devotion.'" Letter to the Editor, *Harvard Alumni Bulletin* (April 26, 1947).

8. "I am not only against a utilitarian memorial, I think it is an imposition—a horrible commercial exploitation of the affection that mothers and fathers have for their boys. The memorial must be a reminder. . . ." Letter to the Editor, *Harvard Alumni Bulletin* (April 26, 1947).

9. For evidence of this trend, see *The American City* (February 1945), p. 64, and (July 1945), p. 5. In July it was reported that a survey of plans of communities for war memorials found that four-fifths of them wanted "living memorials" of various kinds, with dedicatory plaques.

10. *The American City* (February 1946).

11. A similar account would be necessary for the recent glorification in war memorials of the common soldier as against previous idolization of the General on Horseback.

12. An example of such rationalistic bias: "Unless one feels the past war to have been frivolous and all human labor ineffectual, how can one favor the commemoration of the war by expending human labor on a frivolous structure of stone and metal which affects nothing?" Letter to the Editor, *Harvard Alumni Bulletin* (December 13, 1947). The rationalistic bias is probably the inclusive basis of all these partial sources.

13. Some of those who favor the utilitarian memorial see this point. For example, Dean Hudnut, *op. cit.*, says: "I am not for Memorial Convention Halls or Memorial Baseball Fields or Memorial Waterworks . . . there are degrees in dignity. There are buildings which lift the communal life out of the narrow business of getting and spending."

PART FIVE

The Application
of Behavioral Science
to Design

22

The Questions Architects Ask [1]

ROBERT GUTMAN

Although there has been a tendency in American architectural circles to emphasize the "art" of architecture and to regard an alliance between architecture and the sciences as a threat to the design tradition, the fact is that architecture has always been responsive to developments in science. One need only recall the influence of developments in mathematics on Renaissance architecture, the role that the engineering sciences played in the Gothic revival of the nineteenth century, or the significance of advances in environmental control technology to the modern movement in architecture during this century. In each of these periods, developments in basic and applied science influenced the form and esthetic of building and the theory of architectural design, and also transformed the architectural profession's concept of the procedures that should be followed in formulating design schemes, or what is known among architects as the design process.

The kind of alliance that developed in the past between architecture and the natural and mathematical sciences is now developing between architecture, planning, and the behavioral sciences. This development shows up in the extensive care that many architects now give to determining user needs before beginning to work on designs, in the efforts to include sociologists and psychologists as members of the design-building team, and in the growing tendency, both in America and in England, to allow building forms to express behavioral science concepts about the nature of man and society. These developments, and other examples of behavioral science influence on architecture and urban design, are illustrated in the selections included in Part Five.

The following selection is intended to provide a context for interpreting the new "behavioral architecture." It discusses some of the reasons why architects have suddenly found it necessary to familiarize themselves with sociological and psychological knowledge, emphasizing in particular the role played by the emergence of new building types that require a much more thorough and systematic inquiry into user needs than was customary in past centuries. It also deals with the different aspects of user behavior—institutional and personal goals, the organization as a means for achieving goals, and space as a facility for allowing the means to operate—that are relevant to building design and discusses the competence of sociologists to

Reprinted from Robert Gutman, "The Questions Architects Ask," *Transactions of the Bartlett Society,* Bartlett School of Architecture, University College, London 4 (1965–1966): 49–82.

provide data and advice relating to these aspects. The third part of the selection describes the design process and some of the issues that arise when the architect asks the sociologist to help him convert information about the user into a three-dimensional design solution.

Although the selection was written shortly after I first began conducting research into architecture and teaching sociology to architecture students, it was obvious even then that architects and sociologists were often finding their initial contacts disappointing and frustrating. Much of the selection, therefore, is devoted to describing, from a sociologist's point of view, the nature of architectural design, the organization of the design process, and the many important differences between the social role of the architect as practitioner and decision maker and the scholarly, academic, and scientific role of the behavioral scientist. The final part of the selection analyzes these role differences as sources of misunderstanding between the disciplines and sketches a strategy for enabling architects and sociologists to develop more effective forms of cooperation in the future.

□

Introduction

For the last eight months I have had the good fortune to be involved with the world of architects and architecture. During this period I have been stationed at architecture schools, for the first half of the current academic year at Princeton, and since February at the Bartlett. I have taken advantage of this informal association with two important centers of architectural education to listen to lectures and sit in on seminars dealing with a variety of subjects that make up the curriculum of these schools. I have had a chance to visit and observe the work of the studio classes, and from time to time, at the invitation of my hosts, I have been asked to participate as a critic or examiner in review sessions and juries. From my base in the schools, I also have gone out to architectural offices, to talk with architects about their work. Between times I have tried to familiarize myself with the written literature that embodies the architectural tradition, to keep up with the architectural press, and also, of course, to visit buildings, sometimes in the company of the architects who designed them. It goes without saying that these experiences have been stimulating and exciting and I am extremely grateful to my hosts for having given me these opportunities, which will, I hope, be made available to many more sociologists in the future.[2]

My general purpose this past year has been to familiarize myself with what an anthropologist might call the culture of architecture, to learn how the architect works and is trained, in the hope of being able to suggest ways in which sociology can contribute to the problems that today face the profession and the schools. Architecture is beset by a sense of crisis, probably for very good reasons, and so it will come as no surprise to you to learn that the problems I was told about are numerous; there are intellectual problems having to do with the theory and method that guide design, there are organizational problems involving the way the profession finances, arranges and carries out its work, and there are communication problems reflecting the relation of architects to other members of the building team, and to the public.

In view of the magnitude and importance of some of these issues it may seem selfish of me to talk about the subject I have chosen to discuss with you, but it is one with respect to which I can claim some competence, since it is a problem involving my own discipline. I wish to discuss the difficulties that have arisen in the relations between architecture and sociology, as these difficulties have been revealed to me in interviews with practising architects, and in observations of the work of design teams in school studios and in offices. I also have discussed these problems with other sociologists besides myself who have had a chance to collaborate and associate with architects. The problems that have been reported to me resemble other difficulties faced by the architect at present. As happens in his relationship with the engineer or the contractor, the architect is found complaining that the sociologist doesn't tell him what he wants to know and that the sociologist doesn't do what the architect wants him to do. And the sociologist, just like the builder or the engineer, is usually found muttering that the architect doesn't present his requests for information clearly, is not certain about what he wants done, or is asking for impossible things.

I had better admit right at the outset that as a member of one of the parties in the relationship between architecture and sociology, it is hard for me to pose as an objective observer and commentator on the problems of this relationship, but I will try to present a fair view of the issues nevertheless. This isn't easy, but perhaps I can help my case by stating now, at the beginning, that the complaints registered by both sides strike me as grossly oversimplified. Both positions arise from a failure to comprehend the nature of the architect's task and the role of sociology as this task and this role have been defined traditionally.

Why Architects Turn to Sociology

It has been encouraging to me to discover the enormous interest of the architectural profession in sociology. In many schools in England and in the States, students are expected to take at least one course of lectures in sociology, with particular attention to the topics of the city and metropolis, family institutions, bureaucracy, the organization of the professions, and small group behavior. There has even been some experimentation with using sociologists in the design studio as specialist consultants and critics, particularly in relation to problems of urban design and housing. The program of the Bartlett is, of course, outstanding in demanding that the student pass a general examination in social science subjects; and the Bartlett his probably proceeded further than any other school in involving social scientists in studio work.

The use of sociology now is hardly limited to the schools. Town planning architects often consult sociologists in the States especially in connection with urban renewal schemes; and real estate developers of large suburban complexes, such as Reston, Va., and Columbia, Md., have sought the advice of sociologists in formulating their site plans and making provision for community facilities. Although there is perhaps less use of sociology by architects in private practice in the U.K., sociology and the findings of sociological research have been extremely influential in the determination of design standards for public authority housing and for hospitals and other health facilities that are established and administered by the central government. Indeed, one of the most impressive features of the English architectural scene to the American visitor is the presence of professional sociologists on the staffs of the research and development groups in the ministries.

The interest of the architect in sociology arises from the simple but important fact that a building cannot be conceived apart from the human activities it serves to facilitate and encourage. This is what architectural critics and aestheticians have had in mind when they have called architecture the most social of the fine arts. Buildings are objects of use in addition to being objects of pleasure, which offer delight to their beholder. Architecture is so essentially a social art that no architect can talk about his medium or about his schemes without reference to how they will be used by people; and a good deal of the conscious intention behind any design, as well as various decisions about its elements, are expressed in terms of its consequences for social behavior. This social nature has been characteristic of the architectural medium since buildings were first planned and designed and there has never been an architect who was not, in some sense, a student and critic of society. Is it any wonder therefore that once a science was developed whose specific task it is to understand the structure and function of society and to set out the principles that govern group behavior, the architect should turn to this discipline and to people who are learned in it for expert advice and guidance?

340

The current rage for sociology is not fully explained, however, by recognizing the natural ambition of the architect to substitute professional, scientific expertise for the informal, casual interpretation of human purposes and motives which has always been intrinsic to the architectural tradition. It also reflects the emphasis now current in the profession on making buildings that are responsive to the specific and unique needs of their users. It indicates, too, the recognition by architects that modern, complex building types which demand high and efficient levels of services and which shelter groups that undergo rapid changes in organization can be designed only by means of thorough and comprehensive briefs. The emphasis on designing and fabricating buildings that respond to the needs of users is probably stronger in Great Britain, with its tradition of ethical architecture extending back into the last century, than it is in the States. The attention now being paid to sociology cannot, therefore, be held responsible for the widespread discussion of user requirements, even though the interest in sociology may be the contemporary expression of this concern. But I think it can be argued that the interest in commodious built environments now being displayed by architects in America is the direct consequence of the criticisms that many sociologists have made of building schemes. In the States, during the 1930s, it was sociology that launched the attack on simple notions about the influence, say, of the housing environment on behavior. This has resulted in a public housing movement that now is concerned principally with the amenities provided in buildings rather than with building form.[3] The contrast is interesting: British architects are interested in sociology because they have always been fairly good amateur sociologists; American architects have begun to use sociology because the sociologists have been among the leading critics of architecture.

In both countries the interest expressed in sociology has been intensified by the confused state of architectural theory and design methods. Architectural theory is the set of principles that guide the architect in making decisions about the complex problems that arise in translating the requirements of the brief into the design of a building. One can argue over whether theory is necessary for architectural practice—its very emergence can be read as a sign that the traditions of the craft are breaking down. But leaving this issue aside, the current despair over the state of theory is said to arise because the principles of the modern movement did not establish the appropriate priorities among the variety of design elements that are part of any design scheme. It is claimed, say, that recent theory was too occupied with the symbolic and aesthetic functions of the structural system or skin of a building and ignored the function of the building envelope and structure in providing a commodious, workable environment. The criticism is sufficiently well entrenched so that even architects who by personality, experience or intellectual style are disposed to accept theories that emphasize technology or form see themselves on the defensive. They attempt to buttress their design theory by arguing that it is confirmed by the principles and observations of Gestalt psychology; or that it can be "explained" in the language of set theory and finite mathematics. I don't think that it would be right to give sociology the credit for this intellectual revolution; it probably is more accurate to say that the difficulty in which the advocates of a principled architecture now find themselves and the development of sociology are two cultural phenomena, both of which stem from the break down in established intellectual absolutes, the rise of pragmatic philosophy and the general emergence of a scientific ethos as the dominant ideology of Western culture.

Design method is the series of mental procedures that architects adopt in applying their favorite principles to the design problem. Here, too, the scientific ethos has done damage and fewer and fewer architects are willing to defend their application of principles on the grounds of intuition alone. Some of them wish to abandon intuition entirely as a basis for decision-making; others continue to use it because they regard no other method as relevant to the architect's task, but are ambitious to understand what intuition is and how it works; still other architects recognize a place for intuition but wish to narrow the range of decisions within which intuition still must operate. My impression is that one could probably rank architects along a continuum, with those who cling to a belief in the importance of intuition at one end and the proponents of a scientific approach to design located at the other extreme. Architects who are likely to base their design method on intuition will also turn out to be those architects who accept a theory emphasizing the formal dimensions of a building; whereas the advocates of scientific design methods believe that it is important to design building primarily in terms of user requirements. It is the "scientific" architects who are most likely to adopt sociology, in the hope that full knowledge of the user, his needs and his social activities will enable the architect to deduce the design of a building. This view is an extreme one, and to my mind, it is also absurd, because it ignores the essential nature of the problem of building design. A more moderate viewpoint among the "scientific" architects is that design must remain an achievement of the individual architect, requiring the intervention of his creative talents, but sociology can be used to evaluate the proposed scheme in terms of its suitability to user needs.

I said earlier that it is difficult to find an architect who is not a student and critic of society; I would extend this notion further, and add that most architects are also reformers. Indeed, one of the facts that first struck me when I began my encounter with the architectural profession was that architecture is today one of the few fields that keeps alive the utopian tradition of social thought. Many architects hold to a vision of some future social organization that comes closer to achieving goals of justice, humaneness and order than the society we live in now. They regard every building they design as an opportunity for bringing this utopian state into existence. In exploiting this opportunity, architecture in the past has looked to historical studies. Architectural historiography is today under serious intellectual attack on the grounds of having focused its concern on the externalities of building. This criticism is undoubtedly warranted, but in making it, design educators have tended to ignore the stream in art history that not only advocated a particular style of building but that also, by implication, proposed a social vision in the direction of which architecture was or should be moving. Recent examples of this way of using historical studies are Wittkower's book on renaissance architecture and the essays of Colin Rowe.[4] Both Rowe and Wittkower espouse a formal theory of building. They link this view of the design problem with a belief in the possibility of a humane social order founded on reason in which architecture will instruct man by means of its intellectual content rather than its emotional appeal. Most students in the schools do not read these essays now, but the need of the architect to find an intellectual ally who will offer theoretical and philosophical support for his natural determination to change society through building lingers. The survival of this need also helps to explain the current interest in sociology. Sociology, as many an architect defines the discipline, is a field that can not only help him to understand how people behave but also add to his stock of knowledge about how they ought to behave.

Sociology in the Briefing Process

Before discussing the content of the questions that architects tend to address to sociologists, I would like to make two general comments about the situations in which these questions are raised. In the first place, my observations suggest that sociologists are consulted about architectural issues more often by design educators working with students on hypothetical problems in studio classes than by practitioners concerned with actual design and building projects. There are probably numerous reasons for this pattern: the use of sociology is still in an experimental phase, and the schools are a more appropriate setting for experimentation than the world of practice; architects and sociologists are more easily available to each other within the context of a university; the use of consultants is expensive in practice, but collaboration between architects and sociologists within the university can be justified in terms of the academic tradition of interdisciplinary co-operation; design educators and academic sociologists are more disposed and also have more time to overcome the communication barrier that exists between the two fields than are practitioners and independent sociological consultants.

My second general comment is that the expertise of the sociologist is not thought to be relevant to all phases of the building process to the same degree, at least judging by observations of how sociologists have been used by architects and design educators.

We can divide the building process into four stages: the briefing stage, during which the demands of the client and user are presented and articulated to the architect and other members of the building team; the design stage, during which the brief is translated into the design scheme; the building stage, during which the design scheme is transformed into the object we call the building; and the use stage, during which the building is inhabited.

In all of these stages problems arise about which it is conceivable that the knowledge and expertise of the sociologist could be employed and indeed have been sought, but it is interesting that the questions addressed by architects to sociologists deal principally with the briefing and design phases. In so far as questions are raised about the building stage, they have in most instances come to the sociologists from other members of the building team, particularly representatives of the construction industry itself. Questions dealing with the user stage are most often raised by client users, including the ministries and local authorities in this country and large industrial firms in the United States. The fact that persons and groups other than architects are usually the ones to raise questions for sociologists about the problems of a building during the construction and use phases is surely not without significance: it indicates either that architects tend to regard their task as completed once the brief and design schemes have been completed or that the architect himself is regarded as the problem that requires study and treatment.

When the architect turns to the sociologist during the briefing stage, he usually wants three things from him.

1. The architect wants guidance in understanding the purposes and objectives of the client or user. In some situations, he wants guidance because the client has given him almost exclusive responsibility for developing the brief. Before he is able to formulate the schedule of accommodations, the architect wants to feel confident that he knows what the client is aiming to do with his organization, what, say, his ultimate objective is in running a university or building a house. If the architect has been presented with a pretty adequate brief, he wants the sociologist to help him decide whether the objectives stated by the client are valid. Since clients, either in their briefs, or in their talks with architects, usually mention a number of objectives, the architect hopes that the sociologist will help him to select those that deserve greater emphasis. Running right through the encounter with the sociologist in this stage of briefing is the ambition of the architect I mentioned earlier: the ambition to employ the building project as a means for improving the quality of social life. In pursuing this ambition, the contemporary architect often has doubts about the propriety of this ambition. Even if he suppresses his doubt, he still is confused about how to translate general goals of order, justice, and democracy into the particular objectives that can be attained through building schemes. This confusion is less prevalent when the building is a house, a school, a church, or some other building type for which there are many precedents in the architectural tradition. However, almost all architects are baffled by the prospect of translating their general notions about social purpose into a brief dealing with a relatively new, complex building type such as a university for 10,000 or 20,000 students, an air terminal, or a teaching hospital with research functions.

2. Architects also look to sociologists for expert advice to help them decide whether the present or proposed social organization of the client represents a reasonable means for achieving the objectives that are articulated or implicit in the brief. As a result of the critical attitude that seems to be built into the architectural tradition, many of the better architects suspect that clients and users do not arrange their activities in the manner most likely to achieve objectives efficiently and in a humane way. Once more, in the case of established building types, such as private houses, architects are fairly confident of their compe-

345

tence to judge the reasonableness of the client's round of activities; and this is one reason, I suspect, why so many of the important planning and space innovations associated with the modern movement in architecture, such as the open plan of Wright or Le Corbusier's Domino, were explored originally in the designs of large and luxurious private dwellings. The architect's self-confidence diminishes, however, in direct relation to the size and complexity of the project and is particularly fragile when the brief is for a large factory or a new kind of mass transport system.

3. My interviews suggest that outside of the school studio the majority of architects still rely upon their own knowledge, information and skill in evaluating the client's objectives and his social organization. To the degree that sociologists have contributed to the development of real briefs in practice, it has most often been with respect to formulating the schedule of accommodations; that is, the sociologists have often been assigned the task of estimating the spaces required for the client's activities.

The problems that arise when the sociologist is consulted about these three issues during the briefing process can be illustrated by the experience of architects and sociologists concerned with university building. The development of university briefs is a good example to choose because it represents one of those new building types I said are particularly likely to find the architect confused and uncertain about the objectives and demands of the client and user. Furthermore, the newer universities, both in Great Britain and in the States, are committed to the belief that traditional conceptions of university education are archaic and irrelevant to the problems that modern societies now are facing. The ferment in higher education arises from the sense that the universities are not producing individuals with the skills needed to operate the organizations of society and are not creating ways of action and group life that are responsive to the demands of a technologically advanced society.

I have spoken with architects for several of the universities involved in major building projects here and in America and they are agreed that the task of developing university briefs was difficult but also fascinating and exciting. It was difficult because no one involved in the client's organization—not the vice-chancellor or president, not the building committee, the department head, or professor—no one was able to articulate his objectives except in the most vague terms. Was it the aim of the university to improve the quality of undergraduate teaching or was it to increase the volume and competence of scientific research; did the university acknowledge its responsibility to break down the barriers of the established class structure; did the university want to emphasize the virtues of humanistic culture or did it wish to forward the advance of the scientific, technological ethos? Architects who asked questions of this kind—and their ability to do so is an example of the sophisticated kind of utopian thinking that is so often characteristic of architects—often got an indeterminate response. These briefs required the expenditure of a good deal of office and staff time, particularly the time of the project director; the pleasant feature was that it gave the architect a good deal of leeway in proposing objectives and organizational solutions himself. It was fascinating because the architect could feel that he was engaging in genuine innovation, blazing a new trail not only architectonically but also in terms of social organization.

A few of the university architects I talked with had used sociologists to help them in thinking about the purposes of a university or to assist them in determining the objectives that clients and users intended the university to serve. They claim to have found the sociologists helpful in devising the interview schedules and other research instruments by means of which clients and potential users were interrogated; but they report that they were generally disappointed that the sociologists were not more adept in guiding them toward the articulation of university purposes and goals. According to the architects, the sociologists who had been selected as consultants did not know much more about the general issues involved in university planning than the architect himself and often were not very imaginative in proposing objectives.

I am not surprised by these responses. We must keep in mind several characteristics of contemporary sociology that make it difficult for many sociologists to respond to the architect's queries in a positive way. In the first place, we must realize that sociology regards itself as a discipline, divided into various sub-fields of specialized knowledge. All sociologists are trained to have a familiarity with the general principles that regulate group behavior and social organization, but not every sociologist is familiar to the same degree with the norms, values, structures and behavior patterns of the particular groups and institutions out of which a modern society is organized. There are sociologists who know a great deal about the family and its problems, others who are specialists in the organization of religious institutions, others who are expert in industrial organizations, and there are a few sociologists who have conducted research and are acquainted with planning problems in higher education. If the architect has had the misfortune to consult

347

a sociologist who knows a lot about the problems of families, naturally he isn't going to get the best advice in preparing a brief for a university, even though the family sociologist might be useful to him in designing a dwelling unit. The dissatisfaction is therefore similar to that expressed by a man with a kidney ailment who has mistakenly consulted an ophthalmologist.

Secondly, we must consider a more fundamental difficulty, more serious because it is likely to inhibit the relationship of sociology and architecture even if the right specialist has been chosen. Sociology for some time now, ever since the second world war in the United States, and within the last decade in England, has become a scientific discipline that is extremely self-conscious about the distinction between values and facts. Most sociologists tend to believe that the methods their discipline has adopted enable them to describe the way in which people behave with some degree of accuracy and also to foretell the consequences for behavior of particular value choices; but sociologists, on the whole, do not believe their methods are capable of determining which one among a particular range of possible values should be selected. However, it is expert and informed advice about which values and objectives to choose for clients and users that architects so often desire from sociologists; or if they do not expect the sociologist to propose objectives to them, at least they want the sociologist to tell them which of the values the client already holds are worthwhile and deserve to be selected as implicit objectives of building. Presented with these demands by the architect, the sociologist responds by criticizing the architect for his apparent assumption that determinations of values can be objective. This is one reason, I think, why architects so often accuse sociologists of being destructive rather than constructive allies during the briefing process.

In my interviews with university architects I also tried to get them to talk about their experiences in understanding and evaluating the organizations proposed or developed by the client for attaining the objectives of higher education. In general, I discovered that architects felt much easier about this phase of the briefing process than they did when dealing with the objectives alone. The social organization of a client's work has a certain concreteness which makes it more accessible to the architectural imagination than concepts dealing with goals and purposes; clients, too, the architects report, were able to be more intelligent and articulate when discussing the way a research laboratory worked, or how residential activities should relate to eating and to study. There was a substantial backlog of experience around which to construct this portion of the brief: the architects were themselves products of schools of higher education, the clients had spent many years working in different kinds of university situations, and many universities embodying at least some of the goals of the client had been built in the past. However, the more self-critical architects recognized that the availability of this experience and the existence of buildings could be a danger, too, in so far as they led both clients and architects to think in terms of established precedents instead of encouraging them to explore new and original ways of achieving the purposes of a university.

In view of their doubts about planning a new campus on the basis of established building, combined with the desire to be truly innovative, some of the architects I interviewed consulted sociologists or read reports of social research studies dealing with university activities. These studies relate to such diverse facilities as dining halls, research laboratories, residence halls, and classrooms. The architects consulted these sources because they wanted further information about the advantages and disadvantages, say, of planning a common eating facility for all students or providing many eating spaces for smaller numbers of undergraduates; about whether to have undergraduates and graduates eat together or separately; about whether to provide common facilities for faculty and students. They sought further understanding of the preferences of students for one-, two- or three-bedroom units, for assigned work spaces in laboratories, for classrooms giving access to the outside or rooms completely insulated from the natural environment, and so on.

Architects who spoke with sociologists about these questions ran into some of the same difficulties encountered by the architects who sought the advice of sociologists for understanding the objectives of higher education. A frequent complaint is that the sociologist consulted did not have much more expertise on these questions than the architect, or the client himself. Again, here, I think part of the problem was that the architects did not pick the right sociologist. It astonishes me, frankly, that architects are not more aware of the need to consult sociological specialists, and I wonder why this awareness is not more widespread. Is it because the architect regards himself as someone who can design any type of building, and therefore he assumes that other disciplines and professions should be able to exhibit the same degree of generalized skill? If so, it seems to me the architect fails to realize that his own profession has become highly specialized, with some firms and offices devoting themselves primarily to hospital design, others to town planning, others to factory building, and still others to housing. It may be,

349

of course, that the sociologist is at fault; perhaps he does not take advantage of the opportunities offered to him to make clear to the architect the complex division of labor that has developed in the discipline.

As I said, picking the right sociologist is part of the problem, but there is also a more profound issue involved here. Architects who express their disappointment also have in mind the indubitable fact about sociologists that they are much better at describing the activities and organization that already exist in universities than they are at proposing new organizations, or at forecasting the consequences of new organizations proposed by the architect. A typical situation is that in which the architect says to the sociologist: "I gather from what you tell me that students don't like those large impersonal universities made up of undergraduate colleges of 10,000 or 15,000 students. They lead, you tell me, to a sense of isolation, loneliness, apathy and all those other reactions that are said to be responsible for the student revolt at a place like Berkeley. Well, then, can you propose to me a better way for organizing collegiate life?" Many sociologists fail the architect at this point in their collaboration, in part because they are, as I said, not skillful at suggesting new solutions, in part because even when they can conceive of organizational alternatives, they are reluctant to stick their necks out and make forecasts when data to support their interpretation are lacking.

I happen to believe that this incapacity is an unfortunate weakness of contemporary sociology, but I think it is important for the architect and sociologist to understand its basis. It arises from the commitment of sociology to the scientific method. Sociology, as I said earlier, is devoted to the development of principles that will help to describe group behavior in general. Every historical event is the result, however, not only of the operation of principles that are generally applicable, but of specific determinants that work in combination with these principles. In the study of already existing groups or in the investigations of historical episodes these specific determinants can usually be discerned *ex post facto*; but for events still to occur, it is virtually impossible to anticipate the full range of specific determinants that will operate to modify the impact of the general principles. Trained as he is to be as certain as possible of the factors that impinge on an event, the sociologist is incapacitated for the task of estimating outcomes when these factors are, by the nature of the case, not yet ascertainable. However, if he is to be helpful to the architect in providing the information the architect really wants, the sociologist must learn to relax these strictures. I will say more about this later on.

Let me report an odd finding here which may be of interest to you. I have run into a few situations, and I have discussed similar situations with one other social scientist, in which the sociologist undertook to make the leap into the future demanded of him by the architect, only to find himself rebuffed. These situations occurred over the drawing boards in an office in which I, and my colleague, were consulted by the architects about design problems, once about a town center for a new suburban community, another time about a housing project in a central city, a third time about the plan for a new psychiatric hospital. We were asked to propose new organizational solutions for achieving the objectives of these building types; and since we were bent over the drawing board, naturally these proposals could not be expressed without revealing immediately their implications for spatial organization, without, that is, our talking about them in the language of form. In all three cases, our proposals were met with cold stares by the architects involved and as one of the architects later reported to a friend of mine: "That damn sociologist thinks he's a designer!" But surely this is what sociologists will indeed become if they begin finally to respond to the questions of the architect.

Architects who have consulted social research studies in dealing with the organizational aspects of universities say of these studies that they were hard to find, that their results are often diffuse and contradictory, and that they would like to find available a compendium or manual that summarizes the findings and relates them to problems of university design. It certainly is true that a greater effort should be made to inform architects about the available sources and to collate them, but I think it will be less easy to resolve the confused interpretations to which these studies easily can give rise. The contradictions, after all, emerge because each study, even when it was concerned with establishing generalized knowledge, nevertheless dealt with a particular historical event.

Incidentally, for the record, I perhaps ought to make it clear that the university architects whose comments I have reported were working in England and dealing with new university campuses in which the brief was very informal. This seems to be a common situation in this country, in spite of the program of the architecture development group of the University Grants Committee. These problems are handled quite differently in the United States now, especially in the large state systems, such as the University of California, with its master plan providing for the establishment of twenty-four campuses by the year 2000, compared to the nine campuses already built or in the construction stage. California and other state systems have major administrative units concerned exclusively with planning the organization of each campus; the existence of these offices undoubtedly transforms the way in which the social sciences contribute to the briefing process.

As I said, of the three fundamental issues raised in briefing, sociologists have enjoyed their principal opportunity to demonstrate the relevance of their expertise by helping to develop the schedule of accommodations. This seems to have been the case with regard to the formulation of university briefs, too. The architects I talked with, even when they did not consult sociologists or social research studies in determining objectives and appropriate university activities, did make use of sociology for ascertaining the floor area for student rooms, the furniture and other equipment that should be installed in these rooms, the kinds of wall surfaces to construct, the size and number of places for refectory dining, the floor plan for student rooms, and an almost endless number of details involving spatial requirements and the provision of amenities.

The architects I met were no more enthusiastic about the contribution of sociologists to the resolution of their problems in this stage of briefing than they were about their role in the other stages. Their specific criticisms, however, were different. It was in this context, for example, that they raised the traditional complaint about social research, that it tells a good deal about what people want but does not offer sufficient guidance about the weight that should be given to these desires. The architects said that the sociological surveys they had sponsored might tell them how much space students now were using in existing dormitories, how satisfied or dissatisfied students were with this space, but little about how much space students ought to have. They complained too that the sociologists were not able to translate their information about student activities and organization into the spatial organization these activities required. Faced with these deficiencies in sociological research, it is obvious that the architects proceeded much as they have in the past when faced with the problem of developing a schedule of accommodations, except perhaps with a better sense of the possibilities for modification and criticism. Instead of developing wholly new schedules on the basis of sociology, ergonomics or anthropometrics, they examined previous university residence halls, took into account the design standards established by the UGC, corrected them on the basis of taste, experience and the available budget, and formulated their design scheme accordingly.

I can well understand the disappointment of the architects I spoke to; if anything, I am surprised that it was not more keen. For the fact of the matter is that even though there are sociologists, say, who know a great deal about higher education, its goals and organizations, there are extremely few individuals within any sociological specialty who have given thought to, or who have conducted research about, the way in which these goals and organizations can be facilitated and served through building. How should a building be defined in order to make this phenomenon most accessible to sociological inquiry? What are the social functions that buildings perform in a society? Which elements of a building are of primary significance for particular kinds of social activities? At what point along the continuum over which any behavior pattern extends is the building likely to become a significant determinant of the pattern? How wide a range of behavior within any single behavior pattern is compatible with a particular spatial organization? These are not questions that many sociologists have thought about or discussed, and therefore little in the way of a "conventional wisdom" is available.

In reporting the dissatisfaction of the private university architects with the sociologist's contribution to the schedule of accommodations, we ought not to overlook the fact that many of the research and development groups in the central government ministries in Britain seem to be quite pleased with the role of the sociologist in this phase of briefing. I am not sure of the reason behind this more favorable response but I suspect it has something to do with the manner in which the sociologist makes his contribution to the work of these groups. He acts as a gentle critic to architects who are accustomed to reviewing the components of schedules of accommodation and it may well be that gentle criticism, administered in the right setting, is more valuable than the answers that can only be obtained through the development of the complex intellectual apparatus of systematic social research.

Sociology and the Design Process

I said earlier that the interest of architects in sociology has been concentrated on its possible contribution to the development of the brief and to the formulation of the design scheme. In reviewing the questions architects ask, it has struck me, too, that questions raised with respect to designs have a different character from those asked with regard to briefs. For example, architects naturally, and quite legitimately, anticipate that their design schemes will have certain social consequences. But they rarely invite the sociologist to comment on the validity or propriety of these consequences; instead they only ask his opinion about whether the design scheme is likely to *result in* the intended consequence.

Let me give an example. About a year ago an architectural firm in the United States asked me to help with the design of a major privately developed housing scheme to involve 15,000 housing units with an expected population of 60,000 residents. When I arrived at the office, I first was shown an elaborate series of slides, drawings and models to acquaint me with the scheme, the same presentation, incidentally, that previously had been shown to the leaders of the city in which the speculative builder was hoping to install this complex. The chief architect, his staff, and I then spent several hours discussing the drawings and models in more detail while they peppered me with questions about the likelihood that the particular scheme would result in the formation of what the team called "community spirit among the residents." I was happy to give my opinion about the virtues and deficiencies of the scheme in terms of this criterion, but as the discussion proceeded, I injected questions of my own in an effort to get a better, more rounded idea of the site, the social and political structure of the existing city, its social problems, the general social objectives of the team, and the ambitions of the developer. The more I found out about this city and its problems, the harder it was for me to keep my mind focused on the questions being addressed to me, because it soon became obvious that the designers, who had been ingenious, resourceful and sophisticated in imagining a variety of alternative design solutions to their problem as stated, had never once subjected their objective— the production of community spirit—to critical examination. Yet it was in fact questionable whether this was the appropriate objective for new housing in this particular city: it was a city with a Negro population of almost 40 per cent, with one of the highest unemployment rates in the whole United States; the average per capita income in the city, for both whites and Negroes, was one of the lowest of any city in the State; the public physical plant, including schools, public transportation, and hospitals, was in bad condition, and the statistics indicated a long-run trend of deterioration. Civic morale was low, and evidence of political corruption was high. The intensification of what the designers called "community spirit" in their proposed enclave could only result in its further reduction in the city as a whole, since the developers in fact were asking the city to endow their project with special resources, in excess of those being provided in the older parts of the city. Furthermore, the production of community spirit could only be achieved through a series of design elements and amenities that would turn the attention of the residents inward on to themselves away from the problems of the city as a total community. I stated some of these probable consequences to the architects; as good, decent, liberal Americans they recognized the point immediately, although they admitted they never had before doubted the validity of their single objective, nor, they confessed, was this the kind of issue about which they expected advice from the sociologist. We then spent another few hours reviewing objectives that the design scheme conceivably could try to implement in addition to the original objective of "community spirit"; and then went back over some of the design elements to consider how they would enhance or inhibit the achievement of these objectives. I think that by the time I left for the airport we had achieved a certain meeting of minds. However, all of us were very aware that to plan a housing development that met the needs of the total community might result in a scheme that would be uneconomical for the developer and that therefore could be achieved only with additional subsidies from the city and federal governments. The issues are still being discussed among the parties and it will be some time before a resolution will be determined.

Cases of the sort I have described are legion in the experience of social scientists who have worked with planners, architects and private developers in the United States. I cite it to illustrate in capsule form the simple fact that once the process of building has reached the design stage the interest of the architect in understanding social objectives which he displays so forcefully during briefing tends to be relaxed, and intellectual energy is concentrated instead on finding the most efficient means in terms of design elements for achieving social objectives that are assumed *a priori* to be valid. To put it in another way, I would say that during the briefing stage there is a great willingness to consult others, including the client and the sociologist, about ends and means; once the design stage is reached, the architect chooses the ends, and asks the help of others in evaluating the means.

I would like, in the presence of this audience, to be able to say that my experience here in England is inconsistent with the generalization I have just made, but unfortunately it has confirmed it. Indeed, what is especially striking is that many of the same criteria are used by architects here as in the States to justify design schemes, including the objective of developing community spirit. Apparently, throughout Western democratic society there is a strong feeling that we have lost many of the social virtues that were present in the rural and pre-industrial village; architects regard it as their responsibility, and believe that it is within their competence to redevelop these virtues. Frankly, this finding surprises me. As I said earlier on, the architectural tradition in Great Britain is distinguished by its concern for the public interest; and design education is notable, in contrast to the education of architects in the States, for teaching students to be concerned with the needs of users and the social consequences of building. Therefore, one is led to look for the source of the critical deficiency of the designer not in the social role of the architect in a particular culture but rather in the universal nature of the architectural enterprise. What is it about this enterprise that leads the architect, who often is open-minded to the possibility of design alternatives, to be set in his determination to evaluate these alternatives in terms of their contribution to the attainment of a previously chosen, single objective?

Many features of the design task are probably relevant here. The architect is pressed for time; especially if he has been industrious in compiling the brief, he must get on with the job of designing and building and he cannot afford to re-examine social objectives all along the way. His training is not one that encourages him to devote as much energy to the consideration of objectives as he devotes to the development of a design scheme; in most schools the student is rewarded for design performance rather than for analytical skill. Regardless of the rewards, the curriculum of the schools does not give him the background in analytical philosophy, in social thought or in politics that conceivably could improve his sophistication in weighing the desired social consequences of designs. To the extent that these concerns are emphasized at all, the emphasis is all stated in the context of improving briefing competence. The tradition for briefing is so vague anyway that when dealing with briefs the architect is open for guidance and advice from any quarter. When he begins to design, however, the tradition comes to his rescue. What if the tradition is imprecise in the way in which it relates the vocabulary and language of form to the categories of social thought, at least a tradition is available. I am always struck by how architectural students and practitioners will talk as if they know what people want or should have; seldom in their training, except perhaps here at the Bartlett, is this informal language of user needs and user behavior ever subjected to critical scrutiny. The self-confidence of the architect is often shaky and febrile in the composition of the brief and in the encounter with the client, but it rises to a plateau of authority when he is at the drawing board, back at the office, alone or with his peers.

The demands imposed by the design phase of any building project are so stringent that it may, indeed, present almost insuperable diffi-culties to the critic who still wants to reconsider the social objectives implicit in the design during this phase. Many of the more radical edu-cators and practitioners now recognize this fact, and this is one reason, I think, why so much attention is given to getting the social objectives and activities of the user crystal clear during the briefing process. This is all to the good, but there are problems still to be mentioned even here. In the first place, as we all know, it is impossible in practice to separate the briefing process from the design process. Much of what is unclear about the client's requirements is revealed only well after the sketches, the working drawings and the specifications are produced. Secondly, how is the sociologist to react when he is consulted only after the design process is well under way and he then discovers that, from his point of view, the brief has been prepared inadequately? Should he suppress his awareness and not point out to the architect the serious social consequences that may follow from the architect's failure to con-sider a broader range of design objectives? Some architects seem to be asking the sociologist to forget about these issues and to attend only to the questions that the architect poses within the confines of his estab-lished frame of reference. It would be judicious, however, for the archi-tect to recognize that the sociologist's commitment to the canons of his discipline are as firm and compelling as those of the architect to his ethical code, and a new strategy must be developed to persuade both parties in the relationship to overcome the constraints imposed by the principles that govern their professional and scholarly lives.

I have said that when the architect becomes involved in the design stage the scope of the questions he addresses to the sociologist is nar-rowed. He asks the sociologist to evaluate the social and behavioral consequences of alternative building plans that he, the architect, pro-poses. I would like for the moment to ignore the sociologist's disposi-tion to urge upon the architect the re-examination of the objectives im-plicit in his proposed scheme and to consider, instead, the problems that emerge when the architect and the sociologist agree about the validity and propriety of the chosen objective.

One problem that emerges is that the architect asks the sociologist to estimate the probable social consequences of a proposed scheme without allowing the sociologist to consider a variety of other alter-natives for achieving the same objective. In a situation in which the agreed objective is to produce a sense of belonging in a housing project, the architect will ask the sociologist to weigh the advantages of two different schemes for producing this feeling of "rootedness." One scheme will be described as a building having a linear shape; and the other scheme will be described as a group of buildings arranged around a courtyard. "Which of these two," the architect will say, "is more likely to give the residents a feeling of responsibility for the community?" The response of the sociologist to this kind of query is a mixture of bafflement and disdain. A wealth of sociological research has already shown that the shape of buildings and site plans is a relatively insignificant determinant of social interaction, compared, say, to the positive effect that follows from the provision of such amenities as a nursery school for the area, or a community hall. Even more important as a factor contributing to the emergence of community spirit than either the shape of the building or the amenities it contains is whether the building is owned by the residents or only rented. If it is owned, they have an economic stake in maintaining it, and through the act of maintaining it they are brought together with other owners into what one might call a community.

A second difficulty emerges when the architect responds to this kind of criticism from the sociologist by saying, quite legitimately, that he, the architect, is still faced with the question of deciding whether the building should be of linear shape or arranged around a courtyard. "Do you mean to tell me," the architect says, "that there is nothing the sociologist can offer in the way of advice about which of these two is better for the inhabitants?" The sociologist can offer advice but it is usually with respect to effects that don't interest the architect who asks the question.[5] Every aspect of a building certainly does have consequences, but not all aspects of buildings are relevant to a particular consequence. Thus, in the example mentioned, it probably is wrong to assume that a relevant criterion for evaluating the form of a building is whether or not it contributes to community spirit, for the simple reason that building form is not something that is capable of determining a complex social interaction of this kind immediately and directly. If the architect is interested in influencing community spirit he is better advised to pay attention to the amenities he provides in the building and the pattern of ownership. If he continues to require objective social criteria for evaluating building form then he must consider other possible effects, such as the consequence of efficient or inefficient land use. In this respect, he will discover, as Martin and March have recently pointed out, that building form is important.[6] Courtyard buildings, they show, apart from whatever other virtues or deficiencies they may possess, can be justified on the grounds that they constitute an economical means for utilizing urban land.

I have been chided so often by thoughtful and intelligent architects for making these or similar comments that I had better take a few moments to clarify what I am not saying as well as what I do intend to imply. First of all, let me point out that the formal alternatives I referred to in the comparison of the courtyard to the linear building were both high blocks with eight storeys, in one case distributed around a large open green space, in the other situated and set along a street. The courtyard, in other words, offered by one alternative was not the intimate inner space of a French *hôtel*. I am perfectly willing to recognize the probability that buildings that differ significantly in scale are going to constitute significantly different kinds of living environments.

Even were the comparison between two buildings of different scale, I still would be inclined to argue that given the architect's intention to create a residential group exhibiting community spirit, it is more important to pay atttention to the amenities in the area and the pattern of ownership than to issues of building form. Not that building form does not matter or does not make a difference, but, I would argue, it makes a difference only initially, in the first few weeks or months after the residents move in and over the long run, after residents have lived there for a generation. But I don't think that the planners of contemporary housing developments are concerned with the initial response or the generational reaction: they want to produce communities that will work well over the next five or ten years. Human communities with this particular planning trajectory are best achieved, if they can be planned at all, by concentrating attention on community facilities and ownership patterns.

I think the irritation architects display when this view of the matter is presented is directly related to the fact that building form exerts a lasting impact only gradually; as I put it, rather arbitrarily, over the period of a generation or more. Building forms are capable of expressing an intention; and if the designer of the building is what we call a good designer, the form he designs will express that intention. But the fact of the matter is that the designer's intention is not immediately obvious to most people, although it may be clear to the designer and to the *cogniscenti* who are familiar with the language through which architecture tries to communicate its intention. The populace of a democratic society can, however, eventually come to understand the architect's intention but it will take a very long time. They can understand it if they use the building often enough; or they can understand it if they are taught how to use it in the way the architect intended; or they can understand it if the architect's vision of society which is intended by the form of his building catches on and is reproduced in the form of other new building in the society; or if his vision is consistent with the intention of buildings already established in the society and is thus reinforced by the forms generally visible and present in the built environment. In other words, the architect can be didactic, he can instruct, but like most of the messages put forth by the good teacher, some lessons can be learned easily and others are too subtle to be understood until long after the students have left the school, or the teacher has resigned, or the teacher is dead, or the students are dead, or the building itself perishes.

Still another difficulty that typically arises when the architect approaches the sociologist for advice about the social consequences of particular design proposals must be mentioned. I have in mind here numerous occasions on which I have been asked to evaluate specific elements in schemes that, I thought, should not have been specific to begin with, but should rather have consisted of generalized solutions. Perhaps two examples will serve to illustrate what I mean. An architectural firm in the United States was preparing as part of an urban renewal plan the design for a large housing project in a section of Chicago noted for its high juvenile delinquency rate. The basic elements of the scheme were groups of row houses surrounding on three sides a large central green space, the space to be used as a common area for children's play, recreation and informal community activities, such as picnics, fairs, etc. I was asked to comment on a number of features of the scheme, including whether it was advisable to fence off the open end of the green space, providing a private locked gate which could be opened only by a key belonging to the residents. The architect was confused about what to propose. He felt that if the space were open, the area could easily become a "turf" for the gangs of the surrounding neighborhood; if it were closed, the fence might discourage visiting among the residents of different groups within the project. A closed space, he suspected, would also confirm their fears that the area was located in a hazardous section of the city, and thus would discourage the sale or rental of the dwelling units. I agreed with the view that the fence could be interpreted in the way the architect suggested but I said that it was almost impossible to anticipate the contribution of these interpretations to the overall satisfaction of users with the proposed scheme. "Why not," I said to the architect, "design the housing and green area in such a way that the residents could later decide for themselves whether they wanted to put up a fence, or take the fence down if one were put up. Or establish fences in some of the groups and have no fences in others to begin with." The architect, I discovered, was unwilling to accept this flexible arrangement and insisted upon reaching some conclusion ahead of time about the proper or improper way to build the fence into the scheme.

A second example that casts light upon the same issue is this one. A group of architects responsible for the design of university residence halls for a campus of a new college within a large American state university were uncertain about the proportion of one-, two- and three-bedroom units they should provide. They asked me whether there was any guidance I could give them on the basis of the social research done on housing that would help them to make a decision on this matter. It so happens, as you know, that this is one of the best researched areas within the general field of user requirements in university building; but, as I commented earlier, there is little agreement among the conclusions of these studies.[7] A larger proportion of the students in colleges in the Eastern states seem to prefer communal units; in the West there is a greater preference for single units. Private college students prefer large units, state university students, smaller units. Apart from generalizations of this sort, however, it is really impossible on the basis of these studies to recommend in more precise terms the proportions in which large and small, single or communal, units should be incorporated into a new campus. I recommended that the buildings should be designed so that the units could be altered in size depending upon the university's experience with their students in the halls. I am sorry to say I was not able to convince the architects of the reasonableness of my suggestion and they have gone ahead to plan a fixed proportion of units of different size.

I find these cases very interesting. They exemplify what I regard as the unwarranted ambition of many architects to find specific solutions in building designs even when these specific solutions are incompatible with the pattern of user behavior or client needs relevant to the building type being considered. I am aware, of course, that the entire question of indeterminate building, building of generalized spaces, endless building, etc., is a controversial subject in the design studio these days, and that there are serious and important issues involved in deciding what should be fixed and what indeterminate in any building, and in assessing the problems for which indeterminate solutions are applicable. Nevertheless, it is clear that the significance of the issue being debated has made little impact so far on the practical work of the architectural profession. The possibility of variable or flexible solutions interests me, too, because it shifts part of the burden for dealing with the contradictions of the findings of sociological research back on to the shoulders of the architect. Thus, it can be argued that the inconsistency of sociological findings is not only an indication of the necessary historicity of all studies of past behavior but also a sign that not all future behavior of building users is determinable through social research. The population of students who use residence halls is likely to be different from one year to another; and the same students are often likely to change their desired requirements for space from one year to another. Buildings and architectural designs should somehow be able to accommodate this characteristic of building users.

Sources of Misunderstanding

Throughout this selection I have discussed not only the questions architects address to sociologists but also the attitudes these questions generate in architects and sociologists. The attitudes are generally a mixture of disappointment, irritation, and sometimes of horror, on both sides. Architects, the sociologists seem to be saying, don't ask the correct questions at the right time; and the sociologists, according to the architects, don't tell us what we really want to know. At various places I have suggested some of the reasons that may help to account for the poor relationship, the misunderstanding, which now seems to prevail. I want to conclude now by reducing these reasons to their fundamental sources. There are three sources I want to discuss: (A) The requirements of design; (B) The nature of building and groups; and (C) The social roles of architects and sociologists.

A. The building the architect is responsible for designing must, as Vitruvius implied, meet standards of firmness, commodity and delight: it must stand up as a work of structural engineering, it must meet the needs of its users in a reasonably satisfactory fashion, and it should conform to established or original standards of beauty or aesthetic integrity. More recently, the architectural tradition has pointed to this same trichotomy of building by saying that the architect must be skillful in developing the technology, the program and the form of the building. If we recognize building as made up of these three dimensions, it might be said that the dilemma of architecture's relationship to sociology emerges from the fact that the architect must be concerned with all three dimensions during the design process, whereas sociology relates to only one of them, namely, the program.

Because sociology only deals with one of the elements that the architect must respond to and that he must manipulate in the design of the built environment, information about the objectives of users and about the activities the building must shelter cannot conceivably by itself be used to dictate a design solution. Most architects, of course, recognize this point: I don't think that the architectural tradition, for example, has ever seriously argued that a design method could be formulated in terms of the program, any more than architects really believe that structure, technology or form alone can be used to prescribe the design scheme, in spite of the pretence within the Modern Movement to argue sometimes as if this were possible. What those architects have meant who have stressed in the past, or argue today, that form or technology is the means to solving design problems is rather that the language of form or the vocabulary of technology provides a medium for grasping the totality of the architectural problem; or that the pursuit of one of these elements should be given priority in organizing the remaining elements.

I regret to say that sociologists are often not aware of the threefold nature of building design and this is often the reason why they evidence so much difficulty in responding positively to the questions stated by architects. They do not realize, in other words, that while the architect is asking questions about the program, he is trying to balance the sociologist's answers with what he knows about the demands imposed on the design scheme by the elements of form and technology. Nor does the sociologist realize that the content of the question posed by the architect, or the way in which it is stated, is often determined by the previous experience of the architect in grappling with the formal and technological elements of the building. I frankly do not know what attitude to take toward this situation: in part, I would think it demands that the sociologist somehow become conversant with the technological and formal elements that have determined the statement of the problem by the time it is presented to him; at the same time, I have sometimes felt that the architect has given more weight to these demands than they deserve and that more fruitful collaboration between the fields could have been developed had the sociologist been consulted earlier during the design process.

I think the nature of building design has an additional implication for the sociologist's response to the architect—what I am going to say may seem patronizing, but it certainly is not stated with this intention. I think that there is a sense in which the sociologist takes the architect's questions too seriously. Just because a building is more than the solution to the problem represented by the program, it cannot hope to satisfy the demands of the program fully. There is no design that works equally well for builders, engineers, clients, and users; there is no building that can hope to serve the needs of all its potential users to the same degree; there is no building that can achieve a maximum effect as form, as technique, and as user environment. The good designer knows this, or if he doesn't, he certainly should. Therefore, the good designer who turns to the sociologist really wants approximate answers rather than precise ones. He wants to know whether one proposed feature of a particular scheme will be better or worse than some other proposal: he does not demand that it should be the best of all possible alternatives. Since he has to juggle so many features and dimensions of building simultaneously, the responsible designer just wants to make sure that he is not too far off in the solution he is proposing to deal with a particular problem.

Sociologists may find it hard to understand this mood in which the architect addresses them, and even if they do understand, it often is difficult for the sociologist to respond on these terms. Sociology prides itself today on being a scientific discipline that investigates problems systematically and that aims to provide systematic answers. It is hard for the sociologist to relinquish the methods of work that these standards impose on him, just as the architect apparently finds it difficult to do the opposite, namely to abandon his impulse to find design solutions in favor of a careful, analytical examination of a problem. Yet I have found that the sociologists who have been most successful in their dealing with architects are those who are willing to adopt a somewhat more casual attitude toward their own discipline. When presented with a problem, they don't as sociologists so often tend to do, propose a research project; instead, they try in a responsible way to give the architect their best judgment about the issue, based on their accumulated experience in conducting research, teaching, and reviewing the research of others.

B. The subject matter of sociology is social groups, society and human activities; the subject of architecture is building. There are fundamental distinctions between the essential nature of these phenomena, building and society. Buildings are physical objects but societies and groups are social and cultural facts. One important difference between physical objects and social facts is that physical objects can be sensed directly through the eye and by touching them; values, norms, statuses, classes, and social roles are ascertainable indirectly, only by inferring their existence from the behavior patterns that they regulate and determine. I think that many of the difficulties that develop between architects and sociologists arise from these differences in the way in which one learns about the nature of objects and social facts. For example, physical objects have form; inescapably they are sculptural phenomena. Anyone who works with them regularly in a professional capacity, as the architect does, becomes sensitive to variations in form and to the capacity of forms to communicate significant information. Sociologists don't spend their time considering objects as part of their occupational routine. I think this is one important reason why sociologists often do not understand the architect's emphasis on formal and aesthetic considerations in building, or why they are puzzled when the architect poses questions about the social consequences of formal differences. It works the other way, too, I would guess. For the reason that he is necessarily busy dealing with the world of form, the architect tends to anthropomorphize forms, to endow them with life, and to search out their possible social significance. The architect finds it difficult to accept the fact that phenomena with such potent tactile qualities do not have an important immediate influence on many patterns of social action. The sociologist, on the other hand, devotes himself full time to inferential activities; since values, norms, statuses and classes cannot be perceived by the eye, he develops a capacity to guess at their existence even though they are not immediately apparent. It is not at all difficult for him to believe that the important determinants of human action are not available to touch or to look at; and he is frankly suspicious of anyone who, in his view, is so simple-minded as to equate what is visible with what is influential.

The differences between the nature of building and the nature of social groups is of greater fundamental significance than is implied by only pointing to the intellectual styles they engender in architects and sociologists respectively. Buildings behave differently than people do. Buildings are generally fixed in space, whereas groups can and do move about easily. The simplest illustration of this difference is that the same family in the course of a generation can occupy several different dwelling places, but only rarely is a building transferred from one location to another. Social groups are reorganized more easily and can shift their elements more speedily than is possible for the units that make up a building. For example, compare the high turnover rate in the staff of industrial work groups with the difficulties encountered in renovating a Victorian factory. Furthermore, groups can be enormously resourceful in finding new means for achieving established goals. But a building has no sensorium. It cannot by itself learn its shortcomings, communicate this knowledge to part of itself, and then reform itself in order to maintain its capacity under new external conditions to achieve its original purpose.

These differences in the natural capacity of buildings and social groups impose serious limitations on the power of buildings to influence social action. A building is not capable of outwitting a recalcitrant or unsympathetic user. The user can leave it and maintain his established mode of behavior intact. The inhabitant can alter the building, making it respond to his needs, and the building cannot fight back. If the facilities provided by the building somehow manage to frustrate a user in attaining or maintaining a way of life, this is only temporary; the user can find new means, independent of the building, for achieving the same objective. This is very odd, because again judging by looks alone, buildings should be more powerful than people. They are heavier, can withstand more physical assault, and are usually bigger. But men have capacities for survival that buildings don't have and this makes all the difference. So long as buildings are different from groups in these respects—and even the ambition of the architects of indeterminism to make buildings grow, change, and generally behave like people is unlikely to transform their fundamental nature—it will continue to be difficult to forecast the effect that buildings will have on society.

C. The act of designing necessarily demands information about other matters than user requirements, but nevertheless all of us would recognize that a conscientious concern for the program is an essential ingredient of good design. The nature of buildings, on the one hand, and of human beings and groups, on the other, however, suggest that our understanding of the program and how the building can be used to fulfill it will always remain imprecise. The information and the theory that the designer must use thus will always fall short of meeting the standards of exactness and certainty that some designers desire and that most sociologists recognize as essential for the further progress of their own discipline.

As a sociologist, given my background and training, I find it amazing and wonderful that architects are willing and able to design buildings given the fragmentary character of the knowledge in terms of which they must proceed. I have asked myself how it is possible for them to do it. The answer I give to this question is itself sociological. Architects are able to be good designers because our society has thrown up the culture of architecture and created a social role in which the individual who adopts this culture and fulfills its demands is rewarded. If the individual who is an architect manages to design buildings that work reasonably well, that stand up and are pleasant to the eye he gets paid a regular salary, he can become a member of a chartered society, and he earns the respect of colleagues and the admiration of the nation. If he should prove incapable of proposing a building that meets these standards, if he balks at the fact that he is being asked to commit himself to a plan without sufficient knowledge on which to base that plan, then he doesn't get a job as an architect, he doesn't get the respect of his colleagues, and he cannot put the initials ARIBA or AIA after his name. To put it in another way, we can say that the social role, "architect," and the culture, "architecture," are organized in a way that is particularly appropriate for encouraging individuals to assume the responsibility of making design decisions.

The culture and role structure of sociology and the sociologist are very different. Architects seem not to realize, for instance, that sociology is the name of a particular scholarly discipline and sociologists traditionally have been members of learned societies rather than professional associations. Academic rewards do not go to the sociologist who plans or builds a society on the basis of fragmentary knowledge about human needs, social structure and technology, but to the sociologist who studies an important social problem in a new way, or who develops a theory that explains a variety of apparently unrelated facts. Many sociologists are members of the teaching profession, but this is something else; in their role as sociologists they are researchers, students and analysts. Judgments about their competence as sociologists are made privately, by other sociologists rather than, as is so often the case in architecture, by clients, users and tourists who are not expert in the subject of building. Sociologists are not compelled to serve social purposes immediately or to provide solutions to problems on short notice.

I am aware, of course, that the distinction I have introduced is exaggerated and idealized, and no longer describes adequately the condition either of sociology or architecture. In fact, at the urging of the other professions, including architecture, sociology is gradually being forced to assume the kind of responsibilities traditionally associated only with the professions. And architecture, in order to merit its admission into the British university structure and to demonstrate its relation to modern scientific philosophies, is becoming more like a discipline. Still these changes are developing only gradually, and I don't think it is seriously proposed that architecture will ever be anything other than a highly skilled and subtle craft, no matter how sophisticated it becomes as a profession, or that sociology will ever abandon its status as a learned, scholarly enterprise. In admitting this fact about their essential nature, however, sociologists must continue to explore the possibility that sociology would be a better and more competent discipline if some sociologists at least had the experience of applying their information in the context of professional problems; and if they from time to time assumed the burden of decision making that goes along with being a professional person. Just as architects must strive to make architecture a more perfect craft by having some of their colleagues devote themselves to social research.

But do we really believe these commands? Statements of the kind I just offered are often espoused on suitable ritual occasions, such as this one, when architects, educators and social scientists meet together. If we do honestly believe them we must consider much more carefully than we have up to now how the curriculum of architectural schools should be revised; and how faculties and departments of sociology can begin to acquaint postgraduate and research students with the culture and dilemmas of architecture. What kind of sociology should architecture schools teach? Who should teach it for them? What kind of architecture should be taught to sociology students? Who should teach it to them? In what ways should we restructure the context in which architects now make use of sociology? How can we ensure that research on buildings conducted by sociologists will make maximum use of the experience, knowledge and wisdom of the architect? How, in other words, are we to produce a true social architecture and a genuine architectural sociology? These are the questions that architects and sociologists should ask.

NOTES

1. I wish to thank the Rutgers University Research Council and the Russell Sage Foundation for the support that made it possible for me to undertake the research on which this selection is based.

2. I am especially grateful for the hospitality extended to me in the U.S.A. by Professor Robert Geddes, Dean, School of Architecture, Princeton University; and in England for the help given me by Professor Lord Llewelyn-Davies (Professor of Architecture), Mr. John Madge (Director of the Sociological Research Unit) and Mr. Peter Cowan (Director of the Joint Unit for Planning Research), all of University College, London.

3. Alvin Schorr, *Slums and Social Insecurity*, U.S. Department of Health, Education and Welfare, Social Security, Administration, Division of Statistics, Research Report No. 1, Washington 25, D.C., 1963.

4. Rudolf Wittkower, *Architectural Principles in the Age of Humanism*, London: Tiranti Ltd., 1962.

Colin Rowe, especially, "The Mathematics of the Ideal Villa," *Architectural Review*, March 1947, pages 101–104; and "Mannerism and Modern Architecture," *Architectural Review*, May 1950, pages 289–298.

5. Social research dealing with the influence of the built environment on social action is discussed in my paper, "Site Planning and Social Behavior" in Joachim Wohlwill and Robert Kates, eds., "Man's Response to His Environment," *Journal of Social Issues*, October 1966.

6. Sir Leslie Martin and Lionel March, "Land Use and Built Forms," *Cambridge Research*, April 1966, pages 8–14.

7. Sim Van der Ryn, *et al.*, *The Ecology of Student Housing: A Case Study in Environmental Analysis and Design*, Berkeley, Calif.: University Students Co-operative Association, no date.

23

The Room, A Student's Personal Environment

SIM VAN DER RYN AND MURRAY SILVERSTEIN

It could easily be inferred from the tone of many of the selections in this book that although there is a growing awareness of the relevance of the behavioral sciences to architecture, little has as yet been done to apply the concepts and research techniques of these sciences to actual design projects. However, the situation is otherwise; both in this country and in Europe one can point to a variety of program documents, design proposals, and in some cases, finished building projects, that have utilized sociology and psychology as collaborative disciplines.

The following selection by Van der Ryn and Silverstein deals with a dormitory program and design proposal. Presented with the problem of formulating basic program information and generating building specifications for student housing for the University of California, these two architects decided that, before beginning to work on the program, they would study how space in existing dormitories was being used and try to determine the degree and sources of satisfaction or dissatisfaction among the occupants. Their data consisted of observations of the pattern of space use, activity logs which indicated the students' schedules and the kinds of activities that took place in the dormitories or elsewhere on campus, and interviews to identify the attitudes of students toward existing facilities.

One of the most interesting features of the inquiry is that Van der Ryn and Silverstein made practical use of many of the behavioral science concepts discussed earlier in this volume, such as personal space, territoriality, and privacy. These concepts helped them anticipate the possible sources of tension and strain in the existing dormitories, and the questions included in the interviews and the types of behavior observed were focused around these concepts. These concepts also served as dominating ideas to guide the spatial organization and the choice of materials incorporated in the design schemes. In this sense, it may be appropriate to regard the building specifications included in the text as early examples of what may well be an emerging trend in contemporary architecture, namely an architecture whose form

Reprinted from Sim Van der Ryn and Murray Silverstein,
Dorms at Berkeley: An Environmental Analysis, Center for
Planning and Development Research (Berkeley, University of
California Press, 1967), pp. 31–34; 36; 38; 70; 72–75.

and style can be traced to a behavioral science view of human nature and man's principal social needs.

The selection reprinted here deals only with the room environment. In the larger work on dormitory design from which the selection is taken, the authors also discuss their findings and proposals as they relate to common rooms, lounges, food facilities, and other amenities appropriate to student housing.

☐

Our activity logs and interviews indicate that students spend one-third of their waking hours in their rooms. The total time spent in the room is greater than that spent anywhere else. The design of the individual student room and its immediate surroundings is the key planning element in college housing.

The Berkeley high-rise dorms are a good example of the most prevalent plan in student housing over the past twenty years: a multi-story building, each floor with a central corridor lined on both sides with identical two-student-to-a-room quarters. It was this plan that David Reisman and Christopher Jencks had in mind when they wrote, "At an average cost of roughly $4,000 per student, the typical student residence joins two students, two beds, two bureaus, two desks, two straight chairs, and two hundred square feet of floor in an effort to produce enlightenment." [1] Creating conditions where students can achieve privacy and solitude has yet to be achieved by most housing planners. The literature of student housing is rich with phrases such as "experience in group living," "social adjustment," etc. Such rhetoric may be a justification for the fact that typical dormitory plans do not resolve the prime student need for *individual* living. Sociologist Marvin Trow, in a keynote speech to a workshop discussing life in the residence halls, stressed that one of the three functions he saw as essential for dorms was, "the opportunity to be alone, to think, to read, to work, or to just be alone." [2]

The concept of "personal space realm" or "personal territory," which has been understood by students of animal behavior for some time,[3] and studied more recently by anthropologists and social psychologists,[4] provides a clue to the nature of student irritation with the room. Whether it is expressed by the song bird who warbles in defense of her nest, or by the urban gang defending its "turf," both men and animals exhibit the need for a personal territory. The student wants to establish a unique home territory that is fixed in space and that is the locus of those activities most important to him. The room is the focal point of private and semi-private activities. For students it is "home" territory.

When personal space characteristics are not available, problems result. Control over personal space is of special importance in a large, urban university like the Berkeley campus; the new student, overwhelmed by the size and impersonal nature of the campus, needs some kind of place to identify with and hang his hat in. There is some evidence that in circumstances that require the individual to adapt to drastically altered cultural settings, "home" and its amenities assume ever greater importance than when the social and physical environment is familiar.

The room is one place where an individual, at-home feeling ought to be available for the student, since most other areas in the residence hall housing must be shared with others. Lounges and date rooms serve 200 students. The recreation rooms are "about as homey as a Greyhound depot," as one student put it.[5] The bathroom, which in the family home is one haven for privacy, serves about 25 students on each floor. One girl who moved out of the dorm said of apartment life, "where else could you sit in the bathtub for hours and read the *Tropic of Cancer?*" [6]—certainly not in the dormitory.

Perhaps the greatest single deterrent to adequate privacy is sharing less than 200 square feet of space with someone else for 35 weeks. Clashes between incompatible roommates appear commonplace, and probably affect a student's approach to his work. Over half of the students we interviewed simply told us, "I can't stand my roommate." Sleep, study, and intimacy are activities which require personal territory, while other needs may be met by degrees of common space.

Even when two roommates are compatible, there are irritations inherent in sharing private space. One girl said, "You don't have privacy in a dorm when you have a roommate"; another, "It's impossible to be able to be by yourself in the dorms; you go to campus if you want this." No one has measured the psychic stress or the effect on student well-being or academic performance caused by the strain of living in close quarters. We have, however, documented some of the ways students adapt to the double occupancy situation. The most obvious adaptation is that one roommate is forced out of the room. Students often have incompatible schedules. Spot checks and analysis of activity log data indicate that both students seldom are studying together in the room at the same time. Thus the supposed economies of two-to-a-room occupancy planning tend to shift the burden of providing places for study, solitude, and relaxation to other facilities on campus.

The individual room is most responsive to differing schedules. A realistic look at schedule determinants would show a rich set of variations. Some university work can only be done at a particular place and time (certain libraries, for example); some work, while it is due at a special time, is left to each individual to complete as his time permits; other types of study demand peculiar conditions and special environments, while some are dependent on nothing more than a place to sit with good light; exam schedules vary from class to class, and exam preparation time will differ correspondingly. Every student has a slightly different schedule imposed on him from campus, and this schedule effectively structures much of his time. Furthermore, each student has a personal or idiosyncratic schedule. Of course the personal schedule will often respond to the campus schedule—if a student contracts for a class at 8:00 a.m., he presumably will give up his habit of sleeping in—but personal schedules should not be overlooked. With increased emphasis on individual work and independent research, college housing must be designed to tolerate eccentric schedules.

Henry Wriston, a college president for many years, sums it up this way:

If I had been able to find money enough, every dormitory I had anything to do with would have been made up of single rooms—no doubles, much less suites for three or four. Single rooms constitute no danger that undergraduates will not learn how to live with other people. Their lives are much too gregarious; even if they have one room where privacy is possible, they will still have enough group experience to avoid becoming anti-social.[7]

Along with shared living space, noise is a great enemy of privacy. Loud noises carry along the corridor and through adjacent rooms. Complaints about noise were numerous in the group interviews and in unsolicited comments written on the student logs. Rooms next to lounges, across from the elevator, laundry or bathroom suffer from lack of sufficient wall insulation and sealing around doors. Rooms at the ends of the hall are reputed to be quieter, and the residents experience fewer interruptions. Slamming doors, conversations, radios, and hi-fi's are common problems at night. One student observed that "because of the 'community living,' there seems to be a constant low-volume noise. This can be very irritating at times."

Another source of irritation is the awareness that one might disturb others. "It would be nicer if the rooms were soundproof. For instance,

373

when I practice ballet or play my guitar, there is always someone complaining that they are trying to study."

Girl students are particularly sensitive to the feeling of being watched while in their rooms. In a letter to the *Daily Cal*, one girl wrote, "The men from the neighborhood dorm have no need for social events and mixers for they have already met us with binoculars and telescopes." [8] It may be that there are various thresholds of visual invasion. The residence halls at Berkeley seem to fall short here, as more than once they have given rise to comments that dorm life is like "living in a crowded fish bowl." [9]

Another related source of irritation comes from wanting to protect one's possessions. There have been a number of cases of thefts of clothing and other equipment. Most often such losses are the result of leaving rooms unlocked during dinner. During one dispute about maid service, a student charged that he had found a maid looking through his belongings. It turned out that she had briefly glanced at a newspaper he had left open on his desk.[10] A trivial incident perhaps, but indicative of conditions which can destroy the feeling of security in one's personal environment.

Inflexibility of room equipment and regulations pertaining to its use are a major source of student discomfort. Two issues that are cited continually are wall surface decoration and built-in furniture. One girl who had moved from the dorm to an apartment put it quite clearly: "We've got space. . . . I can hang things up if I want to, and rearrange the furniture . . . everything!" [11]

When new students move into the dorm, they are, of course, eager to hang prints and clippings, even paint the walls. The University responds by prohibiting "tacking, taping or otherwise marring the wall finish." It is the Housing Administrators' point of view that, while students come and go, the building remains and must be kept up at reasonable expense. As a result, decorating is confined to a small 12" x 24" cork-board, placed behind the door. (However, many students ignore the rule; hence, unannounced inspections are necessary.) This is typical of student housing on many campuses. One student explained how to cope with the situation: "I put a lot of posters, etc. on my ceiling to decorate the place a little . . . the bulletin board, the little thing it is, is located behind the door, so when the door is open— it covers the bulletin board completely! Hanging stuff from those stupid hooks at the ceiling corners is ridiculous."

Psychiatric observations suggest that the rooms for women are seen as extensions of their physical persons.[12] It becomes as important to dress the room as to dress oneself. One girl remarked during Spring 1964 that she planned to leave because, "the dorms are just too much like home, having everything done for you." [13]

Rules which prohibit room decoration, while motivated in part by the desire to maintain a clean and uniform front, are dictated by administrative decisions to avoid damage to wall finishes. While much effort has gone into promulgating rules, little seems to have gone into finding innovative solutions to the problem. Student rooms should be designed so that residents can make non-permanent changes. One approach is to line permanent wall elements with a surface that can be decorated and replaced periodically at a cost not exceeding routine painting and maintenance.

With regard to the inflexibility of room arrangement and equipment, the program for the design competition for these dormitories was quite specific:

Bedrooms: *Each bedroom shall have a floor area of 182 square feet net. The bedrooms shall have no built-in furniture or fixed equipment of plumbing fixtures. Items of moveable furniture (the design of which is not part of this program) with their respective dimensions are as follows:*

2 beds each 6'-8" x 3'-0"
2 wardrobe units each 2'-0" x 5'-0"
2 chests of drawers each 21-12" x 28" x 45" high
2 desks each 26½" x 41½" x 30" high
2 chairs

It is desired that each student have the maximum opportunity to arrange this furniture as he pleases. The owner, through experience, has found that room dimensions of 14' of exterior wall by 13' in depth have provided such maximum opportunity. These room dimensions are strongly recommended. [14]

The assumption about moveable furniture appears to be well-founded. We discovered that a great variety of furniture arrangements were created by students, although many of these arrangements fell into identical patterns. It appears that roommates rearrange furniture as often as once every ten weeks.

Two out of three of the women's arrangements were represented by one plan, in which desks faced away from each other and towards the wall and beds were placed against the wall with the head at the corner. Men's room arrangements tended to be more asymmetrical and represented a wider variation of arrangements. The fixed relationships in the room (closet, window, mirror, wall lamps and door) eliminated many arrangement possibilities. However, we conclude that in the double occupancy situation, roommates try to create their own territory; they try to escape each other's field of vision; they seek spatial isolation while sleeping.

The desire for personal territory is expressed in room arrangement in a number of ways. An analysis of room arrangement patterns shows that 94 per cent of the sample group arranged furniture completely on one side of a hypothetical line that splits the room into two equal halves, in spite of the fact that many other arrangements are possible. The inference we draw from this is that the desire to create personal territory is stronger than the desire to share space with a roommate. Another finding concerns the desire of students to study without being observed by their roommates. In the majority of rooms, students re-arranged desks so that when they are at their desks their angle of vision excludes one another from view. It is likely that when students share a room, they prefer not to be observed by one another.

In the Berkeley dorm, moveable furniture *alone* does not provide the degree of flexibility or convenience that students would prefer. Our interviews and questionnaires revealed a seemingly endless list of specific complaints about features of the room design, which we will not recount here. Our hunch is that many of these complaints were generated by basic social and psychological dysfunctions of double occupancy.

Equipment that must, by its nature, be fixed should be placed conveniently; one student notes that "it would be nice if the phone were located differently, so that people coming in the door don't run into you while you're talking on the phone." Another student added, "under the present conditions it is impossible to open the door when someone is standing at the [book] shelves." Inadequate space is another source of complaints; "I need room for the phonograph, it bothers the person next door when next to the wall."

A woman student noted that "the rooms are too small for any convenient arrangement giving both occupants sufficient privacy, typing or studying late for example." Another woman student added a short, unsolicited essay on the same subject at the end of our questionnaire:

There simply isn't enough space in this room. My phonograph sticks out into the middle of the room, and I had to turn my dresser sideways to make room for a guitar. Also we would appreciate having curtains that could be opened without our having to stand on the beds and pull them. A light in the middle of the room instead of one small one over the back mirror would be a big improvement; so would moveable mirrors. It would also be nice if the phone was located differently, so that people coming in the door don't run into you while you're talking on the phone. The location of the light switch is also inconvenient—it makes the use of one bookshelf impossible. We also feel that a different type of window sill would be a great improvement if possible; the metal sills now make it impossible to sit on your bed and lean against the window. Therefore, we are almost forced to have just one room arrangement. . . . Other than that, the rooms are fine, other than the fact that if we wish to adjust the heat we have to either crawl under our desks or move our beds, depending on the room arrangement. Thank you for giving us the chance to air our complaints.

The trend in student housing is away from moveable furniture and towards built-in furnishings. This is unfortunate because built-in systems further limit the potential for variety and the ability of students to shape their room space to meet personal needs. It is clear that just as there is no ideal student, there is no ideal fixed room arrangement; what is important is that students make a place their home by asserting their own preferences and changing it. Periodic furniture rearrangement may also be a way of letting off steam, trying to achieve variety in an otherwise monotonous environment, and expressing frustration with difficult social conditions. It may be that if the room and its surfaces lent themselves to other forms of personalization, the need to have moveable furniture might not be as great.

However, many administrators have substantial reasons for holding other views. Although moveable furniture may be financed through Federal College housing loan programs, some lenders follow the practice of considering only built-ins as part of the real estate package. Secondly, free standing furniture pieces are commonly of heavier construction and use more material than built-in systems (which can use walls for structural support), and thus are often more expensive. It is claimed that it is more efficient for maids to clean around the built-in equipment which is wall-hung and has no dust-collecting floors beneath it. Built-in equipment gives the room a neater appearance than free-standing furniture, and damage due to moving furniture around is minimized.

While these views are reasonable, they ignore the realities of student living as we have seen them. Many precedents for college housing administration and planning are derived from hotel management. Yet the student room is not a hotel room for a transient, it is the student's home for at least 200 days. Thus a fixed furniture arrangement which may be fine for the casual guest becomes an irritant to a resident over a period of time. The wish of a hotel keeper to show off a neatly arranged room to the public is reasonable, but the dorm is not a hotel. We question whether routine cleaning is not better left to residents rather than outside help. Finally, with respect to furniture, resistance to wear in relation to first cost has usually been the prime criterion. Tolerance and recovery from wear are equally important criteria. It may be appropriate in some instances to deliberately choose inexpensive furniture with a short use life. Pieces can be replaced periodically, over the life of the building, at no higher annual cost than expensive highly resistant furnishings.

Administrators, of course are not unaware of these points. Their professional journals show them to be continually interested in the products of modern materials research. Chester Winter, writing in *College and University Business,* emphasizes the importance of a personal and personally determined student room environment. He states that

. . . students were genuinely concerned with regimentation. . . . The opportunity, though limited, to move furnishings as an expression of the student's personal living habits appeared to be very important. . . . Furnishings and decor deserve special attention. The details of the finishing touches largely set the tone of the room and make the difference between a homelike atmosphere and the stilted, barren character typical of much college housing.[15]

Finally, the results of a survey at St. Olaf's College correspond to our Berkeley findings:

. . . after a certain point is reached, the effort to find a perfectly efficient size and arrangement for a dormitory room is not fruitful . . . the rooms in Ellingson Hall in St. Olaf were planned to provide what is generally agreed to be a lucid, logical and efficient space for two students. In them there is one arrangement of furniture which exploits this potential to its fullest. In an inspection of forty-one rooms two weeks after school began in September, 1962, however, only six were found to be remaining in the original efficient arrangement. In the others the furniture had been rearranged in an almost baffling variety of ways. This sort of thing could be found in any dormitory where rooms are all identical to each other. The obvious conclusion is that "functional" efficiency is not a very important thing in the mind of the student. . . . One way for him to assert uniqueness is to arrange his room differently from that of his neighbors . . . and he does this at the expense of efficiency, which his vitality can compensate for, and sometimes at the expense of any at all.[16]

The old Las Casitas housing on the Santa Barbara campus of the University of California is reported to have been heavily favored by students over accommodations of better physical quality. The housing officer on the campus suggests that the reason for this popularity was that students could do what they wanted to their rooms. Similar results are reported for the rather cramped trailer units used at Santa Cruz for temporary housing.

The editor of the *Daily Californian,* in an editorial on the students' apparent preference for apartments, states that "people will put up with a lot when on their own as compared to being at home or in a dorm." [17]

• • •

Our evaluation at Berkeley and additional surveys of student housing conditions across the country lead us to some conclusions about student housing needs and how they may be met through design. Following are user needs and performance specifications for (1) room furnishings and personal space arrangement and (2) the room itself.

• • •

Furniture and Equipment

USER NEEDS:

1. Students want to rearrange their furniture from time to time.

2. Bed is a popular study location.

3. Desks must permit comfortable study involving two or three books, typewriter, and papers.

4. Desk chair must permit free shifting, tilting, leg stretching, etc., comfortably; when students cannot make such adaptations they are likely to have less productive study sessions.

5. Students occasionally try to visually "break-up" their room-space. Moveable closets provide a needed barrier.

6. Students want to extensively "personalize" their rooms; this involves tacking, painting, hanging, etc., on wall surfaces.

7. Because student residents come and go, housing administrators want to periodically return rooms to original conditions at minimum cost.

SPECIFICATIONS:

1. All components are moveable (e.g., all furnishings may be rearranged by two freshman girls).

2. The bed unit can be either free standing or hung from the wall (at student's discretion), bed unit includes adjustable backrest, integral lighting fixture, swing-away night table.

3. Desk unit has minimum dimensions:

45" long   24–30" wide   28–30" high

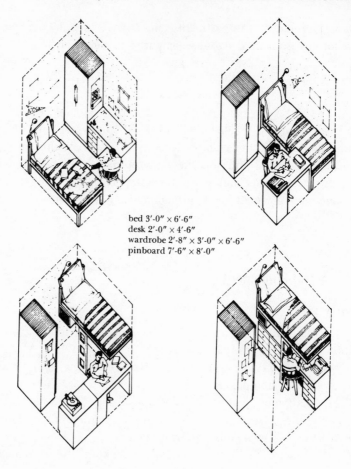

bed 3'-0" × 6'-6"
desk 2'-0" × 4'-6"
wardrobe 2'-8" × 3'-0" × 6'-6"
pinboard 7'-6" × 8'-0"

Figure 23–1 Typical Unit Furnishing Arrangements in 7' × 6" by 7' × 6" Space.

There is adequate clear-space beneath desk for stretching and crossing legs; desk unit includes soft-covered tilt-back chair (doubles as an easy chair).

4. The closet unit is free-standing and moveable; it may contain drawers and double as a dresser; optional free-standing bureau (compatible with desk height for added surface). Some minimum dimensions for closet unit:

Full length hanging space: 60" high   20–30" wide
½ length hanging space: 30" high   16" wide
24" closet depth

The external surface of closet (back, sides, front) is usable as tackboard surface.

5. Wall surface panels provided for painting, hanging, etc.; panels are moveable and are dimensioned 7'6" x 4 or 7'6" x 8; panels may be installed and replaced without complicated tools.

Room

USER NEEDS:

1. For the most part students want single rooms; a few, usually incoming freshmen, will prefer double rooms; some students will accept roommates to reduce costs.

2. Some students will want to change from double to single accommodations as they progress through school.

3. In general, students want choice in the cost of their accommodations; they want to choose from a variety of living conditions; various amenities, single or double, etc., according to their pocketbook needs.

4. Student residents will want to put up an occasional visitor; off-campus commuters may want to rent sleep and study space for one or two days/week only.

5. Even when sharing a room students want a personal space (capable of containing all their furnishings and equipment) that is visually separate from their roommate.

6. Students prefer privacy in bathrooms; for the most part they resist "gang bathrooms."

7. Students want to have visitors in their quarters without inconvenience to others.

8. Acoustical privacy is an essential students require of their rooms; double doors with buffer space is a sure way of providing this kind of privacy.

9. Students may want to come and go in their private space without running into others from their shared living space.

10. Total space per student should not, for economic feasibility, exceed 250 square feet or $5000.

Specifications:

1. All rooms are of three types:
   a) strictly single rooms   b) optional, single or double rooms
   c) strictly double rooms
   (Note: types b and c can accommodate visitors, e.g., commuters needing an occasional sleep/study space.)

381

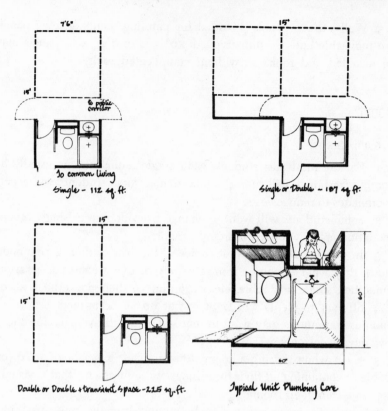

7'6"

15'

to public
corridor

To common living

single - 112 sq. ft.

15'

Single or Double - 187 sq. ft.

15'

15'

Double or Double + transient space - 225 sq. ft.

Typical Unit Plumbing Core

60"

60"

1. Single Occupancy—112 Square Feet

2. Single or Double Occupancy—187 Square Feet

3. Double Occupancy (with guest space)—225 Square Feet

4. Typical Unit Plumbing Core

Figure 23–2   Typical Unit Plans.

2. All rooms are based on a 7′6″ module; each module capable of containing complete personal territory for one student; bed, storage, and desk in a visually protected space.

3. Each room has its own bathroom core.

4. Each room has two entrances:

    a) one entrance directly onto public passageway;

    b) one entrance to common living space shared by several other rooms.

5. Each entrance has two doors separated by a usable acoustic buffer space.

6. Each room receives natural light from at least one window; the window is at eye level for a person both sitting and standing.

382

NOTES

1. Jencks, Christopher and David Reisman, "Patterns of Residential Education: A Case Study of Harvard," in Nevitt Sanford, ed., *The American College* (New York: John Wiley and Sons, 1964), p. 732. Average cost in 1967 is closer to $6000 per student.

2. Trow, Martin, "Reflections on the Residence Hall Program," unpublished speech given at Residence Hall Workshop, Berkeley, October 1961.

3. See works by John B. Calhoun, Robert Ardrey, H. Hediger, H. Tinbergen, C. R. Carpenter, K. Lorentz.

4. See works by Edward T. Hall, Robert Sommer, Humphrey Osmond.

5. *Daily Californian*, October 20, 1961.

6. *Daily Californian*, November 10, 1961.

7. Wriston, Henry, *Academic Procession* (New York: Columbia University Press, 1955), p. 192, quoted in Trow, *op. cit.*

8. *Daily Californian*, February 17, 1964.

9. *Daily Californian*, February 6, 1964.

10. *Daily Californian*, March 1, 1965.

11. Friedlander, Neal and Alan T. Osborne, "Apartments for Women," *Comment*, University of Pennsylvania, Philadelphia, Pa., Fall 1965, p. 8.

12. See Theodore Reik, *Of Love and Lust: On the Psychoanalysis of Romantic and Sexual Emotions*, or Jurgen Ruesch and Weldon Kees, *Non-Verbal Communication* (Berkeley: University of California Press, 1956).

13. *Oakland Tribune*, February 6, 1964.

14. Program for the competition for dormitories written by John Lyon Reid.

15. Winter, Chester N., "Full-Scale Model Gives Room a Trial Run," *College and University Business*, Vol. 37, No. 6, December 1964, pp. 47–49.

16. University Facilities Research Center and Educational Facilities Laboratories, *High Rise or Low Rise? A Study of Decision Factors in Residence Hall Planning*, New York, November 1964, p. 44.

17. *Daily Californian*, March 13, 1964.

24

Old People's Flatlets at Stevenage

MINISTRY OF HOUSING AND LOCAL GOVERNMENT

Architectural design has been described as a process of successive approximation in which the architect proposes a series of tentative hypotheses stating a reasonable fit between the shifting needs of building users and the environments they plan to inhabit. If this view of the design process is valid, then the behavioral sciences must be involved in a continuing collaborative relationship during the design process. In practice, this means that in addition to helping develop basic program information, sociologists and psychologists should also have a hand in translating the program into a design scheme and in evaluating completed projects. The aim of this form of collaboration should be to use the information about user response turned up in the building evaluation as a basis for improving the quality of future design.

This total approach to cooperation between architecture and the behavioral sciences has been tried with some success in England, particularly by the research and development groups in the national ministries responsible for building. Teams made up of architects, sociologists, cost estimators (the British call them quantity surveyors), and engineers work together in the same office. They assess existing environments, use this information in the formulation of programs (in British usage, briefs), collaborate on the design of the project, assess the design once it is built, and then use this information for the subsequent round of design and construction.

The following selection reports on such a combined effort made by the Ministry of Housing and Local Government to develop a scheme for old people's housing in the new town of Stevenage, outside London. The Ministry had been concerned with housing for the aged since the 1950s, when it first published general recommendations for architectural standards for such housing. In 1962 it issued reports of two studies (made in 1960 and 1961) that had assessed user response to some of the existing old people's housing in England, and on the basis of these inquiries developed a new set of standards and design recommendations. The Stevenage housing, which made use of these studies, was built in 1962, and the Stevenage report, from which the selection reprinted here is taken, is a reassessment of the standards and basic schemes that emerged from the 1960 and 1961 studies.

Reprinted from Ministry of Housing and Local Government
Design Bulletin 11—*Old People's Flatlets at Stevenage* (London:
HMSO, 1966), pp. 3–6. Reprinted by permission of the
Controller of Her Britannic Majesty's Stationery Office.

Two features of the assessment studies are especially worthy of note. One is the wide range of user needs and requirements that were included in the project brief and evaluated in the finished units. These requirements include elements relating to basic biological needs, such as sanitary facilities, heating, ventilation, lighting, and sleeping accommodations, as well as elements relating to social needs, such as the design of common rooms and the provision of facilities for social life. The second is the deliberate effort on the part of the research and development group to incorporate the design of social conveniences into the physical design. For example, the initial assessment studies of 1960 and 1961 indicated the importance of providing a warden in old people's housing and of making sure the warden would be available to deal with the emergencies that continually plague the elderly. Accommodation for a warden, usually a woman and often a woman whose husband is responsible for the physical maintenance of the building, was included in both the basic project brief and the recommended design schemes. This amenity seems to have worked out quite well in meeting the needs of the old people, although the warden herself could have used more privacy.

□

Introduction

1. For some years the Ministry of Housing and Local Government has urged local authorities to build more dwellings of all kinds for old people and to provide grouped flatlets, with full-time resident wardens, for those old people who may sometimes need a helping hand. The Ministry's recommendations on the design of grouped flatlets were published in 1958 and 1960.[1]

2. During 1960 and 1961 the Ministry carried out more detailed studies of the problems of old age. The results of these studies were published as two of the Ministry's series of design bulletins.[2] In particular, Design Bulletin 2, which will be often referred to in this bulletin, embodied a survey of the first six blocks of flatlets for old people constructed by local authorities in this country.

3. The intention of these studies was that they should be put to practical effect, and the Ministry had decided to undertake, as a development project, the design and construction of a grouped flatlets scheme. The Stevenage Development Corporation, who were at the time about to make further provision for old people, agreed to be the client authority for the development project. The Ministry's architects thus acted in effect as private architects to the Corporation.

4. The Corporation's Architects' Department collaborated with the Ministry and advised on the project. Their quantity surveyors, with

385

their detailed knowledge of local conditions, were responsible for general cost advice and undertook the preparation of the cost plan and analyses and of the bills of quantities. The Corporation's landscape architect carried out the design of the landscaping.

5. The development team within the Ministry consisted of architects, an administrator, a sociologist and a housing manager. The advice in *Flatlets for old people* and *More flatlets for old people* was taken as a starting point, but it was implicit in the terms of reference for the project that the detailed suggestions in those two handbooks would be modified where necessary to take account of the team's surveys and investigations.

6. The ever-lengthening time needed to carry out building contracts, the scarcity of site labor and increasing shortages of technical staff highlighted the need for the development of a component system of construction. Although this was not part of the original brief, it was undertaken as part of the project. A nominated contractor was appointed to collaborate during the design period.

7. The project included a social appraisal made after the flatlets, now called Ross Court, had been occupied for 18 months. The summary which follows juxtaposes in parallel columns the findings of Design Bulletin 2 and the other preliminary studies, the requirements of the project brief, and the evaluation of the project brief in the appraisal survey. This makes it possible to see, in outline, what the user requirements were, how far they were planned for and what lessons are to be learnt from them.

8. At the same time, sweeping conclusions should not be drawn from either the project or the appraisal. Design Bulletin 2 was compiled from only six local authority flatlet schemes and the number of elderly residents interviewed was ninety-nine. The appraisal discussed here is based on interviews with only twenty. Thus the requirements in the project brief and the findings of the appraisal survey reflect the views of a minute sample of elderly people. And no two schemes of this type are exactly similar in site, cost, methods of selecting tenants, etc.

9. However, many of the lessons to be drawn from the Stevenage project, such as elderly people's extreme sensitiveness to draughts and their sturdy refusal to do just what they were expected to do in such matters as placing their beds, are probably of general application. Since 1960, when the study embodied in Design Bulletin 2 was carried out, many more local authorities have embarked on flatlet schemes

and will have encountered similar problems to those which faced the Development Group's architects. But others, who are contemplating schemes, may find the account of the Stevenage project and the lessons to be learnt from it of value.

The Surveys

SURVEY FOR USER REQUIREMENTS

10. At the outset, in 1960, the sociologist carried out a survey of the first six blocks of flatlets built by local authorities in different parts of the country. Information was gathered by observation and by interviews with housing managers, wardens and tenants. The results of the survey are published as Design Bulletin 2.

11. In addition, visits were made to accommodation of all types, from self-contained dwellings to welfare homes. The views of managements and designers, as well as those of old people themselves, were heard, and the quantity, size and arrangement of furniture were studied. The information was recorded and used during the planning stage.

12. Little information about the physical dimensions of old people was available. As this design information was urgently needed a small pilot study of these dimensions was commissioned. The results are set out in Design Bulletin 1.

APPRAISAL SURVEY

13. In the winter of 1963–1964, when the flatlets had been occupied for some 18 months, as many tenants as were willing were interviewed by a team of sociologists and architects. Two married couples out of four were interviewed, and sixteen people out of twenty living on their own. The sociologists used a prepared questionnaire, and the architects drew sketches of the furniture arrangement and recorded the amount of furniture in each flat.

The Summary

14. The following paragraphs contain a summary of the findings of the studies for user requirements; the project brief which emerged from them; and the evaluation of the project's design in the appraisal survey.

Study Findings	*Project Brief*	*Evaluation*

15. Warden

The success of any flatlets scheme for old people depended largely on the qualities of the warden. The wardens visited had widely different backgrounds, from nursing to housekeeping. Most were kindly and understanding with sympathy for the difficulties of old age, and willing to be helpful in most situations.

The scheme to be planned with accommodation for one warden, looking after twenty people living alone in bed-sitting rooms and four couples in one-bedroom flats.

The warden's duties are described in detail in Design Bulletin 2 (pages 2–3). In general, they exercised inconspicuous supervision, gave good-neighborly day-to-day assistance to the tenants, helped them in emergencies and acted as the link with the management.

The accommodation of the warden to allow easy access to the tenants.

This was achieved, but the warden should have been given more privacy.

The contact between warden and tenants was easier where covered and heated circulation space was provided between the flatlets and the warden's house.

Link warden's house and the flatlets with heated corridor.

Successful.

---

16. Number of Tenants

Twenty people living alone and four married couples.

The total number appeared satisfactory, but there were too few men living alone to be company for each other.

---

17. One-Person Bed-Sitting Rooms

Minimum-sized rooms of 140 sq. ft. caused some dissatisfaction, but rooms of 170–180 sq. ft. satisfied almost all tenants.

Bed-sitting rooms to be at least 170 sq. ft.

The bed-sitting room of 166 sq. ft. proved adequate in size, but was designed too specifically for a preconceived quantity and arrangement of furniture. Bulkier furniture than was expected sometimes obscured low windows.

Study Findings	Project Brief	Evaluation
		A design suited to a greater variety of furniture arrangement would have been preferable.
It was evident that a bed recess gave a more convenient arrangement of furniture, but there were complaints about ventilation and the absence of a window in the recess.	A well-ventilated bed recess with a window and an interesting view to be provided.	Ventilation and lighting of the bed recess were found satisfactory, although the position of the windows did not allow air movement across the bed recess. Often the head of the bed was placed out of reach of the light switch and bell pull, and study is needed of other ways of placing these so that they can be used from different positions. An optional curtain to draw across the bed recess would have been appreciated. The considerable demand for separate bedrooms should be borne in mind in future schemes.
Sound reduction between corridor and flatlet was inadequate where front doors from the corridor opened directly into the bed-sitting room.	A lobby should be provided between corridor and bed-sitting room.	The only disturbing noise heard from the corridor was doors banging. Door fittings to prevent this are needed.
18. Storage Provision for linen and brooms was often inadequate.	All dwellings to be fitted with hanging space for clothes and with linen and broom cupboards.	Adequate, but a shelf needed in the broom cupboard. In general, more shelving would have been appreciated.
19. Kitchens Cupboard kitchens in bed-sitting rooms were generally criticized for lack of storage and food preparation space, and for the difficulty of eliminating cooking smells.	Separate kitchens required.	The separate kitchens were found satisfactory, but storage capacity was often insufficient and the food cupboard was too near the hot water cylinder.

Study Findings	Project Brief	Evaluation
Top shelves were sometimes beyond the reach of tenants, working tops at unsuitable heights, and sinks too wide for comfortable reach to the taps.	Anthropometric data to be used to determine optimum heights and widths for fittings and sinks.	No person in normal health had any difficulty in reaching any shelves.

20. Shared Sanitary Facilities

In flatlets, only half the tenants used the bath. This was usually due to physical disability rather than to any objection to sharing. Some tenants with skin disorders were worried about the possibility of passing them on.	Baths to be shared in the ratio of one to four persons. A variety of arrangements and aids to be provided for different physical disabilities. The shower to be designed for easy use.	The number of baths was ample, and sharing did not lead to any difficulties. The aids were useful, but in a small scheme of this kind not so many different ones were needed. The shower was used by a handicapped man, but otherwise not liked or used at all.
In flatlets where handbasins were not provided, only one-fifth of the tenants used those provided in the shared bathrooms and w.c.s: they preferred to use their own kitchen sinks.	Each flatlet to have a handbasin.	This was generally used.
Although there were few objections to sharing a w.c., it was clear this was inconvenient to some tenants, particularly at night, and encouraged the use of pots.	Each flatlet to have a w.c. (The Development Corporation felt that in any case the housing standards of the New Town demanded this.)	The individual w.c. was much preferred to more space in the flatlet. The internal w.c. compartment, though occasionally criticized, was satisfactory.

21. Common Room and Social Life

Wardens explained that, though most old people enjoyed watching television, it had limited the use of the common room for other social activities and caused some arguments over program selection.	The common room to have two separate spaces, one for television viewing, the other for other social activities.	In practice, one large subdivisible room would have been more useful than the two rooms.
It was observed that in flatlet blocks the corridor was used as a social meeting place.	Informal sitting spaces to be provided in the corridor.	These spaces were well-sited and well-justified.

390

Study Findings	Project Brief	Evaluation
Most guest rooms in flatlet schemes were large, and none had been used for accommodating visitors.	Only minimum provision to be made for guests.	In fact, no provision was made for guests, as the idea of using the small common room also as a guest room could not be carried out because it was a through room. The tenants of the flatlets expressed no wish for guest rooms, but they usually had relatives living near who could presumably put up guests. The warden, however, would have appreciated a spare room for guests.
A common room in the center of the building with a view of life going on was more popular than a secluded one. Planning the warden's flat next to the common room encouraged the warden to help things along from her kitchen when necessary.	The common room to overlook the center of interest, and to adjoin the warden's accommodation.	The common room was well placed in the center of the flatlets, but it was unnecessarily disturbing to have it as a corridor from the front door to one wing of the flatlets.
22. Call-Bell Most flatlets were provided with a warning bell system connected to the warden's home, but some indicator boards did not identify the flat which needed help. Very few schemes made provision for someone to deputize when the warden left the building.	Devise efficient call-bell system enabling a tenant to deputize for the warden.	The warden would have liked the call-bell to sound in her bedroom or her garden, by a switchover. And a supplementary indicator outside rooms could have been provided. The deputizing system worked well.
23. Heating Central heating was the service most highly valued in the flatlets studied. Tenants had many problems with open fires, which are described in Design Bulletin 1, page 4.	Provide the kind of central heating best suited to the physiological needs of old people.	The off-peak electric floor-warming system was chosen to ensure warmth throughout without stuffiness and to avoid the effects of dust-laden air on sufferers from respiratory complaints. (As the first floor is timber, under floor heating could not be used there.)

391

Study Findings	Project Brief	Evaluation
		It succeeded in this, but as operated initially did not yield sufficient heat in a very cold winter. Even so, it was too much at night for many tenants. Owing to the cold it was used to provide a higher temperature than originally calculated, and this, together with a structural defect, resulted in the running costs being higher than originally estimated. Costs were reduced in the second year, but were still high. At first the level of heating was uneven through the week but this has been adjusted.
24. Communal Food Stores In centrally heated flatlets there were problems of keeping food cool.	Investigate the provision of communal refrigerators.	Provision of communal refrigerators has been justified, although the milk is not delivered directly to them. However, the refrigerators should be on the same floor level as the flats.
25. Laundry Survey suggested that about one-third of the tenants were able to do all their own washing, about a quarter were not doing any at all, and the remainder were washing small items at home and sending the larger wash to the laundry. The scheme where the highest percentage of old people did all their own washing was well equipped with washing and drying machines. Where constant advice and assistance was given by the warden, all the old people used the machines; in schemes	Investigate provision of suitable washing machines, and outdoor and indoor drying facilities.	One type of washing machine installed proved easy to operate, but the other type did not and is being replaced. Their provision was justified by their use, but more outdoor drying facilities are needed.

Study Findings	*Project Brief*	*Evaluation*

where explanation and encouragement were not given, the complexity of the machines tended to discourage the old people from using them. There were very few complaints about drying arrangements when both indoor and outdoor facilities were provided within easy distance of the flats.

26. Floor Preference

Most of the tenants interviewed lived on the ground floor and only a few would have preferred to live any higher. The preference of some tenants for the first floor is discussed in Design Bulletin 2, page 10; with increasing age and disability this preference naturally decreased.	Most of the accommodation to be provided at ground level.	No one was dissatisfied with his floor level, and there was ample room on the ground floor for all who could not manage stairs easily.

NOTES

1. Ministry of Housing and Local Government. *Flatlets for old people*. HMSO 1958 (2s. 6d) and *More flatlets for old people*. HMSO 1960 (2s.).

2. Ministry of Housing and Local Government. Design bulletins: 1. *Some aspects of designing for old people*. HMSO 1962 (2s. 6d.) and 2. *Grouped flatlets for old people: a sociological study*. HMSO 1962 (5s.).

25

Typology and Design Method

ALAN COLQUHOUN

The use of the behavioral sciences in architecture is often based on the assumption that the architect, by relying on the techniques and concepts of the behavioral sciences, will be able to circumvent some of the traditional difficulties of arriving at design solutions. One such difficulty, present in every design situation, is that of closing the gap between the information contained in a building program and the final organization of three-dimensional space that constitutes the constructed artifact. Many architects and designers who use the behavioral sciences in their work often seem to be arguing that their solutions can be derived more or less directly from the program, or if this is not possible, that the gap can be closed and the solutions obtained from the interaction of the program's content with the architect's intuitive, creative ability.

In the following selection Colquhoun argues against this doctrine. He is concerned with the application of the biological and engineering sciences to design, what he calls biotechnical determinism, but his position is equally relevant to architectural solutions based upon sociological or psychological data. His argument is that both the belief in a scientifically determined architecture and the belief in an architecture based on the combination of science and intuition rest on false premises. With regard to the former doctrine Colquhoun cites the autobiographical statements of several architects who have tried to use objective data and mathematical techniques in their own work. These statements make it quite clear that the designer is always faced with making voluntary decisions and that these decisions are based on intentions and purposes that exist prior to the development of the program. In other words, Colquhoun is contending that architects or planners who claim, in the manner of evolutionary theorists, that their solutions follow from their data in a teleologically determined manner, simply do not understand the mental processes they experience during the process of design.

Colquhoun's argument against the significance of free intuition is based upon anthropological findings, in particular the structuralist theories of Lévi-Strauss. According to Lévi-Strauss the images and representations that develop in a society are not simply derived from objective facts—there is, Lévi-Strauss argues, no discernible biological basis for explaining the variety of kinship systems that emerge in different societies or the preferences

Reprinted from Alan Colquhoun, "Typology and Design Method," in Arena, The Architectural Association Journal, London (June 1967): 11–14, by permission of the editor.

people exhibit for particular kinship forms. Instead, kinship systems are arbitrary systems of social interrelationships whose sources can be found in the histories and rule systems of particular cultures. Although these rules exhibit certain regularities, the regularities exist at the level of culture and cannot be reduced to biological or technical principles. Colquhoun cites the conclusions of Lévi-Strauss to support his assertion that the freedom of the individual imagination is a fiction, a fiction built into modern architectural thinking. In his view it derives from the expressionist phase in modern architecture, which was so popular in Europe during the 1920s and is still pervasive in American design circles. This may explain why it is that the behavioral science approach has been more popular among those American architects who identify themselves with the modern movement than it is among those still committed to conventional styles of building.

Given the fact that design solutions cannot be based entirely on scientific knowledge about people's needs and behavior or on the fusion of this knowledge with the designer's creative ability, Colquhoun turns to the much maligned tradition of "building typologies" as a source of design solutions. Building typologies, in his use of the term, are sociospatial organizational schemata, which through time have yielded forms appropriate for sheltering human activities. Since, given the nature of architectural phenomena, reliance on these typologies is, in Colquhoun's view, inevitable, designers would be better off to admit their influence. Only to the degree that the importance of typologies is made manifest, and their influence made the subject of discussion and evaluation, can one hope to achieve a rational architecture, that is an architecture that is neither deterministic or intuitive, but one that makes the most appropriate use of both scientific knowledge and the individual designer's creative ability. Colquhoun is astute enough to recognize the possibility that his theory will be taken to justify a conservative stance toward building and the rejection of advances in the use of scientific knowledge and innovations in building form, but he obviously believes that an intelligent use of his approach can avoid these pitfalls.

□

During the last few years a great deal of attention has been given to the problem of design methodology, and to the process of design as a branch of the wider process of problem solving.

Many people believe—not without reason—that the intuitive methods of design traditionally used by architects are incapable of dealing with the complexity of the problems to be solved, and that without sharper tools of analysis and classification, the designer tends to fall back on previous examples for the solution of new problems—on type solutions.

One of the designers and educators who has been consistently preoccupied by this problem is Tomas Maldonado. At a recent seminar at Princeton University, Maldonado admitted that, in cases where it was

395

not possible to classify every observable activity in an architectural program, it might be necessary to use a typology of architectural forms in order to arrive at a solution. But he added that these forms were like a cancer in the body of the solution, and that as our techniques of classification become more systematic it should be possible to eliminate them altogether.

Now, it is my belief that beneath the apparently practical and hard-headed aspect of these ideas lies an aesthetic doctrine. It will be the purpose of this selection to show this to be the case, and, further, to try and show that it is untenable without considerable modification.

One of the most frequent arguments used against typological procedures in architecture has been that they are a vestige of an age of craft. It is held that the use of models by craftsmen became less necessary as the development of scientific techniques enabled man to discover the general laws underlying the technical solutions of the preindustrial age.

The vicissitudes of the words "art" and "science" certainly indicate that there is a valid distinction to be drawn between artefacts that are the result of the application of the laws of physical science and those that are the result of mimesis and intuition. Before the rise of modern science, tradition, habit and imitation were the methods by which all artefacts were made, whether these artefacts were mainly utilitarian or mainly religious. The word "art" was used to describe the skill necessary to produce all such artefacts. With the development of modern science, the word "art" was progressively restricted to the case of artefacts that did not depend on the general laws of physical science, but continued to be based on tradition and the ideal of the final form of the work as a fixed ideal.

But this distinction ignores the extent to which artefacts have not only a "use" value in the crudest sense, but also an "exchange" value.

The craftsman had an image of the object in his mind's eye when starting to make it. Whether this object was a cult image (say a sculpture) or a kitchen utensil, it was an object of cultural exchange, and it formed part of a system of communications within society. Its "message" value was precisely the image of the final form which the craftsman held in his mind's eye as he was making it and to which his artefact corresponded as nearly as possible. In spite of the development of the scientific method we must still attribute such social or iconic values to the products of technology, and recognize that they play an essential role in the generation and development of the physical tools of our environment. It is easy to see that the class of artefacts that continue to be made according to the traditional methods (for example paintings or musical compositions) have a predominantly iconic purpose, but such a purpose is not so often recognized in the creation of the environment as a whole. This fact is concealed from us because the intentions of the design process are "hidden" in the overt details of performance specification.

The idolization of "primitive" man, and the fundamentalist attitude which this generates, have also discouraged the acceptance of such iconic values. There has been a tendency since the eighteenth century to look on the age of primitive man as a golden age in which man lived close to nature. For many years, for instance, the primitive hut or one of its derivatives has been taken as the starting point for architectural evolution, and has been the subject of first-year design programs, and it would not be an exaggeration to say that frequently a direct line of descent is presumed to exist from the noble savage, through the utilitarian crafts to modern science and technology. In so far as it is based on the idea of the noble savage, this idea is quite baseless. The cosmological systems of primitive man were very intellectual and very artificial. To take only kinship systems, the following quotation from the French anthropologist Claude Lévi-Strauss will make the point clear: "Certainly," he says, "the biological family is present and persists in human society. But what gives to kinship its character as a social fact is not what it must conserve of nature; it is the essential step by which it separates itself from nature. A system of kinship does not consist of objective blood ties; it exists only in the consciousness of men; it is an arbitrary system of representations, not the spontaneous development of a situation of fact." [1]

There seems to be a close parallel between such systems and the way modern man still approaches the world. And what was true of primitive man in all the ramifications of his practical and emotional life—namely the need to *represent* the phenomenal world in such a way that it becomes a coherent and logical system—persists in our own organizations, and more particularly in our attitude towards the man-made objects of our environment. An example of the way this applies to contemporary man is in the creation of what are called sociospatial schemata. Our sense of place and relationship in, say, an urban environment, or in a building, are not dependent on any objective fact that is measurable; they are phenomenal. The purpose of the aesthetic organization of our environment is to capitalize on this subjective schematization, and make it socially available. The resulting organization does not correspond in a one-to-one relationship with the objective facts, but is an artificial construct which *represents* these facts in a socially recognizable way. It follows that the representational systems which are developed are, in a real sense, independent of the quantifiable facts of the environment, and this is particularly true if the environment is changing very rapidly.

No system of representation, no meta-language, however, is totally independent of the facts which constitute the objective world. The modern movement in architecture was an attempt to modify the representational systems which had been inherited from the pre-industrial past, and which no longer seemed operable within the context of a rapidly changing technology. One of the main doctrines at the root of this transformation was based essentially on a return to nature, deriving from the romantic movement, but ostensibly changed from a desire to imitate the surface of natural forms or to operate at a craft level, to a belief in the ability of science to reveal the essence of nature's mode of operation.

Underlying this doctrine was an implied belief in bio-technical determination. And it is from this theory that the current belief in the supreme importance of scientific methods of analysis and classification derives. The essence of the functional doctrine of the modern movement was not that beauty or order or meaning was unnecessary, but that it could no longer be found in the deliberate search for final forms. The path by which the artefact affected the observer aesthetically was seen as short-circuiting the process of formalization. Form was merely the result of a logical process by which the operational needs and the operational techniques were brought together. Ultimately these would fuse in a kind of biological extension of life, and function and technology would become totally transparent. The theory of Buckminster Fuller is an extreme example of this doctrine.

The relation of this notion to Spencerian evolutionary theory is very striking. According to this theory the purpose of prolonging life and the species must be attributed to the process as a whole, but at no particular moment in the process is it possible to see this purpose as a conscious one. The process is therefore unconscious and teleological. In the same way, the bio-technical determinism of the modern movement was teleological because it saw the aesthetic of architectural form as something which was achieved without the conscious interference of the designer, but something which none the less was postulated as his ultimate purpose.

It is clear that this doctrine contradicts any theory which would give priority to an intentional iconic form, and it attempts to absorb

398

the process by which man tries to make a representation of the world of phenomena back into a process of unconscious evolution. To what extent has it been successful, and to what extent can it be shown to be possible?

It seems evident, in the first place, that the theory begs the whole question of the iconic significance of forms. Those in the field of design who were—and are—preaching pure technology and so-called objective design method as a sufficient and necessary means of producing environmental devices, persistently attribute iconic power to the creations of technology, which they worship to a degree inconceivable in a scientist. I said earlier that it was in the power of all artefacts to become icons, no matter whether or not they were specifically created for this purpose. Perhaps I might mention certain objects of the nineteenth-century world of technology which had power of this kind —steamships and locomotives, to give only two examples. Even though these objects were made ostensibly with utilitarian purposes in mind, they quickly became *gestalt* entities, which were difficult to disassemble in the mind's eye into their component parts. The same is true of later technical devices such as cars and airplanes. The fact that these objects have been imbued with aesthetic unity and have become carriers of so much meaning indicates that a process of selection and isolation has taken place which is quite redundant from the point of view of their particular functions. We must therefore look upon the aesthetic and iconic qualities of artefacts as being due, not so much to an inherent property, but to a sort of availability or redundancy in them in relation to human feeling.

The literature of modern architecture is full of statements which indicate that after all the known operational needs have been satisfied, there is still a wide area of choice in the final configuration. I should like to quote two designers who have used mathematical methods to arrive at architectural solutions. The first is Yona Friedmann, who uses these methods to arrive at a hierarchy of organization in the program. In a recent lecture, in which he was describing methods of computing the relative positions of functions within a three-dimensional city grid, Friedmann acknowledged that the designer is always after computation, faced with a choice of alternatives, all of which are equally good from an operational point of view.

The second is Yannis Xenakis, who, in designing the Philips Pavilion while he was in the office of Le Corbusier, used mathematical procedures to determine the form of the enclosing structure. In the book which Philips published to describe this building, Xenakis says that calculation provided the characteristic form of the structure, but that after this logic no longer operated; and the compositional arrangement had to be decided on the basis of intuition.

From these statements it would appear that a purely teleological doctrine of technico-aesthetic forms is not tenable. At whatever stage in the design process it may occur, it seems that the designer is always faced with making voluntary decisions, and that the configurations which he arrives at must be the result of an *intention,* and not merely the result of a deterministic process. The following statement of Le Corbusier tends to reinforce this point of view. "My intellect," he says, "does not accept the adoption of the modules of Vignola in the matter of building. I claim that harmony exists between the objects one is dealing with. The chapel at Ronchamp perhaps shows that architecture is not an affair of columns but an affair of plastic events. Plastic events are not regulated by scholastic or academic formulae, they are free and innumerable."

Although this statement is a defense of functionalism against the academic imitation of past forms and the determinism it denies is academic rather than scientific, it none-the-less stresses the release that follows from functional considerations, rather than their power of determining the solution.

One of the most uninhibited statements of this kind comes from Moholy-Nagy. In his description of the design course at the Institute of Design in Chicago, he makes the following defense of the free operation of intuition. "The training," he says, "is directed towards imagination and inventiveness, a basic condition for the ever-changing industrial scene, for technology in flux. The last step in this technique is the emphasis on integration through the conscious search for relationships. The intuitive working methods of genius give a clue to this process. The unique ability of the genius can be approximated by everybody if one of its essential features be apprehended: the flashlike act of connecting elements not obviously belonging together. If the same methodology were used generally in all fields we could have *the* key to the age—seeing everything in relationship.[2]

We can now begin to build up a picture of the general body of doctrine embedded in the modern movement. It consists of a tension of two apparently contradictory ideas—biotechnical determinism on the one hand, and free expression on the other. What seems to have happened is that, in the act of giving a new validity to the demands of function as an extension of nature's mode of operation, it has left a vacuum where previously there was a body of traditional practice. The whole field of aesthetics, with its ideological foundations and its belief in ideal beauty, has been swept aside. All that is left in its place is permissive expression, the total freedom of the genius which, if we but knew it, resides in us all. What appears on the surface as a hard, rational discipline of design, turns out rather paradoxically to be a mystical belief in the intuitional process.

I would like now to turn back to the statement by Maldonado which I mentioned at the beginning of this selection. He said that so long as our classification techniques were unable to establish all the parameters of a problem, it might be necessary to use a typology of forms to fill the gap. From the examples of the statements made by modern designers it would seem that it is indeed never possible to state all the parameters of a problem. Truly quantifiable criteria always leave a choice for the designer to make. In modern architectural theory this choice has been generally conceived of as based on intuition working in a cultural vacuum. In mentioning typology, Maldonado is suggesting something quite new, and something which has been rejected again and again by modern theorists. He is suggesting that the area of pure intuition must be based on a knowledge of past solutions to related problems, and that creation is a process of adapting forms derived either from past needs or on past aesthetic ideologies to the needs of the present. Although he regards this as a provisional solution—"a cancer in the body of the solution"—he none the less recognizes that this is the actual procedure which designers follow.

I suggest that this is true, and moreover that it is true in all fields of design and not only that of architecture. I have referred to the argument that the more rigorously the general physical or mathematical laws are applied to the solution of design problems the less it is necessary to have a mental picture of the final form. But, although we may postulate an ideal state in which these laws correspond exactly to the objective world, in fact this is not the case. Laws are not found in nature. They are constructs of the human mind; they are models which are valid so long as events do not prove them to be wrong. They are models, as it were, at one remove from pictorial models. Not only this. Technology is frequently faced with different problems which are not logically consistent. All the problems of aircraft configuration, for example, could not be solved unless there was give and take in the application of physical laws. The position of the power unit is a variable, so is the configuration of the wings and tailplane. The position of one affects the shape of the other. The application of general laws is a necessary ingredient of the form. But it is not a sufficient one for determining the actual configuration. And in a world of pure technology this area of free choice is invariably dealt with by adapting previous solutions.

In the world of architecture this problem becomes even more crucial because general laws of physics and the empirical facts are even less capable of fixing a final configuration than in the case of an airplane or a bridge. Recourse to some kind of typological model is even more necessary in this case.

It may be argued that, in spite of the fact that there is an area of free choice beyond that of operation, this freedom lies in the details (where, for instance, personal "taste" might legitimately operate). This could probably be shown to be true of such technically complex objects as airplanes, where the topological relationships are largely determined by the application of physical laws. But it does not seem to apply to architecture. On the contrary, because of the comparatively simple environmental pressures that operate on buildings, the topological relationships are hardly at all determined by physical laws. In the case of Philips Pavilion, for example, it was not only the acoustic requirements which established the basic configuration, but also the need for a building which would convey a certain impression of vertigo and fantasy. It is in the details of plan or equipment that these laws become stringent, and not in the general arrangement. Where the designer decides to be governed by operational factors, he works in terms of a thoroughly nineteenth-century rationalism, for example in the case of the office buildings of Mies and SOM, where purely pragmatic planning and cost considerations converge on a received neoclassic aesthetic to create simple cubes, regular frames and cores. It is interesting that in most of the projects where form determinants are held to be technical or operational in an avant-garde sense, rationalism and cost are discarded for forms of a fantastic or expressionist kind. Frequently, as in the case of "Archigram," forms are borrowed from other disciplines, such as space engineering or pop art. Valid as these iconographic procedures may be—and before dismissing them one would have to investigate them in relation to the work of Le Corbusier and the Russian constructivists which borrowed the forms of ships and engineering structures—they can hardly be compatible with a doctrine of determinism, if we are to regard this as a *modus operandi,* rather than a remote and utopian ideal.

The exclusion by modern architectural theory of typologies, and its belief in the freedom of the intuition, can at any rate be partially explained by the more general theory of expression which was current at the turn of the century. This theory can be seen most clearly in the work and theories of certain painters—notably Kandinsky, both in his paintings and in his book *Point and Time to Plane,* which outlines the theory on which his paintings are based. Expressionist theory rejected all historical manifestations of art, just as modern architectural theory rejected all historical forms of architecture. To it these manifestations were an ossification of technical and cultural attitudes whose *raison d'être* had ceased to exist. The theory was based on the belief that shapes have physiognomic or expressive content which communicates itself to us directly. This view has been subjected to a great deal of criticism, and one of its most convincing refutations occurs in E. H. Gombrich's book *Meditations on a Hobby Horse.* Gombrich demonstrates that an arrangement of forms such as is found in a painting by Kandinsky is in fact very low in content, unless we attribute to these forms some system of conventional meanings not inherent in the forms themselves. His thesis is that physiognomic forms are ambiguous, though not wholly without expressive value, and that they can only be interpreted within a particular cultural ambience. One of the ways he illustrates this is by reference to the supposed affective qualities of colors. Gombrich points out in the now famous example of traffic signals, that we are dealing with a conventional and not a physiognomic meaning, and maintains that it would be equally logical to reverse the meaning system, so that red indicated action and forward movement, and green inaction, quietness and caution.[3]

Expressionist theory probably had a very strong influence on the modern movement in architecture. Its application to architecture would be even more obvious than to painting, because of the absence, in architecture, of any forms which are overtly representational. Architecture has always, with music, been considered an abstract art, so that the theory of physiognomic forms could be applied to it without having to overcome the hurdle of anecdote representation, as in painting. But if the objections to expressionist theory are valid, then they apply to architecture as much as to painting.

If, as Gombrich suggests, forms by themselves are relatively empty of meaning, it follows that the forms which we intuit will, in the unconscious mind, tend to attract to themselves certain associations of meaning. This could mean not only that we are *not* free from the forms of the past, and from the availability of these forms as typological models, but that, if we assume we are free, we have lost control over a very active sector of our imagination, and of our power to communicate with others.

It would seem that we ought to try to establish a value system which takes account of the forms and solutions of the past, if we are to gain control over concepts which will obtrude themselves into the creative process, whether we like it or not.

There is, in fact, a close relationship between the pure functionalist or teleological theory that I have described, and expressionism, as defined by Professor Gombrich. By insisting on the use of analytical and inductive methods of design, functionalism leaves a vacuum in the form making process. This it fills with its own reductionist aesthetic—the aesthetic that claims that "intuition," with no historical dimension, can arrive spontaneously at forms which are the equivalent of fundamental operations. This procedure postulates a kind of onomatopoeic relationship between forms and their content. In the case of a biotechnico/determinist theory the content is the set of relevant functions—functions which themselves are a reduction of all the socially meaningful operations within a building—and it is assumed that the functional complex is translated into forms whose iconographical significance is nothing more than the rational structure of the functional complex itself. The existent facts of the objective functional situation are the equivalent of the existent facts of the subjective emotional situation, in the case of expression theory. But traditionally, in the work of art, the existent facts, whether subjective or objective, are less significant than the values we attribute to these facts or to the system of representation which embodies these values. The work of art, in this respect, resembles language. A language which was simply the expression of emotions would be a series of single-word exclamations; in fact language is a complex system of representation in which the basic emotions are structured into an intellectually coherent system. It would be impossible to conceive of constructing a language *a priori*. The ability to construct such a language would have to presuppose the language itself.[4] Similarly a plastic system of representation such as architecture has to presuppose the existence of a given system of representation. In neither case can the problem of formal representation be reduced to some pre-existent essence outside the formal system itself, of which the form is merely a reflection. In both cases it is necessary to postulate a conventional system embodied in typological solution/problem complexes.

My purpose in stressing this fact is not to advocate a reversion to an architecture which accepts tradition unthinkingly. This would imply that there was a fixed and immutable relation between forms and meaning. The characteristic of our age is change, and it is precisely because this is so that it is necessary to investigate the part which modifications of type solutions play in relation to problems and solutions which are without precedent in any received tradition.

I have tried to show that a reductionist theory according to which the problem/solution process can be reduced to some sort of essence is untenable. One might postulate that the process of change is carried out, not by a process of reduction, but rather by a process of exclusion, and it would seem that the history of the modern movement in all the arts lends support to this idea. If we look at the allied fields of painting and music, we can see that, in the work of a Kandinsky or a Schoenberg, traditional formal devices were not completely abandoned, but were transformed and given a new emphasis by the exclusion of ideologically repulsive iconic elements. In the case of Kandinsky it is the representational element which is excluded; in the case of Schoenberg it is the diatonic system of harmony.

The value of what I have called the process of exclusion is to enable us to see the potentiality of forms as if for the first time, and with naivety. This is the justification for the radical change in the iconic system of representation, and it is a process which we have to adopt if we are to keep and renew our awareness of the meanings which can be carried by forms. The bare bones of our culture—a culture with its own characteristic technology—must become visible to us. For this to happen, a certain scientific detachment towards our problems is essential, and with it the application of the mathematical tools proper to our culture. But these tools are unable to give us a ready-made solution to our problems. They only provide the framework, the context within which we operate.

NOTES

1. Claude Lévi-Strauss. *Structural Anthropology*. Basic Books, New York, 1963.
2. L. Moholy-Nagy. *Vision in Motion*. Paul Theobald, Chicago, 1947.
3. It is interesting that, since his book came out, the Chinese have in fact reversed the meanings of their traffic signals.
4. For the study of language as a system of symbolic representation see Cassirer, *Philosophy of Symbolic Forms*. Yale University Press, 1957. For a discussion of language in relation to literature (metalanguage) see Roland Barthes, *Essais Critiques*. Editions du Seuil, Paris, 1964.

405

26

The City as a Mechanism for Sustaining Human Contact

CHRISTOPHER ALEXANDER

In the previous selection Colquhoun argues that to believe that design solutions can be derived from scientific data alone runs the danger of misrepresenting the nature of architectural phenomena and the process through which buildings in fact get designed. From the point of view of the behavioral sciences the current interest in applying the findings of these disciplines to design runs another risk. It would appear from the way in which architects and planners tend to make use of sociology and psychology, that they do not allow these disciplines to deal with the full range of building and design issues to which they are potentially relevant.

Probably the most striking instance of this underutilization is the tendency of many architectural users of sociology or psychology either to assume that the behavioral scientist is proficient only in providing technical assistance in gathering data about user requirements, which the architect or client will then use for his own purposes, or, at the other extreme, to assume that the sociologist or psychologist is in all situations an ideologically committed representative of the neglected, and in many cases impoverished, user, and should therefore be employed in the design process as the users' spokesman. Both of these views are caricatures. In practice, most sociologists would argue that their competence to serve as technical assistants for identifying user requirements is limited, primarily because the discipline has only recently become interested in group activities in space. And many certainly eschew the role of serving as political representative for one group or class in society, even though the organization of our society today has made many people conclude that it is the poor and the blacks whose opinions and preferences are most easily overlooked in the design and building process, and who must therefore receive extra attention and support.

A more reasonable view of the potential contribution of the behavioral sciences is to regard them as concerned with the examination of the ends and purposes implicit in programs and design schemes and the evaluation of these ends, not just in terms of the needs of the user population, but from

This is an abridged version of Christopher Alexander's article,
"The City as a Mechanism for Sustaining Human Contact,"
which appeared in *Environment for Man*, edited by William R.
Ewald (Bloomington: Indiana University Press, 1967), pp. 60–102.
© 1967 by Indiana University Press. Reprinted by permission
of the publisher.

the perspective of the needs of the community as a whole. The behavioral sciences should also be regarded as capable of dealing with the full range of means, both physical and social, on which architectural solutions depend if their intentions are to be fulfilled. Used in this way the behavioral sciences are not, as they are sometimes accused of being, antithetical to the utopian tradition in architecture. Rather they offer the possibility of establishing fundamental reforms of the social and physical order on a more rational basis.

It is his sensitivity to the possibility of using behavioral research to deal with both the ends and means of design that makes Alexander's selection interesting. Its subject is the problem of loneliness, anomie, and alienation in the contemporary urban environment; the author, consistent with good sociological practice, redefines this problem as the absence of human contact. Alexander summons a substantial body of empirical research to show that the lack of human contact is the cause of many individual and social pathologies, such as psychosis and juvenile delinquency. He also discusses the evidence for the view that anomie is largely the consequence of the highly fragmented social and physical organization of urban society.

In the final portion of his selection, Alexander proposes a design scheme for reducing the amount of loneliness in the city. This scheme is an amalgam of twelve separate design elements, each of which is derived from a rational analysis of the lack of good fit between social needs and existing urban environments. The rational analysis is based on the behavioral research reported in the earlier portions of his selection. It uses a model that assumes that social pathology is the consequence of need frustration, and explains the frustration of needs in terms of the absence of compatibility between buildings and urban forms and basic psychological or group process requirements. Each of the twelve design elements proposed is justified in terms of the likelihood that it will eliminate or minimize the poor fit, thus hopefully reducing the need frustration, and, in turn, again hopefully, leading to the reduction of neurosis and anomie. The solution considered as a totality is reminiscent of many solutions developed by avant garde architects in this country and in Europe over the last 50 years: high-density housing; self-designed dwelling units; multilevel streets, corridors, and parks; abundant private and semiprivate spaces; and separate pedestrian and high-speed vehicular traffic flow systems.

Students of the relationship of architecture to behavior will be made uncomfortable by Alexander's ambition to control or influence activity patterns by providing just the right fit between the physical environment and human needs; the degree of indeterminacy in the interaction between man and the environment is a major issue which demands further investigation. From the point of view of many sociologists and architects it may be preferable for architects to design spaces with very general qualities and characteristics, on the assumption either that the users will know best how to accommodate their needs to the spaces after occupancy, or that a wide range of human activities can use similar spatial organizations. It is also somewhat disturbing to find that Alexander makes no recommendations for the social and administrative programs that might be required if his model of urban form is to achieve the desired aims. Both these shortcomings illustrate what one might call the tragedy of architecture today, namely that when he is forced to consider his designs in terms of their social consequences, even an architect with a sophisticated grasp of the behavioral sciences and committed to rational analysis tends to fall back on the assumption of architectural determinism. The note that Alexander has written for this abridged version of his original article indicates that he has become aware of this difficulty and that he looks upon his selection as a more general proposal than a literal interpretation of his model of urban form would suggest.

☐

Author's Note: I wrote this article five years ago, and I see its shortcomings very clearly now. I believe that the two central insights, concerning the need to strengthen children's primary groups, and the need to make informal dropping-in more common among adults, are still correct.

However, I should like to make it clear that the configuration of houses that I proposed to accommodate these two needs is no more than a diagram, and as I now realize—a very exaggerated diagram. In 1965 I was anxious to show that physical design could be drawn directly from social problems— and this led me to make a much more literal diagram than I should make today. The two central needs are real needs—but they can be used to shape a far more subtle, and more humane, kind of housing than I showed in my diagram.

People come to cities for contact, yet almost all the people who live in cities suffer from endless inner loneliness. They have thousands of contacts, but the contacts are empty and unsatisfying. *What physical organization must an urban area have, to function as a mechanism for sustaining deeper contacts?*

Before we can answer this question, we must first define exactly what we mean by "contact" and we must try to understand just what it is about existing cities that prevents the deepest contacts from maturing. This selection therefore has four parts: In the first part I shall define the most basic, and most urgently needed kind of contact, *intimate contact*. In the second part I shall present evidence that strongly suggests that the social pathologies associated with urban areas—delinquency and mental disorder—follow inevitably from the lack of intimate contact. In the third part I shall describe the interplay of phenomena that causes the lack of intimate contact in urban areas today. These phenomena are facets of a single complex syndrome: *the autonomy-withdrawal syndrome*. I shall try to show that this syndrome is an inevitable by-product of urbanization, and that society can only re-create intimate contacts among its members if they overcome this syndrome. In the fourth part I shall show that in order to overcome the autonomy-withdrawal syndrome a city's housing must have twelve specific geometric characteristics, and I shall describe an arrangement of houses that has these characteristics.

Intimate Contact

Modern urban society has more contact and communication in it than any other society in human history. As metropolitan areas grow, society will become even more differentiated, and the number and variety of contacts will increase even more. But as the total number of the individual's contacts increases, his contacts with any one person become shorter, less frequent, and less deep. In the end, from a human point of view, they become altogether trivial. It is not surprising that in just those urban centers where the greatest expansion of human contacts has taken place, men have begun to feel their alienation and aloneness more sharply than in any pre-industrialized society. People who live in cities may think they have lots of friends, but the word friend has changed its meaning.

Intimate contact, by which we mean that close contact between two individuals in which they reveal themselves in all their weakness, without fear, is very rare. It is a relationship in which the barriers that normally surround the self are down. It is the relationship that characterizes the best marriages, and all true friendships. We often call it love. It is hard to give an operational definition of this kind of intimate contact, but we can make it reasonably concrete by naming two essential preconditions without which it can't mature.

These conditions are: (1) The people concerned must see each other very often, almost every day, though not necessarily for very long at a time. If people don't meet almost every day—even if they meet once a week, say—they never get around to showing themselves; there are too many other things to talk about. (2) They must see each other under informal conditions. Many people meet every day at work. But here the specific role relationship provides clear rules about the kinds of things they talk about, and also defines the bounds of the relationship. The same thing is true if they meet under "social" circumstances, where the rules of what is proper make deep contact impossible.[1]

It may help to keep in mind an even more concrete criterion of intimacy. If two people are in intimate contact, then we can be sure that they sometimes talk about the ultimate meaning of one another's lives; and if two people do sometimes talk about the ultimate meaning of their lives, then we are fairly safe in calling their contact an intimate contact.

By this definition, it is clear that most so-called "friendly" contacts are not intimate. Indeed, it is obvious that the most common "friendly" occasions provide no opportunity for this kind of contact to mature. Let us therefore begin by asking what social mechanism is required to make contacts intimate.

In pre-industrial society, intimate contacts were sustained by primary groups. "A primary group is a small group of people characterized by intimate face to face association and cooperation." [2] The three most universal primary groups are the family, the neighborhood group of elders, and the children's playgroup. These three primary groups have existed in virtually every human society, and they have been primary in forming the social nature and ideals of the individual. It is clear that the contacts that these primary groups created do meet the two conditions I have named. The members of a primary group meet often—almost daily; and they meet under unspecialized conditions, where behavior is not prescribed by role, so that they meet as individuals, man to man.

Because primary groups have, so far, always been the vehicles for intimate contact, and because intimacy is so important, many anthropologists and sociologists have taken the view that man cannot live without primary groups. [3] Many architects and planners have therefore tried to recreate the local primary group artificially, by means of the neighborhood idea. They have hoped that if people would live in small physical groups, round modern village greens, the social groups would follow the same patterns, and these artificial groups would then once more provide the intimate contact that is in such short supply in urban areas today. [4] But this idea of recreating primary groups by artificial means is unrealistic and reactionary: it fails to recognize the truth about the open society. The open society is no longer centered around place-based groups, and the very slight acquaintances that do form round an artificial neighborhood are once again trivial; they are not based on genuine desire. [5] Though these pseudo-groups may serve certain ancillary purposes (neighbors may look after one another's houses while they are away) there is no possible hope that they could sustain truly intimate contact, as I have defined it.

The only vestige of the adult primary groups that still remains is the nuclear family. The family still functions as a mechanism for sustaining intimate contact. But where the extended family of pre-industrial society contained many adults, and gave them many opportunities for intimate contact, the modern nuclear family contains only two adults. This means that each of these adults has at most *one* intimate contact within his family. (Although the contact between parent and child is, in a colloquial sense, an intimate one, it is not the kind of contact that I am discussing here; it is essentially one-sided; there can be no mutual revealing of the self between adults and children.) Furthermore, one-third of all households in urban areas contain only one adult (either unmarried, widowed, or divorced).[6] These adults have *no* intimate contacts at all, at home.

Modern urban social structure is chiefly based on secondary contacts—contacts in which people are related by a single role relationship: buyer and seller, disc jockey and fan, lawyer and client.[7] Not surprisingly, the people who find themselves in this dismal condition try madly to make friends. It is not hard to see that this is an inevitable consequence of urbanization and mobility. In a society where people move about a lot, the individuals who are moving must learn to strike up acquaintances quickly since they often find themselves in situations where they don't know anybody. By the same token, since deep-seated, old, associations are uncommon, people rush to join new associations and affiliations, to fill the gap they feel. But the very life stuff of social organization is missing.

People may not be ready to admit that most of their contacts are trivial, but they admit it by implication in their widespread nostalgia for college days, and for army days. At college men and women had an experience that many of them never have again: they had many intimate friends; intimate contact was commonplace. The same is true of army days. However grisly war may be, it is a fact that the vast majority of men never forget their army days. They remember the close comradeship, the feelings of mutual dependence, and they regret that later life never quite recreates this wonderful experience.

All the recent studies of dissatisfaction when slum dwellers are forced to move say essentially the same.[8] These people are moving from a traditional place-based society into the larger urban society where place-based community means nothing. When they make the move they lose their intimate contacts. This is not because the places they go to are badly designed in some obvious sense that could be easily improved. Nor is it because they are temporarily uprooted, and have only to wait for the roots of community to grow again. The awful fact is that modern urban society as a whole has found no way of sustaining intimate contacts.

Some people believe that this view is nothing but nostalgia for an imaginary past and that what looks like alienation is really just the pain of parting from traditional society, and the birth pang of a new society.[9] I do not believe it. I believe that intimate contacts are essential for human survival, and, indeed, that each person requires not one, but several intimate contacts at any given time. I believe that the primary groups which sustained intimate contact were an essential functional part of traditional social systems and that since they are now obsolete, it is essential that we invent new social mechanisms able to sustain the intimate contacts that we need.

Expressed in formal terms, this belief becomes a fundamental hypothesis about man and society: *An individual can only be healthy and happy when his life contains three or four intimate contacts. A society can only be a healthy one if each of its individual members has three or four intimate contacts at every stage of his existence.*[10]

Every society known to man, except our own, has provided conditions that allow people to sustain three or four intimate contacts. If the hypothesis is correct, the very roots of our society are threatened. Let us therefore examine the evidence for the hypothesis.

Evidence

Unfortuately, the only available evidence is very indirect. Individual health is hard to define; social health is even harder. We have no indices for low-grade misery or sickness; we have no indices for fading social vitality. In the same way, the relative intimacy of different contacts is hard to define and has never explicitly been studied. The evidence we really need, showing a correlation between the intimacy of people's contacts, and the general health and happiness of their individual and social lives, does not exist.

In a strictly scientific sense, it is therefore only possible to examine an extreme version of the hypothesis: namely, that *extreme* lack of contact causes *extreme* and well-defined social pathologies like schizophrenia and delinquency. Several large-scale studies do support this extreme form of hypothesis.

Faris and Dunham studied the distribution of mental disorders in Chicago in the 1930s. They found that paranoid and hebephrenic schizophrenias have their highest rates of incidence among hotel residents and lodgers, and among the people who live in the rooming house districts of the city. They are highest, in other words, among those people who are most alone.[11]

Faris and Dunham also found that the incidence of schizophrenia among whites was highest among those whites living in predominantly

Negro areas, and that the incidence for Negroes was highest among those Negroes living in predominantly non-Negro areas.[12] Here again, the incidence is highest among those who are isolated.

Alexander Leighton and his collaborators, in their Nova Scotia study, found that people in a disintegrated society, that is, people with no personal contacts of any sort, have substantially higher rates of psychophysiological, psychoneurotic, and sociopathic disorders, than people who live in a closely knit traditional community.[13]

Langner and Michael, studying the incidence of mental disorders in Manhattan, found that people who report having less than four friends have a substantially higher chance of mental disorder than those who report having more than four friends.[14] They also show that membership in formal organizations and clubs, and contact with neighbors, have relatively slight effect on mental health—thus supporting the idea that the contacts must be intimate before they do much good.[15]

Many minor studies support the same conclusion. Most important are the studies reporting the widely known correlations between age and mental health, and between marital status and mental health. Various studies have shown that the highest incidence of mental disorders, for males and females, occurs above age 65, and, indeed, that the highest of all occurs above 75.[16] Other studies have shown that the incidence rates for single, separated, widowed, and divorced persons are higher than the rates for married persons. Rates per thousand, for single persons, are about one-and-a-half times as high as the rates for married persons, while rates for divorced and widowed persons are between two and three times as high.[17]

Of course, the disorders among old people may be partly organic, but there is no getting away from the fact that old people are almost always more lonely than the young and that it is usually hard for them to sustain substantial contacts with other people. In the same way, although the disorders among divorced and single people could actually be the source of their isolation, not the cause of it, the fact that the rate is equally high for widowers and widows makes this unlikely.

So far we have discussed only cases of adult isolation. It is very likely that the effects of social isolation on children are even more acute, but here the published evidence is thinner.

The most dramatic available results come from Harlow's work on monkeys. Harlow has shown that monkeys isolated from other infant monkeys during the first 6 months of life are incapable of normal social, sexual, or play relations with other monkeys in their later lives.[18]

413

Although monkeys can be raised successfully without a mother, provided they have other infant monkeys to play with, they cannot be raised successfully by a mother alone, without other infant monkeys, even if the mother is entirely normal.[19]

In Harlow's experiments, the first 6 months of life were critical. The first 6 months of a rhesus monkey's life correspond to the first three years of a child's life. Although there is no formal evidence to show that lack of contact during these first 3 years damages human children—and as far as I know, it has never been studied—there is very strong evidence for the effect of isolation between the ages of 4 and 10.

The most telling study is that by Herman Lantz.[20] Lantz questioned a random sample of 1,000 men in the United States Army who had been referred to a mental hygiene clinic because of emotional difficulties. Army psychiatrists classified each of the men as normal or as suffering from mild psychoneurosis, severe psychoneurosis, or psychosis. Lantz then put each man into one of three categories: those who reported having five friends or more at any typical moment when they were between four and ten years old, those who reported an average of about two friends, and those who reported no friends at that time. The results are astounding: Among men who had five friends or more as children, 61.5 per cent had mild cases, while 27.8 per cent had severe cases. Among men with no childhood friends, only 5 per cent had mild cases, and 85 per cent had severe cases.

It is almost certain then, that lack of contact, when it is extreme, has extreme effects on people. There is a considerable body of literature beyond that which I have quoted.[21] Even so, the evidence is sparse. We cannot be sure the effect is causal, and we have found evidence only for those relatively extreme cases that can be unambiguously counted. From a strictly scientific point of view, it is clearly necessary to undertake a special, extensive study, to test the hypothesis in the exact form that I have stated it.

However, just because the scientific literature doesn't happen to contain the relevant evidence, doesn't mean that we don't know whether the hypothesis is true or not. From our own lives we know that intimate contact is essential to life, and that the whole meaning of life shows itself only in the process of our intimate contacts.[22] The way of life we lead today makes it impossible for us to be as close to our friends as we really want to be. The feeling of alienation, and the modern sense of the "meaninglessness" of life, are direct expressions of the loss of intimate contact.

414

The Autonomy-Withdrawal Syndrome

As far as we can judge, then, people need three or four intimate contacts at every moment of their lives. It is therefore clear that every human society must provide social mechanisms that sustain these intimate contacts in order to survive as a society. Yet as we know, the historic mechanisms that once performed this function for our own society are breaking down.

I shall now try to show that we are not merely faced with the collapse of one or two social mechanisms, but rather with a massive syndrome, a huge net of cause and effect in which the breakdown of primary groups, the breakdown of intimacy itself, the growth of individualism, and the withdrawal from the stress of urbanized society, are all interwoven. I shall call this syndrome the *autonomy-withdrawal syndrome*.

In pre-industrial societies the two institutions that sustained intimate contacts between adults were the extended family and the local neighborhood community. These two primary groups have almost entirely disappeared, and the modern metropolis is a collection of many scattered households, each one small. In the future, individual households will probably be even smaller and the average size of urban areas even larger.[23] We must therefore ask how, in a society of scattered, mobile individuals, these individuals can maintain intimate contact with one another.

The first answer that comes to mind is this: since friendships in modern society are mostly based on some community of interest, we should expect the institutions that create such friendships—work place, golf club, ski resort, precinct headquarters—to provide the necessary meeting ground. It sounds good, but it doesn't work. Though people do meet each other in such groups, the meetings are too infrequent and the situation too clearly prescribed. People achieve neither the frequency, nor the informality, that intimacy requires. Further, *people can only reach the true intimacy and mutual trust required for self-revelation when they are in private.*

Frequent, private, almost daily meetings between individuals, under conditions of extreme informality, unencumbered by role prescriptions or social rules, will only take place if people visit one another in their homes. It is true that occasional meetings in public places may also be very intimate, but the regular, constant, meetings that are required to build up the possibility of intimacy cannot happen in public places.

415

In a society of scattered mobile individuals people will therefore only be able to maintain intimate contacts with one another if they are in the habit of constant informal visiting or "dropping-in."

In modern American society dropping-in is thought of as a peculiar European custom. Yet in fact, dropping-in is a normal part of life in every pre-industrial society. In part it has to be because there are no telephones in pre-industrial society. But dropping-in is not merely the pre-industrial version of what we do by phone. The very notion of friendship demands that people be almost totally exposed to one another. To be friends they must have nothing to hide; and for this reason, informal dropping-in is a natural, and essential, part of friendship. This is so fundamental that we may even treat it as a definition of true friendship.

Why is dropping-in so rare in mobile urban society? The first reason, of course, is still mechanical. Two people will not sustain a pattern of daily dropping-in unless they live within a few minutes of each other, ten minutes at the most. Although the car has enormously enlarged the number of people within ten minutes' distance of any given household, most of the people in the metropolis are still outside this distance. Potential friends see each other very rarely—at most once or twice a month for dinner—and when they do meet, it is after careful invitation, worked out in advance. These kinds of evening contact have neither the frequency, nor the informality, that intimacy requires.

However, distance alone, though it is a serious obstacle, does not fully explain the loss of intimacy. There is another reason for it, far more devastating, and far more profound: when people get home, they want to get away from all the stress outside. People do not want to be perpetually exposed; they often want to be withdrawn. But withdrawal soon becomes a habit. People reach a point where they are permanently withdrawn, they lose the habit of showing themselves to others as they really are, and they become unable and unwilling to let other people into their own world.

At this stage people don't like others dropping in on them, because they don't want to be caught when they aren't ready—the housewife who doesn't like anyone coming around except when she has carefully straightened up her house, the family which doesn't like to mix its friends and has them to visit one couple at a time in case the couples shouldn't get along. Afraid of showing themselves as they really are, such people never reach a truly intimate degree of contact with others.

This fear is partly caused by stress. The man who lives in modern urban society is exposed to innumerable stresses: danger, noise, too many strangers, too much information, and above all, the need to make decisions about the complexities of personal life without the help of traditional mores. These stresses are often too much to bear, so he withdraws from them. Even when they are in public, people behave as though the other people who surround them are not there. A woman cheerfully wears curlers in the street because, although she is curling her hair for people who are real to her, the people who surround her don't exist; she has shut them out.

In its extreme form, this withdrawal turns into schizophrenia: that total withdrawal into the self, which takes place when the outside world is so confusing, or so hard to deal with, that the organism finally cannot cope with it and turns away.[24] Schizophrenics are completely individualistic; the world they live in is their own world; they do not perceive themselves as dependent on the outside world in any way, nor do they perceive any interaction between themselves and the outside world. Nor indeed, do they enter into any interaction with the world outside.[25]

The stress of urban life has not yet had this extreme and catastrophic effect on many people. Nevertheless, what is nowadays considered "normal" urban behavior is strikingly like schizophrenia: it is also marked by extreme withdrawal from stress, and this withdrawal has also led to an unrealistic belief in the self-sufficiency of individuals.

Any objective observer comparing urban life with rural or pre-industrial life must be struck by the extreme individualism of the people who live in cities.[26] Though this individualism has often been criticized by non-Americans as a peculiarity of American culture, I believe this view mistaken. Individualism of an extreme kind is an inevitable by-product of urbanization—it occurs as part of the withdrawal from stress—and is very different from healthy democratic respect for the individual's rights.[27]

An obvious expression of this individualism is the huge amount of space that people need around them in the United States. Edward Hall has suggested that each person carries an inviolable "bubble" of personal space around with him and that the size of the bubble varies according to the intimacy of the situation.[28] He has also shown that the size of bubble required varies from culture to culture. Apparently people need a larger bubble in the United States, for any given situation, than in any other country; this is clearly associated with the fear of bodily contact, and with the fact that people view themselves as isolated atoms. This isolation of the individual is also expressed clearly by the love of private property in the United States, and the wealth of laws and institutions that keep people's private property inviolate.

Another form of extreme individualism, which threatens the development of intimate contacts, is the exaggerated accent on the nuclear family. In modern urban society it is assumed that the needs for intimate contact that any one individual has can be completely met in marriage. This concentration of all our emotional eggs in one basket has gone so far that true intimacy between any friends except man and wife is regarded with extreme suspicion.

It is true that this exaggerated arrogant view of the individual's strength is a withdrawal from stress. But it could never have happened if it weren't for the fact that urbanization makes individuals autonomous. The extreme differentiation of society in an urban area means that literally any service can be bought, by anyone. In material terms, any individual is able to survive alone.

Of course these isolated, apparently autonomous, individuals are in fact highly dependent on society—but only through the medium of money. A man in a less differentiated rural economy is constantly reminded of his dependence on society, and of the fact that his very being is totally intertwined with the being of the social order, and the being of his fellows. The individual who is technically autonomous, whose dependencies are all expressed in money terms, can easily make the mistake of thinking that he, or he and his family, are self-sufficient.

Now, naturally, people who believe that they are self-sufficient create a world that reinforces individualism and withdrawal. In central cities this is reflected in the concept of apartments. Though collected together at high densities, these apartments are in fact, like the people themselves, totally turned inward. High density makes it necessary to insulate each apartment from the world outside; the actual dwelling is remote from the street; it is virtually impossible to drop in on someone who lives in an apartment block. Not surprisingly, recent studies report that people who live in apartments feel more isolated than people who live in any other kind of dwelling.[29]

But autonomy and withdrawal, and the pathological belief in individual families as self-sufficient units, can be seen most vividly in the physical pattern of suburban tract development. The houses stand alone—a collection of isolated, disconnected islands. There is no communal land, and no sign of any functional connection between different houses. If it seems far-fetched to call this aspect of the suburb pathological, let us examine the results of a study made in Vienna in

1956. The city planning department gave a questionnaire to a random sample of 4,000 Viennese to find out what their housing preferences were. Most of them, when asked whether they would rather live in apartments or in single family houses, said they preferred apartments, because they wanted to be near the center, where everything was happening.[30]

A Viennese psychiatrist then gave the same questionnaire to 100 neurotic patients in his clinic. He found that a much higher proportion of these patients wanted to live in one-family houses, that they wanted larger houses relative to the size of their families, that they wanted more space per person, and that more of them wanted their houses to be situated in woods and trees. In other words, they wanted the suburban dream. As he says, "The neurotic patients are marked by a strong desire to shun reality and to isolate themselves."[31]

Most people who move to suburbs are not sick in any literal sense. The four main reasons people give for moving to the suburbs are: (1) Open space for children, because children can't play safely in central urban areas.[32] (2) More space inside the house than they can afford in the central city.[33] (3) Wanting to own a house of their own.[34] Ownership protects the owner from the uncertainties of tenancy and from reliance on others, and creates the illusion that the owner and his family have a world of their own, where nobody can touch them. (4) More grass and trees.[35]

Each of these is a withdrawal from stress. The withdrawal is understandable, but the suburb formed by this withdrawal undermines the formation of intimate contacts in a devastating way. It virtually destroys the children's playgroup.

As we saw earlier, the intimate contacts in pre-industrial society were maintained by three primary groups: the extended family, the neighborhood group, and the children's playgroup. The first two, those that maintain intimate contacts between adults, are obsolete—and need to be replaced. But the third primary group—the children's playgroup—is not obsolete at all. Little children, unlike adults, do choose their friends from the children next door. It is perfectly possible for children's playgroups to exist in modern society just as they always have; and indeed, it is essential. The children's playgroup sets the whole style of life for later years. Children brought up in extensive playgroups will be emotionally prepared for intimate contacts in later life; children brought up without playgroups will be prone to individualism and withdrawal.

On the face of it, the suburb ought to be a very good place for children's playgroups—it has open space and safety. Yet, paradoxically, this children's paradise is not a paradise at all for little children.

If you drive through a subdivision, watching children play, you will see that children who are old enough to have school friends do have local playgroups of a sort. But if you look carefully, you see the smallest children squatting forlornly outside their houses—occasionally playing with an older brother or sister and occasionally in groups of two or three, but most often alone. Compare this with the situation in a primitive village, or in a crowded urban slum: there the little children are out on the street fending for themselves as soon as they can walk; heaps of children are playing and falling and rolling over one another.

Why are suburban playgroups small? There are several reasons. First of all, suburban density is low and little children can't walk very far. Even if every house has children in it, the number of two- and three-year olds that a given two-year-old can reach is very small. Secondly, even though the suburb is safer than the central city, the streets still aren't entirely safe. Mothers keep their two- and three-year-olds off the street, inside the individual yards, where they can keep an eye on them. This cuts the children's freedom to meet other children. Further, many suburbs have no common land at all in them, not even sidewalks. There isn't any natural place where children go to find each other; they have to go and look for each other in one another's houses. For a child this is a much more formidable enterprise than simply running out to see who's on the street. It also makes the children hard to find and keeps the size of groups down, especially since many parents won't allow large groups of children in the house. And finally, when children play in one another's yards, parents can control the playmates they consider suitable.

It is small wonder that children who grow up in these conditions learn to be self-reliant in the pathological sense I have described. As they become adults they are even less able to live lives with intimate contacts than their parents; they seek even more exaggerated forms of individualism and withdrawal. As adults who suffer from withdrawal they create a world that creates children who are even more prone to suffer from withdrawal, and more prone to create such worlds. This closes the cycle of the syndrome, and makes it self-perpetuating.

The autonomy-withdrawal syndrome is not a unique American phenomenon. It is true that it is, so far, more acute in the United States than in any other country; but this is merely because urbanization is more advanced in the United States than anywhere else. As massive urbanization spreads, the syndrome will spread with it. I believe this syndrome is the greatest threat to social human nature that we face in this century. We have already seen that it can create misery and madness. But in the long run its effects are far more devastating. An individual human organism becomes a self only in the process of intimate contacts with other selves. Unless we overcome the syndrome, the loss of intimate contacts may break down human nature altogether.

Solution

How can cities help to overcome the syndrome? If the city is to be a mechanism for sustaining intimate human contact, what geometric pattern does the mechanism need?

Of course, no amount of geometric pattern in the environment can overcome the syndrome by itself. The syndrome is a social and psychological problem of massive dimensions; it will only be solved when people decide to change their way of life. But the physical environment needs changing too. People can only change their way of life if the environment supports their efforts.

There are two fundamentally different approaches to the problem. On the one hand we may decide that intimate contact can only be sustained properly by primary groups; we shall then try to create new kinds of primary groups that might work in our society. On the other hand we may decide that adult primary groups are gone forever, and that it is unrealistic to try to re-create them in any form whatever in modern society; in this case we must try a more radical approach, and create a social mechanism that is able to sustain informal, daily contact between people without the support of a primary group.

It may be that the first of these approaches is the more hopeful one. This is what T-groups try to do, it is the idea behind the groups of families that Aldous Huxley describes in *Island,* and above all, it is the idea behind group work. If work can be reorganized, so that people band together in small work groups of about a dozen, and each group is directed toward a single concentrated socially valuable objective, then the dedication and effort that develop in the group are capable of creating great intimacy, which goes far beyond the working day.

However, so far none of these methods has met with any great success. So far the forces that are breaking primary groups apart have been stronger than the efforts to build artificial primary groups. In this selection I shall therefore assume that more radical steps will have to be taken: that although children's playgroups can be saved, adult primary groups are doomed, and that adults will have to sustain their intimate contacts in a new way, by frequent casual visiting. I shall now describe the reorganization of the housing pattern that is required by this approach.

At present, people have two main kinds of housing open to them: either they live in apartments or they live in single family houses. Neither helps them overcome the autonomy-withdrawal syndrome. I shall now try to show that, in order for them to overcome the syndrome, the houses in a city must have twelve specific geometric characteristics, and that these twelve characteristics, when taken together define a housing pattern different from any available today.

1. Every dwelling must be immediately next to a vehicular through street. If there are any multi-story buildings with dwellings in them—like apartments—then there must be vehicular through streets at every level where there are entrances to dwellings.

In the modern city, many houses, and almost all apartments, are some distance off the street. Yet people live so far apart they have to move around by car or motor bike. Informal dropping-in will only work properly if all dwellings are directly on the street, so that people in the dwelling can be seen from a passing car.

It may be said that this is unnecessary since people who want to visit one another informally can telephone ahead and ring the doorbell when they get there. This argument is superficial. People will only make a regular habit of informal visiting if they can be certain they are really wanted when they get there. A phone call in advance does not convey enough information to make this possible, and this will be true even with TV-telephones. But if you go and knock on someone's door and it turns out to be a bad moment, your visit is already too far advanced for you to withdraw gracefully.

It is therefore essential to see the people you intend to visit inside their home, from your car. You wave to them; you sound the horn; you shout a few words. By then you have had a chance to assess the situation, and they have had a chance to react. If it is the right moment for a visit, they will invite you in. If it is not, you talk for a few moments, without leaving your car—and you can then drive on, without embarrassment to either side. It is therefore essential that the house be directly on a through street, and that some part of the house be transparent and directly visible from passing cars.

2. Each dwelling must contain a transparent communal room with the following properties: on one side the room is directly adjacent to the street, on the opposite side the room is directly adjacent to a private open air court or garden. Since the room is transparent, its interior, seen against the garden, and the garden itself, are both visible from the street.

The part of the house that is visible must be indoors so that it can be used year round, and since it is indoors it must have windows both on the street side and on the far side, so that people inside can be seen from the street. The room must be designed in such a way that people will go there whenever they are feeling sociable and likely to welcome a casual visitor. But if the room is merely facing the street, people won't want to sit there; the street is far less pleasant than it used to be. The transparent room, though visible from the street, must therefore be oriented toward a private court or garden, with a view beyond. Under these circumstances it will be a natural place for people to go for family meals, to read the paper, to have a drink, to gossip. In warm seasons they may also sit in the court beyond, where they will still be visible from the street.

3. The transparent communal room must be surrounded by freestanding, self-contained pavilions, each functioning as a bed-living unit, so arranged that each person in the family, or any number of people who wish to be undisturbed, can retire to one of these pavilions and be totally private.

If the communal room is visible from the street, and open to passing friends, then the private rooms must be far more private than they are today, so that their privacy is not infected by the openness of the communal room. Each of these private rooms must be a more or less self-contained pavilion, where people can be entirely undisturbed—

either alone, or in twos, or in a group. People who live in such a house must learn to distinguish deliberately between being accessible and being inaccessible. When they want to be accessible, they go to the communal room; when they want to be inaccessible, they go to one of the private pavilions.

4. The street immediately outside the dwelling must be no more than about 1,000 feet long, and connected to a major traffic artery at each end.

The house must be so placed that people can drive past it easily, without having to go too far out of their way. This means that the house must be on a street that is reasonably short, and connected at each end to a traffic artery that plays a major part in the overall traffic system.

5. There must be a continuous piece of common land, accessible and visible from every dwelling.

Suburban yards are far too private. They only allow small groups to form, they make it hard for children to find each other, and they allow parents to regulate the other yards their own children may visit. In order to give children the chance to meet freely in groups, there must be common land where they can go to find each other.

In some of the older and denser suburbs, the wide sidewalks provide such common land. However, most suburban tract developments have very narrow sidewalks, or no sidewalks at all, and anyway most middle-class parents consider even the sidewalk dangerous, or rule it out on the grounds that "well brought up children don't play in the street." Most important of all, even in the suburbs parents still feel very protective about the smallest children. They will only allow these children to play freely on common land if they are convinced the children will be completely safe while playing there.

This means, first of all, that the access to the common land must be direct from every house; it must not be necessary to cross streets or other public thoroughfares to get there. Second, the common land must be visible from the house itself so that parents can, if they want to, watch their children playing there. Third, the common land must be so placed that a child cannot get to any vehicular street without going through a house. Finally, the common land must be disassociated from the street, and clearly meant for play, so that it has no connotation of "playing in the street." If all these conditions are met, parents will allow the little children—even toddlers—to roam freely on and off the common land, and playgroups have a good chance of forming.

6. This common land must be separated from the streets by houses, so that a child on the common land has to go through a house to get to the street, for reasons given under 5.

7. The common land, though continuous, must be broken into many small "places," not much larger than outdoor "rooms," each surfaced with a wide variety of ground surfaces, especially "soft" surfaces like earth, mud, sand, and grass.

This condition must be met to make sure the children really like the common land and don't end up preferring their own yards, or other places. Little children do not enjoy playing in great big open areas. They seek small corners and opportunities for secrecy, and they seek plastic materials—water, earth, and mud.[36]

8. Each house must be within 100-yards walk of 27 other houses.

Let us assume that there are two children per household (the modal figure for suburban households) and that these children are evenly distributed in age from 0 to 18. Roughly speaking, a given preschool child who is x years old, will play with children between $x-1$ and $x+1$ years old. In order for playgroups to form, each child must be able to reach at least five children in this age range. It can be shown that for each child to have a 95 per cent chance of reaching five such potential playmates, he must be in reach of 27 households.[37]

If we assume that preschool children are not able, or allowed, to go more than about 100 yards in search of playmates, this means that each house must be within 100 yards of 27 other houses. To achieve this density in a conventional suburban layout, house lots would have to be less than 40 feet wide, about half the width and twice the density they are today.

9. Overall residential densities throughout the metropolitan area must be as high as possible.

There is a second reason why residential densities must be higher than they are today. Informal daily dropping-in will not take place between two households that are more than about 10 minutes apart. Since average door-to-door speeds in urban areas are about 15 m.p.h., 10 minutes is about 2½ miles, thus putting each person in reach of about 20 square miles, or about 100,000 people at current metropolitan densities. This is a tiny fraction of the population of a metropolitan area—a twentieth of a small one, a hundredth of a large one. Since we have started out with the axiom that a person's best friends may live anywhere in the metropolitan area, this means that people are within dropping-in distance of no more than a twentieth of their potentially closest friends.

Obviously vehicle speeds and streets can be improved. But it seems unlikely that average door-to-door speeds will more than double in this century. This means that people in the largest metropolitan areas will still be within informal distance of less than one-twentieth of the population. While transportation must be improved, it is clear that overall mean densities must *also* be raised as far as they can be.

Many planners believe that high density is bad for man. This is based on the fact that high density is often correlated with the incidence of crime, delinquency, ill health, and insanity. If this belief were justified, any attempt to increase the density of population would obviously be ill advised. However, though the belief has a long history, the evidence available today does not support it.

There seems little doubt that overcrowding—too little living space per person—does cause damage. Calhoun has shown this dramatically for rats;[38] Loring, Chombard de Lauwe, and Lander have shown that it is true for humans.[39] It is clear that people who are now forced to live in crowded conditions either need more income or need ways of reducing the square foot costs of living space. But this does not imply that the density of population per square mile should be reduced. Even dwellings that are individually very large can still be arranged at high population densities without overcrowding.

426

It is true that there is often a positive correlation between high population density and various indices of social disorder like crime, delinquency, ill health, and insanity rates.[40] However, it seems almost certain that these effects are caused by intervening variables and are not directly caused by density. There are places—Boston's North End and Hong Kong, for example—which have exceptionally high densities, and exceptionally low indices of social disorder.[41] Unless we assume that Italian-Americans and Chinese are organically different from other people, this means that density, as such, cannot be the source of trouble in the cases where a correlation does exist.

The following hypothesis fully explains all the observed correlations: those social disorders apparently caused by density, are in fact caused by low income (combined with poor education) and by social isolation. People who are poor, and badly educated, tend to live in high density areas. People who are socially isolated also tend to live in high density areas. Both variables are associated with high indices of social disorder. Although some published studies of density have controlled for one or the other of these variables, no study has controlled them both. Lander has shown that the correlation between *overcrowding* and delinquency, when controlled for these two variables, vanishes altogether.[42] Schmitt has published a table showing that the correlations persist when income-education is controlled, but also showing a strong negative correlation between household size and social disorder (larger households are less prone to social disorders), which suggests strongly that social isolation may be responsible for the persistent correlation.[43] The fact that there are very few social disorders in Boston's North End and in Hong Kong is clearly due to the existence of close knit extended families—the lack of social isolation. I predict that the partial correlation between density and social disorder, when controlled for income-education *and* for social isolation, will disappear altogether.

This hypothesis explains all the available data. Although it is untested, there is no published evidence that contradicts it. As far as we can tell, the high density called for by the need for contact is perfectly safe.

10. The entire exterior surface of the residential area must be an undulating hillside, covered with grass and flowers and trees; the houses are set immediately under the surface of this hillside.

427

We cannot expect people to live at high densities just because they have certain social benefits. The low density of suburban tracts has been created by demands far more important to consumers than the point of view I have presented. Unless these demands can be satisfied equally well at higher densities, there is not the slightest hope that overall densities will ever be increased.

The pattern of density in an urban region is created by the conflict between two basic tendencies: the desire for land and the desire for easy access to central areas. For a given income, each person can choose less land at the center, or more land further from the center. When a population of individuals tries to resolve this conflict for itself, a characteristic pattern of density comes into being: density declines exponentially with distance from the center according to the equation: $d_r = d_o e^{-br}$.[44] This relation holds for cities all over the world.[45] What is even more surprising, the relation is almost entirely fixed by absolute population, and by the age of the city. This means that in a free market, neither the overall mean density of a city, nor the densities at different distances from the center, can be controlled by planning action.

They can, however, be controlled indirectly. If we can make land more useful, so that a person can get a given level of satisfaction from a smaller piece of land than he needs to get that satisfaction now, then the desire for access will balance differently against the desire for land, and densities will increase.

Land is valuable for two basic reasons. First of all, it is the prime building surface. Secondly, it provides open space. The first is replaceable. The second is not. It is easy to create artificial building surfaces at many levels. But the area of open space cannot be increased beyond the area of the land. Yet this basic natural resource is almost entirely wasted in urban areas today. Fifty per cent is wasted on roads and parking lots, and 15 per cent is wasted on roofs; none of these need it. The 25 per cent of open space left over is chopped up and useless.

If a city were built so as to conserve this resource, with all roofs covered with grass and trees, and all roads roofed over, so that the total exterior surface of the city was a parkland of grass and flowers and bushes and trees, people could have the same amenities they have today, at far higher densities. To make it work, the surface would have to undulate like a range of rolling hills, so that windows in the hillsides can get daylight to the houses under the surface.

How much useful open land does a family in a suburban tract command? At a gross density of 5,000 persons per square mile, each family has a lot of about 70 feet by 100 feet, 7,000 square feet in all; 2,000 square feet go to the house and another 1,000 square feet to the driveway, leaving about 4,000 square feet of open land, or about 1,000 square feet per person. If the entire exterior surface of the city were artificial open land, it would be possible to house 25,000 people per square mile, and still give them the same 1,000 square feet of open land per person.

11. Each house must be on an individual load-bearing pad, which doesn't touch any other pad, and which may be clearly visualized as a piece of private property. The pad has its own open space, and allows the owner to build and modify his house as he wishes.

So that people can get the same feeling of ownership and the same opportunity to build what they want and the same private open space they get in the suburbs, the houses under the hillside must be built on individual artificial lots. To avoid the half-hearted feeling of ownership that condominium apartments offer, each lot must be totally separate from the other lots, and so made that the owner can build what he wants to on his own lot. Each lot is an individual load-bearing pad, large enough to hold a 2,000 square foot house with a private garden.

CENTER⟶

12. The hills vary in height and slope according to their location in the urban region. They are highest and steepest near commercial centers, and low and flat near the periphery.

Since density will still vary with distance from urban centers, even if the land-access equation changes, the hills must vary in height and slope. The highest and steepest hills, whose density is greatest, will be near the urban centers, the low flat hills at the periphery.

It now remains to find a single concrete configuration of dwellings, in which all of these twelve relations are simultaneously present. The drawings that follow show such a configuration.

The residential area of the city is a continuous series of rolling linear hills. The hills are about 700 feet long, connected at each end to major traffic arteries. They change in height and slope according to their dis-

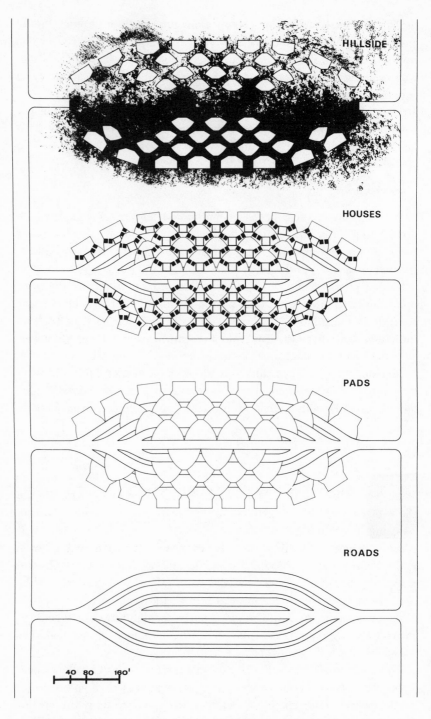

HILLSIDE

HOUSES

PADS

ROADS

40 80   160'

Figure 26–11   Four Hills in Plan, with Different Amounts Cut Away.

tance from the major urban centers. The outer surface of these hills is publicly owned common land, covered by grass and trees and bushes and flowers. Each house is built on a pad immediately under the surface of the hill. The outer half of this pad is a private, fenced garden, which connects directly with the outer surface of the hill. Daylight for the house comes from the garden. The common part of the hill, which surrounds the private gardens, is broken down to form a series of small places, connected by slopes and stairs. Each house is served by a street inside the hill, at its own level. The house is immediately next to its street. Each house has two basic components: a communal room, and a number of private pavilions. The communal room, which is next to the street, between the street and the garden, is open to the street, and transparent, so that the garden is visible through it, and so that people inside this room are visible against the light. The private pavilions are arranged around this communal room, under the roof provided by the hillside above.

This configuration contains all twelve relations specified. Although it can be varied in many details without damaging any of the twelve relations, I do not believe it is possible to find a configuration that differs fundamentally from the one I have described, and still contains all of the twelve. However, I should not like this configuration to be thought of as a building. Many problems still need to be worked out before it can be built. The configuration must be thought of simply as a partial specification of what a city has to be to function as a mechanism for sustaining human contact.

Let me once more repeat the central argument. It is inevitable that urban concentrations create stress. Our first reaction to this urban stress is to move away from it; to turn our backs on it; to try to escape it. This is very natural. Yet the remedy is worse than the disease. The ills of urban life which are commonly attributed to density and stress, are in fact not produced by the original stress itself, but by our own actions in turning away from that stress. If urban society is to survive, we must overcome this over-reaction. If people do not expose themselves, if they do not dare to make themselves vulnerable, life will become more and more intolerable, and we shall see more and more of the signs of dissociation which are already far too evident. The pattern of twelve relations that I have presented has only this one objective. It brings people out of hiding, and lets them expose themselves to the larger fabric of the city and to society and to their friends. In such a city there is some chance of breaking down the autonomy-withdrawal syndrome. In our own cities there is no chance at all.

NOTES

1. Of course, people do occasionally have intimate contact with one another, even when these two conditions are not fulfilled. This happens between old friends who now live 3,000 miles apart and see each other every few years for a day or two. But even in these cases, there must have been some period in the past when the two conditions *were* satisfied.

2. C. H. Cooley, *Social Organization* (Glencoe, Ill.: 1956), pp. 23–31.

3. See, e.g., Edward A. Shils, "The Study of Primary Groups," in Lerner and Lasswell, *The Policy Sciences* (Stanford: 1951), pp. 44–69; W. I. Thomas, *Social Behavior and Personality*, ed. E. H. Volkart (New York: 1951); George Homans, *The Human Group* (New York: 1950); Ralph Linton, *The Study of Man* (New York: 1963), p. 230.

4. For instance, Clarence Stein, *Towards New Towns for America* (Chicago: 1951).

5. Melvin M. Webber, "The Urban Place and the Nonplace Urban Realm," in Webber *et al.*, *Explorations into Urban Structure* (Philadelphia: 1964), pp. 79–153; Ikumi Hoshin, "Apartment Life in Japan," *Marriage and Family Living* 26 (1964), pp. 312–317; Rudolf Heberle, "The Normative Element in Neighborhood Relations," *Pacific Sociological Review* 3, no. 1 (Spring 1960), pp. 3–11.

6. Ruth Glass and F. G. Davidson, "Household Structure and Housing Needs," *Population Studies* 4 (1951), pp. 395–420; S. P. Brown, *Population Studies* 4 (1951), pp. 380–394. This is also the same as saying that one-fifth of all adults in urban areas are either single, separated, widowed, or divorced. See U. S. Census, Vol. 1, *General U.S. Statistics* (1960), Table 176.

7. Emile Durkheim, *The Division of Labor in Society*, trans. by George Simpson (Glencoe, Ill.: 1949); Cooley, *op. cit.*; Louis Wirth, "Urbanism as a Way of Life," *American Journal of Sociology* 40 (1938), pp. 1–24; James M. Beshers, *Urban Social Structure* (New York: 1962); Janet Abu-Lughod, *The City is Dead, Long Live the City* (Berkeley: 1966).

8. H. Gans, *The Urban Villagers* (New York: 1962); Michael Young and Peter Willmott, *Family and Kinship in East London* (London: 1957); M. Fried and P. Gleicher, "Some Sources of Residential Satisfaction in an Urban Slum," *AIP Journal* (1961), pp. 305–315.

9. Abu-Lughod, *op. cit.*

10. The numbers three and four have no special significance. I have chosen the range three to four, simply because one or two are too few, and more than about five too many to sustain at the level of intimacy I have defined.

11. R. E. L. Faris and H. H. Dunham, *Mental Disorders in Urban Areas* (Chicago: 1939), pp. 82–109.

12. *Ibid.*, pp. 54–57.

13. Alexander Leighton, *My Name is Legion*, The Stirling County Study, Vol. I (New York: 1959); Charles C. Hughes, Marc-Adelard Tremblay, Robert N. Rapoport, and Alexander Leighton, *People of Cove and Woodlot*, The Stirling County Study, Vol. II (New York: 1960); Dorothea Leighton *et. al.*, *The Character of Danger*, The Stirling County Study, Vol. III (New York: 1963). See esp. Vol. II, pp. 267 and 297, Vol. III, p. 338.

14. T. S. Langner and S. T. Michael, *Life Stress and Mental Health* (New York: 1963), p. 285.

15. *Ibid.*, pp. 286–289.

16. Neil A. Dayton, *New Facts on Mental Disorders* (Springfield, Ill.: 1940), p. 464; C. Landis and J. D. Page, *Modern Society and Mental Disease* (New York: 1938), p. 163; Benjamin Malzberg, *Social and Biological Aspects of Mental Diseases* (Utica: 1940), p. 70; Benjamin Malzberg, "Statistical Analysis of Ages of First Admission to Hospitals for Mental Disease in New York State," *Psychiatric Quarterly* 23 (1949), p. 344; H. F. Dorn, "The Incidence and Future Expectancy

of Mental Disease," *U.S. Public Health Reports* 53 (1938), pp. 1991–2004; E. M. Furbush, "Social Facts Relative to Patients with Mental Disease," *Mental Hygiene* 5 (1921), p. 597.

17. Malzberg, *op. cit.* (1940), p. 116; Landis and Page, *op. cit.*, p. 69; L. M. Adler, "The Relationship of Marital Status to Incidence of and Recovery from Mental Illness," *Social Forces* 32 (1953), p. 186; Neil A. Dayton, "Marriage and Mental Disease," *New England Journal of Medicine* 215 (1936), p. 154; F. J. Gaudet and R. I. Watson, "Relation Between Insanity and Marital Conditions," *Journal of Abnormal Psychology* 30 (1935), p. 368.

18. Harry F. Harlow and Margaret K. Harlow, "The Effect of Rearing Conditions on Behavior," *Bull. Menninger Clinic* 26 (1962), pp. 213–224.

19. Harry F. Harlow and Margaret K. Harlow, "Social Deprivation in Monkeys," *Scientific American* 207, no. 5 (1962), pp. 136–146.

20. Herman R. Lantz, "Number of Childhood Friends as Reported in the Life Histories of a Psychiatrically Diagnosed Group of 1000," *Marriage and Family Living* (1956), pp. 107–108. See also Anna Freud and Sophie Dann, "An Experiment in Group Upbringing," *Readings in Child Behavior and Development*, ed. Celia Stendler (New York: 1964), pp. 122–140.

21. R. E. L. Faris, "Cultural Isolation and the Schizophrenic Personality," *American Journal of Sociology* 40 (September 1934), pp. 155–169; R. E. L. Faris, *Social Psychology* (New York: 1952), pp. 338–362; R. E. L. Faris, *Social Disorganization* (New York: 1948), ch. 8; Paul Halmos, *Solitude and Privacy* (New York: 1952), pp. 88–92; Carle C. Zimmermann and Lucius F. Cervantes, S. J., *Successful American Families* (New York: 1960); R. Helanko, "The Yard Group in the Socialization of Turku Girls," *Acta Sociologica* 4, no. 1 (1959), pp. 38–55; D. Kimball, "Boy Scouting as a Factor in Personality Development," Ph.D. thesis, Dept. of Education, University of California, Berkeley, 1949; Melvin L. Kohn and John A. Clausen, "Social Isolation and Schizophrenia," *American Sociological Review* 20 (1955), pp. 265–273; Dietrich C. Reitzes, "The Effect of Social Environment on Former Felons," *Journal of Criminal Law, Criminology and Police Science* 46 (1955), pp. 226–231; E. Gartly Jaco, "The Social Isolation Hypothesis and Schizophrenia," *American Sociological Review* 19 (1954), pp. 567–577; Aldous Huxley, *Island* (New York: 1963), pp. 89–90; Arthur T. Jersild and Mary D. Fite, "The Influence of Nursery School Experience on Children's Social Adjustments," *Child Development Monographs* 25 (1939); Helena Malley, "Growth in Social Behavior and Mental Activity After Six Months in Nursey School," *Child Development* 6 (1935), pp. 303–309; Louis P. Thorpe, *Child Psychology and Development* (New York: 1955); K. M. B. Bridges, *Social and Emotional Development of the Pre-School Child* (London: 1931); W. R. Thompson and R. Melzack, "Early Environment," *Scientific American* 194 (1956), pp. 38–42.

22. This is, in effect, the same as the classic thesis of Cooley and George Herbert Mead, which says that the individual self appears only as a result of interaction with others, and that it is liable to disintegrate when these interactions are not available. Mead, *Mind, Self and Society* (Chicago: 1934); Cooley, *op. cit.*

23. Glass and Davidson, *op. cit.*, p. 400.

24. "The person who is diagnosed as suffering from schizophrenia perceives himself as bombarded by a multiplicity of personal and family problems he is not able to handle." L. H. Rogler and A. B. Hollingshead. *Trapped: Families and Schizophrenia* (New York: 1965).

25. Robert Sommer and Humphrey Osmond, "The Schizophrenic No-Society," *Psychiatry* 25 (1962), pp. 244–255.

26. Durkheim, *op. cit.*, pp. 283–303.

27. J. G. Miller, "Input Overload and Psychopathology," *American Journal of Psychiatry* 116 (1960), pp. 695–704; Richard Meier, *A Communications Theory of Urban Growth* (Cambridge, Mass.: 1960).

28. E. T. Hall, *The Hidden Dimension* (Garden City: 1966).

29. Ministry of Housing, *Families Living at High Density* (London: 1966), pp. 29–33; John Madge, "Privacy and Social Interaction," *Transactions of the Bartlett Society* 3 (1964–1965), p. 139.

30. Leopold Rosenmayr, Wohnverhältnisse und Nachbarschaftsbeziehungen, Der Aufbau, Monograph No. 8 (Vienna: 1956), pp. 39–91.

31. Hans Strotzka, Spannungen und Lösungsversuche in Städtischer Umgebung, Der Aufbau, Monograph No. 8 (Vienna: 1956), pp. 93–108.

32. Nelson Foote, Janet Abu-Lughod, Mary Mix Foley, and Louis Winnick, *Housing Choices and Housing Constraints* (New York: 1960), pp. 107 and 392.

33. *Ibid.*, pp. 223–263 and Peter H. Rossi, *Why Families Move* (Glencoe, Ill.: 1955).

34. *Ibid.*, pp. 187–193 and Irving Rosow, "Homeownership Motives," *American Sociological Review* 13 (1948), pp. 751–756.

35. Center for Urban Studies, "Tall Flats in Pimlico," *Aspects of Change* (London: 1964), ch. 8; Santa Clara County Study, unpublished, 1966.

36. L. E. White, "The Outdoor Play of Children Living in Flats," *Living in Towns*, ed. Leo Kuper (London: 1953), pp. 235–264.

37. The problem may be stated as follows: In an infinite population of children, one-sixth are the right age and five-sixths are the wrong age. A group of r children is chosen at random. The probability, $P_{r,k}$ that these r children contain exactly k right-age children is given by the hypergeometric distribution. The probability

that r has five or more right-age children in it is $1 - \sum\limits_{k=0}^{4} P_{r,k}$.

If we now ask what is the least r that makes $1 - \sum\limits_{0}^{4} P_{r,k} > .95,$

r turns out to be fifty-four, requiring twenty-seven households.

38. J. B. Calhoun, "Population Density and Social Pathology," *Scientific American* 206 (1962), pp. 139–146.

39. William C. Loring, "Housing Characteristics and Social Disorganization," *Social Problems* (January 1956); Paul Chombard de Lauwe, *Famille et Habitation* (Paris: 1959); B. Lander, *Towards an Understanding of Juvenile Delinquency* (New York: 1954).

40. Robert C. Schmitt, "Delinquency and Crime in Honolulu," *Sociology and Social Research* 41 (March–April 1957), pp. 274–276 and "Population Densities and Mental Disorders in Honolulu," *Hawaii Medical Journal* 16 (March–April 1957), pp. 396–397.

41. Jane Jacobs, *The Death and Life of Great American Cities* (New York: 1961), pp. 10 and 206; Robert C. Schmitt, "Implications of Density in Hong Kong," *AIP Journal* 29 (1963), pp. 210–217.

42. Lander, *op. cit.*, p. 46.

43. Robert C. Schmitt, "Density, Health and Social Disorganization," *AIP Journal* 32 (1966), pp. 38–40.

44. Brian J. L. Berry, James W. Simmons, and Robert J. Tennant, "Urban Population Densities: Structure and Change," *Geographical Review* 53 (1963), pp. 389–405; John Q. Steward and William Warntz, "Physics of Population Distribution," *Journal of Regional Science*, Vol. 1 (1958), pp. 99–123.

45. Colin Clark, "Urban Population Densities," *Journal of the Royal Statistical Society*, Series A, 114 (1951), Part 4, pp. 490–496; Berry, *op. cit.*

Annotated Bibliography

ROBERT GUTMAN AND BARBARA WESTERGAARD

I. Behavioral Constraints on Building Design

1. BASIC APPROACHES TO THE BEHAVIORAL STUDY OF ARCHITECTURE

Dubos, René. *Man Adapting*. New Haven: Yale University Press, 1965. An exploration of "some of the biological and social implications of man's response to his total environment." States of health or disease are seen as the results of the organism's success or failure in its attempts to respond adaptively to environmental challenge.

Frankl, Paul. *Principles of Architectural History*, translated and edited by James F. O'Gorman. Cambridge: The M.I.T. Press, 1968. First published in German in 1914, this history of architectural principles is distinguished by its unusually systematic approach, by its method of treating several architectural properties simultaneously, and, above all, by its specific interest in the functional properties of architecture.

Gutman, Robert. "Site Planning and Social Behavior." *Journal of Social Issues* 22, no. 4 (October 1966): 103–115. A summary of research that has tried to answer the question, "How does the spatial arrangement of dwelling units influence the residents of a site?" The empirical evidence that site plans influence individual behavior or collective social action is not very strong, but the author suggests that the studies have not investigated a wide enough variety of site plans, and have ignored many of the behavioral mechanisms through which social organization and architecture are connected.

Proshansky, Harold M., Ittelson, William H., Rivlin, Leanne G., eds. *Environmental Psychology: Man and His Physical Setting*. New York: Holt, Rinehart and Winston, 1970. A collection of readings intended to define and establish the substantive and conceptual boundaries of the field of environmental psychology. As a new but rapidly growing field that is highly interdisciplinary, its literature is consequently widely dispersed, and the collection is intended to be useful to both students and practitioners.

RAPOPORT, AMOS. *House Form and Culture*. Englewood Cliffs, N.J.: Prentice Hall, 1969. A comprehensive attempt using behavioral science material to provide a conceptual framework for looking at a wide variety of house forms and types and the forces that affect them. On the basis of an examination of the primitive and vernacular architecture of many countries, the author concludes that given the various constraints of climate, technology, and the like, house form depends finally on people's views of the ideal life.

SELLS, S. B. and BERRY, C. A., eds. *Human Factors in Jet and Space Travel*. New York: Ronald, 1961. A collection of articles dealing with some of the problems involved in maintaining individuals in hostile and unusual environments. Included are discussions of the effects of such environments on perception, physical functioning, performance of skilled tasks, and group behavior.

2. ANATOMICAL AND PHYSIOLOGICAL FACTORS IN DESIGN

DREYFUSS, HENRY. *The Measure of Man*, 2nd ed. New York: Whitney Library of Design, 1967. Includes anthropometric data charts, life-size figure charts, a space standards check list, and a bibliography listing sources of anthropometric data. Written from the point of view of an industrial designer.

GOROMOSOV, M. S. *The Physiological Basis of Health Standards for Dwellings*. Public Health Papers no. 3, Geneva: WHO, 1968. Physiological aspects of home comfort and health, with discussion of thermal comfort, air circulation, illumination, noise, and the characteristics of new materials. The bibliography includes many Russian items.

LE CORBUSIER [JEANNERET-GRIS, CHARLES ÉDOUARD]. *The Modulor; A Harmonious Measure to the Human Scale Universally Applicable to Architecture and Mechanics*, translated by Peter de Francia and Anna Bostock. Cambridge, Mass.: Harvard University Press, 1954; *Modulor 2, 1955*, translated by Peter de Francia and Anna Bostock. Cambridge, Mass.: Harvard University Press, 1958. A description by Le Corbusier of the development and uses of the modulor, a measuring tool "based on the human body and on mathematics." He argues that the modulor, because it is a measure based on man, should be used as a basic design tool, and describes his use of it for many projects, including the Unité d'Habitation at Marseilles and his plans for the U.N. buildings. The second volume includes the reactions and corrections of architects and other users of the modulor.

436

Morgan, Clifford T. *et al.*, *Human Engineering Guide to Equipment Design*. New York: McGraw-Hill, 1963. Intended as a handbook of design principles. Chapters include discussions of man-machine systems, visual and auditory presentation of information, speech communication, man-machine dynamics, the design of controls, the layout of workplaces, the arrangement of groups of men and machines, designing for ease of maintenance, and the effects of the environment on human performance. There is also a chapter of anthropometric data.

Ramsey, Charles G. and Sleeper, Harold R. *Architectural Graphic Standards*. New York: John Wiley & Sons, 5th ed., 1963. A handbook for architects, engineers, decorators, builders, draftsmen, and students. Drawings and specifications are presented that provide information on such items as construction with different materials; details such as stairs, fireplaces, and doors; and space standards for homes and schools.

3. CULTURAL VARIATIONS IN ENVIRONMENTAL STANDARDS

American Public Health Association, Committee on the Hygiene of Housing. *Planning the Neighborhood*. Chicago: Public Administration Service, 1960. A reprint, with an expanded bibliography, of a 1948 manual of environmental standards on the neighborhood scale, including discussions of the physical setting in which homes should be located and the basic health criteria that should guide the planning of the residential neighborhood.

Dore, Ronald Philip. *City Life in Japan: A Study of a Tokyo Ward*. Berkeley: University of California Press, 1958. A neighborhood study of one section of Tokyo, consisting of about 300 households, made during a period of social change. Chapter 4, "Houses and Apartment Blocks," describes housing standards and conditions and illustrates the capacity of those in other cultures to live under much more crowded conditions than are considered acceptable in the United States.

Fitch, James M. and Branch, Daniel P. "Primitive Architecture and Climate." *Scientific American* 203, no. 6 (1960): 134–144. A study of the high performance of primitive architecture designed for extreme climatic conditions and usually with meager resources. American designers tend to ignore the physical environment and overestimate their technical competence, often producing buildings with poorer performance.

Sonnenfeld, Joseph. "Variable Values in Space and Landscape: An

Inquiry into the Nature of Environmental Necessity." *Journal of Social Issues* 22, no. 4 (1966): 71–82. The kind of landscape that people prefer varies with culture, sex, age, personality, occupation, and environmental experience. The author argues that man could adapt to much less space than he now has, since people accept what they have grown up with.

TAUT, BRUNO. *Houses and People of Japan.* London: John Gifford Ltd., 1938. A thorough but highly personal study of housing design in another culture. The author's attempt to explain Japanese residential architecture is in part historical and sociological, but primarily he sees housing design in Japan as a response to climate.

WEBBER, MELVIN M. "Culture, Territory, and the Elastic Mile." In Regional Studies Association *Papers and Proceedings* 13 (1964): 59–69. The author states that space perception is culturally specific. He speculates on the space-related behavior of intellectuals, summarizes some empirical findings on working class behavior in relation to space, and offers suggestions for research into space-related behavior.

4. THE CONCEPT OF PERSONAL SPACE

CONDER, P. J. "Individual Distance." *Ibis* 91 (1949): 649–655. A description, based largely on the author's observations but with references to the literature, of individual distance as it occurs among birds. The relation of individual distance to territory is clarified.

LITTLE, KENNETH B. "Personal Space." *Journal of Experimental Social Psychology* 1 (August 1965): 237–247. Includes a summary of the literature on personal space and a report of the results of a study done by the author. The author's study attempted to assess the effect that degree of acquaintance would have on interaction distance in different settings.

SIMMEL, GEORG. "Discretion." In *The Sociology of Georg Simmel,* translated and edited by Kurt H. Wolff. Glencoe, Ill.: The Free Press, 1950, pp. 320–324. An early statement of the concept that was to become known as "personal space." Simmel discusses the sphere that surrounds each personality and the distance that separates great men from others.

SOMMER, ROBERT. *Personal Space, the Behavioral Basis of Design.* Englewood Cliffs, N.J.: Prentice-Hall, 1969. A plea for basing building design on the concerns of those who will use the building. The author describes some of his empirical work on the concept of personal space and discusses the use of space in mental hospitals, schools, taverns, and college dormitories.

WOHLWILL, JOACHIM F. "The Emerging Discipline of Environmental Psychology." *American Psychologist* 25, no. 4 (April 1970): 303–312. A discussion of the relationship between the field of psychology and the general increase in interest in the physical environment. Until recently, psychologists have not concerned themselves with the physical environment but have concentrated instead on social and interpersonal influences. The author reviews the work being done, the potential benefits to both psychology and the field of environmental management, and some of the institutional problems of doing research in this area.

5. THE PHENOMENON OF TERRITORIALITY

BOURLIÈRE, F. *The Natural History of Mammals.* New York: Alfred A. Knopf, 1954. Chapter 3, "Home, Territory, and Home Range," discusses the concept of territory, and cites evidence for the lack of territory among some animals. Apparently territory is not as important for mammals as it is for birds.

CARPENTER, C. R. "Territoriality: A Review of Concepts and Problems." In *Behavior and Evolution,* edited by A. Roe and G. G. Simpson. New Haven: Yale University Press, 1958, pp. 224–250. Also in C. R. Carpenter. *Naturalistic Behavior of Nonhuman Primates.* University Park, Pa.: Penn State University Press, 1964, pp. 407–429. Bibliographical article, which reviews the development of the concept of territoriality historically and discusses its varying nature for different animals and its evolutionary and behavioral significance.

LIPMAN, ALAN. "Territoriality: A Useful Architectural Concept?" *RIBA Journal* 77, no. 2 (February 1970): 68–70. An attempt, based on past studies and the author's experience with old people's homes, to define the concept of territory, a term borrowed from animal studies, so that it can be meaningful and useful to architects and designers.

STEA, DAVID. "Space, Territory and Human Movements." *Landscape* 15, no. 1 (Autumn 1965): 13–16. A discussion of the way in which territories are affected or shaped by the designed environment; if the environment changes, the territory may too. Conversely, changes in behavior may produce territorial changes. Illustrated with examples from real and hypothetical business offices.

SUTTLES, GERALD D. *The Social Order of the Slum; Ethnicity and Ter-*

ritory in the Inner City. Chicago: University of Chicago Press, 1968. An intensive participant-observer study of a mixed ethnic community on the near West Side of Chicago. Negroes, Italians, Puerto Ricans, and Mexicans live in different sections of the area, and the importance of territory to the ordering of the social structure is stressed.

6. STUDIES AND DISCUSSIONS OF SENSORY STIMULATION

BROWNFIELD, CHARLES A. *Isolation: Clinical and Experimental Approaches.* New York: Random House, 1965. A semipopular review of the subject and literature of isolation with an extensive bibliography. The point is made that changing and varied stimulation are necessary to the organized functioning of the human organism.

HEBB, D. O. *Organization of Behavior.* New York: John Wiley & Sons, 1949. Psychology text that is in large part responsible for psychologists' increased interest in the importance of the physical environment. Introduced work on sensory deprivation into the mainstream of psychology.

HERON, W. "The Pathology of Boredom." *Scientific American* 196, no. 1 (1957): 52–56. A description of the famous McGill University experiments, under Hebb's leadership, which first showed the cognitive, perceptual, and emotional impairment that result from prolonged exposure to a completely monotonous environment.

RAPOPORT, A. AND KANTOR, R. E. "Complexity and Ambiguity in Environmental Design." *Journal of the American Institute of Planners* 33 (1967): 210–221. The authors base their argument that there is a need to provide more interesting visual fields on the psychological literature. Ambiguity (that is visual nuance allowing alternative reactions to the same building) is suggested as a way to achieve the desired complexity.

SOLOMON, PHILIP, *et al.,* eds. *Sensory Deprivation.* Cambridge, Mass.: Harvard University Press, 1961. Papers from a symposium, covering perceptual, cognitive, and motor effects of sensory deprivation, including the effect on adults of childhood sensory deprivation.

VENTURI, ROBERT. *Complexity and Contradiction in Architecture.* New York: Museum of Modern Art, 1966. An architect's attempt to present both a theory of architectural criticism and an apologia for his own work. Venturi stresses the importance of complexity and contradiction, and believes that esthetic simplicity is the result of inward complexity and that richness of meaning is more important than clarity of meaning.

440

II. Spatial Organization and Social Interaction

7. SPATIAL ORGANIZATION AS A BEHAVIOR DETERMINANT

ALEXANDER, CHRISTOPHER. "A City is Not a Tree," *Architectural Forum* 122, Part I (April 1965): 58–62 and Part II (May 1965): 58–61. To reduce confusion and ambiguity, people tend to organize situations into nonoverlapping units. This habit of mind, when it occurs among planners and designers, is responsible for producing unsuccessful planned cities, since natural cities are made up of overlapping units.

BARKER, R. G. "On the Nature of the Environment." *Journal of Social Issues* 19 (1963): 17–38. A Kurt Lewin memorial address, urging that psychologists study behavior in its natural setting and showing how both the relation of the individual to his actual social and physical environment and the effect of that environment on the individual can be handled scientifically.

CAPLOW, THEODORE, *et al. The Urban Ambience.* Totowa, N.J.: Bedminster, 1964. An empirical study of twenty-five neighborhoods in San Juan, Puerto Rico, which led both to refinements in the theory of the neighborhood and to practical information for the San Juan city planners. Included are sociometric charts of interaction networks for each neighborhood, and analyses of the relationship between the intensity and extensity of interaction, of the conditions that determine residential satisfaction and stability, and of the bases on which neighbors choose each other for interaction.

GULLAHORN, J. T. "Distance and Friendship as Factors in the Gross Interaction Matrix." *Sociometry* 15, nos. 1–2 (1952): 123–134. A study of the social organization of clerical workers: even where work did not require cooperation, the gross interaction rate was largely determined by distance.

OLSSON, GUNNAR. *Distance and Human Interaction: A Review and Bibliography.* Regional Science Research Institute Bibliography Series, no. 2. Philadelphia: The Institute, 1965. A review of the literature and a bibliography of the role of distance in human interaction. Special attention is paid to the spatial patterns of location theories, migration and diffusion models, and gravity and potential models.

STRODTBECK, F. L. AND HOOK, L. H. "The Social Dimensions of a Twelve-Man Jury Table." *Sociometry* 24, no. 4 (1961): 397–415. A sociometric study of the influence of spatial position on small group

441

interaction. Participation is probably determined more by visual accessibility than by actual distance.

8. THE SOCIAL CONTEXT OF ENVIRONMENTAL PLANNING

FESTINGER, LEON, SCHACTER, STANLEY, AND BACK, KURT. *Social Pressures in Informal Groups.* New York: Harper and Brothers, 1950. The classic study of the effect of propinquity on interaction. The authors studied interaction and communication in a married students housing project and found that group cohesion was largely determined by the ease of interaction (measured in terms of both physical nearness and the position of the house within the court).

GANS, HERBERT J. "Planning and Social Life, Friendship and Neighbor Relations in Suburban Communities." *Journal of the American Institute of Planners* 27 (May 1961): 134–140; also in *People and Plans.* New York: Basic Books, 1968, pp. 152–165. Propinquity may influence interaction, particularly in a new community, but friendship depends more on homogeneity of interests, background, and the like. The site planner should not try to impose a particular pattern of social relationships, but should rather introduce sufficient diversity in house types and siting to make sure the residents can choose their own patterns of social relationships.

KUPER, LEO, ed. *Living in Towns.* London: Cresset, 1953. A collection of research papers in urban sociology. Two-thirds of the book is taken up with a report of the editor's sociological field study of two low-income neighborhoods in Coventry, one an old neighborhood and the other a new public development, from which he concludes that planned environments do not in themselves directly influence behavior.

LITWAK, EUGENE. "Voluntary Associations and Neighborhood Cohesion." *American Sociological Review* 26 (April 1961): 258–271. An attempt to consider some of the large-scale organizational factors that influence community cohesion. The author believes that voluntary associations help integrate individuals into local groups, and thus large corporations by encouraging local community participation increase local cohesion.

MERTON, ROBERT K. "The Social Psychology of Housing." In *Current Trends in Social Psychology,* edited by W. Dennis. Pittsburgh: University of Pittsburgh Press, 1948, pp. 163–217. A general discussion of the use of social psychology in the field of housing and a report on studies carried out in three housing developments. In one of

442

these studies it was found that propinquity was a strong determinant of interaction.

WEBBER, MELVIN M. "Order in Diversity: Community without Propinquity." In *Cities and Space,* edited by Lowdon Wingo, Jr. Baltimore: Johns Hopkins Press, 1963, pp. 23–54. The argument is made that the city derives from cultural, not spatial, factors. Its essence is specialization, which leads to interdependence and interaction; urban order therefore lies not in spatial, mappable patterns, but in complex social organization.

WILNER, DANIEL M., WALKLEY, ROSABELLE PRICE, AND COOK, STUART W. *Human Relations in Interracial Housing.* Minneapolis: University of Minnesota Press, 1955. A study of four housing projects to determine whether the interaction coming from proximity in integrated projects led to increased harmony between races or increased antagonism. Opportunities for contact plus a favorable social climate produced the most improvement in relations.

9. CULTURAL VARIATIONS IN SPATIAL RELATIONSHIPS

ERIKSON, ERIK H. "Inner and Outer Space: Reflections on Womanhood." *Daedalus* 93, no. 2 (Spring 1964): 582–606. Although the article is intended as an analysis of the fundamental nature of women, there is discussion of what Erikson sees as basic differences in the attitudes of men and women toward space.

HALL, EDWARD TWITCHELL. *The Hidden Dimension.* Garden City, N.Y.: Doubleday, 1966. The major book-length discussion of "proxemics," or man's use of space as a specialized elaboration of culture. Cultural differences in attitudes toward personal space are described. Particular attention is paid to the stress that results from overcrowding.

HALLOWELL, A. IRVING. "Cultural Factors in Spatial Orientation." In *Culture and Experience.* Philadelphia: University of Pennsylvania Press, 1955, pp. 184–202. A discussion of cultural variability in spatial orientation with a detailed description of the spatial orientation of the Saulteaux.

ROSENGREN, W. R. AND DEVAULT, S. "The Sociology of Time and Space in an Obstetrical Hospital." In *The Hospital in Modern Society,* edited by E. Freidson. New York: The Free Press, 1963, pp. 261–292. People's interactions are not adequately defined by their status and roles; the interactions also depend on the physical setting. In the interstitial areas of the hospital (hallways, corridors) behavior was less stereotyped and more informal social organizations prevailed.

WATSON, MICHAEL AND GRAVES, THEODORE. "An Analysis of Proxemic Behavior." *American Anthropologist* 68, no. 4 (August, 1966): 971–985. An empirical study, using Arab and American students at the University of Colorado as subjects. The authors collected proxemic data and tested Hall's notation and the validity of his impressions of Arab-American differences. They did indeed find that Arab interaction distance is less than American.

10. COMMUNITY AND PRIVACY

ALEXANDER, CHRISTOPHER AND CHERMAYEFF, SERGE. *Community and Privacy.* Garden City, N.Y.: Doubleday, 1963. Urban areas must be designed so that everyone has the opportunity to be private and yet retain the advantages of living in a community. A list of categories for solving the problem of fitting private housing into an urban pattern is developed and several cluster plans are evaluated in terms of these categories.

HALMOS, PAUL. *Solitude and Privacy: A Study of Social Isolation; Its Causes and Therapy.* London: Routledge & Kegan Paul, 1952. An inquiry into the problem of social isolation based on extensive reading in psychological and other literatures and on the author's empirical study. Society, as it is presently organized, frustrates man's attempts to achieve a satisfactory group life, but without the proper balance between community and privacy, neurosis results.

MADGE, CHARLES. "Private and Public Spaces." *Human Relations* 3, no. 2 (1950): 187–199. A discussion of one type of social decision—the subdivision of living spaces, both public and private. The problem is to balance the need for privacy against the dangers of withdrawal, and the author considers the social and psychological consequences of too much and too little privacy.

MADGE, JOHN. "Privacy and Social Interaction." *Transactions of the Bartlett Society* 3 (1964–1965): 123–141, Bartlett School of Architecture, University College, London. A review of some of the psychological and sociological reasons for the need for privacy, with some design suggestions for achieving it. The author argues that the home must make allowance for both privacy and social interaction, particularly since most people's jobs today require that they remain accessible to others at all times.

SIMMEL, ARNOLD. "Privacy." *International Encyclopedia of the Social Sciences,* Vol. 12. New York: Macmillan and The Free Press, 1968, pp. 480–487. Comments on changing ideas about the right to privacy, a discussion of the determinants and indicators of privacy, a functional analysis of privacy, and a discussion of the law of privacy.

SIMMEL, GEORG. "Secrecy" and "The Secret Society." In *The Sociology of Georg Simmel*, translated and edited by Kurt H. Wolff. Glencoe, Ill.: The Free Press, 1950, pp. 330–376. A classic discussion of the role of secrecy (and privacy) in social life, both for the individual and for the group.

WESTIN, ALAN F. *Privacy and Freedom*. New York: Atheneum, 1967. Drawing on the sociological and psychological literature, the author presents a thorough discussion of the function of privacy for the individual and the group, including the nation. There is an extensive bibliography.

11. CRITIQUES OF ARCHITECTURAL DETERMINISM

BROADY, MAURICE. *Planning for People*. London: National Council of Social Service, 1968. A collection of essays in which the author attempts to integrate social planning with land-use and economic planning. He offers positive advice to planners in an effort to counter his rejection of architectural determinism.

GANS, HERBERT J. *The Levittowners*. New York: Pantheon, 1967. A report of the two years the author spent in Levittown, N.J., in the attempt to find out how a new community comes into being, how people change when they leave the city, and what their lives and politics are like in suburbia. The author found that the nature of the community depended upon the nature of those who moved there, that most suburbanites were happy, and that life in the suburbs was not the competitive wasteland pictured in the suburban myth.

GANS, HERBERT J. "The Potential Environment and the Effective Environment." In *People and Plans*. New York: Basic Books, 1968, pp. 4–11. The physical environment is relevant to behavior insofar as it affects the social system of those who will use it. However, what the urban designer plans is only a potential environment; the way in which it is used makes it into an effective environment. Planned facilities should take this distinction into account.

KELLER, SUZANNE. *The Urban Neighborhood*. New York: Random House, 1968. A thorough review of the different meanings of the concept of neighborhood and of the evidence for the effect of physical planning on neighborhoods. The author is generally pessimistic about the role the physical planner can play in encouraging the development of a sense of neighborhood.

445

MICHELSON, WILLIAM H. *Man and His Urban Environment.* Reading, Mass.: Addison Wesley, 1970. A sociological approach to the question of how much and how the physical form of the city shapes the lives of its inhabitants. A synthesis of past research relating life style, stage in the life cycle, social class, values, and pathology to the urban environment.

WILLMOTT, P. AND COONEY, E. "Community Planning and Sociological Research: A Problem of Collaboration." *Journal of the American Institute of Planners* 29, no. 2 (May 1963): 123–126. A general discussion of the difficulties of coordinating architectural practice and sociological research, plus a brief description of a study designed to see if sociological research on physical planning could be useful. Although people reported differences in sociability, privacy, and isolation with buildings of different types, the difficulty of weighing, for example, the benefits of privacy against the costs of isolation remains.

III. Environmental Influences on Health and Well-Being

12. HOUSING AND PHYSICAL HEALTH

LEVINE, SOL AND SCOTCH, NORMAN A., eds. *Social Stress.* Chicago: Aldine, 1970. A collection of essays reviewing the sources of social stress (family, work, class, degree of urbanization) and the consequences to the individual (including physical and mental illness and social pathology). Theoretical models and problems of research methodology are also discussed.

LORING, WILLIAM C. "Housing Characteristics and Social Disorganization." *Social Problems* 3, no. 3 (1956): 160–168. Description of a pilot study by the housing authority of metropolitan Boston to discover just what aspects of density and bad housing have a causal effect on health and social disorganization. The conclusion is that the number of social roles played by people per given amount of space determines whether or not housing will be harmful.

MARTIN, A. E. "Environment, Housing and Health." *Urban Studies* 4, no. 1 (February 1967): 1–21. A history of the relation between housing and health and a discussion of the research methods that could show the influence of housing and environment on mortality and health. The British literature is reviewed, and methodological problems, which are considerable in this area, are discussed.

POND, M. ALLEN. "The Influence of Housing on Health." *Marriage and*

Family Living 19, no. 2 (May 1957): 154–159. A short, clear summary of the relationship of housing to health including sections on communicable diseases, chronic diseases, mental illness, accidents, and overcrowding. The characteristics of healthful housing are reviewed, and a plea is made for more research.

SCHORR, ALVIN LOUIS. *Slums and Social Insecurity.* Washington, D.C.: Government Printing Office, 1963. Also London: Nelson, 1964. A thorough review of the interrelation between bad housing and poverty and of the need for coordination between physical and social planning. Housing affects one's perception of oneself, contributes to or relieves stress, and affects health.

SELYE, HANS. *The Stress of Life.* New York: McGraw-Hill, 1956. Includes a history of the concept of stress and a description of the body mechanisms involved. The discussion of the medical aspects of stress includes material on diseases of adaptation, that is, diseases caused by failures in the stress-fighting mechanisms (*e.g.* digestive disorders, heart failures).

13. ACOUSTICAL AND VISUAL FACTORS IN HEALTH AND WELL-BEING

BLACK, JOHN W. "The Effect of Room Characteristics upon Vocal Intensity and Rate." *Journal of the Acoustical Society of America* 22 (March 1950): 174–176. Rate and intensity of reading are affected by reverberation time and the size of a room, not by its shape. The rate is slower in larger and less reverberant rooms, the vocal intensity is greater in smaller and less reverberant rooms, and intensity increases as reverberation decreases.

GLASS, DAVID C., SINGER, JEROME E., AND FRIEDMAN, LUCY N. "Psychic Cost of Adaptation to an Environmental Stressor." *Journal of Personality and Social Psychology* 12, no. 3 (July 1969): 200–210. Description of two experiments that led to the conclusion that unpredictable noises lower a person's tolerance for frustration and his performance efficiency. The effect is greater the louder the noise but is smaller if the person thinks he is controlling the noise. Predictable noises do not have this effect.

HOPKINSON, R. G., PETHERBRIDGE, P., AND LONGMORE, J. *Daylighting.* London: Heinemann, 1966. Handbook for students and practitioners based largely on research done at the Building Research Station in England. The approach is essentially psychophysical, that is, the emphasis is on *good* lighting, not on quantitative standards. The final chapter gives examples of designing for daylight to illustrate the use of the techniques.

MANNING, PETER, ed. *Office Design: A Study of Environment.* Liverpool University, Pilkington Research Unit, 1965. A study of the design and performance of office buildings and office spaces and people's attitudes toward their offices. An attempt is made to present a picture of the total environment of the office, rather than separating the requirements for heating from the requirements for lighting, and so on.

RODDA, MICHAEL. *Noise and Society.* Edinburgh and London: Oliver & Boyd, 1967. An attempt to make present knowledge about noise available to laymen. The major problem for most people is not a loss of hearing acuity but annoyance and possibly lower efficiency. The worst noise sources are domestic equipment, advertising, automobiles, and airplanes; airplanes are likely to prove most troublesome in the future.

WELLS, B. W. P. "Subjective Responses to the Lighting Installation in a Modern Office Building and their Design Implications." *Building Science* 1 (1965): 57–68. Examines conditions under which subjective needs and comfort are met, not the levels of illumination physiologically necessary for clerical work. People think they need daylight and a view from a window; actually they tend to think they have more daylight than they in fact do; therefore buildings could be deeper without lowering office workers' comfort.

14. THE BEHAVIORAL EFFECTS OF ESTHETIC CONDITIONS

BERLYNE, D. E. *Conflict, Arousal and Curiosity.* New York: McGraw-Hill, 1960. A psychological study primarily concerned with the motivation of perceptual and intellectual activities, which includes material on the role of sensory deprivation as an influence on the formation of esthetic judgment.

BIRREN, FABER. *Light, Color, and Environment.* New York: Van Nostrand Reinhold, 1969. Contains a summary of research on the effect of color on plants and animals, historical material on the use of color, and a discussion of the psychological and emotional effects of color. Practical suggestions are given for the use of color in offices, industrial plants, hospitals, and schools.

DEWEY, JOHN. *Art As Experience.* New York: Capricorn, 1959. An attempt to understand art and its role in civilization in terms of the continuity between esthetic experience and the normal processes of living. An argument against the separation of works of art and everyday life.

448

PARR, A. E. "Psychological Aspects of Urbanology." *Journal of Social Issues* 22, no. 4 (1966): 39–45. A discussion of the psychological effect of visual monotony and enclosure, qualities the author believes are typical of today's cities.

SEGALL, MARSHALL H., CAMPBELL, DONALD T., AND HERSKOVITS, MELVILLE J. *The Influence of Culture on Visual Perception.* New York: Bobbs-Merrill, 1966. A report of a research project designed to determine the role that culturally determined experience plays in visual perceptions. The research demonstrated that there are cross-cultural differences in the perception of illusory line drawings, based on different habits of visual inference learned by people in different visual environments.

15. THE BUILT ENVIRONMENT AND MENTAL HEALTH

FARIS, ROBERT E. L. AND DUNHAM, H. WARREN. *Mental Disorders in Urban Areas; an Ecological Study of Schizophrenia and Other Psychoses.* Chicago: University of Chicago Press, 1939. A pioneer study in the social aspects of mental disorder. Social isolation was found to produce mental breakdown, but different types of mental illness were found in different areas of the city or in specific types of communities. The basic data are from Chicago, but there is comparative data from Providence.

GUTMAN, ROBERT. "Population Mobility in the American Middle Class." In *The Urban Condition,* edited by Leonard J. Duhl. New York: Basic Books, 1963, pp. 172–183. A discussion of the movement of population to the suburbs—both old established suburbs and new developments—and an attempt to answer three questions: How do suburban settlements react to middle-class whites after they've moved in, how do the migrants respond to the settlements, and what is the impact of mobility on the migrants themselves?

HARE, E. H. AND SHAW, G. K. *Mental Health on a New Housing Estate.* London: Oxford University Press, 1965. A comparative study of health in two districts in Croyden, one a new housing estate and the other an older neighborhood. Mental health in the two populations was roughly the same, suggesting that either the lack of amenities on the new estate did not lead to problems or that it was compensated for by other factors.

KANTOR, MILDRED B., ed. *Mobility and Mental Health.* Springfield, Ill.: Charles C Thomas, 1965. Proceedings of a conference on community mental health. Part I contains previously unpublished research deal-

449

ing with mobility and mental health by workers in psychiatry, epidemiology, sociology, psychology, and demography; part II contains discussion papers and a summary prepared after the conference.

PLANT, J. S., "Some Psychiatric Aspects of Crowded Living Conditions." *American Journal of Psychiatry* 86 (March 1930): 849–860. A discussion, based on clinical evidence, of the effects of crowded living conditions, particularly on children. The author suggests that it is difficult for children raised in crowded conditions to develop a strong sense of individuality.

SROLE, LEO, *et al. Mental Health in the Metropolis* 1. The Midtown Manhattan Study. New York: McGraw-Hill, 1962. LANGER, T. S. AND MICHAEL, S. T., *Life Stress and Mental Health* 2. The Midtown Manhattan Study. New York: The Free Press, 1963. A large-scale empirical study, made in midtown Manhattan, of the relationship between mental disorder and the sociocultural environment. Volume 1 deals with the relationship of demographic factors to mental disorder; volume 2 with the relationship of stressful experiences, lack of close friends, and mental worries to mental disorder.

16. THE SOCIAL CONSEQUENCES OF OVERCROWDING

CALHOUN, JOHN B. "Population Density and Social Pathology." *Scientific American* 206 (February 1962): 139–146. Rats conditioned to eat in company develop a tendency to congregate in one place, leading to what is called a "behavioral sink." The article describes the disruption of nesting, sexual, aggressive, and feeding behavior caused by the overcrowding.

CHOMBART DE LAUWE, PAUL. *Famille et Habitation.* Paris: Editions du Centre National de la Recherche Scientific, 1959. A thorough empirical study of three postwar French housing estates, including one by Le Corbusier. The architects' decisions seem to have been based more on government regulations than on users' needs, and the resultant overcrowding, bad soundproofing, and lack of amenities produced family strains, particularly for the children.

CHRISTIAN, J. J. "Endocrine Adaptive Mechanisms and the Physiological Regulation of Population Growth." In *Physiological Mammalogy,* edited by William V. Meyer and Richard G. Van Gelder. Vol. 1, Mammalian Populations. New York: Academic Press, 1963, pp. 189–353. Purely behavioral or social interaction acting through the central nervous system produces an endocrine response, which is described in the first section. The second section reviews the physiology of endocrine adaptation in different mammalian populations, including descriptions of lab populations of fixed and growing size and reports of natural populations.

GRAHAM, HUGH DAVID AND GURR, TED ROBERT, eds. *Violence in America; Historical and Comparative Perspectives.* Washington, D.C.: U.S. Government Printing Office, 1969, 2 vols. A staff report to the National Commission on the Causes and Prevention of Violence, the book attempts a descriptive and analytical history of violence in the United States and Western Europe. Chapter 21 deals with the connection between overcrowding and aggression.

SCHMITT, ROBERT C. "Implications of Density in Hong Kong." *Journal of the American Institute of Planners* 29 (1963): 210–217. Hong Kong has one of the highest overall density rates in the world without high rates of death, disease, or social disorganization. This is partly a result of Chinese tradition, partly because the refugees are accustomed to worse conditions, and partly a result of the fact that there are not many cars.

WINSBOROUGH, H. H. "The Social Consequences of High Population Density." *Law and Contemporary Problems* 30, no. 1 (Winter 1965): 120–126. An attempt to help the city planner by disentangling (with confusing results) the effects of density on health from the effects of other, associated variables.

IV. The Social Meaning of Architecture

17. ENVIRONMENTAL PERCEPTION

GREGORY, R. L. *Eye and Brain.* New York: McGraw-Hill, 1966. A clearly written examination of the physiological and psychological problems involved in seeing: how is information from the eyes coded into neural terms, into the language of the brain, and reconstituted into the experience of surrounding objects?

HOWARD, I. P. AND TEMPLETON, W. B. *Human Spatial Orientation.* London: John Wiley & Sons, 1966. A thorough discussion of those aspects of human behavior that are determined by the angular position of the body or head with respect to any stable, external reference system. The development of orientation in children is also discussed. There is an extensive bibliography.

LOWENTHAL, DAVID, ed. *Environmental Perception and Behavior.* University of Chicago, Department of Geography, Research Paper no. 109, 1967. A collection of essays, of uneven quality, dealing with people's attitudes toward the environment, particularly the subjective, often unconscious, and culturally dominated forces that play a major role in determining how people see the environment and how they act in it.

LYNCH, KEVIN. *The Image of the City.* Cambridge, Mass.: The Technology Press and Harvard University Press, 1960. A seminal work dealing with the mental image of the city held by its citizens, particularly the clarity or legibility of that image. A good environmental image produces a sense of emotional security, and the argument is made that we should build our cities to encourage, not discourage, our tendencies to organize our environment.

PIAGET, JEAN AND INHELDER, BÄRBEL. *The Child's Conception of Space,* translated by F. G. Langdon and J. L. Lunzer. New York: W. W. Norton, 1967. A study of the development of the child's conception of representational (not perceptual) space. The child starts with certain primitive topological relationships such as proximity and separation, order and enclosure, which are necessary to his subsequent grasp of Euclidean notions.

RAPOPORT, AMOS AND HAWKES, RON. "The Perception of Urban Complexity." *Journal of the American Institute of Planners* 36, no. 2 (March 1970): 106–111. Complexity, defined in terms of the maximum rate of usable information received and processed by the individual, is a desirable quality for an urban environment. The significance of information provided by any object or event depends not just on the object but also on the individual's culture, personal experience, learning, and current emotional and motivational states.

THIEL, PHILIP. "A Sequence-Experience Notation for Architectural and Urban Spaces." *Town Planning Review* 32, no. 1 (April 1961): 33–52. An attempt to develop a system of graphic notation to represent the perception of architectural and urban spaces. Since architecture must be experienced in time, the planner, to understand his material, needs a tool analogous to dance notation.

18. THEORY OF ARCHITECTURAL SYMBOLISM

CHOAY, FRANÇOISE. *The Modern City: Planning in the Nineteenth Century.* New York: George Braziller, 1969. A history of nineteenth-century urban planning that makes use of semiological theory to account for the chaotic condition of twentieth-century urban forms. The author believes that twentieth-century urban planning is still heavily influenced by nineteenth-century modes of thought.

CONSTANTINE, MILDRED AND JACOBSON, EGBERT. *Sign Language.* New

452

York: Reinhold, 1961. They show, mainly by pictures, how signs can contribute to the total effect of a building or cityscape. "Properly understood, placed and designed, all of our signs can become a new kind of heraldry, enriching the structures and the landscape."

GOODMAN, PAUL. "Seating Arrangements: An Elementary Lecture in Functional Planning." In *Utopian Essays and Practical Proposals*. New York: Vintage Books, 1951, pp. 156–181. Current seating arrangements in, for example, houses of parliament, reflect cultural attitudes; future seating arrangements could be planned in terms of what one wishes to accomplish rather than by convention.

JENCKS, CHARLES AND BAIRD, GEORGE, eds. *Meaning in Architecture*. New York: George Braziller, 1969. A crude and not always successful attempt to apply the principles of semiology to the understanding of architecture. The book includes alongside each article a running commentary by the editors and other contributors with an occasional rejoinder by the author.

WOHL, R. RICHARD AND STRAUSS, ANSELM L. "Symbolic Representation and the Urban Milieu." *American Journal of Sociology* 63, no. 5 (March 1958): 523–532. Cities are so complex that people must represent them by devices that simplify and evoke images and sentiments. The article describes the manner and means whereby city people organize their perceptions of the environment to achieve social perspective on urban life.

19. THE RELATION OF ARCHITECTURE TO PERSONALITY DYNAMICS

BACHELARD, GASTON. *The Poetics of Space*. New York: Orion Press, 1964. A study by a French phenomenologist of many aspects of attitudes toward space. Of particular interest are the chapters on the house, in which Bachelard examines the special qualities of the image of the house.

BALINT, MICHAEL. "Friendly Expanses—Horrid Empty Spaces." *International Journal of Psychoanalysis* 36, part 4/5 (1955): 225–241. People can be divided into two groups in terms of their attitudes toward space: those who enjoy a temporary loss of security and those who hold on to firm ground. For the first the world consists of friendly expanses dotted more or less densely with dangerous and unpredictable objects; for the second the world consists of objects separated by horrid empty spaces.

BROWER, SIDNEY N. "Territoriality, The Exterior Spaces, The Signs We Learn to Read." *Landscape* 15, no. 1 (Autumn 1965): 9–12. Four different kinds of territory are distinguished, according to the degree of restriction of admission and controls over action within the territory. It is important that the design communicate clearly what kind of territory is involved.

FLÜGEL, J. C. *The Psychology of Clothes.* London: Hogarth, 1930. An analysis by a prominent psychoanalyst of the functions served by clothes other than mere protection. The method of analysis could be used for a similar study of the functions served by architecture.

GOLDFINGER, ERNO. "The Elements of Enclosed Space" and "Urbanism and Spatial Order." *Architectural Review* (November 1941): 129–131, (December 1941): 163–166, (January 1942): 5–9. A series of three articles which focus particularly on the implications arising from the fact that buildings (and cities) enclose space. What makes up the sensation of space and the ways in which high-speed travel has changed our urban perceptions are also discussed.

HARTMAN, CHESTER W. "Social Values and Housing Orientations." *Journal of Social Issues* 19, no. 2 (April 1963): 113–131. One cannot judge residents' attitudes toward housing simply on the basis of its physical condition. In Boston's West End 80 per cent of those in an area condemned by the housing authority as a slum liked their housing; the objective quality of the apartment mattered only to those who were not attached to the neighborhood.

RUESCH, JURGEN AND KEES, WELDON. *Nonverbal Communication.* Berkeley and Los Angeles: University of California Press, 1956. An attempt to analyze what we mean when we discuss the "atmosphere" of a house or a section of a city. Includes discussion of what is being expressed by the arrangement of furniture in a house or merchandise in a shop window.

SEARLES, HAROLD F. *The Nonhuman Environment.* New York: International Universities Press, 1960. The author, a psychiatrist dealing primarily with schizophrenic patients, believes that the nonhuman environment, far from being of little or no importance to the development of personality, is one of the most important ingredients of human psychological existence. Each individual has a strong sense of relatedness to his nonhuman environment, which he ignores at his psychological peril.

20. ARCHITECTURAL PROPERTIES AND SOCIAL STATUS

CHAPMAN, DENNIS. *The Home and Social Status.* London: Routledge & Kegan Paul, 1955. An empirical study of the interaction of family and social status; differences in social status were found to be reflected in differences in the pattern of use of the home, in material, cultural, and esthetic equipment, and in location.

FORM, WILLIAM H. AND STONE, GREGORY P. "Urbanism, Anonymity, and Status Symbolism." *American Journal of Sociology* 62 (March 1957): 504–514. Status symbolism is important to urban sociology, because in the city, unlike the small town, the individual must deal with so many other individuals that there is no time for the kind of social contact that enables status to be bestowed in terms of rights and duties. The authors examine the variation in the symbolism used by different socioeconomic groups to bestow status on anonymous others.

MACK, RAYMOND W. "Ecological Patterns in an Industrial Shop." *Social Forces* 32, no. 4 (May 1954): 351–356. A case study applying ecological analysis to an industrial situation. A man's residential location within certain physical boundaries was taken as a status symbol and became a datum in defining his social relations, in this example extending from residence to work.

SEELEY, JOHN R., SIM, R. ALEXANDER, AND LOOSLEY, ELIZABETH W. "Shelter." In *Crestwood Heights, A Study of the Culture of Suburban Life.* New York: Basic Books, 1956, pp. 42–62. A chapter from a study of a middle-class Canadian suburb, in which the special role of the house is discussed. Particularly relevant is the discussion of the psychocultural functions of the house: the house as property, the house as stage, the house as home.

WERTHMAN, CARL, MANDEL, JERRY S., AND DIENSTFREY, TED. *Planning and the Purchase Decision.* University of California at Berkeley, Institute of Urban and Regional Development, Center for Planning and Development Research, Preprint no. 10 (July 1965). A study to find out what people who bought into planned communities thought they were buying and why. The class image of the community and the investment potential of a home were found to be important and intertwined considerations. Furthermore, the choice of a home also involves a choice of social identity.

21. THE SOCIAL FUNCTION OF ARCHITECTURAL SYMBOLISM

DURKHEIM, ÉMILE. *The Elementary Forms of the Religious Life,* translated by Joseph Ward Swain. New York: Macmillan, n. d. Durkheim's classic study of comparative religion, which includes discussion of the social role of religious beliefs and practices.

ELIADE, MIRCEA. *Images and Symbols,* translated by Philip Mairet. New York: Sheed & Ward, 1969. Includes a discussion of the universal nature of the idea of the city as sacred because it lies at the center of the universe. The idea of the city as the place where the cosmic mountain, with roots in the earth and the summit on heaven, is to be found is also discussed, and examples from a wide range of cultures are used as illustration.

FIREY, WALTER. "Sentiment and Symbolism as Ecological Variables." *American Sociological Review* 10, no. 2 (April 1945): 140–148. Space is not only an impediment but also a symbol. Locational activities are not just economizing agents but bear sentiments that influence the process of location. An argument against economic ecology, illustrated with examples from Boston.

GUTMAN, ROBERT. "Library Architecture and People." In *The Library Building Consultant Role and Responsibility*, edited by Ernest R. De Prospo, Jr. New Brunswick, N.J.: Rutgers University Press, 1969, pp. 11–29. An analysis of library buildings in terms of five properties considered significant for the relation of buildings to society and behavior: ambiance, amenity, communication net, symbol, and architectonic space. Many of the difficulties that arise in the relationship between library architects and library planners can be traced to the failure to admit that symbolism is an inescapable element in building design.

V. The Application of Behavioral Science to Design

22. PROBLEMS OF APPLYING THE BEHAVIORAL SCIENCES IN THE DESIGN PROCESS

GUTMAN, ROBERT. "What Architectural Schools Expect from Sociology." *AIA Journal* 49, no. 3 (March 1968): 70–77. A review of the kinds of sociology courses typically taken by architectural students in the United States and Britain, and the kinds of questions architectural students tend to expect sociologists to be able to answer. Some of the reasons why the interaction between architectural students and sociologists is not always successful are also discussed.

HIGGIN, GURTH AND JESSOP, NEIL. *Communications in the Building Industry.* London: Tavistock Publications, 1965. A report of a study of the building industry made by a specialist in operations research and a social psychologist with recommendations for research projects that would help the industry. The difficulties in communication faced by the industry are seen as consequences of the fact that the resource controllers are technically interdependent and organizationally independent.

LIPMAN, ALAN. "The Architectural Belief System and Social Behaviour." *British Journal of Sociology* 20, no. 2 (June 1969): 190–204. An examination of the way in which the architect's belief that he can influence social behavior helps him resolve some of the difficulties in his working situation. Because he sees himself as satisfying profound needs, it is not so upsetting that he makes money from his clients, nor that there is a gulf between his esthetic ideas and those of the public.

NORBERG-SCHULZ, CHRISTIAN. *Intentions in Architecture.* Oslo: Universitetsforlaget, 1966. An attempt to assimilate sociological and psychological concepts into the tradition of architectural criticism. The book presents a theory that would encompass both the study of building tasks and the finished building, and then uses it to analyze the state of contemporary architecture.

SOMMER, ROBERT. "Can Behavioural Studies be Useful as Well as Ornamental?" *Transactions of the Bartlett Society* 5 (1966–1967): 47–65, Bartlett School of Architecture, University College, London. A discussion of the difficulties faced by designers trying to incorporate social science findings in their work. Unless these findings are translated into a form that shows how they affect design, they may be only of interest, not of use.

23. BEHAVIORAL APPROACHES TO DESIGN SOLUTIONS

BROLIN, BRENT C. AND ZEISEL, JOHN. "Mass Housing: Social Research and Design." *Architectural Forum* 129, no. 1 (July–August 1968): 66–71. An attempt to apply social science principles to the design of mass housing. The authors believe that architects should not impose their ideas of proper social organization on other people. Using Gans' observations on the Italian-Americans in Boston's West End, the authors suggest ways in which housing could be designed to support the group's existing way of life.

GOOD, LAWRENCE R., SIEGEL, SAUL M., AND BAY, ALFRED PAUL, eds. *Therapy by Design.* Springfield, Ill.: Charles C Thomas, 1965. Part I is a report of a project carried out at the Topeka State Hospital in which the influence of architecture on mental patients was studied. Part II contains the proceedings of a conference of social scientists and architects called to discuss the project.

HOLE, W. V. AND ATTENBURROW, J. J. *Houses and People: A Review of*

457

User Studies at the Building Research Station. London: HMSO, 1966. A review of British research showing people's reactions to planning and facilities in existing mass housing. Meant as a guide to design, the book considers family activity patterns and their effect upon room use and suggests likely future trends in user needs.

LANGDON, F. J. *Modern Offices: A User Survey.* Ministry of Technology, Building Research Station, National Building Studies, Research Paper no. 41. London: HMSO, 1966. A report of a survey on attitudes toward offices. The physical environment was found to be much less important to satisfaction than the intrinsic characteristics of the job, but this did not mean that it was totally unimportant.

RAVEN, JOHN. "Sociological Evidence on the House." *Architectural Review* 142, no. 845 (July 1967): 68–72, and 142, no. 847 (September 1967): 236–240. A review in two parts of the empirical sociological evidence on housing, both British and American. The first article deals with space within the dwelling, the second with what people expect of their home environment and the influence it exerts on them.

STOKE, STUART M. *et al. Student Reactions to Study Facilities.* Amherst, Mass.: 1960. A report of a study made at four New England colleges as part of the planning for a new college. The spaces used by students to study and their reactions to these spaces were investigated. There was a clear preference for small spaces, and most studying was done in the student's room.

24. ENVIRONMENTAL ASSESSMENT

"BUILDING APPRAISAL: ST. MICHAEL'S ACADEMY, KILWINNING." *Architects' Journal* 151, no. 1 (January 7, 1970): 9–50. A study by the Building Performance Research Unit, an interdisciplinary team at the University of Strathclyde, of a school in Scotland. The team is trying to develop techniques of appraisal in use and appraisal in design so that it will be possible to predict how a building will work.

"HOUSING RESEARCH AND DEVELOPMENT." *Architectural Design* 36 (August 1966): 379–402. A report on the work of the British Ministry of Housing and Local Government Research and Development Group. An explanation is given of the methods they use for preparing briefs, designing projects, and evaluating finished projects, and examples are shown of some of the projects they have undertaken.

MICHIGAN, UNIVERSITY OF, SCHOOL ENVIRONMENTS RESEARCH PROJECT. *The Effect of Windowless Classrooms on Elementary School Children.* Ann Arbor: Architectural Research Laboratory, Department of Architecture, University of Michigan, 1965. A report of a case

458

study of the effect of windowless classrooms on primary school children. Windowless rooms decreased outside distractions and increased available wall space and apparently had little effect on learning ability.

RAE, JOHN. "Heathrow." *Architects' Journal* 151, no. 20 (May 20, 1970): 1243–1262 and 151, no. 21 (May 27, 1970): 1323–1338. An evaluation study of an airport terminal. The article compares the actual use of the building with the architects' intentions and examines the relationship of the planning concepts to the finished building.

TRITES, DAVID K. "Radial Nursing Units Prove Best in Controlled Study." *Modern Hospital* 112, no. 4 (April 1969): 94–99. A description of a hospital deliberately constructed in order to test alternative floor plans. The follow-up study questioned patients, nurses, doctors, administrators, and visitors, and found a clear preference for a radial design, a preference substantiated by some of the objective measurements made in the study.

WHITE, R. B. *Qualitative Studies of Buildings.* Ministry of Technology, Building Research Station, National Building Studies, Special Report no. 39. London: HMSO, 1966. A study of the long-term durability and functional performance of the De La Warr Pavilion in Bexhill-on-Sea and the Gilbey Building in London in relation to their owners' and designers' intentions.

25. PROBLEMS OF SCIENTIFIC DESIGN METHODOLOGY

FRAMPTON, KENNETH. "The Visionary vs the Utilitarian." *Architectural Design* 38 (March 1968): 134–136. An analysis and comparison of the Palais des Nations competition designs of Hannes Meyer and Le Corbusier. The complex relationship between utility and iconography is discussed, and the point is made that a building that is "automatically determined" from the program may in fact turn out to be less utilitarian than one built according to an esthetic founded on utopian idealism.

JONES, J. CHRISTOPHER AND THORNLEY, D. G., eds. *Conference on Design Methods.* Oxford: Pergamon, 1963. A collection of papers presented at a conference on systematic and intuitive methods in engineering, industrial design, architecture, and communications. The conference brought together people from different fields in an attempt to establish systematic methods of problem solving, particularly with respect to design, and to consider how design could best be taught.

RYKWERT, JOSEPH. "The Sitting Position, A Question of Method." In

Meaning in Architecture, edited by Charles Jencks and George Baird. New York: George Braziller, 1969, pp. 233–243. The author's argument that the whole of the environment is a tissue of symbolic forms is illustrated by a discussion of the chair. The dependence of comfort on social convention severely limits the usefulness of ergonomics to design.

STUDER, RAYMOND G. "The Dynamics of Behavior-Contingent Physical Systems." In *Design Methods in Architecture*, edited by G. Broadbent and A. Ward. New York: Wittenborn, 1969, pp. 55–70. An elaborate model for locating the important junctures at which human behavior and the physical environment interact. The relevance of the model to solving design problems is discussed and a strong stand is taken in favor of working with behaviorally oriented definitions of human needs and social organization rather than relying on typological solutions to design problems.

SUMMERSON, JOHN. "The Case for a Theory of Modern Architecture." *RIBA Journal* 64 (1957): 307–311. An extremely influential article among contemporary designers. The author argues that modern architecture is distinguished by a new concern for the program, in particular for the qualitative aspects of the program. Designers are no longer content to work from a list of quantitative requirements.

26. FUTURE ROLES OF THE BEHAVIORAL SCIENCES
   IN THE DESIGN PROCESS

ALEXANDER, CHRISTOPHER. *Notes on the Synthesis of Form*. Cambridge, Mass.: Harvard University Press, 1964. Design problems have become so complex that a way must be found to break them up into smaller problems that can be understood. Part I contains an account of the nature of design problems and Part II a method of representing design problems so that they can be broken up into solvable units; the appendix shows how the method works in practice.

DEASY, C. M. AND BOLLING, R. D. *Actions, Objectives and Concerns*. Los Angeles, 1969. (Available through Educational Facilities Laboratory, New York, N. Y.) An experiment in the use of behavioral science techniques for architectural objectives. Before preparing the program for a student union building at California State College in Los Angeles, the architects, with the help of a social psychologist and the college building coordinator, made a study of actual and desired student activity patterns.

GANS, HERBERT J. "Social Planning: A New Role for Sociology." In *Neighborhood, City, and Metropolis*, edited by Robert Gutman and

David Popenoe. New York: Random House, 1970, pp. 920–932. There is a need for sociologists to become more involved in city planning. They should work at developing theoretical schemes to guide planning, at improving the methods for deciding on social goals, at formulating programs for achieving these goals, and at conducting research to evaluate action programs.

MOORE, GARY T., ed. *Emerging Methods in Environmental Design and Planning.* Cambridge, Mass.: The M.I.T. Press, 1970. Proceedings from the first international conference of the Design Methods Group. The conference was concerned with finding new methods for solving the problems of the physical environment. The subjects covered include building layout models, problem structuring, computer aided design, evaluation systems, and applications of systems engineering. There is also considerable theoretical discussion.

PERIN, CONSTANCE. *With Man in Mind. An Interdisciplinary Prospectus for Environmental Design.* Cambridge, Mass.: The M.I.T. Press, 1970. An attempt to bridge the gap between what we do when we design and change the environment and what people really want from the environment. The author puts forth the concept of the "behavioral circuit" as a framework for bridging the gap and also suggests concrete proposals that can be carried out now, in particular by social scientists and building users, to make the environment more responsive to people's desires.

Index